INTERNATIONAL AID:
A SUMMARY

HUGH L. KEENLEYSIDE

INTERNATIONAL AID:
A SUMMARY

WITH SPECIAL REFERENCE TO
THE PROGRAMMES OF THE UNITED NATIONS

H JAMES H. HEINEMAN, INC., NEW YORK

First Printing 1966
James H. Heineman, Inc.,
60 East 42nd Street, New York, New York 10017

Library of Congress Catalogue Card No. 66–22154
Canadian Publishers: McClelland and Stewart Limited

Much of the material used in Chapter VI is taken from
or based on a paper entitled "Administration Problems of
the United Nations Technical Assistance Administration"
which was awarded the Haldane Medal of the Royal Institute
of Public Administration in 1954, and published in the
Journal of the Institute, *Public Administration* (Autumn, 1955).

PRINTED IN GREAT BRITAIN

———

THIS BOOK IS DEDICATED
WITH ADMIRATION AND GRATITUDE
TO
ALL MY COLLEAGUES IN
THE TECHNICAL ASSISTANCE ADMINISTRATION
WHOSE
IDEALISM, INTELLIGENCE AND INDUSTRY
DID SO MUCH TO HELP SO MANY PEOPLE
IN SUCH DIVERSE PARTS OF THE WORLD,
AND, IN PARTICULAR, TO
MY CLOSEST ASSOCIATES
AND MOST STEADFAST FRIENDS
GUSTAVO MARTINEZ CABAÑAS
AND PHOEBE ROSS KIDD

CONTENTS

Preface and Acknowledgements

In view of the vast number of books being produced annually every prospective author should be prepared to explain, and if possible to justify, his appearance in that role. In the present case I hope that the explanation may itself be accepted as the justification.

My purpose in writing this book can be quickly stated.

In the years since the end of the Second World War a great deal of attention has been given to the multitude of complicated problems covered by the general term international aid. Many articles and books have been published on one or more of the diverse aspects of this subject. But so far as I am aware no one has attempted to bring together in one place and in summary form

— first, a review of the contemporary circumstances which have made it imperative that aid programmes should be established and maintained;

— second, a historical review of earlier forms of international assistance;

— third, a description of how the current programmes have been developed and of the ways in which they work; and

— finally, a listing of the steps that should be taken if future action is to be built constructively on past experience.

That most of the book is devoted to the assistance activities of the United Nations is a reflection of my belief that while these operations are by no means the largest in scale—that honour belongs easily to the United States—they are the most significant in character, and hold the greatest promise for the future. It is also due, of course, to the fact that I have been more intimately acquainted with the mutual aid programmes of the United Nations than with the comparable activities of a regional or bilateral character.

Many of the general books and articles that have been written about technical and financial assistance have either omitted entirely, or have given only brief attention to, the population problem. As this is, in my opinion, next to the danger of nuclear war the most important and indeed frightening issue facing the world, its consideration has been incorporated as an integral part of the essential background against which the aid programmes have been developed.

The chapter on the Technical Assistance Administration of the United Nations has been included because the history of that department of the United Nations Secretariat illustrates in concrete form a great many of the problems that must be faced by all those who are engaged in the provision of international aid. Here again my personal involvement is an additional reason for the choice of TAA rather than of some other agency of comparable experience.

It is perhaps advisable to draw attention to the fact that I have violated what has now become an almost hallowed convention by referring to the under-developed countries as under-developed countries. This was not the result of carelessness or accident. That it was done from a lack of sympathy or understanding of the governments and peoples concerned I hope that the whole substance of the book will refute. I have also used the conventional and generally favoured locution "developing"; but only for variety (and in spite of the fact that when used in a general sense it is inexact because some of the under-developed countries are retrogressing rather than developing). I have also in some cases used the words "poor", "emerging", "backward", "indigent", "less fortunate", and so on, when they seemed appropriate. The antipathy to the term under-developed did not arise until the 1950's when some politically-minded participants in the United Nations' affairs decided that it might be considered offensive by the representatives of the countries to which it was being applied. This seemed to me to be nonsense, and it still does. In a considerable experience I have still to meet a serious representative of any of the less-developed countries who had the slightest objection to its use. The general reaction was that if the representatives of the more advanced countries would be more concerned with trying to meet the needs of the under-developed areas and less afflicted with gentility in the words they employed, everyone might profit.

In the preparation of this book I have had a great deal of assistance. Much of the factual material has been collected and placed in draft form by Professor Gerald Hodge, now of the University of Toronto. Mr. David Blelloch, to whom a number of references are made in the text, was most helpful in the critical review of certain important sections of the typescript. The same was true of Dr. Henry S. Bloch, whose direct experience both at the United Nations Headquarters and on temporary emergency assignments in the field, gave him a great store of valuable experience. Dr. Philip M. Hauser read the chapter on population and gave me most useful advice on many; aspects of that complicated subject. Mrs. Phoebe Ross Kidd who, as Programme Control Officer of the Technical Assistance Administration, was intimately associated with every project handled and almost every problem faced by that organization, has given me assistance that has been as helpful as it has been continuous. Dr. Albert Lepawsky, who has had a wide practical experience of many aspects of technical assistance and who has written extensively on related subjects, has also read part of my text with an admirably critical eye. While I have been most grateful for the advice given by these good friends, I have not in all cases acted upon it and they should not be held responsible for any persisting errors of fact or interpretation.

As the book has had to be done in spare time—of which there has been very little—it has meant the disruption of many evenings and weekends that might otherwise have been devoted to family pleasures. In her willing acceptance of this burden, as well as for her direct, discriminating assistance in connection with many aspects of the work itself, I must gratefully record my deep continuing indebtedness to my wife.

For uncomplaining acceptance of the added burden of producing repeated drafts of a difficult text, I warmly thank my secretary Miss Frances West. I also record my appreciation of similar technical assistance received from Mrs. Jean FitzSimons of the Victoria staff of the British Columbia Hydro and Power Authority, Mrs. Beatrice Kendrick, and from my skilful daughter Sara Lynn Jackson.

HUGH L. KEENLEYSIDE

United Nations Agencies
and Their Respective Abbreviations

ACC	Administrative Committee on Coordination
CCAQ	Consultative Committee on Administrative Questions
ECA	Economic Commission for Africa
ECAFE	Economic Commission for Asia and the Far East
ECE	Economic Commission for Europe
ECLA	Economic Commission for Latin America
ECOSOC	Economic and Social Council
IBRD	International Bank for Reconstruction and Development
IFC	International Finance Corporation
IMCO	Intergovernmental Maritime Consultative Organization
IMF	International Monetary Fund
NGO	Non-Governmental Organization
TAA	Technical Assistance Administration
TAB	Technical Assistance Board
TAC	Technical Assistance Committee
UNICEF	United Nations Children's Fund
UNRRA	United Nations Relief and Rehabilitation Agency
UPU	Universal Postal Union

CHAPTER ONE

Change in Modern Times

The greatest change in the recent history of humanity has been the fact, the diversity and the velocity of change itself. And in all material matters the old aphorism "plus ça change, plus c'est la même chose" is now spectacularly false.

For many thousands of years prior to the industrial revolution, the basic characteristics of human life—the forms and patterns of living, the intrinsic nature of the ideas, beliefs and motivations of society—had altered with glacial slowness. Repetition and stagnation were the most salient characteristics of the race. Through a myriad of generations it was only by infrequent and infinitesimal steps that men adjusted themselves to and extended their control over the natural forces by which they were encompassed. Then suddenly, after immobile conservatism had persisted so long that any other mode of living was to the ordinary man almost beyond conception, within a moment of historic time, the material structure of human society began to alter.

Anthropologists believe that it took half a million years for man the hunter to become man the farmer. It was only after this essential change had occurred that it became possible for large numbers of people to gather together in some of the great river valleys and for material progress, and innovations in social organization, gradually to ensue. The easy productivity of the lush, warm valleys of the Nile, the Euphrates and the Yangtze made possible the gradual accumulation of the surplus food and other necessities which in turn allowed a small but significant number of men and women to devote themselves to the strange and novel tasks of thought, invention, and the cultivation of the arts. Slowly, over the centuries new and at first primitive forms and aspects of civilization developed in Mesopotamia, China, India and Egypt.

The gradual development of the characteristic pressures and complications of organized society resulted in many false starts and in the consequent and sometimes rapid decline—as Toynbee has shown—of these experimental societies. Inexperience, incapacity, ignorance, greed, and the general infirmity of virtue which has always marked mankind, made set-backs many and progress slow. Nevertheless, a slow accumulation of experience, and an occasional flaring of individual genius, did take place and new communities arose on somewhat surer foundations as in such dramatic instances as China, India, Greece and Rome, Slowly too, an increasing number of individuals began to develop the curiosity, the impatience, the sceptical spirit that later spread into many parts of the world, most notably in the Renaissance, the Reformation and the so-called Expansion of Europe. The gradual growth of commerce, and the cultural intercourse which accompanied its development, contributed heavily to the intellectual activity from which they arose. The great trade routes have always been the main channels for ideas as well as for goods.

But in spite of these phenomena, as late as the eighteenth century the scientific spirit had infected only a relatively insignificant number of persons and they had done little to influence the policies of governments, or to change the generally prevailing way of life. On almost all issues both politics and religion were adamant in their organized opposition to change. And above all, the apparently instinctive hostility of the average human mind to any innovation—and especially to any new idea—made for leaden progress. Inertia, habit, prejudice, lack of imagination, have almost always delayed or blocked the application of new concepts or inventions. Throughout human history it has been normal for ideas to die because the intellectual climate has been adverse. Hero of Alexandria devised a steam-engine, but in a slave society it seemed of no more use than a toy; block printing developed in China many centuries before its introduction in the West but in that highly relaxed and contemplative society it was put to little use.

A · The Acceleration of Material Progress

Within the last two hundred years the annals of human society have recorded a dramatic change. In comparison with what had gone before, the material progress of some segments of humanity since the middle of the eighteenth century has been almost incredible in its force and scope. Previously, European and Asian alike—whether lord or peasant—were working and living and thinking in ways but little changed from those of their predecessors in the tropical valleys of five thousand years before. But the contrast between their knowledge and activities and those of the mechanized farmer of Saskatchewan or Minnesota, or those of the factory worker of Manchester or Detroit, or, above all, of those of the modern scientist in chemistry, biology or physics, is as dramatic as that between the hoe and the self-propelled combine; between the ox-cart and the supersonic jet; between the parish rumour and world-wide aural and visual communication.

Even the most highly educated man, even the scientist, of 1750 A.D. would today be completely lost in the most elementary courses in astronomy, chemistry, physics or geology. Outside the arts, only the lawyers and the theologians would still feel at home. William Pitt, George Washington, Benjamin Franklin, or Louis XV would have been more at ease with Hippocrates or with the builders of the pyramids than with Enrico Fermi, Sir John Cockcroft, or Dr. Wilder Penfield. The average high-school student of today knows far more of the physical facts of the universe than was known to the combined intelligence of statesmen and scholars during the young manhood of Abraham Lincoln, William Ewart Gladstone, or Sir John A. Macdonald.

B · The Extraordinary Changes Since 1750

The revolutionary surge in material achievement which suddenly developed between two and three hundred years ago was the result of an increased interest and consequent inventiveness in the technical arts. The initial achievements of the industrial revolution, as had been the case with the widely-spaced inventions of the past, were the results of individual curiosity, accident or practical experiment rather than of the conscious and organized application of new theories in speculative science. The major accomplishments in concentrating power, characterized by Watt's steam-engine and Cartwright's loom, were developed quite independently of work then being started in fundamental research and scientific enquiry. But as the practical benefits of the new inventions became apparent, a rapid increase took place in the practice of systematic experiment and original research. By the beginning of the nineteenth century a self-conscious scientific technique was being applied to the selection of objectives and was increasingly the explanation of progress in technical change. Today, of course, the relationship between pure research and practical application is so intimate that they can almost be accepted as the inseparable components of a single process.

This fact is of tremendous importance for the future of humanity. It can now be assumed that technological innovation at a progressively more rapid pace will continue indefinitely into the future—if humanity can refrain from using its new-found powers for self-destruction. The effects that this will have on the organization of society and the life of the individual is the most important conundrum now facing mankind. The one thing certain is that the remarkable developments since 1750 in agriculture, in industrial development, in transport and communications, in medical knowledge, in almost every material aspect of life, will soon be recognized as only the slow beginnings of what science will reveal and invention will provide for mankind.

While this is not the place for an extended summary of the recent history of human progress, the problems facing the world today can be seen in better perspective if some aspects of this history are kept in mind. The possibilities of the present and of the immediate future can, in this way, be more realistically appraised.

In agriculture, the last two hundred years have seen scientific principles applied to the inventory of the resources available for cultivation, to more effective methods of production, and to improved modes of utilization, with astonishing results. Plant fertilization, aided by the discovery of how the industrial fixation of nitrogen can be economically effected, has vastly increased the productivity of field-crops, especially on poor or marginal lands. The introduction of insecticides, new methods of crop rotation, of irrigation, of cultivation and harvesting, the beginnings of the practice of hydroponics, and the development of new varieties of seeds such as the winter wheats of Canada and hybrid corns, have all contributed to a radical change in the world food-picture. The whole character of protein production has also been transformed by new methods of animal husbandry, culminating for the moment in the practice of artificial insemination, and by almost fantastic innovations in the harvesting of food from the sea. Not only the improved organization of production but new techniques of transportation, preserving and marketing have made it possible for even the most isolated rural communities to be in ready contact with far-distant sources of varied supplies. Japanese shell-fish, Danish cheese, Arabian dates and Argentinian beef can be bought from Bolivia to Nepal and from the valley of the Zambesi to the valley of the Peace.

The dismal future for the human race forecast by Malthus has been staved off for almost two centuries by improvements in technology and by the opening of new lands to cultivation. Indeed, until comparatively recently the over-all food supply has increased somewhat more rapidly than has the world's population. This is not true today, and if present trends continue it will be very far from true tomorrow. With population in large areas of the earth now expanding at over three per cent a year it is obvious that the production of food and related necessities cannot continue to keep pace with this spectacular and rapidly accelerating growth. Perhaps the hydrogen bomb is nature's method of contradicting the gloomy English cleric.

In communications it is a commonplace that journeys which in 1750 took months can now be completed in hours; messages that used to require weeks can now be exchanged as rapidly as tongues can talk, fingers can move, or eyes can read. The miraculous velocity which characterizes so many aspects of the contemporary world grew out of man's ability to amass and focus power: steam for the locomotive and steamship; internal combustion of fuels for the motor car and the older aircraft; electricity for the telephone, telegraph, and wireless. Nuclear power has already disclosed new possibilities of movement and contact. It is possible that even interstellar space will soon be within the reach of man—although it is at least arguable that humanity should learn to control itself and its present domain before taking its diseases, its greed and its odious addiction to war, prejudice and injustice to other, perhaps less noisome, worlds.

Increased facilities for travel and communications are not, of course, ends in themselves. They have real value only insofar as they contribute to human needs, and to the support of human values through the provision of increased opportunities for the interchange of people, goods and ideas. Today it is unnecessary for any community to be ignorant of cultural processes outside its immediate vicinity; no longer need an industry employ antiquated techniques for lack of specialized knowledge; no individual has to be denied the intellectual contacts which stimulate speculation and—it is to be hoped—the slow growth of wisdom.

In the history of medicine it is clearly recorded that as late as 1750, the illnesses of even the well-to-do and most sophisticated families were being treated by methods singularly resembling those employed by the physicians of King Hammurabi or those of the Hsai dynasty of China. In both those eras the medical profession understood the use of simple herbs but frequently applied remedies of quite spurious value. At the end of the seventeenth century, Sir Thomas Browne, one of the ablest, most enlightened and compassionate men of his time was nevertheless an active defender of the belief in witchcraft and dealt with certain types of patient accordingly. The celebrated and humane Quaker, Dr. John Lettsom, who was enjoying an income of £12,000 per annum when he died in 1815, is said to have described his methods in the following verse:

> When any sick to me apply
> I physicks, bleeds, and sweats 'em;
> If after that they choose to die
> What's that to me, I Lettsom.*

---

* This technique may account for the fact that the author was said to have treated as many as 82,000 patients in a year.

Operations were performed without anaesthetics, and diseases were treated without any detailed knowledge of anatomy or any suspicion of the existence of germs. The handling of patients suffering from mental illness was as revolting as it was ineffective.

In the last two hundred years medical knowledge and practice have undergone amazing changes. As a result of the theoretical formulations and practical experiments of such scientists as Hunter, Bernard, Pasteur, and Hopkins, an understanding of anatomy, physiology, bacteriology and biochemistry is today a basic component of an acceptable medical education. In day-to-day practice anaesthetics are available to facilitate operations (even the Church's determination that women should suffer in childbirth has now been generally abandoned); vaccines are administered and environmental sanitation has been developed to prevent disease; specialized drugs and antibiotics of remarkable potency are available for curative purposes; and insecticides combat the spread of infection. Life expectancy is steadily increasing and the prospects of a healthy existence for the ordinary man or woman have become immeasurably brighter than ever before. As late as 1840 life expectancy in England was forty years for men, forty-two for women. One hundred years earlier it was probably in the neighbourhood of thirty-five for each. The comparable figures today are sixty-eight and seventy-two. (It has been suggested that the sex differential is nature's way of assuring that the woman will have the last word.)

The great material progress of the period under review is reflected with equal clarity in many aspects of domestic life. In a remarkable variety of instances new tools have been introduced directly into the household itself; in others, changes in family practice have been the indirect result of developments outside the immediate household. In both cases the effects have been profound. Except perhaps in bed and at the table, the domestic life of the early eighteenth century in Europe or America had more in common with Pharaonic Egypt than with the household of a contemporary family in London, Montreal, or New York. It can be argued that the food has not been conspicuously changed and that when changes have been made and in spite of increased knowledge of nutritional values, they have not always been for the better. But there has been a radical development in much of the physical equipment employed in family and community life. A great deal of contemporary clothing is made from materials unknown two centuries ago and the external environment, except for the weather, is almost completely changed. The habits of the ordinary citizen, especially as they have been influenced by the automobile and the various applications of electricity, have altered almost beyond recognition.

In almost every other material aspect of life, changes similar to those already cited have taken place. And this process of change is not slowing down; on the contrary, it is still accelerating with unexampled rapidity. The time between the great discoveries has become shorter and shorter until today each decade sees more scientific, technical, and material progress than marked the previous century. Representing man's separate existence on earth as twenty-four hours, there has been an infinitely greater material change in the last thirty seconds than in the whole preceding period.

C · The Moral Lag

In view of the radical nature of these material innovations, and of the shattering impact that they have had on human behaviour, it is not surprising that mankind is finding difficulty in adjustment. The speed and profundity of the changes have far exceeded the human capacity for rapid social adaptation. Man's endowment of wisdom, intelligence, flexibility and goodwill has been inadequate to meet the problems his inventions have so suddenly engendered.

As nothing is harder for a human being to accept than a new idea, so nothing is harder to change than an established social practice. Through many millenia, human history has been characterized by the sluggish evolution of thought and custom. This has been a tragically inadequate preparation for the demands that have been made on the individual and on society in modern times. Having been patently unable to solve many of the problems of the last two hundred years, the prospect of humanity being successful in coping with the trials that will inevitably be created by the changes still to come is far from reassuring. In the light of human history it is natural to expect that frustration, resentment and irrational responses will be among the results when familiar conditions are destroyed and when men and their organizations are faced with the necessity of acquiring new habits and practising new skills. The years immediately ahead threaten to tax the adaptive capacity of mankind's nervous and social systems as never before.

It is, of course, true that mankind can learn from experience and that today more conscious consideration and more serious and informed study are being given to problems of human behaviour than in the past. And the results of these researches are being applied with a rapidity unequalled in the history of the species. The danger lies in the fact that comparatively rapid as these adjustments are, they are far out-raced by the speed, impact and frequency of material innovations. Apparently it is much easier to make and apply scientific and technical discoveries in the material world than it is to harmonize social concepts and behaviour with the conditions that the new revelations create. Today the scientific knowledge of the twentieth century is, in many ways and in many cases, synchronized with the moral outlook and the behaviour patterns of the distant past. Thus, Hitlerite Germany combined the knowledge of Einstein and the insight of Sigmund Freud, Karl Marx and Thomas Mann with the morality of the followers of Tamerlane or Genghis Khan. Since the discovery of the methods of nuclear fusion and fission and the perfection of the techniques of biological and chemical aggression, humanity, for the first time, has acquired the power of universal self-destruction. Unfortunately, there is little in the past record of the species to justify the belief that it will not be used.

It cannot too often be recalled that among all the higher forms of life on this planet only human beings have been engaged, from the beginning to the present day, in a deadly, constant, organized effort to destroy each other. It has more than once been suggested that the present situation can be realistically interpreted only on the assumption that humanity is collectively insane.* Even wolverines and tigers are less viciously ferocious; and gorillas can justly despise their less hirsute relations.

Viewing the last twenty years in historical perspective, and comparing them with what has happened in advance of earlier international conflicts, it is difficult to avoid the conclusion that humanity is approaching another major war, a war which may prove to be the ultimate catastrophe. A recent head of the Civil Defence Administration of the United States endorsed this conclusion when, in prophesying an inevitable conflict, he said, "The weight of human nature and human experience runs

---

* In another place the author has made the following comments:

"That the human race is predominantly insane, and that insanity peculiarly affects its chosen or accepted leaders, would seem quite plain to any intelligent visitor from another planet.

"How else could such a stranger explain the fact that as soon as we leave the innocence of childhood, as soon as we attain the power to reason and to influence events, we begin to plan ways of killing each other?

"How else explain that in the thousands of years of recorded history there has been hardly a day in which human beings have not been engaged in organized war against each other?

"How else explain the fact that most of our national communities are spending about twice as much on past and present war—euphoniously called national defence—as on all other purposes combined?

contrary to the hope of peaceful settlement." Unless some profound change takes place, unless sanity returns to those in high places (and to the peoples whom their propaganda has perverted and inflamed), at some point, by accident or design, the tension will almost certainly explode in nuclear conflict. Anyone who doubts the reality or the severity of the prevailing nervous strain should visit the Strategic Air Command Headquarters in the United States—and presumably the same crackling tension prevails in the corresponding centre in the u.s.s.r. Not all of Dr. Strangelove is theatrical fantasy.

Churchill's hope that war will be averted by mutual terror may prove to be well-founded, and recent events appear to give it some support. But as long as scientists, urged on by military and political leaders, continue to prostitute their genius to the contrivance of more and more inventive methods of killing human beings, and as long as the major powers continue to compete in the development of offensive weapons, the prospects of peace grow more and more insubstantial. Robert Oppenheimer's description of the chief protagonists in the present venomously divided world as being dangerously "like . . . scorpions in a bottle" is as true as it is graphic. Nor is the prospect made more hopeful by the probability that two or three more nuclear scorpions will shortly be added. What will happen when the number rises to ten or twelve—as seems to be clearly foreshadowed—can be better imagined than described.

Although this serious lag exists in the application of technical knowledge to the solution of social problems, it would be false to argue that there has been no moral progress during the generations that have experienced the recent and phenomenal material changes. It is hard to resist the conclusion that those who mouth the old platitude that "human

---

"How else explain the fact that we can discuss without a qualm the idea of incinerating hundreds of thousands or millions of women and children whom under normal conditions we should be glad to cherish, and in whom we should find gentleness and delight, except by recognizing that, being insane, we have devised political and economic and religious reasons to justify burning them to death.

"Perhaps the final proof of our insanity is the fact that we have so prostituted our scientists—that great fraternity of men and women whose lives should rationally be devoted to the search for truth in all its aspects and its use for human welfare—that an ever-growing number of them concentrate all their knowledge, all their imagination, all their industry, all their skill, on the invention of ever more horrible means of killing their fellow men. Science has become the tool of human madness; too many of our scientists, the adept and complaisant panderers to human depravity."
(H. L. Keenleyside: Address to the National Committee for the Control of Radiation Hazards, Montreal, 1960.)

nature never changes" have never read history. Appalling as have been the cruelties—the cold, calculated, vicious cruelties—of the present and the recent past, there is a vast body of evidence to support the view that humanity as a whole has made some real progress in the correction of its moral deformities. Against the record of two world wars and all the bestialities that accompanied and followed them, can be balanced the history of public decency and private kindness that has marked social welfare projects in many lands, the various missionary movements, the work of the great foundations, the national and international technical assistance programmes, and the innumerable personal sacrifices for good causes that have increasingly marked—although they have fallen far short of dominating—the organized conduct of humanity in recent generations. Even the most cynical observer can hardly deny the obvious fact that never before in human history have so many individuals and such diverse groups been giving an affirmative answer to the ethical and universal question, "Am I my brother's keeper?"

But accepting the fact of notable progress in social practice, it still remains true that humanity as a whole is not morally equipped to handle the tremendous responsibilities that have been placed upon it. Even if the repeated assertion that the vast majority of people in all lands are prepared for the substitution of decency and kindness for naked and brutal power in their relations with their neighbours is true, there is still no assurance that this goodwill is so preponderant as to be generally effective. Indeed the degree to which governments desert all recognizable standards of ethical conduct when their so-called national interests are involved, is only exceeded by the enthusiasm of the support they secure from the people they rule—except on the infrequent occasions when, as in the case of the Suez crisis in Great Britain in 1956, the innate decency of the people prompts them to resist the temptation to support the official line without regard to the merits of the case. The squalid and persistent lying that has marked official statements of the governments of the major powers in recent years would shock Ananias.

D · The Paradoxical World of 1965

That the contemporary world possesses enormous material wealth and has a vast potential for further production is as clear to the scientist as it is tempting to the exploiter. This opulent world, however, is still characterized by great inequalities and injustices amongst its peoples, and there are gross variations in the use that is being made of the scientific and technical knowledge that should be employed to ensure the use of nature's manifold resources for the benefit of all and not just a limited segment of mankind. Indeed the world of the 1960's is, above all else, a world of harsh and shocking paradox.

Over half the people on earth are illiterate, thus providing fertile soil for the weeds of superstition, prejudice, and fanaticism. Of the remainder —those to whom are open the infinite opportunities that come from knowledge of the written word—a sad proportion confines, or is confined in, its reading to material that is almost certain to increase rather than to reduce ignorance, bigotry, and ill-will. Illiteracy could be practically abolished in a single generation if the problem were attacked vigorously, with wisdom and determination. And the possession of the tool of literacy might reasonably be expected to lead—eventually at least— to its beneficial use. Without it any significant and sustained social progress is virtually impossible.

Over half the people in the world are chronically ill, though most of them could be cured and many of the most prevalent diseases could be permanently eradicated by the use of medical knowledge already available. The current contrasts are nowhere more apparent than in the variations in life expectancy in the different regions of the earth. Persons who are born and reside in New Zealand or Canada or Sweden can expect to live, on the average, nearly seventy-five years if female, just over seventy if male. But in over twenty countries including some of the largest in the world, the average life expectancy is less than forty years!

A large proportion of the people in the world are hungry most of the time and are confined to diets that invite disease. Yet by applying even present knowledge to the problem of production and distribution of food it would be possible to come close to ensuring reasonable standards of nutrition for everyone—although this condition will not last long if the population of the world continues to grow at its present rate of increase.

Most of the people in the world cannot afford decent clothing, housing and recreation. In the wealthiest of nations, the United States of America, the average income per capita is just over $2,900 per year, which means that the great majority of its people must do with less than that. Recent studies have demonstrated that of the 190 million people in the United States nearly 40 million are living in poverty. But almost two-thirds of the people in the world, living in over seventy-five different countries, have a per capita income of less than $250 per year and suffer accordingly. Yet in the industrial countries many factories stand idle, many work only part of the time, and many are devoted to the production of weapons of destruction. In wide areas of the earth fields lie untilled and seas teem with a harvest ungarnered. In comparative terms at least, this situation is getting worse rather than better, as the gap between the more comfortable and the indigent nations is widening rather than closing. Indeed, this understates the situation. Today the average per capita income in the industrialized nations as a whole is $1,900 per annum. In the under-developed countries it is $130. But the World Bank has estimated that in twenty-five years, if present trends continue, the comparable figures will be $4,000 for the industrialized countries and, because of population growth, the average in the under-developed countries will have been forced down to $80 per capita. (George D. Woods: Address to the Canadian Club of Toronto, *Financial Post*, November 28, 1964. p6.)

Finally, a large proportion of humanity is affected by injustice in one or more of its manifold forms: slavery, peonage, forced labour, political despotism, racial prejudice, religious persecution and legal corruption.

While these conditions persist, the governments of the major powers quarrel increasingly over forms of political, social, and economic organization. In a rational world the real task facing humanity would be recognized as the need for an immediate, united and concentrated search for a way to abandon these deadly and imbecile obsessions and to develop a universal programme that would abolish the conditions of ignorance, disease, hunger, poverty and injustice by which so large a part of the race is perpetually afflicted. That such a programme would be technically feasible there is no longer any doubt. If the scientists who have been so fantastically successful in devising means of destruction were now permitted and encouraged to devote their amazing talents to the problems of peace, it is reasonable to believe that there are no material problems that could not be successfully resolved.

If this is true it requires no great imagination to envisage a time when it will be within the power of mankind to make it possible for all men everywhere to live freer lives, no longer shackled by the bonds of ignorance, want, and fear. The immediate task is to eliminate those conditions of material under-development which are so prevalent in so many parts of the world. This, of course, is no small undertaking for by whatever criterion under-development is judged, amelioration of the lot of the poor and afflicted will involve concern with well over half of the people of the world.

The geographic distribution of under-development is an element of the present situation, of which the significance is not always recognized. If on a map of the world all those countries with an annual per capita income of less than $100 are coloured in black, and in grey all those with incomes running between $100 and $250, it will be clearly seen that economic and social under-development are tropical and semi-tropical diseases. (See *Figure 1*.)

The hot countries have not always been the slums of the world. In the

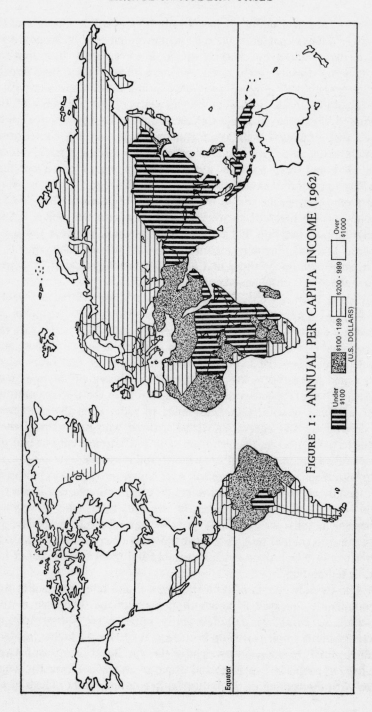

FIGURE 1: ANNUAL PER CAPITA INCOME (1962)

Under $100

$100 - 199

$200 - 999

Over $1000

(U.S. DOLLARS)

Equator

earliest history of mankind, as has already been noted, it was only in the hot river valleys that an economic surplus could readily be produced. Life in these valleys was uncomfortable, but even with their primitive methods and the narrowly restricted knowledge of their time, the inhabitants could still produce substantial crops, and a leisure class could develop and persist. Inevitably the majority of the members of this privileged class behaved as most of the people in such groups always behave: they exploited their less fortunate neighbours and concentrated on maintaining and extending their power for selfish and often anti-social ends. Here and there, however, a man, a family or a group utilized their privileged position to extend the bounds of knowledge, to produce works of art or to engage in and to exchange the subtleties of thought. The scholar and the theoretician were less common than the soldier and the feudal despot, but they did exist, and as a result, progress towards a civilized life was gradually recorded. The magnificent achievements of such early cultures as those of China, Babylon, Egypt and Crete were among the more conspicuous results.

Over the centuries men gradually came to know a little more about the ways of nature and to increase their knowledge of the techniques by which nature's laws could be utilized for individual and social purposes. Families, clans, and incipient nations began to live in the temperate zones. Here, when the basic problems of sustenance had been solved, they found it possible to live lives of greater industry and to enjoy more consistent health. Whereas their contemporaries in the tropics continued their relatively slothful ways, continued to suffer from the characteristic debilitating and enervating diseases, those who had adapted themselves to the temperate regions made slow and intermittent but real progress toward a more healthful and a more productive life.

In both tropics and temperate zones, of course, progress was repeatedly stultified by recurring wars, and sometimes these brought desolation that required centuries to redress. But, in the end, those who lived where persistent activity was not only possible but relatively agreeable, surpassed in the gradual progression toward a civilized life those who lived in regions in which disease was inevitable and indolence an almost irresistible temptation.

While the inhabitants of both the tropical and temperate zones were predominantly engaged in agricultural pursuits the difference in their standards of living was not necessarily pronounced. The greater productivity in the tropics made up in some measure for the higher incidence of disease and the oppressive weight of the sun. But the contrast between the lives of people in temperate and tropic zones reached dramatic dimensions with the coming of the Industrial Revolution. In an industrial age, the strangling enervation of tropical life combined with the physical demands of the factory techniques to place an almost insuperable burden on the working populations of the torrid regions. Their progress could not keep pace with that achieved in more temperate zones. It would certainly be an exaggeration to say that the Industrial Revolution flourished in England because the workers preferred employment even in an eighteenth- or nineteenth-century English factory to facing the cold and damp of the English climate, but there is a real element of truth in the emphasis on climate in the interpretation of industrial history. Eventually as the peoples of the temperate zones increased in numbers and power, many areas in the tropics were reduced to colonial status (or its economic equivalent) and in this role acted as the suppliers of raw materials for the great productive communities of Europe and America, and as controlled markets for their manufactures.

It is perhaps true that in years to come certain by-products of recent scientific progress may swing the balance somewhat back towards the warmer countries. The conquest of tropical diseases such as malaria, yellow fever, yaws, and hookworm; the improvement of tropical clothing and footwear; the introduction of air conditioning, and the control of indoor humidity, may all, work to re-direct the tide of progress. This change, however, is still in its primitive beginnings.

It is also true that there has been a "racial" (to use that much abused word in its colloquial sense) or colour distribution of ignorance, poverty, and disease. This is not, of course, absolute; rapidly progressing Japan is a "coloured" country, whereas Greece with an annual income of about $200 per capita is inhabited by white Europeans of most notable ancestry. It is, however, a fact that the bulk of today's problems of under-development occur in the so-called "coloured" countries. That there is nothing inherent or necessarily permanent in this situation hardly requires noting. All informed observers have long abandoned the idea of any innate differences in the intellectual or physical capabilities of the different races. An Indian, or Sudanese, or Paraguayan has the same chance of being intellectually superior—and runs the same hazard of a less fortunate endowment—as any of his differently pigmented contemporaries.

If the belief in the existence of innate variations in human capacity based on race or colour is scientifically inaccurate, it becomes still less plausible when viewed under the microscope of history—a most useful criterion. Even an elementary knowledge of the story of our human race should have a sobering effect on the racial bigots—if such persons were open to the persuasive influence of reason.

Four thousand years ago the Mesopotamians and the Egyptians, both coloured (though in slightly different shades) might be excused, in view of their lack of scientific training in biology, for believing that they represented permanently "superior" races. There was at that time no reason to feel that the barbarous Greeks, or the predecessors of the people who established the great Empire of Rome, would ever be able to match the cultural achievements of Memphis or of Babylon; of Amenemhet I or of the great law-giver Hammurabi.

A few centuries later the Assyrians or the Chinese might easily have felt that Providence had designed *them* as the permanently highest example of the creative art.

About the same time the Hebrews made their conviction of Jehovah's discrimination in their favour a basic tenet of their religion. In view of their general cultural backwardness at that time, this was possibly the supreme example of the human capacity to substitute faith for probability.

The Bible provides some interesting illustrations. In Genesis it is said "The Egyptians might not eat bread with the Hebrews: for that is an abomination unto the Egyptians." And in the New Testament we read "The Jews have no dealings with the Samaritans" and "Into any city of the Samaritans enter ye not."

During the years of "the glory that was Greece and the grandeur that was Rome," who could have imagined that the half-naked, superstitious, woad-stained savages who lurked in the forests of Germany and the swamps of Britain could ever become anything more than dull-witted slaves to be slowly taught some of the more essential tasks required by civilized man—such as how to kill one's neighbour?

And then the Moors. At a time when Western Europe was going through a period of barbarism of which squalid, bestial, and perpetual war was about the only technically developed activity (a period we have flatteringly called the Dark Ages) these deeply coloured African peoples were developing the mathematical sciences and organizing a civilized community life that made Europeans seem the uncouth barbarians that most of them were.

Coming nearer to the present time, it was only fifty years ago that the Russian peasant—the stupid mujik—was a stereotype for everything that was degraded, doltish and beyond the reach of civilized thought. Yet tomorrow this peasant's grandson may be laughing at the western world from the moon. Or threatening from Mars!

It can be shown, by way of illustration, that the currently most socially backward element in the population of the u.s.a. is almost purely Anglo-Saxon in origin.

It is historical accident, disease, and variations in opportunity that have caused existing disparities to occur. But for the present, the fact that there is a *colour/under-development* coincidence adds a serious complication to the task of those who are striving to make the advances of science available for the benefit of all men in all countries.

E · The Present Waste of Talent and Resources

Apart from the inherent danger of universal destruction through war, the contemporary world is bedevilled by the enormous waste of material and human resources on the production of an array of military hardware that is as costly as it is menacing and inventively ingenious. With few exceptions these monstrous devices have no value for any purpose other than killing. Never before in history has humanity devoted so much of its substance and its talent to the preparations for human annihilation. Over fifty per cent of all the natural scientists in the United States are engaged directly or indirectly on "defence" projects. The percentage in the Soviet Union is generally estimated to be still higher.

In the light of these facts, many interesting computations have been made of the benefits that could be brought to humanity by a sane use of the resources now being perverted to these malevolent ends.

Achieving the maximum beneficial results for mankind through applied intelligence and morality is by definition a reasonable objective, but with humanity in its present state of moral immaturity even its practical acceptance as a goal is more than can realistically be expected. The incongruities in the policies and practices of even the wealthiest country in the world indicate the dimensions of the obstacles that must be overcome, as well as the rewards that might be secured, if the objective should be accepted and eventually achieved. The United States is today spending on medical research an amount that is less than one-tenth of one per cent of the money that it allocates for military purposes. Or again, if the United States were to spend on housing its people and schooling its children one-half of what it now spends on military affairs, it could, in three years, provide a fund which would ensure every family a decent house and every child a decent school.

To take a smaller example of the irrationality of present practice, Canada, which must by any standard be considered one of the more fortunate and more enlightened of modern nations, currently spends on military and related projects something like 1½ billion dollars a year. If two-thirds of this sum were to be devoted to social purposes Canada could in one year build and pay the operating costs of twenty new universities each large enough to provide facilities for ten thousand students. Alternatively, the use of one year's savings would enable Canada to

build and operate a national theatre in Ottawa and a provincial theatre in each provincial capital
   and
build a series of libraries supported by a mobile book service that would meet the needs of every province
   and
provide full maintenance for 50,000 graduate students in Canadian universities
   and
provide full maintenance for 200,000 undergraduate students in Canadian universities
   and
still have about $200 million left over to use for some other good causes.

Or if Canada should decide to use $1 billion of its savings to assist in the development of the poorer countries of the world the Canadian contribution alone would equal about five times the total sum now being spent annually on technical assistance and related projects by the United Nations and all the Specialized Agencies.

In a material sense the whole world could be completely transformed in a single decade if even one-half of the money now being wasted on armaments were to be devoted to programmes of economic and social progress. The effect on individual lives and on society as a whole would be of such a character and of such dimensions as to mark a wholly new era in human affairs.

Of course there is no likelihood of any such revolution occurring— in spite of the fact that most of the people of the world would undoubtedly approve a change of this kind if they could be convinced that no "enemy" would be enabled thereby to gain in relative strength. But old fears and old hatreds, ingrained custom and habit, the stolid inertia of the existing systems of national politics and international relations, the influence of the interests vested in the "military-industrial complex" against which even President Eisenhower in the end warned his fellow-countrymen, all make such a development almost infinitely remote.

If humanity were as reasonable in its collective organizations as are most of the individuals of which it is composed, some programme of this kind would become a practical possibility. But in its political groupings mankind is as yet palpably incapable of such rational behaviour. Until some effective form of world federation—or world government based on accepted laws—has been established, the present extravagant and dangerous folly is almost certain to continue.

F · The Significance of the Programmes of Mutual Aid

While the prospect of any radical and comprehensive change in organized human conduct of the character that is so obviously desirable is tragically remote, it is appropriate to consider and assess certain salutary changes in international conduct that have occurred in recent years. The most important of these and the most encouraging in their implications for the future are undoubtedly those comprised in the many programmes of reciprocal assistance for economic and social progress.

So long as these programmes of mutual international aid continue on their present scale, while infinitely greater sums are wasted by the richer states on armaments and other less dangerous but still non-essential ends, it will be difficult to convince that large proportion of the people of the world who still suffer from poverty, ignorance, and disease that their plight is a matter of serious concern to their more opulent neighbours. In view of their obvious inadequacy, much of the praise that has been lavished on these programmes is as exaggerated in substance as it is offensive to good taste.

Nevertheless, meagre and grudging as they are, these joint activities are something new in the world and they have evoked a human and political response of such significance that, whereas twenty years ago their conception would have been scorned as visionary and utopian, today it is inconceivable that they should ever be abandoned. At even the lowest estimate they are proof that the world's problems are recognized as they have never been in the past. As a result, in many regions hopes are rising; the paradoxes of poverty in plenty, of unused knowledge and skills, are becoming less and less acceptable to men and women of intelligence and goodwill. Eventually, it must be believed, through these and other means, many of the cruellest problems facing humanity today will find solutions. *Quote this*

In the end it may even be true, as Arnold Toynbee has said in his often-quoted comment, that if humanity can survive the dangers by which today it is so gravely threatened, this era will be remembered "not for its horrifying crimes or its astonishing inventions but because it is the first age since the dawn of history in which mankind dared to believe it practical to make the benefits of civilization available to the whole human race." Having dared to believe, perhaps mankind will soon dare, effectively, to act.

It is to describe and assess the need for, and the first tentative steps towards, such action that the remaining chapters of this book are addressed.

CHAPTER TWO

What is Meant by Under-Development

A · Development and Under-development

Inadequate as have been the steps that have so far been taken to meet the problem of the unequal distribution of the benefits of modern civilization, there is a general and growing concern over the persistence of those conditions of poverty, ignorance and disease which afflict so large a proportion of mankind. This concern is not significantly limited or channelled by considerations of race, nationality or religion. Even the old distinction between "civilized" and "uncivilized" peoples has been generally abandoned as closer knowledge of the facts has led to an appreciative recognition of some of the values of the cultural traditions of even the most primitive peoples. So far has this gone that even the descriptive term "under-developed" has come to have a pejorative connotation that is alleged to be abrasive in its effect on the sensibilities of certain people in some of the countries to which it is usually applied. How far this is generally true and how far it is confined only to some members of the small element in the population that occupy representative and political posts is at least open to question.

The changing attitudes and behaviour that reflect the growing concern with human misery have been illustrated by a conscious effort to avoid giving offence in relations between peoples living in contrasting economic and social circumstances. It is also due to a belated recognition of the fact to which reference has already been made of the equality in intrinsic ability of all racial or national groups. It is true that to many people in the less sophisticated classes* in even such countries as Canada, Great Britain and

---

* To limit this criticism to the unsophisticated is not wholly accurate. It was only a few years ago that the chief lobbyist in Ottawa of Canada's largest church—a man of ability and of wide classical training—scornfully commiserated with the Commissioner of the Northwest Territories because the latter was so "ignorant and naive" as to argue that given adequate opportunities Canada's northern Indians and Eskimos would be no less susceptible

the United States, as well as to Germans, South Africans and others who are still obsessed by the traditional prejudices, the belief in racial inequality is still as widespread and virulent as it is unjustified and erroneous. Anthropologists, psychologists, and members of all other scientific disciplines that are concerned with this problem are now in general agreement:

a/*that there is no such thing as a pure race*, and

b/*that the various groupings into which mankind can be divided*, whether based on colour, head form, hair structure, or any of the other criteria that once were employed to distinguish different "races," *have no significant continuing relationship to either intellectual or physical capacity.*

In these circumstances such words as "developed" and "underdeveloped" are useful terms to use in the attempt to define differences that do exist between current conditions—particularly economic conditions—in some parts of the world as compared with those in others. So, without using the terms to indicate a belief in any permanent or inherent inequality or as being applicable to all aspects of any racial or political grouping, they can reasonably be employed as a rough means of identifying areas and peoples that for any of many possible reasons have made less progress than some others in applying contemporary knowledge to the solution of their communal problems.

"Under-development" is obviously a comparative term. It is equally obvious that it is an inexact one. A nation or society may have an enormous income, as is the case of some of the Arabian sheikdoms, yet have little claim to being considered highly developed. Alternatively, the people of some of the most economically depressed nations have retained or developed cultural traditions and practices of continuing social value. David Blelloch, a long-time champion of international aid as well as one of the severest critics of its current standards of practice, has suggested a useful definition of the term "developed":

The distinguishing feature of a developed society is that it has evolved a social and administrative organization, a system of education, a relationship between classes and sexes, a set of habits and customs, a way of life and a scale of values which are compatible with modern

---

to the influences of education than any other Canadians. Fortunately the Canadian government was not influenced by the misguided cleric and the results of an enlightened northern administration have already gone far to justify this decision. Even more convincing proof of Eskimo capacity is available in the experience of Denmark and Russia.

industrial technology and the mass production and distribution of commodities which it implies. (David Blelloch: *Some Problems of Aid for Development, Civilisations,* VIII, 1958, p. 36.)

In another place the same acute and experienced observer has made a further comment on this theme:

Thus, though the whole of mankind has been developing, and developing in a single direction, the course of development has been far from even and uniform, both as among the various independent political units into which the world's area and population are divided and also within the boundaries of those units. A developed society is only incidentally an affluent society: it is also a society characterised by such traits as a general belief in both the possibility and the desirability of achieving affluence, at whatever cost; a general sense of belonging to, and of obligation towards, the political unit of which one is a citizen, and of solidarity with one's fellow-citizens; an efficient and honest public administration; universal literacy, and a complete public education system. No nation, however highly developed, can claim perfection in respect of any of these traits; on the other hand, no nation in which any one of them is completely absent can be regarded as having reached a stage of development fully compatible with industrialisation; and, be it noted, none of them can be either bought or taught—all of them must be acquired by an arduous effort of collective will and discipline. (David Blelloch: *Technical Co-operation and the Development Decade;* United Nations Association, London, 1964, p. 4.)

The distinction between a developed and an under-developed society does not consist alone of a contrast in material circumstances. It involves the quality as well as the degree of the integration of social and political institutions with modern means of industrial production. In an economically and socially advanced nation there will normally exist a unity of purpose as well as both an opportunity and a capacity for a beneficial choice of means in promoting social and economic growth. Thus, in spite of such obscene but temporary aberrations as that of Hitlerite Germany and the widespread current obsession with nuclear and biological instruments of war, the highly developed countries of North America and Europe have demonstrated a steadily growing sense of responsibility to their own peoples—and, to a lesser degree, to others.

On the other hand nothing is more disheartening in visiting the less developed countries than to observe the almost total lack of interest in the welfare of their poverty-stricken compatriots that is displayed by a varying but usually considerable proportion of the customarily small group who possess wealth and exercise authority. Similar contrasts between extremes of wealth and poverty have of course marked the history of some of the nations that are today among the most highly developed, and a similar callousness on the part of many of the most affluent individuals is still to be found in the generally progressive societies of Europe and America. But today this characteristic is particularly evident in the under-developed areas. In many countries, in Latin America for example, the most violent social revolutions are now almost inevitable unless there is a rapid and radical change in the attitude and behaviour of the ruling classes. A visit to such a city as Rio de Janeiro with its luxury apartments and its unspeakable slums in one of the most richly endowed countries in the world is a revolting experience for any sensitive observer. Even in countries in which some serious effort is being made to improve the general lot it would appear that this is often, although certainly not always, the result of fear of the consequences of doing nothing rather than of the influence of either a sense of responsibility or a feeling of compassion. Nevertheless, the more this apprehension can be aroused the more hope there may be of progress. The fear of death has been known before now to encourage virtuous behaviour.

Since the material foundation of a developed country rests on modern technology, such a country is inevitably subject to rapid change, for change is a salient characteristic of that technology. Thus a developed sociey is a dynamic society and this dynamic quality is perhaps its most obvious indentification. An under-developed country by comparison is likely to be socially static and economically stagnant.

In a dynamic society economic and social growth are both self-sustaining and closely integrated. Gunnar Myrdal in his admirable study entitled *An International Economy* lays great stress on this attribute of "integrated growth" that marks the developed countries to which he refers as the "progressive and highly integrated nations." (Gunnar Myrdal: *An International Economy*, New York, 1956, p. 20.) He emphasizes in the contrasting histories of the developed and under-developed nations the differences in the interrelationships of the factors that affect growth, such as capital, technology, trade, administration, social custom and political institutions. In the growth of a country's economy all of these factors tend to interact with cumulative effect.

Whether a country achieves rapid progress through integrated growth, or moves slowly with torpid and disparate growth, is sometimes influenced by the fact that its economy has received—by accident or design —an effective impetus through a stimulant affecting several of the controlling factors simultaneously. The cumulative effect of such a stimulation is likely to by a dynamic, self-sustaining pattern of progress which constantly reinforces itself through rising levels of such things as real income and industrialization, through improvement in standards of administrative practice, and through a declining incidence of ignorance and disease. Without at some point receiving such an initial impetus the converse is likely to be true. What Evan Luard has described as "The law of cumulative inequality" comes into operation. (Evan Luard: *Nationality and Wealth*, London, 1964, p. 216.) Capital formation is impossible because of poverty and thus the country is unable to finance the introduction of advanced technologies or the training and employment of competent administrators. With the output of goods and services low and inefficient, with administration incompetent and generally corrupt, poverty and its accompanying social ills are perpetuated.

As an instance of how these various negative factors combine to stultify hopes and plans for national progress perhaps no better example can be found than that of Bolivia. The conditions there were sharply summarized in the 1950 Report of the United Nations Mission of Technical Assistance which, after a comprehensive study, described the situation that existed at that time in part in these terms:

> *It is clear that Bolivia has within its boundaries all the resources necessary to provide a sound economic foundation for a national life distinguished by a wide diffusion of culture, by progress and prosperity. But these results have not been achieved. . . .*

> *The conditions of life for the great majority of the people, heirs of more than one brilliant civilization and inhabiting a country of vast potential resources, are harsh, static and largely devoid of present satisfaction or future hope. . . .*

> *A large part of the population is illiterate and ill, and infant mortality is appallingly high. . . .*

> *It was the first duty of the United Nations Mission to find a satisfactory explanation of this paradoxical contrast between the potential wealth of Bolivia and the failure of its people to translate that wealth into the concrete evidences of a prosperous national economy. . . .*

> *The failure to develop a firm, competent and responsible system of government has been the result as well as the cause of Bolivia's economic under-development. Whatever the priority, today governmental weakness and economic debility form the two segments of a single vicious circle; each supports and contains the other. . . .*

*The members of the Mission believe that Bolivia's economic develop-
ment could be assured, and the national standards of living progressively and substantially improved, if foreign and native skills
and capital could be offered appropriate conditions for harmonious
and mutually confident co-operation. . . .*

*The rapid development of Bolivian resources requires the applica-
tion of technical and professional skills that are almost entirely
lacking within the country itself. Of equal and parallel importance
is the necessity for the maximum mobilization of domestic financial
resources and of the foreign exchange income of Bolivian industries
for economic development. This effort, however, will not be sufficient and must be supplemented by the inflow of foreign capital.
Without the employment of technical skills and a vast increase in
capital investment Bolivia cannot expect the results that, with these
aids, could mark an era of unexampled achievement. . . . (Report of
the United Nations Mission of Technical Assistance to Bolivia,* United
Nations, New York, 1951, pp. 2–3.)

The basic problem facing those who are concerned with promoting the
progress of the under-developed areas of the world is to ascertain what
steps can most effectively be taken and what difficulties must most carefully be avoided or overcome if the sinister obstacles to national growth
are to be surmounted. It is difficult now to realize that prior to about 1950
very little concentrated attention had been directed towards the finding
of generally applicable answers to such problems. It is only within the
last few years that any serious and persistent research has been undertaken. Fortunately a good deal is now being done. An admirable illustration of how seriously the subject is being studied is found in the summary
of outstanding research needs of the next decade, compiled under the
editorship of Robert E. Asher and entitled *Development of the Emerging
Countries—An Agenda for Research.* In reviewing this excellent book
Marion Clawson, himself one of the most active and intelligent students
of the subject, said that what impressed him most was:

*. . . the scholarly restraint, one might almost say humility, with
which each of these authors views the process of economic development. This is obviously complex, and no one realizes it better than
those closest to it. Would that legislators, political figures, popular
writers, and even administrators had the kind of basic understanding
this book reveals! Or, better yet, that they might have had it fifteen
years ago, when the United States first began large scale development
assistance. Some, at least, of the subsequent frustrations and mis-*

*understandings could have been avoided. But the problems of econo-
mic development will remain with us for many decades and serious
research on an adequate scale can help mightily. International
Development Review, June 1964, p. 31.)*

That there is no single or simple solution to the problem of economic
development is now obvious to everyone who has had a hand in what
has become a rapidly expanding field of study. It is becoming more and
more clear that the complex interrelationship of many factors has cumulative results in stimulating progress or in confirming inertia. Using an
individual illustration, a worker in an under-developed country may not
get enough to eat; by being under-nourished his health will be weakened;
ill-health will lead to a lower working capacity; as a result of faulty work
he will remain poor; poverty-stricken he will not obtain enough to eat.
The breaking of such an evil chain is likely to involve more than just
the provision of additional food supplies or of medical care. Good health
may require more than merely adequate quantities of food. Work may
not be available even though the worker is strong and willing. If work is
available his training may not fit him for the job.

In many parts of the world it is impossible to take immediate and full
advantage of a beneficial change in one facet of the prevailing condition
of under-development, because synchronized and complementary progress
is impossible in some other but definitely related field. Thus, to per-
petuate a temporary increase in food supplies resulting from some special
circumstances of fortune or charity may require the development of an
improved system of distribution which, in turn, may be dependent on
improved administrative practices and physical facilities. These it may be
impossible to provide because of a lack of trained personnel or because
of financial limitations. As an illustration of this problem consideration
might be given to the results that would have followed had the United
States government, in its relations with Puerto Rico, instead of supporting
an intelligent and comprehensive development programme, confined its
assistance to the provision of adequate food supplies for the whole population over a prolonged period. The effect of such a limited programme
might have been economic decay and social disaster in the commonwealth. By assisting in a multi-pronged attack on Puerto Rico's problems
the United States made possible the remarkable development that has
taken place in that country.

In summary it can be said that an under-developed country is one
which, for any one or more of a hundred different reasons, has been
unable to apply modern scientific knowledge to the creation of an
economy which will produce and distribute those ideas and commodities

that are required to provide the material basis of a healthy community life. Without such an economy it is impossible to organize a society that will foster knowledge, promote competent administration, stimulate intellectual and cultural activity, and encourage co-operation for the general good.

Before leaving this subject, reference should be made to the rather surprising frequency with which large under-developed areas are to be discovered within the borders of what is, in general, an advanced and prosperous country. Such regions as Sicily, the Province of Newfoundland, or the State of Mississippi, are shocking anomalies in such countries as Italy, Canada and the United States. So also, of course, are the nauseating conditions that are tolerated in the still expanding slums of the wealthiest of cities—including New York, site of the headquarters of the United Nations.

B · The Problem of Economic Stagnation

There are many ways of measuring under-development but the most frequently used and the most convenient, if not the most accurate, criterion is that of the average annual income of the residents in the area under review. This, of course, is not an exact or scientific touchstone. It is axiomatic that no final verdict on the state of development of any national community can be based on the per capita income alone. Otherwise Kuwait might be considered more advanced than Israel, Costa Rica or Yugoslavia. The internal distribution of income is of the greatest importance in trying to decide on the general level of economic and social progress. Nevertheless the index of income per capita is broadly indicative of the state of material development of a nation and its people. The population with a high average income will generally have the ability to meet its essential needs. Conversely, the countries with low average incomes are unable to provide many of the necessities of personal and national life, and even less able to accumulate the capital resources required to start and sustain an expanding economy, or to foster social progress. Today over sixty-five countries with a per capita income of less than $200 per year, and with an aggregate population exceeding 1,500 millions, are in this category.

What are the causes of this continuing poverty and of the general stagnation in these countries at a time when such tremendous changes have been taking place in other parts of the world? There are many answers, or partial answers, which apply in varying degrees to each of the nations in this category. Some of them can be quickly summarized.

CLIMATE/ In the early history of humanity, the major preoccupation was the struggle for food, and the provision of shelter against the elements. It was for these reasons that the initial advances in organized civilization occurred and were sustained in the river valleys where a surplus of food could most easily be produced, and in the tropics where the provision of dress and housing were of minor importance. Thus, as has already been pointed out, the valleys of the Nile, of the Tigris-Euphrates, and of the great rivers of Central and Southern China became the earliest centres of population increase and of human progress.

Today, however, there are few of the under-developed countries outside the torrid zone, while there is no real example of a highly developed economy between the tropics of Capricorn and Cancer. Modern science is beginning to make tropical life more bearable, but climate is still one of the handicaps that most of the currently under-developed countries must face. Air conditioning is not enough.

DISEASE/ Tropical climatic conditions also have a direct economic effect through the contribution they make to the incidence of disabling disease. Even the Eskimos live healthier lives than do many of the residents of tropical countries such as Sierra Leone, Haiti or Ceylon. When coupled with such related factors as malnutrition, the result of tropical living is that a large percentage of the people of the under-developed areas suffer frequently or continually from ill-health. Malaria, yaws, dysentery, tuberculosis, bilharziasis, trachoma and other parasitic and respiratory afflictions are normal aspects of life in the poorer countries. The individual effects are a life of misery and the probability of an early grave. Economically, illness reduces productive capacity and thus hardens the iron band of under-consumption, disease and low productivity. In some countries the costs of industrial development are vastly increased by such an incidence of absenteeism due to disease that two men must be employed for every job.

LIMITED NATURAL RESOURCES/ Although further and more reliable surveys may change the picture in some cases, it is clear that in general the under-developed countries are poorly endowed with useful resources. Except in the few instances in which conditions are propitious for the profitable production of cereals or fruits, or in which large supplies of oil or other minerals are available for exploitation, there is in most of these countries only a narrow range of known resources that can be developed for either export or domestic use. Even in the few cases in which extensive areas of land are available for cultivation it is usually found that this cannot be effectively utilized because of climatic handicaps, soil impoverishment or, most serious of all, because of the lack of the most vital of all resources, water.

There are also many instances of present poverty resulting from past mistakes or greed. In some of the most renowned and historic regions of the world—Asia Minor for example—forests have been destroyed and soils degraded or eroded as a result of centuries of wasteful and unscientific use. This is one of the major problems with which the peoples and governments in many regions must contend in their struggle for economic progress. Solutions will require scientific knowledge, time, capital, domestic initiative and, in many cases, international co-operation.

COLONIAL HERITAGE/ Most of the under-developed parts of the world were ruled for generations or centuries by foreign powers. This external control was not universally and exclusively detrimental. To go a long way back, the civilizing and generally beneficial effects of Roman conquests can be recalled. Some of the legacies of modern colonialism have also been salutary as, for example, the administrative tradition left in Pakistan, India, Malaya and elsewhere by the departing British. In the case of Malaya, for instance, a recent student of the government of that country has written that within a "framework of parliamentary government was . . . to be found one of the most effective and efficient bureaucracies" in Southeast Asia. . . . "By the time of the creation of the greater Malaysian Federation this bureaucracy was largely indigenous in composition. . . . These happy circumstances were not entirely accidental nor were they exclusively a product of the period of political independence. . . . [It] is a synthesis of the colonial experience as it acted, reacted and interacted within the indigenous environment of a tropical, plural, Southeast Asian society." (Robert O. Tilman: *Bureaucratic Transition in Malaya*, Duke University Press, 1964, p. vi.) The sad record of such newly independent countries as Indonesia and the Congo shows some aspects of the other side of the colonial picture. The importance of successful training in administrative practices is demonstrated by the contrasting histories of, for example, Tunisia and Morocco. The former is almost devoid of useful resources, but it did have the advantage of a sound administrative tradition. Morocco was much more lavishly endowed by nature but its people learned little of how to administer their affairs. Since becoming independent Tunisia has made considerable progress; Morocco's record has been pathetically bad.

In assessing the effects of colonial rule it should be recalled that while the colonial relationship was often marked by gross and sometimes hideous examples of human exploitation it did on other occasions result in the provision of capital for development projects which in certain cases brought limited or peripheral benefits to the indigenous populations.

Characteristically, however, colonial rule, even comparatively good colonial rule, usually meant a quick and concentrated exploitation of the most readily usable resources of the subject territories. Even more important is the fact that external control almost inevitably resulted in a prolonged delay in the development of the inherent capabilities of the subject peoples for self-government.

The economic results of colonialism were patterns of development which brought only incidental benefits, if any at all, to the people of the country concerned. They reflected instead the interests of the businessmen of the metropolitan power. Modern techniques were introduced and high levels of productivity were attained in the utilization of raw materials from plantations, mines and forests. But these projects normally gave employment to only a small part of the local population. Owned, developed and processed by foreigners, the products were usually exported and the profits were commonly invested (or squandered) abroad. This practice was traditional even in those infrequent cases in which the chief owners and exploiters were nationals of the country concerned— as in the spectacular case of the Patiños of Bolivia. The immense fortune of this depressing family, dug by peon labour from the rich tin deposits of the Andes, was almost entirely spent or invested abroad instead of being used for the beneficial development of the country and people that had made it possible.

Industrial or trading enclaves established in colonial territories were traditionally isolated from the surrounding areas and had little relationship to the remainder of the national economy. The latter often operated on what was practically a subsistence basis and much of it was even outside the money system. The segregation of the externally-owned or externally-influenced projects also had the effect of delaying the transfer of technical skills and the experiences of business enterprise to the subject peoples.

The monopolistic practices which marked the relationship of the metropolitan countries to their colonies were usually established by legislation and fortified by administrative practices which produced what Myrdal calls an "enforced bilateralism." This, in modified form continues to exist even now in certain areas, particularly in some of the ex-colonies of France and of Britain which can be described as commercially independent only if compared with such political, social and economic slums as the tightly controlled colonies of Portugal. The influence of the metropolitan powers naturally tended to work for the preservation of the social and economic *status quo* in their colonial territories, and as Myrdal goes on to say, "From one point of view, the most important effect of colonialism was related to the negative fact that the dependent nation was deprived of effective nationhood." (Myrdal, *op. cit.* p. 54.) Moreover it was usually simpler and more profitable for the governing power to sustain but control the existing rulers, than to encourage or to permit the introduction of democracy, socialism or even a new ruling group. The metropolitan government usually decided that a dictator, or a puppet who would "stay bought," was the most convenient and effective tool for the administration of a colony.

No consideration of the colonial system would be complete that failed to mention the socially and morally bad effects of colonialism on the metropolitan powers, and their peoples. No economic benefits could off-set the evil results—arrogance, intolerance, insensitivity, social prejudice—that inevitably resulted from allowing one people to rule another. Colonialism like slavery degraded both masters and servants.

Today, as the newly-independent countries endeavour to establish their own patterns of development, they embark on this difficult task with the inheritance of the bad, as well as of the sometimes good, features of the colonial systems.

EXCESSIVE POPULATION/Kept within rational limits a large population can be considered a national asset. But what are rational limits? There is no single or universal answer to such a question. In any given case it will depend upon such factors as the form of social and economic organization of the community; the ratio of population to developed and potential resources; the present character and stage of development of the people themselves, their degree of industrialization, and their relations with their neighbours and with the world. Belgium or England today can support, in decency, a denser population than China, Indonesia or Ceylon.

But judged by any defensible standard it must be clear that there are now many parts of the world that are already grossly "over-populated," no matter what the definition of that term. Most of this pressure is in the under-developed countries, yet in many of these same areas the population is growing almost twice as fast as it is in most industrialized societies. The sudden flaring of population that has marked the last hundred years, and in particular, the last few decades, is rapidly creating a situation that threatens to destroy the hopes of those who are working for the progress of the less advanced nations. It is now clear that unless drastic measures are soon employed, grim disaster will menace humanity. In the under-developed countries the hope of any significant improvement in the standards of human well-being is almost certain to be thwarted unless a solution can be found for the problems created by their exploding populations. In many countries it is true, as the Red Queen said to Alice, that "here, you see, it takes all the running you can do to keep in the same place. If you want to get somewhere . . . you must run at least twice as fast as that." The significance of the population problem will be considered in greater detail in the next chapter.

LACK OF DOMESTIC CAPITAL / Under normal conditions the rate of economic development of a country depends in large part upon how much of its current income can be diverted to the creation of real capital—homes, roads, factories, railways, power plants, cultivated lands. In most of the under-developed countries today the accumulation of any sizable surplus is almost impossible. Any favourable balance is usually small and of what is available the major part is likely to fall into the hands of those who have little interest in using it to promote the general progress of their country. With most of the population living at or near the subsistence level, as is generally the case, and with much of it entirely outside the money economy, the ability to mobilize any significant amount of domestic capital is likely to be beyond the national capacity.

Recent figures indicate that the *developed countries* of the West are adding to their productive investment every year at the rate of about ten per cent of their annual income. This means that an average of something like $90 per capita is going into the purchase of new plant and equipment, which in turn results in the creation of more wealth. In the *pre-industrial countries* of Asia and Africa, on the other hand, the total per capita *income* is only about $75 per year. In other words, the people of the industrialized countries are saving more than the peoples of Asia and Africa are receiving for all purposes. It is not, therefore, surprising that the gap between the haves and the have-nots is steadily widening. The extent of this gap can be gauged from the fact that the industrial nations of the West with only one-third of the world's population and one-quarter of its land area produce eighty-six per cent of its manufactured goods. And the rich are steadily increasing their riches; the only luxury of the poor is procreation.

It is not inconceivable that the Marxian belief in the inevitable widening of the gap between rich and poor, with the ultimate complete impoverishment of the latter, having been proved false as between classes in western industrial society, may yet demonstrate an unexpected validity on the international scene. This is a theme to which both Dr. Hans Singer and Dr. Raul Prebisch, among others, have made interesting contributions.

The disparity between the developed and the under-developed parts of the world is aggravated in many ways. Professor Blackett, one of the most perceptive and most thoughtful of contemporary observers, emphasized this point in the course of a remarkable presidential address to the British Association when he said that,

> . . . most new scientific and technical discoveries or developments tend to widen the gap still more, just because the already rich countries have the capital to make full use of them, but the poor countries have not. (P. M. S. Blackett: Technology and World Advancement, Nature 180, Sept. 7, 1957.)

Even in countries where there is, or might be, a useful margin of savings, much of this surplus is likely to be used for unproductive purposes. Wasteful and sometimes intentionally and callously conspicuous consumption by individuals, or by the State itself, drains off resources in a manner that very often is as morally offensive as it is economically mischievous. It is not only in the crude forms of individual or class extravagance that the tendency towards unwise expenditure is displayed. Spectacular investment in public buildings, luxury hotels, or a "status-symbol" steel industry may all have the same adverse effect on the national economy.

Perhaps the most harmful as well as the most extreme example of unwise expenditure by governments of under-developed countries is the outlay of many of these governments on military establishments. In some of the most backward countries—states in which a large part of the populace lives at what should be considered a sub-human level—as much as sixty per cent of the national income is spent on military, naval, and air "defences." In certain cases governments have recently spent enormous sums on military aircraft, while a large proportion of their children have no schools. Such prestige expenditures are not only negatively harmful; they introduce a whole wide range of positive evils, not the least of which is the strengthening of a privileged class of service personnel, whose social ignorance is normally matched only by their political ambitions and their individual and group venality. The Batista regime in Cuba, that of Pérez Jiménez in Venezuela, and that of the Ngo family in Vietnam, are only three of many recent and widely reported examples.

Moreover, one of the most serious dangers in contemporary society arises from the fact that in many of the less-developed countries the only really efficient foreign aid that is being received—judged both by quantity and quality—is in the realm of military equipment and training. This fact carries a clear threat to democratic institutions, where these exist or might otherwise evolve. It may well result in establishing or confirming military dictatorships because only the military will have derived effective benefit from the application of modern technology. A twentieth-century army in an otherwise mediaeval society can hardly fail to produce an imbalance that will make democratic practices improbable, if not impossible. It is not often that a general or an admiral is found to be economically sophisticated, or to be greatly concerned with human rights and political proprieties.

While such criticism of military expenditures by poverty-ridden countries is fully justified, it should not be allowed to stand alone. The insanity of waste that marks the current "defence" policies of the wealthier states, is no more morally defensible than is the behaviour of their indigent neighbours.

Another of the major handicaps that interferes with the progress of the under-developed countries is the fact that, as the gap between the rich and poor nations widens, the cost of catching up is correspondingly increased. The expense of equipping a worker for modern industrial employment is vastly greater today than ever before in history—and the cost is still rapidly rising.

Discussion of the problem created by capital scarcity should not be abandoned without a reference to the ingenious hypothesis of Professor Ragnar Nurkse that contact with more advanced countries may actually retard economic development of their poorer neighbours by encouraging new wants, and thus the propensity to consume, and thereby discourage savings and investment. (Ragnar Nurkse: *Problems of Capital Formation in Under-developed Countries*, London, 1953, pp. 61–70.) It is not necessary to accept in full Professor Nurkse's emphasis on the "international demonstration effect," to recognize this as one among the many problems that face the more backward nations. The temporary enjoyments of conspicuous consumption are as tempting to governments as to individuals.

ABSENCE OF AN EFFECTIVE MIDDLE CLASS/ One of the most striking characteristics of an under-developed country is the meagre size or the total absence of a middle class, and consequently of the enterprising spirit and the managerial capacities that such a class normally represents. To the extent that a middle class does exist, it is usually confined almost exclusively to merchants, agents, soldiers, money-lenders, traders and appointed governmental officials. Such an embryonic bourgeoisie contains very few business entrepreneurs or effective industrial managers. Where such persons are found they have usually been supplied or recruited from outside the national boundaries. Local personnel is not trained for such activities. For centuries, the forebears of those who now constitute the limited middle class of countries like Iran or Peru have traded and sold, have been in the armed services, and have been appointed to office. They have no tradition of industrial organization and management or of involvement in construction or manufacturing. The have manipulated, they have not made.

The historical reasons for this situation are obvious. The larger part of the population in the poorer countries is found in the peasantry. Their lives, in general, are confined to the deadening routine of a comparatively isolated and often unproductive husbandry. Bound by tradition, costive in thought, they have no knowledge of and no incentive towards construction or business management. Until very recently they have believed it to be inevitable that they should always be poor; no avenues have seemed to be open by which they could greatly better their lot.

The small aristocratic class that is characteristic of many of the less-developed nations is equally burdened by history. Traditionally, its members disdained economic pursuits: they could rule, kill, exploit, gamble, waste, plunder, study, but it was beneath their dignity to manufacture or even to trade. The results are illustrated not less by the history of their countries than by the personal defects they so frequently and so repellently display.

Even when the despised members of the local merchant class become wealthy, they do not usually (Japan was a great exception) re-invest their money in productive industrial enterprises. As Barbara Ward has pointed out:

> The merchant tends, as he did in China, to turn his wealth into land and to leave the life of capital-formation behind as soon as his fortune permits the change. Such societies incline of their very nature to be backward-looking, to preserve rather than to create, and to see the highest wisdom in the effort to keep things as they are. Under these conditions no underlying psychological drive impels people to work and to accumulate for the future. . . . In the first stages of a developing business system one finds again and again a pull between the desire to use the new wealth for old forms of privilege . . . and the opposite desire of more adventurous ways of further investment to widen the economic base of the whole society. (Barbara Ward: The Rich Nations and the Poor Nations, New York, 1962, pp 45, 87–88.)

Before leaving this subject a reference should also be made to the obvious fact that in most of the poorer countries native enterprise is greatly inhibited by the lack of a home market with a measurable purchasing power such as might be provided by a prosperous agriculture. The best incentive to production is an active consumer demand.

C · The Problem of Social Debility

Development cannot be discussed in economic terms alone, for the processes of economic growth take place within a social and cultural context. The role of the family, the type of government, the legal system, the skills of labour, the standards of health and education, the character of the prevailing religious beliefs, all influence the form and the quality of the national economy. Indeed, the basic factor in the phenomenon of organized society is the individual human being, the man, the woman and the child who in the aggregate constitute the nation and who as individuals are only too often wracked by disease, haunted by poverty, and bound by ignorance.

In his study of the principles of economic development Professor Charles Kindleberger, a leading theoretician in this field, included as one of its main "ingredients," the capacity of the labour force of a country to participate in and contribute to cumulative economic change, the ability to acquire new productive skills and to be responsive to new opportunities. (Charles P. Kindleberger, *Economic Development*, New York, 1958, pp. 10ff.) Traditional societies, of which the under-developed countries are in general the surviving representatives, are extremely resistant to change in their established modes of thought and behaviour. Such societies characteristically find it exceedingly difficult to mobilize their political, social, and psychological forces for the purposes of national or group development. As a result social debility is typical of their existence.

As in the case of economic stagnation, there is no one cause that explains this social weakness. But here also certain contributing factors can be identified and summarized.

INCIDENCE OF DISEASE/ The geographic and climatic distribution of disease has already been described and reference has been made to its economic effects. But it is also, of course, a social problem. The tragedy and the hope of the present situation are that much of the present misery is unnecessary. By the application of known techniques of treatment and prevention a large part of the current suffering could be relieved and some of the most common and most injurious of the mass diseases could be permanently eradicated.

The preamble of the Constitution of the World Health Organization defines health as "a state of complete physical, mental, and social well-being and not merely the absence of disease and infirmity." The United Nations Charter of Human Rights echoes these phrases, thus recognizing that good health is not just a medical challenge but is also a social goal.

If the general health of a nation can be improved, more effective results from programmes designed to provide better food, better housing, better working conditions, and higher levels of education can be anticipated.

The magnitude of the health problem can be seen, however, in such examples as the estimate that in southern Rhodesia the loss of manpower due to malaria amounts to from five to ten per cent of the total labour force; or in Egypt where bilharziasis alone decreases productivity by thirty-three per cent. (C. E. A. Winslow: *The Cost of Sickness and the Price of Health*, Geneva, World Health Organization, 1951, p. 15.) According to Ritchie Calder (whose writings must surely qualify him as one of the more useful members of his generation) the typical peasant in the tropics has to work a third of his life just to feed his tapeworm. (Ritchie Calder: *Common Sense about a Starving World*, London, 1963, p. 138.)

In the under-developed countries the major barriers to health improvement are those erected by the mass diseases—malaria, bilharziasis, yaws, hookworm, dysentery, tuberculosis, cholera, smallpox, typhus, yellow fever, and the like. Five hundred million people have trachoma. Control of these endemic diseases will provide a better chance for national as well as individual development, but the obstacles to effective control are large. Ignorance and dietary taboos often discourage people from eating the foods that are indispensable for health; religious customs relating to the taking of life have resulted in the appalling burden of the largely useless cattle of India, and have sometimes stalled projects for insect control. In many parts of Africa the witch-doctor is the greatest enemy of the physician. (See Clovis Akindes: *My Number One Enemy is the Witch-Doctor*, World Health, 12, November/December, 1959, pp. 26–27.)

Some progress, however, is being made. The medical profession, including even the confraternity of medicine-men, is more receptive to change than used to be the case. While local witch-doctors still seek to preserve their monopolistic rights, even they are being influenced by the results that flow from the application of new scientific discoveries, and the comparatively recent development of healing and fortifying techniques that have been developed as a result of increased understanding of the human body and its functions. At least it is no longer possible to envisage such a situation as that in ancient Egypt where for over a thousand years doctors were forced on pain of heavy punishment, or even death, to accept the authority and act in accordance with the principles of the Book of the Dead. There are certainly more conscious medical frauds practising today than ever before in human history, but proportionately they have declined in numbers—even in the more backward areas of the world.

SOCIAL TRADITION/ It is broadly true that many of the traditions, customs, and religious beliefs of the people of the under-developed countries are hostile to those attitudes, institutions and activities that are favourable to economic growth and social welfare. Simple examples are the scorn for manual labour and the denigration of the commercial classes.

In religion, the emphasis on contemplation, the influence of the mystic, and the persistent search for contact with a spiritual world may be beneficial to the individual soul but contribute little to the development of an economically viable community. On the other hand the Puritan emphasis on business success as an aspect of religious devotion may have been of dubious moral validity, but it did assist in the rapid economic development of both England and New England. Unfortunately, viewing the situation from a purely materialistic standpoint, there is little of this kind of incentive in most of the less-developed nations today.

Two examples drawn from many in different parts of the world can be used to illustrate the character and the importance of this problem. In Africa, people have lived in tribal communities for many hundreds of years; they are only beginning the slow evolution to nationhood and taking the first limited steps towards industrialization. A fierce tribal spirit, based on blood relationships, which weakens the concept of national unity and which is almost completely incompatible with an industrial economy, still exists in many regions. This divisive influence is fostered by the concomitant guarantee of shelter, food, and comfort which is the tribal cement. Undoubtedly, the vigorous spirit of nationalism will triumph in the end, but meanwhile it must reach a working agreement with persistent tribalism if even a limited progress towards modern forms of commercial and industrial life is to be effected. The great problem will be to achieve this progress while avoiding the danger of leaving the "mass of people without a feeling of unity, of security, of belonging to a group. . . . Otherwise the death of tribalism will kill a vital spark within the spirit" of the African people. (Elspeth Huxley: "Africa's First Loyalty," *New York Times Magazine*, September 18, 1960, pp. 14ff.)

In Indonesia a powerful mysticism became deeply rooted centuries ago and it has never been entirely wiped out by the newer religions. In recent years, there has been a great resurgence of cultism and a virulent associated quackery. This has been attributed by some informed observers to an attempt on the part of the people to escape from the present frustrating "economic turmoil, lack of opportunities, shortages of goods that plague that unhappy country. The nature of this Indonesian mysticism makes its devotees easy prey for corrupting influences, and at the same time makes them less valuable as citizens of a country that desperately needs to marshal all of its resources for economic and social progress." (Bernard Kalb: "Land of Cultists, Mystics and Quacks," *New York Times Magazine*, September 11, 1960, pp. 37ff.)

Also worth considering is the effect on the members of some of the more primitive societies of the obvious association of Christian missionaries with the luxurious life of the countries from which they have come. Edmund Leach, the distinguished anthropologist who is now Provost of King's College, Cambridge, has described in perhaps rather exaggerated terms, a situation that is not without significance in any study of the contemporary world.

A hundred years ago . . . European imperialism and Christian missionary endeavour went hand in hand; justice and virtue were obviously on the side of the big battalions; putting clothes on naked savages was good for morality and good for Lancashire as well.

But colonialism is now in total eclipse and it is permissible to consider, without too much embarrassment, just what the white man's burden looked like from the other side of the fence. In brief, it looked very attractive: it seemed to consist of brick-built houses, motor cars, refrigerators, radios, and all the rest of the technological gadgetry with which administrator, plantation manager, and missionary manage to make life in the tropics worthwhile. Who can blame the poor savage for thinking that it might be nice to have a share of these treasures and that conversion to Christianity was the first step to a material heaven? But singing hymns for the missionaries did not produce refrigerators and, as the image of colonial authority lost its 19th century gloss, heathen and convert alike began to suspect that they had been sold a pup. The missionaries had obviously doled out a fake prescription; they were keeping all the true gifts of the gods to themselves.

This is the context of modern messianic cults, which have a worldwide distribution. The new messiah is usually a "native" who has had close associations with the boss-class Europeans. He has learnt their tricks and admired their gadgets, and he hates their guts. The gospel which he preaches has echoes of Christianity and echoes of older indigenous faith; it assures the faithful that the day of the Lord is at hand, when all manner of blessings shall be their reward and the evil oppressors shall be blotted out. Naturally enough, the messiah very shortly finds himself in gaol accused of sedition and similar beastly practices, though with reasonable luck and persis-

*tence he can also count in due course on becoming the first president
of some newly elected UN member-country. (New Statesman, December 27, 1963, p. 947.)*

LACK OF UNDERSTANDING OF A MONETARY ECONOMY/ If the wide gulf between a barter subsistence and a monetary economy is to be crossed, it
must first be bridged in the minds of the people who are about to make
the change. An economic revolution of this dimension cannot be effected
without a major modification in the social structure of the country concerned. Perhaps the most important change is the acceptance of the idea
that it is necessary to have a job for subsistence; that to survive and progress the individual must participate in the operations of a monetary
economy rather than exist by bartering a few goods with equally indigent
neighbours. He must also be prepared to modify some of his more
cherished customs, such, for example, as the not uncommon celebration
of as many as 150 holidays each year. A reduction in the consumption of
pulque, saki, chicha, beer or some similar intoxicant may also be requried
if a job is to be held.

It is interesting to observe that this idea that it is necessary to work
to eat is being sold to the peoples of the less-developed areas as morally
right and economically essential at the very time that the concept of
the right of everyone to a basic subsistence income is being increasingly
propagated in some of the more advanced countries.* The difference is,
of course, that some of the wealthy countries can afford such an innovation because the vast majority of their peoples are anxious and able
to work, whereas it is a luxury in which the poorer countries cannot
afford to indulge.

The change to a monetary system in an under-developed country will
inevitably mean some dislocation of the prevailing family patterns and
will thus touch the most sensitive of social institutions. In the economically backward regions, the family is normally the basic productive unit,
and the prevailing system of values minimizes the influence of economic
incentives and the individualism which are characteristic of more advanced societies. Within such a social organization the urge to work, save

---

* *A rather amusing if frivolous example of how customs change occurred a
few years ago in Japan. The Christian missionaries in that country had for
generations been preaching against the local custom which took a lenient
view of the exposure of the human, even the feminine, body. So successful
was their teaching that in 1935 the Japanese authorities in Kariwazawa, the
summer resort largely patronized by foreigners, arrested a number of
missionary wives and daughters, who appeared in the streets in shorts and
halters, for "indecent exposure."*

and invest is tempered by the realization that it is always possible to fall back upon the family, the tribe or the village. Moreover, as the lines dividing rich from poor are usually harshly drawn, it is not easy to envisage the benefits that even a proportionately considerable addition to a single income will provide. Thus, individual initiative and the entrepreneurial spirit are discouraged by the weight of tradition, the weakness of imagination, and the absence of any very lively hope. Professor Benjamin Higgins, who has had a wide experience of under-developed areas, has stressed this theme. (Benjamin Higgins: *The Dualistic Theory of Under-developed Areas*, Economic Development and Cultural Change, 4, January 1956, pp. 99–116.)

LACK OF SKILLED LABOUR/ All of the under-developed countries suffer from a shortage of trained artisans and mechanics; in fact this is one of the most characteristic stigmata of their condition. On the other hand, there is almost always a surplus of unskilled labour. In many cases, the size of this surplus is likely to be underestimated because of the various forms of hidden unemployment that are characteristic of the more primitive economies. The historical emphasis on agricultural production in most backward countries is both a cause and an effect of this lack of other labour skills and of the desirable incidence of specialization. Such a society does not even encourage an increase in agricultural skills because, with a surplus of labour, the working-force can be more or less indefinitely supplemented to compensate for individual incompetence.

Manpower, in fact, in most of the under-developed countries is a potential source of economic and social strength, but it is often an immediate burden. The present situation is illustrated by the hordes of office-boys, messengers, attendants, and hangers-on of all kinds, that are usually to be seen in government buildings, business offices and other centres of activity in the less-developed countries. In fact a reasonably accurate estimate of the stage of development of any country can be obtained by noting the number of door-openers on duty and the number of times coffee is served in the course of an hour's visit to a public or private office. The higher the number of attendants and attentions the lower the state of the national economy is likely to be found.

In view of these facts it is important in studying possible development programmes in the poorer countries to place emphasis, at least in the early stages of industrialization, on labour-intensive projects. In such cases automation is as uneconomic as it is anti-social.

D · The Problem of Administrative Incompetence

Partly as a result of the lack of managerial experience and skill, and even more as a result of the inadequacy of private resources of investment capital, there is an inevitable tendency in the under-developed countries for governments themselves to undertake a much larger role in the national programmes for economic development than is customary elsewhere, except in the totalitarian states. Dr. Eugene Staley, who has written perceptively on so many aspects of international aid, has explained this situation in the following words:

> *Private enterprise fails to function effectively in most under-developed countries, not so much because it is repressed or interfered with as because it does not yet exist in the modern sense in which Americans automatically think of it.* (Eugene Staley: *The Future of Under-developed Countries—Political Implications of Economic Development*, New York, 1954. p. 239.)

This reliance on state aid and participation underlines the dangers which flow from the universal shortage of competent administrative personnel in the civil services of the under-developed countries. The gravity of this weakness (which exists in the private sector—to the extent that such a sector exists—as well as in government) would be hard to exaggerate, and it is one of the most difficult of all development problems with which to deal.

Of all the characteristics of national under-development, administrative inadequacy is the most prevalent, the most difficult to overcome, and the least likely to be recognized, or if recognized, to be admitted, by the governmental authorities concerned. There are some things that men and governments confess with ease; others with difficulty, if at all. Public administration suffers from the embarrassment that affects so many of the social sciences; it is a discipline within which almost no one will admit incompetence. Few men or women feel ashamed to acknowledge that they know little of geology, chemistry, astronomy or physics. But equally few will frankly admit doubts of their competence to act or judge in the fields of politics, religion, sociology, literature—or administration. It seems to be an almost invariable rule of human nature that the less demonstrable a conviction, the more firmly it is held. Native conceit seems to have convinced every individual human being of at least two things: that he has an impeccable sense of humour, and that if the opportunity occurred he could successfully manage a government department. If the first were true, it is possible that belief in the second might waver.

It is not surprising that the administrative practices of the economically backward countries should frequently be a source of primary concern to those from abroad who are invited and attempt to assist in the processes of national development. It is difficult to concentrate effectively on proposals for economic and social progress, when it is quite clear that the government of the country concerned will be unable, unwilling, or both unwilling and unable, to execute the desired reforms. Even when administrative weaknesses are identified or admitted, it is not always reasonable to assume that a solution will be accepted. Administrative reform, like other kinds, usually involves at least an initial increase in expenditure. It may result not only in financial burdens for those in control of the government, but in fewer jobs for those they desire to favour. Under such circumstances the fragile fabric of good intent is often inadequate to protect the occupants of the seats of authority against the cold winds of self-interest.

The usual accusations against the administrative practices of the underdeveloped countries are that their organizational arrangements are bad, their personnel inexperienced and inefficient, and their leadership corrupt. Of course, these characteristics are not universally to be found among the poorer countries, nor are any of them entirely unknown among the stronger and wealthier states. Dr. Hans Singer, who has worked intensively on this subject during his long and distinguished service with the United Nations, has neatly summarized the situation:

> Development requires good administration, yet good administration is itself a result of economic development. It is not, of course, a necessary result, for some highly developed countries have very bad administrations. The difference is that once development has been achieved, bad administration can be afforded as a luxury.... (H. W. Singer: "Obstacles to Economic Development," Social Research, 20, March, 1953, pp. 19–32.)

The Report of the United Nations Mission to Bolivia, to which reference has already been made, in describing the public service of that country, emphasized the weaknesses that arose from constant changes in personnel. It was discovered, for example, that no public official then in a senior post had held office for more than four years. As the ministers changed with even greater rapidity the difficulty of developing and maintaining a consistent policy, and of ensuring its effective execution, was obviously insurmountable while these conditions continued to prevail.

Dr. Albert Lepawsky, whose work in the under-developed countries and whose writings about their problems are widely known and highly respected, has pinpointed two of the major public-administration problems of such areas as (1) the historic distrust of government institutions despite a consequent widespread evasion of administrative authority; and (2) the burden of governmental "formalism" that often paralyses administrative action. (Albert Lepawsky: "Technical Assistance: A Challenge to Public Administration," *Public Administration Review*, 16, Winter 1956, pp. 22–32.) *

In the administration of private business in the under-developed countries there is also, in general, a comparable inability to perform efficiently the normal functions of the entrepreneur—functions that elsewhere are simply taken for granted.

The Bolivian report gives a concise description of the problems created and perpetuated by administrative incompetence. The beautiful and richly endowed country which the report describes, epitomizes in many respects the experience and the present condition of a large number of the under-developed nations. Fortunately in recent years Bolivia has differed from many of the other backward societies in having a government that has recognized its responsibilities and has tried—so far, admittedly, with only limited success—to do something to meet them. The report, written in 1950, describes the part that administrative incompetence and instability had played in blocking national progress. It goes on to make a proposal—unique at that time—for overcoming these obstacles:

> It might be possible to disregard the general facts that in 125 years of independence Bolivia has had some 60 Presidents, and that the governmental history of that country has been marked by constant and often violent change, not only in personnel but in policy. Many other countries have had somewhat similar experiences and have at length solved or are solving the problem of governmental instability.

> But there is little evidence of a similar development in modern Bolivia. The recent trends are in the wrong direction. Prospective or possible sources of investment capital will not fail to note that no legally elected Bolivian President has served out his term in the last quarter century; that there have been seven Presidents and eight revolutions in the last ten years; that there have been eighteen Ministers of Labour in four years; that the Corporacion de Fomento Boli-

---

* See also the excellent recent book Development Economics and Administration by the widely-experienced Swedish expert Sune Carlson, Scandinavian University Books 1964.

viano has had five complete changes in its Directorate in the six years of its existence; that there have been eight Ministers of Finance within 18 months. . . .

The instability of Government policies and administration do not arise solely from the frequent changes of the personnel in high office. It is due also to the failure of Bolivia to establish or indeed to make possible, the development of an official administrative service of competence and stability. Bolivia simply does not possess enough senior (or indeed junior) civil servants with ability and experience to handle the problems with which the administrative machine must contend. Yet until this problem is solved Bolivia cannot hope to obtain the raw material of skills and capital that are essential to its welfare and progress.

This situation leads to the first and the most important of all the recommendations upon which the Members of the Mission have agreed. It is a recommendation that has already been accepted with firm approval by the Bolivian authorities and has been adopted in principle by the Technical Assistance Board. It is proposed that the United Nations assist the Bolivian Government in obtaining the services of a number of experienced and competent administrative officials of unquestioned integrity drawn from a variety of countries, and that the Bolivian Government appoint these officials on a temporary basis to positions of influence and authority as integral members of the Bolivian civil service. It is an essential part of the proposal that in order to obtain persons of the required quality, adequate salaries and allowances be paid and that the United Nations provide financial assistance to the Bolivian Government for this purpose.

The persons described above would not in any sense be officials of the United Nations. They would be experts hired by and responsible solely to the Bolivian Government. The United Nations would aid in their recruitment and assist in financing the project, but that is all.

It is intended that the function of these "Administrative Assistants" shall be

1/To perform the duties and exercise the authority assigned to them in the Bolivian civil service;
2/To direct and assist in the training of Bolivian personnel with the object of developing as rapidly as possible a Bolivian civil service of experience, competence and integrity;
3/To aid in ensuring that the terms of the proposed Agreement be-

*tween the Bolivian Government and the United Nations are carried
into effective execution.*

*This proposal constitutes a new development in the methods by
which the United Nations endeavours to extend friendly, and unselfish but mutually beneficial assistance to one of its members. Because
the aid is offered by the United Nations as a whole, and because the
personnel involved—as in the case of the present Mission itself—
will be drawn from a variety of national sources, there can be no
question of any single external authority gaining undue influence
in Bolivia.*

*The proposal is an experiment. But it is an experiment initiated under
the best possible auspices. It is a token of international goodwill towards, and interest in, Bolivia. It will have the vigorous and constant support of the Technical Assistance Board and of the Specialized
Agencies of the United Nations. It has been approved in advance by
the Bolivian Authorities and by representatives of business, labour,
professional and academic life in that country.*

*Above all other considerations is the fact that it seems to offer the
only real hope of success. It is true that economic laws operating on
the abundant resources of Bolivia may eventually produce a stable
and sound economy. But such a result will take generations if not
centuries. It will certainly not develop in time to be of benefit to
the present inhabitants of Bolivia or to their children. By taking this
bold and dramatic step it is the belief of the Members of the Mission
and of their Bolivian collaborators that the national evolution of that
country can be materially accelerated. It is their desire to see results
in this generation, indeed in this decade. They are not content to
allow poverty and ignorance to reign unchallenged one day longer
than is absolutely necessary. It is essential for Bolivia, but it is also
of importance to the prosperity and peace of the rest of the world,
that something be done now. (Report of the United Nations Mission
to Bolivia, pp. 3–4.)*

The proposal thus outlined was based originally on a suggestion made by
Mr. David Blelloch of the United Kingdom who was the labour expert
on the United Nations Mission. It was adopted and elaborated by the
Mission as a whole and, after some initial difficulty and even opposition,
was eventually approved by the Technical Assistance Board and the
Secretary-General of the United Nations. Some years later it was taken
up by the then Secretary-General, Dag Hammarskjold, and became the
basis of an expanded United Nations programme for the provision of

operational and executive personnel to countries requiring and requesting such aid. This OPEX * programme is today a major factor in the
whole scheme of international aid through the United Nations.

Unfortunately, continued political controversy limited the initial successes of the programme in Bolivia but in varying degrees the scheme
introduced in 1950 has persisted even in that still deeply disturbed and
unhappy country.

Although not a universal malady in the governments of under-
developed countries, corruption is sufficiently common to warrant consideration. Apart from the normal human susceptibility to temptation,
there are a number of special reasons for its prevalence in the poorer
nations. In most such countries officials are so badly paid that they are
driven by necessity to seek supplementary employment or to the acceptance of bribes or both. In many countries there is no tradition encouraging probity in office; governments change so often that ministers and
officials are tempted to act on the common assumption that they must
make money while they can. The situation is not improved by the characteristic irreverence with which governments are normally regarded—an
irreverence which stems in part at least from the vast gulf between the
opulent few who establish and profit from official policies, and the miser-
able many who obey them. That in these countries the government is
traditionally controlled by wealthy, landed groups who are likely to have
strong vested interests in the maintenance of the *status quo* is now generally recognized, and is obvious to anyone who has travelled widely in
such areas.

It is not, of course, to be argued that only the under-developed countries suffer from maladministration. Incompetence, inefficiency, and corruption can be found in many parts of the world in many forms, and
in nations at every level of economic development. National material
progress does not necessarily and inevitably result in executive efficiency
or high standards of probity in public office. In dealing with governments
of countries in receipt of technical assistance, it is often embarrassing
for United Nations officials to have to argue the case for organizational
reform and personal integrity in government as a necessary prerequisite
to economic prosperity and social progress, when the daily press is replete
with current examples of administrative weakness and public infidelity
in some of the largest, most modern, and most prosperous of nations.
The world today gives ample proof of the fallacy of the statement of
Alexander Hamilton that "the larger the society the more duly capable
it will be of self-government." The only element of truth in his assertion

* *Programme for the provision of operational and executive personnel.*

is the cold fact that only a strong and wealthy country can for any long period afford a corrupt or inefficient government. Only England could afford Victorian nepotism, only America Boss Tweed and "the Ohio Gang," only Canada such a regime as that of Maurice Duplessis. The fact that such countries can afford corruption does not excuse their indulgence in it. Indeed it makes the behaviour of offenders even more reprehensible for they sin without suffering any real temptation.

These references to corruption should not be interpreted as universally applicable to the under-developed areas. It is not impossible to cite examples of honest, unselfish and determined individuals and governments, who are thoroughly serious in their efforts to establish effective administrations dedicated to the cause of national progress and individual justice. But even in such cases the basic problems are not necessarily conquered. Unfortunately, Jefferson was quite wrong when he said that "the whole of government consists in the art of being honest" —although a more frequent and sustained practice of that art would certainly produce astonishing results in many capitals.

These do not by any means exhaust the list of the causes of the present difficulties, or the roster of continuing obstacles to economic and social progress in the under-developed countries. They merely indicate in a brief and partial manner a few of the more baffling and insistent problems that face those who are trying to assist the progress of the less fortunate peoples.

E · The Historical Precedent?

Some students of the international scene find similarities between the condition of the under-developed areas of today and that of the western world prior to the Industrial Revolution. This comparison has a certain plausibility, especially perhaps in some parts of Latin America, but for most of the world the analogy is quite misleading.

By 1750, when the Industrial Revolution may be said to have begun, the European world was already in possession of many of the material assets, most of the theoretical concepts and, above all, many of the habits of mind, that were to make rapid economic and technical progress feasible. Intellectual curiosity, scientific experimentation, a general concern with new ideas, and an unusual willingness to accept their implications, were widely characteristic of an influential number of the leading thinkers of that period. As Professor Bauer of the London School of Economics has pointed out, "the widespread and pervasive intellectual curiosity, sustained effort and spirit of experimentation in science, industry, and agriculture are obvious from the general literature and the scientific publications of the seventeenth and eighteenth centuries. . . ." (P. T. Bauer: *Economic Analysis and Policy in Under-developed Countries,* Cambridge, 1957, p. 46.) Two hundred years ago the work of Averroes and Bacon, of Galileo and Harvey, of Liebnitz and Newton, had become part of the intellectual framework of the well-educated man. It is true that European society as a whole was scientifically ignorant and complacent in its torpid incomprehension. But as with the cause and the results of the Renaissance, the Reformation and the Expansion of Europe, there was a small group in most western countries whose members were intellectually alive and actively engaged in the search for and dissemination of knowlege. Even in Russia, Peter the Great was trying, though almost single-handed, to break some of the shackles of ignorance, superstition and custom. In England, by the middle of the eighteenth century, the Royal Society was already one hundred years old.

Prior to the Industrial Revolution, long periods of profitable commercial activity had resulted in major accumulations of capital in Western Europe, capital which could be tempted into investment for industrial purposes. Labour was becoming plentiful and was highly mobile, migrating with little formality from place to place, even from country to country, as opportunity beckoned. The Protestant religion, the prevalent faith in the countries that moved most quickly and most effectively into the new industrial era, provided an ethical basis suited to the use of the new techniques. Profit was already becoming a form of piety.

Nor did the western nations of the seventeenth and eighteenth centuries face the handicap of a phenomenal population growth as do the under-developed countries today. The heavy increase in numbers in Europe and America followed the beginnings of the Industrial Revolution, while today the population increase, based primarily on the introduction of medical innovations rather than being stimulated by increased production, has come first.

Perhaps most important of all, as at once a stimulant and a tool, the larger part of Western Europe was integrated in an exchange economy. Thus, an adequate proportion of the ruling classes of the major nation-states were ready, intellectually, emotionally, administratively, and commercially, for the tremendous explosion of material progress that occurred in Western Europe and in Europe's appendages in America and in other parts of the world during the next two hundred years.

This condition stands in vivid contrast with the situation in most of the under-developed countries today. In some cases, as David Blelloch has pointed out, the people of these countries are less prepared for industrial progress than were the inhabitants of Britain or other parts of Western Europe one thousand years ago.

> . . . our industrialisation was the culminating stage in a developmental process whose course can easily be traced over several previous millennia of continuous, if uneven, progress. In terms of some of the essential prerequisites to industrialisation many of the newly developing societies are lower down on the developmental ladder than were our ancestors a thousand years ago: in terms, for instance, of ethnic homogeneity and national consciousness, of literacy, of the prevalence of a market economy, of effective administration, or real per capita income. If left alone, they might reach our present stage of development in a good deal less than a thousand years—or they might fail and perish, as other societies have perished in the past. But in the world of today we can't leave them alone, and they won't leave us alone. For good or ill, worldwide human solidarity and interdependence is no longer either a utopian dream or a patriot's nightmare—it is just one of the facts of life. (Blelloch, op cit., p. 6)

In the same persuasive analysis Blelloch also pointed out a number of the unique difficulties that face the under-developed nations in their current efforts to move ahead. Today,

> . . . even the most favourably situated among the developing societies are confronted by difficulties that our ancestors never had to face, and are denied advantages that greatly facilitated their successful march forward into industrialisation. On the one hand, for instance, they have to cope with the "population explosion" brought about by the medical knowledge we have passed on to them, while the growth of their material resources has lagged far behind; their organised workers, copying ours, can insist on a standard of living far higher than that which our own workers were forced to endure in the early days of our industrialisation; technological progress has rendered their often superabundant labour supply a deadweight rather than an asset; and their industrialisation has to be achieved in a world dominated by nations far stronger than themselves, both militarily and commercially. On the other hand, they have no colonies to receive their surplus population and offer markets to their products; they have not had time or opportunity to build up an efficient and prosperous agriculture such as provided an essential basis for the industrialisation of Western Europe, North America, Australasia and Japan; their populations have learnt to expect "democratic" political institutions, and to resist the imposition of the social

discipline and austerity that are necessary in the early stages of in-
dustrialisation; and the international capital market finds investment
in the developing areas far less relatively attractive than in the past.

Consequently, large areas of the world that we live, and trade, and
travel, and take holidays in will remain part affluent and part slum,
part healthy and part diseased, part orderly and part chaotic, unless
and until we take effective steps to speed up development. (Blelloch,
op. cit., pp. 6–7.)

It is true that some of the presently under-developed countries have
historical traditions of great cultural significance. In many aspects of
art, literature and philosophic thought such countries as Egypt, India,
Iran, and China have made exceptional contributions to human achievement.

But for the most part, though not of course entirely, these contributions have been of an aesthetic or philosophical rather than of a scientific or technical character. In almost every case the social institutions
that accompanied them were not congenial to economic progress. Con-
fucian ethics unquestionably played a major part in delaying economic
progress in China. It is, of course, true that religious barriers to economic
progress are no longer as effective as was once the case. In recent years
some of the countries in which the oriental religions—or Roman Catho-
licism—once were obstacles to economic and commercial development,
have had dynamic records of expansion. Unbridled exploitation, caste
stratification, concentration on war and the military arts, religious
intolerance of scientific enquiry, scorn for all participation in commercial activities and for manual labour, historical accident—all these have
played their part in the ultimate submergence of many of the authentic
values of the ancient heritage of Asia and the Middle East. The enquiring,
curious, sceptical mind and the orderly scientific approach to the study
of nature and humanity, are not commonly today characteristic of the
people of the less-developed areas.

The majority of the inhabitants of the poorer countries are still living
largely outside the social, economic and intellectual fabric that marks
the culture of the more advanced segments of the contemporary world.
Well over a billion people in the under-developed countries are illiterate,
and of those that can read and write very few have access to materials
that make any pretence of giving an objective or useful picture of modern
problems. This is not, of course, intended to suggest that literacy ensures
virtue, or that the intellectual elite are always socially valuable. But the
fact that a tool is badly used is no argument against the tool.

In a few of the under-developed areas of the world almost undiluted barbarism still prevails. There are parts of Africa, Asia, and even of Latin America in which people are living in conditions that have changed little for many hundreds of years. Less than fifty years ago cannibalism was not an uncommon practice in several regions of the world. In certain parts of Africa, it is still the law that meat cannot be sold except with the hide attached—to ensure that the purchaser is not being given human flesh! Slavery, open or only formally hidden, is still known to persist in a number of countries. In fact, regularly organized slave-raiding, usually accompanied by murder, castration and other barbarities, has only recently been stopped, if indeed it has been wholly eradicated even now.

Apart from such extremes, which affect only limited areas, perhaps the most distinctive characteristic of an under-developed country is the fact that subsistence agriculture is the prevailing mode; normal production is for home consumption or for exchange, by barter, in narrowly restricted local markets. Such circumstances prevail in many parts of Asia, Africa, the Middle East and Latin America, yet the development of an inclusive exchange economy is an essential part of any serious national programme for economic growth.

Although it is clear that the presently under-developed countries do not stand on the same threshold of economic progress that the now-established countries crossed some two hundred years ago, it is nevertheless true that in many ways, difficult ground has been broken for them. The basic technology for a high level of productivity exists for both farm and factory; it does not have to be invented again. Man's knowledge and ability to control his environment have been vastly increased. Social machinery has been devised to help cope with the problems of an industrialized society. But a direct and rapid transfer of this knowledge from developed to under-developed societies is neither automatic nor easy; nor in fact is it always desirable that the transfer should be rapidly accomplished. The circumstances of each nation or area must be considered in the light of its own peculiar needs and conditions; there is no single infallible prescription; no path that all must follow.

The great problem of the years ahead is to devise as quickly as possible, taking into account the special circumstances of each particular case, the most effective method by which man's phenomenally rapid growth in knowledge and its use can be translated into the structure of human society, in the developed as well as in the backward nations, and in such a way as to contribute to community progress and to individual growth, (to use the Biblical terms) "in wisdom and stature and in favour with God and man."

CHAPTER THREE

The Population Problem and International Aid

Pessimism about Int. Aid.

It is occasionally argued that until something can be done to solve the problems created by the recent and spectacular rise in the number of human beings in the world, there is little point in trying to raise standards of life in the under-developed countries. It is possible that this pessimistic view may be justified by events yet to come. But whether or not this proves to be the case the population problem cannot be disregarded by anyone who is seriously concerned with the amelioration of the general human lot. Nor can its consideration be safely or justifiably postponed in the Micawberish hope that something will turn up.

A · The Dimensions of the Problem

Of all the human beings who have ever lived, nearly five per cent are alive today.

Although there are no exact figures it is now generally agreed that at the time of Christ there were about 250 million persons in the world. In 1,600 years this number had grown to about 500 million. This had doubled again in a little over two hundred years; that is, by about the time that Queen Victoria ascended the throne, just before Lord Durham wrote his Report, and shortly after the presidency of Andrew Jackson. Today the population of the world is well over three billion and if the present rate of increase continues it will certainly be over seven billion before the end of this century.

Obviously this cannot continue indefinitely. The space available on earth is limited, fixed. The over-all world population is now growing at a rate of just over two per cent per annum. This does not sound very impressive. But if only one couple had been on earth when Christ was born and their numbers had increased at a rate of two per cent annually since that time, the number now on earth would be something like 143 million billion persons. This would work out at about 1025 persons to each square foot of land on this planet. No matter how congenial the inhabitants, this would not be a desirable arrangement.

Not only is the world's population increasing today at a phenomenal and wholly unprecedented tempo, but the rate of increase itself is also sharply rising. Indeed, every time the matter is studied the figures show a new upward surge. United Nations estimates indicated a world population growth of 1.7 per cent in 1961, of 1.8 per cent in 1962, of 2.0 per cent in 1963 and of 2.1 per cent in 1964. If increases on this scale should continue the population of the world would be over fifteen billion by the end of the century, with the annual increase then running at an incredible 6.5 per cent. Of course it can be argued that the changes in the four years from 1961 to 1964 cannot be accepted as proof that the rate of increase will continue to rise in an equally dramatic manner in the future, and that is true. But recollecting what has happened in the past two or three generations it is at least as logical to argue that the rate of increase will accelerate as that it will decline.

Even if it should be assumed that by the year 2000 the population has only increased to six billion and that the rate of increase thereafter is held at three per cent, there would be 115 billion people in the year 2100, which is absurd! In other words, if things go on as they are now the maximum world population that can conceivably be tolerated will be reached long before the year 2100. Children of persons now alive will still be here when an unbearable climax has been reached. Dr. Philip M. Hauser, one of the most widely known and highly respected world experts in this field, who has studied its problem at close quarters in various parts of the world, has summarized the situation in this way:

> In the long run the limiting factor to population growth is, without question, the limit of space on this finite planet. Of the some 200,000,000 square miles of surface on this globe, approximately one-fourth is land. Of the land surface, approximately a tenth is arable and another tenth is potentially arable. The population that can be supported on this earth is necessarily a finite one, limited by the approximately 50,000,000 square miles of land surface on the globe.

> If in addition to the problem of space alone, is introduced the idea of the capacity of the earth to carry population, that is the capacity as measured by ability of the world to provide food, fibres and other requisites of human life, the longer run implications of present rates of growth become even more compelling. The highest estimate of the population-carrying capacity of the globe ever published by a

*responsible scholar is 50 billion. This calculation, by Harrison Brown,
is based on two extreme assumptions. The first is that enough control
of solar and nuclear energy could be achieved so that every "thing"
needed for human life could economically be captured from the sea,
the atmosphere or rock. The second assumption is that mankind
would be content to use algae, or manufactured yeast as his major
foodstuff. At the present rate of world population increase, this
maximum population of 50 billion could be reached well within
200 years!* (Philip M. Hauser: *Population Explosion and World
Politics, World Population Emergency Campaign*. Reprinted in *Study
of Population and Immigration Problems: Population of the World*.
Committee on the Judiciary, Sub-Committee No. 1, House of Representatives, Washington, D.C. U.S. Government Printing Office,
1962, p. 2.)

If, however, the rate continues to rise but is stabilized at three per cent
after 2000 A.D. the 50 billion will be reached about the year 2060.

Professor Harrison Brown, to whom Dr. Hauser referred, has also
said that "Rapid population growth works against practically all the
long-range goals which men and women the world over share. . . .
Of all the problems which confront our unhappy world it is by all odds
the most urgent and the most critical. Yet, ironically it is the problem
which is receiving the least attention." (Quoted in J. M. Jones: *Does
Overpopulation Mean Poverty?* Washington, 1962, p. 27.)

B · *What Can Be Done?*

The appalling situation that would develop within one hundred years—
unless something is done—will not, of course, be allowed to happen. At
some point before such an unendurable condition has been reached a
major change in the situation will certainly have occurred. What that
change will be cannot be forecast with any real assurance but it will have
to come in one, or in a combination of some of, nine forms. Reduced to
brief compass these are :

1/*Some natural law, which has not yet been discovered, will bring into
operation an automatic check on the rate of population growth.*

Forty-odd years ago a distinguished United States biologist tried to
work out a formula to show that all population growth in the animal
kingdom tended to conform to a single pattern that could be described by
a consistent and conventional curve, which after rising in a predictable arc

flattened out to indicate a stable population. (Raymond Pearl: *The Biology of Population Growth*, New York, 1925). Unfortunately it was found that this curve, while it applied with some uniformity in the case of certain insects, was much less accurate when tested against the experience of mankind. In any case, what has happened in the last generation shows conclusively that the curve was not an accurate forecast of what has since happened and is now happening to the human population of the world.

It may be that an automatic check will develop, but there is no present indication of such a convenient solution to the problem.

Disease alone has lost much of its potency as an effective check on population growth. Indeed, as a singularly acute Canadian observer has pointed out, disease is no longer reducing but seriously increasing population pressure. It is part of the essence of man's peril that, having largely eliminated the killing diseases, particularly those of infancy (with the exception of kwashiokor), he finds that the crippling diseases like leprosy, hookworm, bilharzia, tuberculosis, trachoma, the dysenteries and malaria are making it impossible for him to do a full day's work, whilst his capacity to eat and procreate are unimpaired. (Dr. L. S. Anderson: *The Mushroom Crowd*, an address given to the Canadian Medical Association, Vancouver, 1964, MSS p. 5.)

If past experience can be accepted as a guide to the future it is probably true that increased production of food, industrialization and the introduction of various types of social reform, including a widespread postponement of the age of marriage, can be expected to bring about a decline in the birth rate of the areas affected, without requiring any conscious decision on the part of the persons concerned. But this is a slow process and it offers little hope of the radical and rapid change that is required by the present situation if this ominously growing threat to the future welfare of mankind is to be averted.

2/*A single universal catastrophe or a series of major calamities may drastically reduce the current population.*

Some new and widespread pestilence might wipe out much of the human species, or an uncheckable series of universal famines might temporarily rescue the world by annihilating an adequate percentage of mankind. In spite of the many ways in which, even with present knowledge, the production of food could be quickly expanded, the possibility of widespread starvation within the present generation cannot be safely disregarded. On the first of September 1964, Dr. Raymond Ewell, Vice-President for Research of the State University of New York at Buffalo, said that "the most colossal catastrophe in history" in which "hundreds of millions or even billions of human beings" will perish can be expected in the 1970's unless the rich industrialized countries act immediately to give millions of tons of fertilizers to poverty-stricken areas of the world. The deadline beyond which even such gifts will be ineffective is only a few years away. (Associated Press, September 1, 1964.) Dr. Robert C. Cook, Editor of the Bulletin of the Population Reference Bureau pointed out in November, 1964 that the Government of India had estimated that by 1966 India's food-grain production will fall short of the country's needs by 28 million tons a year, and that "no conceivable programme of imports or rationing can meet a crisis of this magnitude." (Quoted by Jay McMullen, *Toronto Star*, November 30, 1964.) As if to underline these warnings the same newspapers that carried Dr. Ewell's statement also reported an urgent appeal from the government in New Delhi for the diversion, to meet emergency famine conditions in India, of grain shipments currently en route to other destinations. In 1965 the situation was rapidly deteriorating and early in 1966 Delhi was begging for emergency aid.

In the light of recent developments it would seem to be rather more than probable that the invention of nuclear weapons and the refinement of chemical and biological techniques of aggression will prove to be nature's insane scheme to provide for periodic reductions in population. If such weapons ever are used in all-out war, however, the result is likely to be the complete extermination of the human race. A milder way of stating a somewhat similar expectation is that of the distinguished American expert, Professor F. W. Notestein, who has said that "it is not at all unlikely that political explosion and the economic disorganization which accompanies it, will provide the major check to population increase in the future." (Quoted in Staley: *op. cit.*, p. 282.) In other words, war and its aftermath will solve the problem.

3/*A continuous state of conventional war, if waged in a sufficiently sanguinary style, might result in a stabilized population.*

As Dr. Anderson and others have pointed out, except in limited areas and for comparatively brief periods, warfare has never exercised a major influence on population growth. (L. S. Anderson, *op. cit.*, p. 3.) This might, however, be changed and conflicts could be arranged in such a way as to result in more or less continuous and heavy casualties but without resort to methods of mass destruction. The closely related practice of genocide might be an effective supplement. After all, Leopold I and his civilized subjects reduced the population of the Belgian Congo by three million in ten years (Ritchie Calder: "Chaos in the Congo," *New Statesman*, December 10, 1960), and Hitler's Germany exterminated some six million Jews in about four years. A periodic selection of certain "racial," religious, geographic or perhaps occupational groups for extermination would be one way of meeting the problem.

4/It is possible that the increasing use of radioactive substances will grow to such dimensions that it will effectively interfere with the reproductive capacity of human beings.

In the last few years there have been many warnings that even working or residing in the vicinity of atomic reactors may adversely affect the sexual capability of the men and women concerned. If these dangers significantly increase in the years ahead they may destroy or radically diminish the desire for sexual intercourse, or the ability of human beings to produce children. There is already some evidence to indicate that this is happening in certain limited areas but it would seem to be likely that increasing knowledge of protective techniques will prevent it from happening on any significant scale, unless it should be decided to use this method of wholesale contraception.

5/Some wholesale system of abortion or some scheme for the deliberate killing of persons after birth may have to be introduced.

Perhaps a variation of the Spartan custom of infanticide by exposure may have to be adopted. Or something like Hitler's scheme for eliminating mental and physical "defectives" and members of "sub-human" racial groups.

6/A widely accepted or, if necessary, a rigorously enforced policy of sterilization might offer a somewhat less drastic method of controlling the number of births.

This has already been started on a voluntary basis in Japan, where it is estimated that something over 100,000 persons are sterilized annually, and it is being practised on a growing scale in India, where the government now pays a sum equivalent to $21 to anyone who submits to this treatment. An additional payment of $1.05 is made to anyone who presents a consenting candidate for the operation. (Associated Press, Vancouver Sun, December 28, 1964.) Fortunately the sterilization technique is now highly refined, the brief operation causes a minimum of discomfort, and subsequent sexual satisfaction is not reduced.

7/A technique may be developed which will permit the transfer of human beings to some other planet in space.

If this could be started not later than about the year 2000 and could be so organized as to remove something like half a million people a day, it might enable the world population to be stabilized at somewhere around seven billion. This would involve the departure of about 3,500 of the largest aircraft every day with persons who would be leaving the earth for permanent residence elsewhere in the universe. So far as can presently be foreseen the development of such a scheme on a voluntary basis is improbable. And as Arthur C. Clarke, Chairman of the British Interplanetary Society, has said, "It would be far easier to make the Antarctic bloom like the rose than to establish large, self-supporting colonies on such worlds as Mars." (Quoted in The Royal Bank of Canada *Monthly Newsletter*, June 1964, p. 4.) Emigration from one part of the earth to another—even if the Antarctic should be turned into a garden—would not provide a means of escape for more than a few years if the rate of population growth continues to accelerate. And few local schemes of reclamation, irrigation and so on have any real value as a lasting solution or even as a method of significantly postponing the problem.

8/*Alternatively, beings or substances from outer space might reach the earth and either intentionally or inadvertently destroy all human life.*

It is not altogether inconceivable that if human beings should land on the moon or on one of the more accessible planets they might bring back with them organic or inorganic substances that would make life on earth impossible. This would be, on a larger and harsher scale, more or less what already happens on earth when exotic diseases are introduced into communities where they have hitherto been infrequent or unknown. The rapid flaring up among the northern Eskimos of such diseases as the common cold and influenza, in the wake of the annual visits of the Canadian supply vessels, is a minor example of how such an event might occur.

9/*The immediate and wholesale adoption of a conscious, deliberate policy of birth control offers the only intelligent and humane method of achieving the objective of a world population adjusted to the resources of this planet.*

Whether this can be designed and brought into effective use in the time left for action is becoming every day more doubtful. Lord Brain, the distinguished British physician, in his presidential address to the British Association for the Advancement of Science, in August 1964, urged the immediate establishment of a United Nations-sponsored organization to develop controls over the world's population. But the implementation of any such proposal is, for the present at least, politically impracticable. Nevertheless, in some way, if catastrophe is to be avoided, means must be found to carry into effect a programme which will result in the discovery or invention of new, inexpensive and acceptable techniques for the avoidance of conception, and the education of thousands of millions of people in their use. While many agencies, national and international— of which the International Planned Parenthood Association is perhaps the most important—are working towards this end, the strength of the opposition to any such programme should not be underestimated. In many parts of the world children are still regarded—against all evidence to the contrary—as socially desirable and economically beneficial. In others, opposition stems from religious or philosophical convictions of a wholly irrational but potent character.

Fortunately there is growing evidence to support the belief that doctrines are changing in the higher ranks of the internationally most influential of birth control's ecclesiastical opponents.

On June 23, 1964, Pope Paul VI in addressing a group of cardinals made it clear that his church could no longer disregard the practical issues raised by the population problem. The question of birth control, he said, "is being subjected to study, as wide and profound as possible, as grave and honest as it must be on a subject of such importance." For the dramatic debate which followed in the third session of the Vatican Council, the ruling of the moderator that the subject should not be discussed in public was disregarded, and strongly conflicting views were expressed. Representing the traditionalists, Cardinal Ottaviani insisted that the idea that married couples could determine for themselves the number of their children could not possibly be approved and was a doctrine unheard of in the Church. On the other hand Cardinal Leger (of Montreal), Cardinal Suenens (of Belgium) and the Patriarch Maximos IV Sayegh came very close to advocating a complete acceptance of the practice of birth control by direct means.

As the Patriarch said, the problem facing the Council was one created by "a lack of alignment between the official doctrine of the Church and the contrary practice of the immense majority of Christian couples. . . . Frankly, might not the official position of the Church on this matter be revised in the light of modern science, both theological and medical, psychological and sociological?" And the Belgian prelate made the emotional plea: "I beg you, my brothers: let us avoid a new Galileo case. One is enough for the Church."

Unhappily the Church cannot be expected to move with rapidity in abandoning its traditional position. The debate has just begun. And although a major change in doctrine is apparently on the way, it would seem to be most unlikely that this change can be accelerated to such a degree as to be effective in blocking the rapidly approaching catastrophe. The church leaders who have for generations been preaching to their followers that birth control is sinful are now, to some degree at least, the captives of their own preachings. It is, of course, obvious that a large proportion of the educated adherents of the Roman Catholic Church have long since given up any pretence of obeying the clerical injunctions on this matter. But even if Rome should modify its rulings it will take a long time, as time must be measured in this context, to bring general practice into conformity with the new authorization. Unfortunately it is the uneducated, the poverty-stricken and the superstitious masses who most need the knowledge of how to avoid the proliferation of the children they can neither support nor educate; it is they who will be the last to learn of the change in Vatican policy and the last to modify the habits that have become ingrained by lifelong indoctrination.*

---

* *The tragic diversity of views that marks the present position of the Roman Catholic membership (including recently the clergy) has been dramatically illustrated by the public debates of the last two or three years. Attitudes have varied from that of Dr. John Rock, Professor Emeritus of Gynaecology at Harvard University, who has asked for a simple but basic change to permit the use of contraceptives (New York Times, January 24, 1964), to that exemplified by M. C. A. Gauthier, Ralliement Crediste Member of the Canadian Parliament who in the House of Commons (Hansard 11. IX. 64 pp. 7936-8), in opposing the modification of the existing law which makes it a criminal offence to give or sell contraceptive information or devices (a law that is flagrantly and constantly violated by almost every chemist shop or drug store in Canada) said in part,*

"*Mr. Speaker, I rise to protest against the passage of this bill.*
I have seen many happenings in the House but this time things have gone too far. When I hear men speak in favour of such legislation, I wonder where the people of Canada are going. This is working towards the destruction of the human race. . . .
The whole of Canada must speak out against those who support this bill. We have no right to put such a dangerous, indeed, such a diabolical weapon into the hands of the people.
Most of us are Christians, and as such, it is our duty to put up as strong a fight as possible against this legislation. . . .
Think of what would happen to our people; in ten years from now, with this system, there would be no people left and the Black and Chinese people would come and replace us in Canada. . . ."
Somewhere between the positions of Dr. Rock and M. Gauthier is that represented by Father Roberts, a member of the Archdiocesan Matrimonial Court of Vancouver who on September 21, 1964 told a public meeting sponsored by the Knights of Columbus that, to quote the Vancouver Times,
"*As a Catholic and a priest I am 100% opposed to the use of contraceptives, but Catholics cannot try to cram down the throats of other citizens their theories on family planning. . . . The present law is violated en masse by responsible people in this country.*" *He added that the govern-*

by a broad and dismal margin to meet the needs of the present population. Today's total production of food, metals, fibres and other essentials would provide a European standard of living for about one-half, or a North American (Canada-United States) standard for about one-sixth of the current population of the world. These figures give a dramatic illustration of how much below the American and European standards the majority of people must now subsist. Even in the wealthiest of countries, according to President Lyndon Johnson, about twenty per cent of the people are living in poverty.

It is moreover true that in those areas of the world in which population is increasing most rapidly, the proportionate production of food is falling most consistently behind. Between 1935 and 1961 the per capita output of grain in Asia *declined* by two per cent; in Latin America it declined by sixteen per cent. In India today, the average food consumption is 1.23 lbs. per day (the corresponding figure in Canada is 4.66 lbs.) and of this eighty-five per cent is rice which is deficient in proteins, fats and vitamins. And in the same country, with twenty per cent of the world's dairy cattle, there are six million people in Calcutta alone who never taste milk. (The Royal Bank of Canada, *op. cit.*, p. 1.)

Persuasive arguments are advanced to show that the production of food could be enormously increased by the application of principles and the adoption of practices already widely known, and this unquestionably is the western world. And after 2000 A.D. the attempt to keep up, if population between now and the end of the century, the food resources of the world will have to be expanded much more rapidly than has ever been done before in even the most affluent and industrialized societies of the western world. And after 2000 A.D. the attempt to keep up, if population continues its present rate of growth, will be completely futile. Even reducing the minimum diet to yeast and plankton will not long suffice.

Population statistics except in the more advanced countries are notoriously inexact but they are gradually improving in precision and coverage and in almost every case in which it has been possible to check the more recent and more accurate figures against earlier estimates, the latter have been shown to be too low. Using with discrimination the tabulations that are now available, it is very clear that not only is the population problem in the under-developed countries at present more serious than it is in the economically advanced areas, but that the contrast is steadily becoming more and more shocking. The following figures illustrate these facts.

Roman Catholic Church is anticipated, it should not be introduced—the acceptance of example—are in themselves of help are as unlikely to make unreliable methods as they are to that the Church has fruitlessly

ment of some practical means of ing coition must be prepared to ternative will *prevent catastrophe?* ust be accepted that moral, ethical no effect commensurate with the control insist on maintaining their and popularize a new and effective e or more of the alternatives outlined ing the lifetime of children now alive ry to choose between preventing conmurder.

orld it might be argued that there is blem. But in contemporary society it o induce a significant number of people l." of Dean Swift that babies—especially ld be fattened and eaten! As Ritchie s a foolish sentiment . . . but we get fond e them to die, and we get attached to our em with us as long as we can." (Ritchie a Starving World, p. 78.)

t humanity is engaged in a race between s probably more accurate in relation to the kind than it is in connection with any other ur. Unfortunately this is an area in which rriers that make the task of education almost

ublic morality with laws such as those forbidding t said the government could not uphold laws on nored the opinion of the majority of Canadians. . . . the illicit quality of a flagrantly violated law." Catholics were too often regarded by their fellow ling back progress. "As Catholics we must look to the community." (Vancouver Times, Sept. 21, 1964.)

TABLE I

Region	Population (Million)	Birth Rate (Thousand)	Rate of Population Increase (%)
Asia (excl. Japan)	1,738	40	2.3
Africa	297	46	2.3
Latin America	240	42	2.7
Europe	440	19	0.8
U.S.S.R.	234	20	1.7
U.S.A. and Canada	214	22	1.6
Australia, New Zealand	14	23	2.1
Japan	98	19	1.0

Present estimates of what is likely to happen between 1975 and 2000 indicate that during those years population in Latin America will probably increase by about four per cent per annum; in Asia by over three per cent; and in Africa by just under three per cent; in North America the growth will be only about 1.2 per cent and in Europe one per cent. These figures are likely to prove to be too low rather than too high. In Latin America today the following rates of natural increase are already being recorded: Chile, 2.3 per cent; Brazil, 3.1 per cent; Nicaragua, 3.4 per cent; Venezuela, 3.0 per cent; Mexico, 3.4 per cent; and 3.2 per cent in Guatemala. In 1963 Costa Rica established an all-time world-record birth rate of 4.9 per cent (*New York Times* report by Tad Szulc, reprinted in the *Vancouver Province*, January 12, 1965). The actual rate of growth in some of the countries of Latin America is higher than these figures suggest because of net increases through immigration. Latin America has the highest growth rate of any region in the world, and is doing less about it.

Why is it that the very countries in which a rapid population growth is least advantageous are those in which it is most characteristic and found in its most exaggerated form?

The obvious, simple, and perhaps the basic reason is that in the poorer countries a larger proportion of the people are ignorant, poverty-stricken, apathetic or reckless (or both) and in bad health. As a consequence, they have less knowledge of how to care for themselves and greater temptations to irresponsibility. It is not unnatural that people thus afflicted should seize on any forms of pleasure that are within reach without giving too much thought to the probable consequences. In such circumstances the one almost insatiable, readily gratified, and thus practically irresistible temptation, is sexual indulgence. And this, because of ignorance and poverty, means more children. In contemporary literature perhaps the most detailed, direct and realistic description of how this works is to be found in *The Children of Sanchez*, the appalling record of how a Mexican slum family lives and thinks, by the anthropologist Oscar Lewis. This family, which was better off than many of those living in the Villas Miserias in Latin America and in Asia, exists in circumstances like these:

> *The room had one bed, in which Faustino and his wife slept. The rest of us slept on pieces of cardboard and blankets or rags spread on the floor. Socorrito slept with her husband and children in the small area between the bed and the wall. Paula and I spread our bedding at the foot of the bed. My sister-in-law Delila and her son slept in the corner near the kitchen. That is the way the thirteen of us, five families, arranged ourselves in that little room.* (Oscar Lewis: *The Children of Sanchez: Autobiography of a Mexican Family*, New York, 1961, pp. 160–161.)

This illustrates, moreover, the threatening fact that in Mexico (as in many other countries) nearly half the population is under fifteen years of age. That even worse conditions are to be found elsewhere is unhappily true. There are places in which, to use the words of a leading British newspaper, there are "children whose eyes stare as if blind, whose legs and arms are like sticks of licorice, who neither cry nor laugh, and who weigh ten pounds at the age of two years." (*The Guardian*, August 12, 1964.)

There are supplementary explanations of the high birth rate in many of the under-developed countries. These can be identified by studying the traditions and social customs of the people in the various regions. As Joseph Marion Jones has pointed out in his admirable summary of the facts of population growth and economic development,

> *Asian cultures produced the "joint family" which included brothers and their wives, and in many cases first cousins, with joint family responsibilities and pooled property and earnings. This system, in turn, gave rise to extremely early marriages and uncontrolled fertility.*
>
> *In contrast, the late Hellenistic, late Hebraic, and early Christian cultures produced in Western Europe a family unit in which a man was responsible for the support only of his wife and their children (and of immediate relatives without means of support), and it was assumed he would not marry until he was in a position to discharge his responsibilities properly. There was strong social pressure*

against "improvident marriages." The results were relatively late marriages and also, as infant and child mortality declined in the late eighteenth century and after, family limitation in marriage and a small family pattern. (J. M. Jones, *op. cit.,* p. 21.)

There is also more than a little truth in the statement of Dr. Calvert Dedrick, Chief of the International Statistical Programs Office of the U.S. Bureau of the Census, that in Latin America, the great area in which the population pressure is most critical, there are strong, deeply rooted cultural forces which defeat efforts to limit fertility. Many Latin Americans, particularly in the rural sections, want large families. The husbands regard many children as proof of their masculinity, and the wives are proud to have virile husbands. Eventually, it may be possible to change such cultural attitudes, but not easily or soon. (Reported by Rev. George H. Dunne, S.J.: "World Peace and the Population Crisis," *Population Bulletin,* February, 1965, p. 13.) If this is correct many of the people of Latin America will have to be educated to desire the contraceptives when they become available, because at present they apparently do not want them. The enlightenment of the women should not be too difficult a task.

If it is true that population growth is a serious world problem and that it is most serious in its effect on the under-developed countries, what bearing does this have on the programmes of international aid through which efforts are being made to improve conditions in the backward areas?

The objective of these programmes is to develop an economic structure and an administrative practice which will make social progress possible. This in turn means a more effective exploitation of resources, including human resources, to provide food, shelter, improved health, education and personal liberty to the benefit of the individual and the advantage of the nation as a whole.

In each case progress of this kind has a direct relationship to the balance between the number of people and in consequence the size of their needs on the one hand, and the extent and exploitability of the national resources on the other. Thus, any increase of population beyond the number that can be adequately supported by existing and usable resources must exert a depressing effect on the national economy and the society it supports.

The effect, in such circumstances, of an increasing population can be summarized as:

1/increasing the number of children who must be fed, clothed and otherwise cared for;

2/increasing the cost of education and other services while reducing the opportunity for the individual child;

3/diverting funds which might otherwise be used for basic and progressive economic development into expenditure on mere survival;

4/raising the pressure on the available productive land with permanent injury to the land itself and to the local and regional economy;

5/adversely affecting the individual and his society by reducing the available per capita food supply, weakening resistance to disease, lowering productivity, encouraging sexual irresponsibility, and thus starting again the malignant cycle.

Mr. Jones has shown in dramatic form the impact of population growth in contradicting optimistic hopes for early and substantial progress in the under-developed areas. Assuming, as is now generally accepted, that an average capital investment of $3.00 is necessary to increase annual output by $1.00, he marks the followings results:

If the population is growing each year by	A country must save and invest each year at least	In order merely to
1 per cent	3 per cent of national income	Maintain per capita income unchanged
2 per cent	6 per cent of national income	which means no improvement in the
3 per cent	9 per cent of national income	average living levels

Obviously, only savings in excess of those required to sustain a growing population at existing levels can be used for investments that will increase per capita income and improve levels of living. Thus:

If the population is growing each year by	A country must save and invest each year at least	In order to achieve an annual increase in per capita income of
2 per cent	9 per cent of national income	1 per cent
3 per cent	15 per cent of national income	2 per cent

Although there are exceptions, under-developed countries characteristically save and invest less than 10 per cent of their national income each year. Obviously, then, improvement in living levels is extremely slow and difficult in most under-developed countries with high birth rates, and in some it is impossible. (Jones, *op. cit.*, p. 29.)

In 1960 Paul Hoffman, then Director of the United Nations Special Fund, pointed out that

*. . . the statistical income per person in the 100 (under-developed)
countries and territories in the year 1950 averaged approximately
$90. It probably reached slightly over $100 per person in 1959. Gross
income grew at the rate of three per cent a year, but because there
were 200,000,000 more mouths to feed in these countries in 1959
than there were in 1950, the net increase in income per person was
only one per cent, that is, about $1.00 a year. This is too slow—
dangerously so.*

He then went on to propose that

*. . . the nations of the world set for themselves the common task of
assisting the people of the under-developed areas to increase the
annual growth of their per capita income from one to two per cent
each year for the next ten years. This means roughly an increase
of $2.00 per head per year, instead of the present rate of $1.00 per
head. . . . This is a modest, but a reasonable and feasible goal.* (Quoted
in Jones, *op. cit.*, p. 30, from Paul G. Hoffman : *One and One-Quarter
Billion People*, Washington, 1960.)

Mr. Hoffman pointed out, however, that to attain the proposed goal it
would be necessary for the under-developed countries to sustain an
economic growth rate of four per cent each year during the decade.

A majority of informed observers would probably agree that in most
of the under-developed areas a growth rate of four per cent per annum
is unlikely to be achieved under any imminent circumstances, and that it
is inconceivable in countries in which population pressures continue
rapidly to rise.

There would probably be even wider agreement on the inadequacy of
Mr. Hoffman's goal itself, if the intention is to bring about a quick and
substantial improvement in the pattern of living. In a country with a
per capita income of $100 per annum, achievement of this objective
would mean an additional $4.00 per person per year, and $4.00 a year will
not go far towards satisfying the demands of people presently living in
poverty and distress. At this rate it could be about the end of the century
before the per capita income of India reached $130 and that figure still
represents what should, by any rational standard, be considered a sub-
human way of life. It is less than the well-to-do Englishman or American
spends annually on his dog. At present India is making no such progress.

If recent experience can be accepted as an accurate guide, a modest
proposal made by the United Nations General Assembly in 1961, that
the objective for the "decade of development" should be an annual
growth rate ten years hence of five per cent in the national income of

each of the under-developed countries, is most unlikely to be followed by effective action. And even if this objective were to be achieved the result would be inadequate by any reasonable criterion.

The influence of population growth on this five per cent proposal of the United Nations would be as follows:

At a population growth rate of	A per capita income of $100 would increase in ten years to
1.5 per cent	$129
2.0 per cent	$123
2.5 per cent	$117
3.0 per cent	$111
3.5 per cent	$106

Realizing that the population in many of the under-developed countries is going to rise by at least two per cent and in some by over four per cent, there is little hope in any of the figures that reflect current or prospective conditions—unless something effective and immediate can be done to halt the proliferation of the human race. The present irresponsible spawning must be stopped if humanity is to be saved.

Few people are as well acquainted with contemporary conditions as Eugene R. Black who, when resigning his post as President of the World Bank in 1961, summarized the situation in his closing address to the Economic and Social Council of the United Nations:

Population growth on this scale [two per cent or more] would be a serious challenge to a country with adequate living standards. Where incomes are low, and economic development is a desperate need, such growth can be a crippling handicap. . . . Unless foreign aid can be increased, a country in this position is faced with a stark alternative. It must reduce its savings, or lower its living standards —although both are already inadequate.

I must be blunt. Population growth threatens to nullify all our efforts to raise living standards in many of the poorer countries. We are coming to a situation in which the optimist will be the man who thinks that present living standards can be maintained. The pessimist will not look even for that. Unless population growth can be restrained, we may have to abandon for this generation our hopes of economic progress in the crowded lands of Asia and the Middle East. This is not a field in which international agencies can do much. But there is scope for governments to act: it is time that they gave earnest attention to this threat to their aspirations.

The industrialized countries have shown their willingness to help. Common humanity and self-interest alike impel them to do so. All the evidence points to a greater flow of aid in the coming years. But I find myself increasingly doubtful whether domestic savings and foreign aid together will be sufficient to allow real progress, if present rates of population growth continue for long.

D · Should the Aid Programmes be Abandoned?

If conditions are as Mr. Black has described them, what should be done? If expanding populations are going to block any significant improvement in the conditions of life in the under-developed areas, why should the international aid programmes be continued? Professor A. V. Hill, recipient of a Nobel Prize for Medicine, put the situation very clearly when, as president of the British Association for the Advancement of Science, he wrote in 1952 :

Had it been possible to foresee the enormous success of this application [of the benefits of science] would humane people have agreed that it could better have been held back, to keep in step with other parallel progress, so that development could be planned and orderly? Some might say yes, taking the purely biological view that if men will breed like rabbits they must be allowed to die like rabbits, until gradually improving education and the demand for a better standard of life teach them better. Most people will still say no. But suppose that it were now certain that increasing population, uncontrolled by disease, would lead not only to widespread exhaustion of the soil and of other capital resources, but also of continuing and increasing international tension and disorder, making it hard for civilization itself to survive: would the majority of humane and reasonable people then change their minds? If ethical principles deny our right to do evil in order that good may come, are we justified in doing good when the foreseeable consequences are evil? (Quoted in Calder : *Common Sense About a Starving World*, pp. 27–8.)

Eugene Black, in arguing that the aid programmes must be continued, used the words "humanity and self-interest," and for the present these terms do apply. The time may soon come, however, when neither can realistically be used. But unless and until the position becomes more desperate the following reasons justify the continuance and the most rapid possible expansion of the programmes of international assistance :

1/If aid is not provided the situation will deteriorate much more quickly than will otherwise be the case. The gap between rich and poor nations will widen with accelerated speed, thus increasing the certainty and severity of local turmoil and the danger of international war. Much of the tension that makes the contemporary world such a dangerous place arises from this disparity in standards of life. So long as North America and Europe, with one-quarter of the world population, enjoy three-quarters of the world's income, while Asia with more than half the population has only ten per cent of the income, this stark and acrid tension cannot be expected to diminish. Even with a significant expansion in the scale of international aid, the pressure on the resources of the under-developed nations is likely to continue to rise with frightening rapidity; without it, this likelihood becomes an immediate and an alarming certainty. The time available in which to seek for a solution to the conflict between population and resources will be very much shorter.

2/Meagre as they are, the aid programmes are doing some direct good. They benefit many individuals and they increase the number of people who can be expected to make use of birth-control techniques when these have been improved, have been greatly simplified, have been made more widely known, and have been made more readily available.

3/One of the most important and in the long run most valuable aspects of the assistance that is now being given is found in its psychological effect on both the donors and the recipients. To the latter it is proof that their needs are known and are not altogether disregarded; that the people of the wealthier countries are beginning to recognize their responsibilities and are making some effort to assist those who are less fortunate. In the case of the donor countries, these programmes, which already represent a radical break with the past, can be considered an effective agency in conditioning the minds of individuals and of governments for far more extensive, more intelligent and more active efforts yet to come. The moral imperative of which they are a result should be as warmly welcomed as it is being increasingly recognized.

4/A final reason for continuing the programmes is that they are instruments of enlightened and universal self-interest. They do something to reduce the incidence of disease, hunger and injustice; they at least tend to strengthen the hope of peace, and, to the extent that they are successful, they raise the demand for the products of the industrialized nations and increase international trade to the benefit of all participants.

These are valid reasons for continuing and for greatly expanding the present programmes. But they do not alter the fact that, in the end, these programmes will fail in their objectives unless some solution is found for the almost unrestrained fertility that debases so large a proportion of the human race.

E · The Need for Action

This is not the place to give detailed consideration to the heavy obstacles that confront those who support the campaigns designed to change population patterns, nor to the practical steps that can and must be taken to reduce the threat inherent in the continuance of present practices. These are matters for the chemists, physiologists, psychologists, physicians, sociologists, and, above all, for those in posts of political responsibility. Here it is only necessary to point out that no acceptable method of solving the problem of birth control in a practical manner and on a significant scale has yet been devised. Many countries—Japan, Formosa, India, Jamaica, Pakistan, Egypt, Turkey, Puerto Rico—have shown rapidly increasing awareness of the problem but for the most part they have been able to make only a meagre start towards an effective system of control. Communist China, after years of boasting that its system of government and of social organization would be able to provide for and profit from an indefinite enlargement of its population, has now begun to work cautiously towards the discovery of means of reducing its sky-rocketing population. It is estimated that an accurate census would record about 730 millions in mainland China and a net annual increase of over 15 million. (*Population Bulletin*, Population Reference Bureau, April, 1964, p. 55.) The Soviet Union has also changed its stand on population problems on several occasions in recent years. In the most recent report to the United Nations it indicated that it accepted the principle that under socialistic economic conditions population increase represents one of the most important factors in the constant growth of social wealth and the prosperity of all members of society. (*Toronto Star*, November 30, 1961.) In the light of current and prospective conditions it would be difficult to conceive of a more irrational statement. However, an early change in Soviet practice—though it is unlikely to be reflected in Soviet dialectic—can confidently be anticipated.

Japan has accomplished more than any other country in the conscious, planned reduction of its rate of increase. But the reliance in Japan on abortion as a major component in its campaign against population growth, especially in early stages of the campaign for family limitation, is one that is unlikely to be widely copied elsewhere, except in desperation. * Safer and more acceptable techniques must be found. At present the recently developed intra-uterine device seems to offer the greatest promise, but much more research is still needed.

An enormous amount remains to be done and the time is very short. If the birth rate is not soon and drastically reduced the death rate will have to be raised. There is no other solution.

With the exception of work for the maintenance of peace—with which it is closely associated—it is clear that in the world today the most important contribution that can be made by governments, by public or private agencies, and by individuals, to the general welfare of the human race is to be found in working towards a solution—through scientific research, education, propaganda, and through raising living standards where that is possible—of the population problem.

(During the time taken to read this chapter the net population of the world rose by about 3,000 persons.)

---

* In Japan until 1948 abortion had been illegal. In the Protection Law of that year it was not legalized but was declared to be, under certain circumstances, "not illegal"! The protective "circumstances" included reasons of health, morals and economics.

CHAPTER FOUR

The History of International Aid

A · Historical Origins

International aid is not, of course, new. It is as old as the history of intercourse between organized communities. It was undoubtedly practised long before writing was invented or the keeping of records began. And the ways in which technical knowledge has been transmitted have been as varied as the circumstances under which the exchanges have taken place.

BY CONQUEST/The simplest, and perhaps for a long time the most frequent, method of acquiring useful knowledge from other communities, was by conquest. To the victors belonged not only the spoils of material possessions but also the techniques of living, the methods of production, the artistic heritage and the scientific knowledge of the conquered. In the Mesopotamian regions a long succession of semi-barbarous invaders—Sumerians, Babylonians, Assyrians—over-ran their predecessors and adopted many of their ways. Later, as the rule of Islam spread over the Middle East and around the southern and western shores of the Mediterranean, and as the nomadic conquerors took up the tasks of established government, they adopted and spread the knowledge acquired from the peoples they had conquered.

Many illustrations of the acquisition of new knowledge and techniques can be readily identified. It is known, for example, that Armenian masons were employed in Palestine and Egypt and also as far west as Morocco and Spain during the period of Arab rule. The major impact of Greek culture on the life of the conquering Romans is so significant an event in the social and intellectual history of the western world that it needs no elaboration. Similarly, when the crude Manchu warriors over-ran China in the seventeenth century they were introduced by the conquered peoples to the arts and sciences of a well-established civilization. Incidentally, for over a hundred years the Manchus refused to permit the modernization of their own land, maintaining Manchuria as a stud farm or breeding-ground for the tough soldiers they needed to enforce their rule in China. They feared, with some justice in view of the times, the softening effects of an easier and more civilized way of life.

Very often the rewards of victory included many of the persons of the defeated community. The great conquerors of history have tradition-ally been served by slaves, men as well as the women seized in war, who brought with them the knowledge and skills acquired in the lands of their birth. Conversely, the conquerors, by the extension of their own domains, frequently brought in new techniques which altered the lives of those subjugated in war. Britain before and after the Roman conquest, and the changes wrought in English society by the ideas and customs that came across the Channel with the Norman conquerors, are obvious instances of this type of cultural migration. A simple North American example of this pattern of change is found in the effect produced on the lives of the Amerinds by the Spanish introduction of the horse.

BY TRADE AND FOREIGN INVESTMENT/In the more peaceful encounters of commerce and trade, new commodities, new crafts, new standards and new dimensions of consumption inevitably spread from nation to nation through the markets of the world. Such was the history of the potato, of tobacco, and of most of the metals. In fact it would be difficult to think of any commodity in general use that has not had a similar record of expansion through the normal channels of commerce. History is vividly coloured by the chronicles of the great trading-centres of the past, and by their initiative in opening and exploiting new routes, new markets, new techniques of barter and sale—and new commodities. The Phoenicians, the Hanseatic traders, the fantastic city states of Venice, Florence and Genoa, and later the merchant adventurers of Spain, Por-tugal, England and France were among the most important instruments in the development and transfer of technical skills and in the general extension of knowledge.

In the modern era private initiative has played a vital and dramatic role in the wide diffusion of ideas and commodities. The immediate pur-pose of free-enterprise investment is, of course, the making of profits through the provision of services, the creation or expansion of commer-cial activities, or the development of industrial enterprises. An integral and most important, if sometimes incidental, aspect of this process has often been the introduction of new ideas and technical training in regions in which experiences of this kind are rare. Foreign oil companies in Venezuela, for example, now recruit less than five per cent of their operational staff from outside that country. In this, as in some other areas, the profits from the exploitation of a natural resource have been employed to underwrite new industrial and commercial ventures. The recent record of Puerto Rico's phenomenal industrial growth is evidence of the widespread utilization of local labour in all phases of the industrial activities of foreign firms. It also illustrates the way in which new techniques can be adopted and applied by indigenous enterprisers and their native employees.

In no country has private commercial initiative played a more prominent role than in Canada. British and American investments made possible the remarkable rise in production and consumption standards that has occurred in that country since the beginning of this century. In 1900 Canada was a weak, insignificant, under-developed, agricultural community with little pride in its past, little expectation of the future. Today it is one of the world's larger industrial and commercial powers. This change has come about in part because of Canada's natural and human resources (which were proportionately no greater, however, than those of some of the currently under-developed countries.) In part, also, it was accelerated by the active mobilization of domestic and the attraction of foreign capital. But above all, it occurred because Canada had the benefit of technical as well as financial assistance—both public and private, and from many countries—in the development of its railways, its mineral, agricultural, and energy resources, and its manufacturing establishments.

BY PERSONAL RELATIONSHIPS AND INITIATIVES/On a somewhat different level, personal friendship between rulers has frequently resulted in the diffusion of knowledge. When King Solomon decided to construct his temple in Jerusalem, he could find no metal-workers in his own country capable of carrying out his plans. In this dilemma, he sent to his friend Hiram, King of Tyre, and asked that an expert worker in brass be sent to his assistance. As a result an artisan, also called Hiram, was sent to King Solomon and, to use the biblical phrase, "wrought all his work." And the Queen of Sheba is alleged to have learned more, to the great advantage of her country than could be acquired in Solomon's bed, at his table, or in his temple. As far back as the ninth century A.D. there is the record of a king of Moravia having asked the Emperor Michael for the help of a comprehensive technical-assistance mission.

Personal relationships have also played a prominent role through the exchange of knowledge between individual scientists and among members of scientific or learned societies. Free professional intercourse between scientists has made an enormous contribution not only to the exchange of present information but also as a stimulant to further progress. The search for knowledge, for the truth, apparently builds up a sense of kinship among those who participate in it. This feeling of brotherhood has repeatedly triumphed over barriers of culture, language, race, nationality, religion, and distance. It has been facilitated, of course, by the existence of a common means of communication as Latin once was, and as English is rapidly becoming. It is an unhappy reflection that the tragic recent prostitution of a large part of the scientific community in many countries, above all in the U.S.S.R. and the U.S.A., has led to a catastrophic decline in the freemasonry of scientific research. In large segments of the systematic disciplines, the search for truth and for means of improving the human lot has been displaced by a secret and concentrated study of methods of human destruction. When a large percentage of the scientists of a great nation are engaged in this denial of the basic principles of their vocation they themselves, their calling, their country, and the world suffer a common degradation.

When invited by a climate of free enquiry, and stimulated by curiosity and imagination, individual initiative has been a potent force in the dissemination of new ideas and new techniques. In the sixth century, two monks returned to Byzantium after adventuring eastward as far as China. They reported to the Emperor Justinian on the practice of sericulture and the methods of processing silk as practised by the Chinese. The Emperor sent them off at once to gather more information and to bring back to the capital of the Empire the basic materials required for the inauguration of a similar industry in the West. When they returned the second time from China, they brought with them a large supply of silkworm eggs, carried in two hollow bamboo poles. It was on this fragile foundation that the subsequent silk industry of Europe was erected.

Centuries later, Peter the Great of Russia, determined to break the bonds of ignorance by which his nation was imprisoned, came himself to the West to see and to learn. In the shipyards of the continent and among the skilled caftsmen of Britain he acquired a personal knowledge of the scientific and technical foundations of modern economic progress. When he returned to Russia he took with him hundreds of specialists competent both to work and to teach.

THROUGH FORCED MIGRATION/In some cases one country has profited by the political or religious intolerance of another. Thus in the seventeenth century England became the leading European centre of the textile industry when France drove out the Huguenots who brought their skills and experience with them across the English Channel. Incidentally it is worth recalling that the exclusion of the Huguenots, with their middle-class commercial and industrial background, from New France was one of the chief factors in making inevitable the triumph of English over French power in North America. In this case tolerance at home might well have meant the establishment of a French rather than a British empire in northern America.

The mere threat of prospective conquest has often played a significant role in the spread of knowledge by creating a class of what are now described as "displaced persons." Thus the gradual westward surge of the Mongols and the Turks, by driving the Byzantines into Italy, Germany, and France, probably did more than any other factor to bring about the revival of learning and the intellectual and artistic excitement of the Renaissance.

In more recent times the appalling threat of Hitler drove countless scientists, businessmen, artists, and others to seek safety in Britain or America, greatly to the advantage of these national communities. A remarkable contribution to the progress of Mexico was made by those who escaped from the Franco terror in Spain.

A very simple contemporary example of how this sort of thing can affect the lives of ordinary people in the recipient country is found in the vast improvement in the quality and variety of the food served in Canada and the United States since the influx of displaced Europeans at the end of the Second World War.

THROUGH COLONIAL ENTERPRISE/Colonial policy has also played a significant role in the spread of technical knowledge. Thus the North American colonies of England and Holland were soon endowed with most of the specialized information that supported the economic life of their mother countries. Similarly, in the conquest of native peoples the ruling powers have occasionally introduced techniques upon which indigenous populations have in time begun to elaborate their own national economies. Long before the British were forced to relinquish their political control of India much of the economic life of that country was based upon industry and trade that was in the hands of the Indians themselves. Ceylon, too, has profited since independence from the tea industry and the coconut plantations that were greatly developed under foreign control. And sound techniques of public administration have on occasion constituted a valuable "export" of some of the metropolitan countries. The British possessions in particular found their transition to independent nationhood made somewhat simpler by the existence of a cadre of their own nationals who had been trained in modern techniques of management.

In recent years the strengthening of colonial economies has become a consciously planned programme through such instrumentalities as the Colonial Development and Welfare Fund and the Colonial Development Corporation established by the Government of the United Kingdom, and similar agencies in France and other countries.

Closely comparable to this kind of relationship between metropolitan powers and their colonial territories has been the long-continued effort of the United States to assist local governments to develop the domestic resources of the countries of Latin America. Here, as in the colonial examples, the work of the government of the more advanced nation has been guided by a mingling of selfish and altruistic motives. Many of the achievements in the field of agricultural development and much of the progress in standards of health and sanitation in Latin America have resulted from the unselfish desire of the people and the government of the United States to aid their less fortunate neighbours. This has been particularly true since the inauguration of the Good Neighbour Policy by President Franklin D. Roosevelt a quarter of a centry ago. Under his stimulus the technical expert soon took the place of the marine as the typical representative of the United States government south of the Rio Grande. Activities of this kind have been increasingly supported by the more enlightened and far-sighted members of the American business community, who have come to realize that a prosperous neighbour is most likely to be a better customer. Unfortunately this is not, of course, the whole picture.

THROUGH NATIONAL AMBITION/In some cases the whole technological basis of national life has been changed by the conscious decision of a government to adopt new methods. The most dramatic example of this kind of planned transformation was undoubtedly that of Japan. In the middle of the nineteenth century that country was forced by the pressure of western power and interest to demolish the walls behind which the people of Nippon had lived in almost complete seclusion for 250 years. The threat carried by Admiral Perry's "black ships" made the government of Japan realize that isolation was no longer a tenable national policy. The menace in the muzzles of the Admiral's guns produced a dynamic reaction in Tokyo which was responsible for the almost incredibly rapid development that saw Japan move in three generations from a static agrarian feudalism to an expanding industrial imperialism. This transformation was made possible only by the conscious, determined, and eclectic use of the principle of technical assistance. The Japanese realized that if they were to escape the fate of China and to survive as an independent nation in the dangerous world of nineteenth-century imperialism, they would have to utilize every tool and skill of modern science and every resource and experience they could acquire from a study of the competitive and threatening nations of the West. Thus they turned to Britain for guidance in industrial techniques and in naval practice. They went to France for a legal code. They obtained help in creating a modern army through advice and materials bought in Germany. They turned to America for guidance in educational methods. At one time, towards the end of the century, over five thousand foreign experts were employed in Japan and about one-third of them were in high official positions. At the same time, many thousands of Japanese students were sent abroad in order to acquire the knowledge that Japan must have if it was to become powerful and remain free.

If it is to succeed in overcoming its present handicaps and achieve the kind of progress that its leaders have announced as their goal, each of the under-developed nations of today must follow the example of Japan in making a firm national resolution to accept whatever sacrifices are necessary to modernize their ways of life. In this they can be greatly helped by far more accessible resources of technical assistance than were readily available to Japan. But no matter how generous are today's offers of aid through the United Nations or from the varied programmes of individual countries, they will produce little effect unless they are employed in the context of a grim national determination to achieve the goals that they may help to make possible.

B · Progress Prior to the First World War

During the nineteenth century there was a notable growth—and in contrast with previous experience a very rapid growth—of international efforts to deal with problems of international concern. Beginning before 1850, the habit of calling intergovernmental conferences to consider issues that could only be solved by joint action became more and more common. As one historian of the movement has pointed out, in almost every decade between 1843 and the outbreak of the First World War, the number of international conferences approximately doubled (9, 20, 77, 169, 309, 510, 1070) in a remarkably regular progression. (C. Howard-Ellis: *The Origin, Structure and Working of the League of Nations*, Cambridge, Mass., 1928, p. 25.) The same writer then went on to point out that:

> With the increase in the number of conferences came the further development in the form of differentiation of the conferences according to the purpose for which they were held. . . . The technical conferences met to frame technical conventions, laying the foundations for permanent co-operation between the interested states . . . this made necessary the setting up of some permanent control machinery . . . which in turn gave birth to institutions. These institutions re-

ceived the generic name of public international unions. The best known are perhaps the International Telegraphic Union, the Universal Postal Union, and the International Public Health Office (. . . by the beginning of this century the number of public international unions and other permanent international bodies was nearly 300). (Idem, p. 26.)

Dr. Manley O. Hudson, one of the early prophets and architects of international co-operation in the modern world, looking back on this same period, wrote:

> For a full 50 years . . . before World War I it had been appreciated that national organizations did not fully meet the demands of a new international society. Beginning with the field of communications, institution after institution had been created to supplement the actions of national Governments. (Manley O. Hudson: Progress in International Organization, Stamford, Conn., 1932, pp. 6–7.)

Important as these developments were, because of their predominantly administrative or political character and the limitations almost invariably written into their terms of reference, these conferences had little direct effect on the problems of world-wide economic debility and social degradation which have since come to be recognized as matters of general concern. The international institutions created in the nineteenth and early twentieth centuries were also almost entirely of an administrative nature. Moreover, the problems they were designed to solve were almost exclusively of a narrowly technical or essentially political character. As a recent writer has described the situation:

> Prior to World War I, there was little international effort to help the so-called "backward areas" to become more highly developed industrially, economically, politically, socially, or otherwise. There were the usually incidental efforts of the great colonial powers for their dependent areas. There were the embryonic efforts of the rudimentary international and regional administrative unions in connection with their regular treaty duties. There were the occasional and periodic efforts of various technical international and regional conferences and bureaus. And there were the non-governmental efforts of such organizations as missionary groups or private profit enterprises, for whom such work was also a by-product of some other primary intentions and considerations.
>
> But there was in no sense any world-wide movement or program or organization, such as is so evident today, in such sporadic and haphazard assistance to socio-economic development as occurred

during the half-century or more preceding the Great Conflagration of 1914. (R. T. Mack, Jr.: Raising the World's Standard of Living, New York, 1953, pp. 6–7.)

The work done during the years before the First World War by the agencies of private capital had only meagre significance as contributions to social progress. By their very nature, the operations of private corporations were concentrated on investment and profit considerations. While the investment of risk capital in enterprises in the under-developed countries in which taxation, tariff, and fiscal policies generally were not genuine value, the more usual result was simple exploitation. At best, only limited sections of the countries concerned were likely to be touched by the benefits of such investment. In the case of successful enterprises the profits were normally withdrawn from the investment areas almost as rapidly as they accumulated. This was particularly true in the colonial countries in which taxation, tariff, and fiscal policies generally were not under domestic control. In most cases these policies were chiefly influenced by foreign financial and commercial interests working through the agency of the metropolitan government. The prevailing attitude of even the best of the colonial powers was thus described by Sir John Maud:

> *Before the last war we hardly ever thought it necessary to help dependent territories for purposes of development—no provision was made for this by Parliament until 1929 when the first Colonial Development Act was passed—and provided only the negligible sum of £1 m. as an annual maximum. As I wandered through Africa South to North in 1932 (with a Rhodes travelling fellowship) it was brought forcibly home to me, I remember, that though we took our role as trustees for colonial territories most seriously, we thought of this only in political terms: we were responsible for teaching them self-government and making ourselves dispensable, but it was not till one reached the Sudan and saw the splendid scheme for growing cotton at Gezira, through public and private enterprise in partnership, that one found an example of our trusteeship interpreted as action to develop economic resources on a grand scale. (Sir John Maud: Aid for Developing Countries, University of London, 1963, p. 10.)*

In non-colonial countries the same results were usually achieved by somewhat less direct means. Here persuasion or bribery of local officials often played an effective role—as, of course, in many instances it still does. In extreme (though not infrequent) cases, gunboat diplomacy produced the desired results and at the same time provided safe and agreeable exercise for naval personnel.

This is not to be interpreted as a wholesale condemnation of all colonial activities, or of all actions of the major powers in their relations with their colonies or with nominally independent but poverty-stricken countries under their influence. In some cases, as has been suggested, metropolitan governments made serious and occasionally intelligent efforts to assist in the economic progress of their dependent areas. In certain instances, more money was put into colonies than was taken out of them. Genuine altruistic purpose was behind some of the policies of some of the major powers in some of their relationships with some of their poorer neighbours.

But this was not the prevailing mode in government policy and it was practically unknown (naturally enough) in the realm of private investment. Even the most ardent apologist for colonial rule can hardly deny that in general the objective of the colonizing power was not local welfare. Colonial programmes were mainly concerned with the maintenance of law and order, and with public literacy and health, chiefly as contributions to economic development for the advantage of the controlling country and its commercial enterprises. For, "whatever the political arrangements (colonial domination, trade concessions, political influences, economic control, etc.) economic development . . . was determined mainly by investment decisions taken in the dominant industrial countries and primarily for the promotion of their trading interests." (J. B. Condliffe and A. Stevenson: *The Common Interest in International Economic Organization: Mankind*, Montreal, International Labour Organization, 1944, Studies and Reports Series B, No. 39, p. 24.)

Perhaps the most truly altruistic of the international activities of the ninetenth century were those associated with the various Christian missionary organizations. The humanitarian impulse that motivated many of those engaged in this movement brought welfare services which were of real benefit to individuals and groups in certain of the backward and impoverished areas. But usually these efforts were of little more permanent value than the occasional Christmas hamper of the traditional Lady Bountiful. Some valuable work was done by the missionary societies in the field of education and to a lesser degree in health; but in general, the missionary's concern was in saving souls, not in righting social injustice or in promoting economic progress. His guiding instruction was "Go ye into all the world and preach the Gospel to every creature." His Bible said nothing about economic progress—although perhaps the injunction to "Love thy neighbour as thyself" might have been given a somewhat wider interpretation than was commonly the case. But undoubtedly the missionary would reply that saving his heathen neighbour's soul was the best proof of his love.

C · The League of Nations and the Beginnings of the Specialized Agencies

Even the long, dragging horrors of the First World War did not produce any very noticeable change in the sensibilities of the politicians and officials of the Great Powers who were responsible for the conduct of international relations at its close. The impact of the wisdom and idealism of a few of those who represented these powers in the negotiations at Versailles soon became dulled as the arguments continued and as cynicism grew at home as well as around the council tables in France. For callous rapacity and irresponsible ignorance it would be difficult to find a counterpart to the typical participant in the negotiations that followed the Armistice of 1918—except in their respective legislatures at home. The "hard-faced men" of the newly-elected Parliament in London had their dull, ignorant but pugnacious counterparts in the capitals of most of the victorious powers. In Washington this element was led by Senator Henry Cabot Lodge who was different only in that his speech was more grammatical and his malevolence more malicious.

But the few men of wisdom, idealism and dedication who fought for the future at Versailles (the Shotwells, the Hendersons and the Cecils) did achieve something. The Covenant of the League of Nations, emasculated and denatured as eventually it was, was better than anything of its kind that had gone before in modern times. The Mandates system at least paid lip service to the idea of the moral responsibility of the metropolitan powers for their dependent areas. And the Covenant did give to the Council and the Assembly a measure of authority to deal with any matter "affecting the peace of the world." But no one at Versailles gave any convincing evidence of a clear recognition of the fact that the three-quarters of the people of the world who were living in hunger, ignorance, injustice, and disease might imperil peace, or that anyone else had any real responsibility for their welfare. Neither President Wilson in his Fourteen Points nor the Covenant of the League suggested that there was any general or specific responsibility to assist in promoting the development of the backward areas of the world.

During the frustrating and often savage years between the wars, the League of Nations was chiefly concerned with problems of European reconstruction. Its efforts to assist the major nations as well as some of the smaller and poorer countries such as Greece, Bulgaria, Hungary, and Estonia, were commendable and, in varying degrees, effective. The League had to cope, however, with periodic crises provoked by the legacies of the war which were aggravated by the economic dislocation and human miseries of the great depression of the thirties. The resulting tensions were raised to the danger-level by the aggression of Japan in Asia, of Italy in Ethiopia, of the Axis powers in Spain, and of Germany in Central Europe. As the fever of insane bellicosity continued to rise, the impotence of those who were trying to make the League an effective instrument of international conciliation became more and more glaringly apparent. The hope of peace and security was submerged in the noise of the explosion arranged by the Japanese army at Mukden, in the howling-down of the Emperor Haile Selassie by moronic Italian jingoes in the Palais des Nations itself, in the bomb-blasts of the Germans' practice incineration of the women and children of Guernica, in the massacre of Nanking, and in the strident screams of the degenerates who seized power in Rome and Berlin.

In spite of these calamities the idea of world unity and of common responsibility for humanity was not wholly forgotten during the inter-war years. Initiatives particularly worth recording were developed by three different agencies: the Mandates Commission, the International Labour Organization, and the Health Organization of the League Secretariat.

Almost from the beginning the Mandates Commission had taken its trust duties with a seriousness that had not been intended by many of those who had consented to its creation. Although at first its concern seemed to be that of a mildly benevolent policeman, by the late 1920's it was beginning to show some anxiety over the economic conditions of areas for which it had, theoretically at least, some responsibility. (See Quincy Wright: *Mandates Under the League of Nations*, Chicago, 1930, especially the final chapter.)

The Commission did make some serious efforts to improve the standard of colonial government and to overcome the old belief that the hallmark of a good colonial administration was the achievement of maximum economic advantage for the home country. The Commission had some success in spreading the idea that the colonial power had at least a minor degree of responsibility for the welfare of the native population. The increase in number of schools and dispensaries and the organization of effective campaigns against sleeping-sickness, malaria and yellow fever, became a yardstick that was increasingly used as a measure of good colonial policy. (League of Nations: *The Aims, Methods and Activity of the League of Nations*, Geneva: Secretariat, 1935, pp. 114–115.) Many prevailing abuses continued in spite of the Commission's efforts and some of them persist to the present day, but the actions of the Mandates Commission did mark a significant development in the subject matter if not in the practice of international affairs.

The International Labour Organization, founded as an autonomous organization at the same time as the League, gradually became aware of its potentiality as more than a clearing-house for labour information. Very shortly after its establishment it commenced the tentative drafting of conventions incorporating desirable standards of labour practice. It also organized research for the collection and analysis of the facts about current conditions and procedures in the labour field.

By 1930, some of the governments who participated in the work of the ILO were beginning to recognize the possibility of using its machinery as an instrument for bringing international experience to bear on their domestic development problems, and an increasingly large number of requests were received for technical assistance missions to advise on labour and related matters. Among the most important advisory missions sent out during this period were those to Greece and Rumania (1930, on social insurance), China (1931, on organization of factory inspectorates), Egypt (1932, for the survey of labour conditions and the organization of a labour department), Cuba (1934, on the organization of a labour department), Venezuela (1936, on labour legislation), Morocco (1937, on the organization of co-operatives), and Turkey (1939, on social insurance). (International Labour Conference, *Technical Assistance*, Geneva, International Labour Office, 1954, p. 4.) By the time the ILO was approaching the end of its second decade, it had accumulated a valuable fund of experience in international technical co-operation which was to be widely copied in the years to come.

The League's programme of technical co-operation with China which began in May, 1931 was a prototype of many of the technical assistance techniques which have since been developed and widely used by international agencies. A bold and broad plan was drawn up to promote Chinese progress by providing aid in public health, road-building and upkeep, communications, hydraulics, and rural economy, the last to cover rural hygiene, rural co-operatives and sericulture). (League of Nations, Council Committee on Technical Co-operation Between the League of Nations and China, Report on a Mission in China by the Secretary of the Council Committee, October 2, 1935.) The original architects of this scheme were Dr. Ludwig Rajchmann of the League's Health Organization, who had already pioneered in malaria control and epidemiological reporting in under-developed parts of the world, and T. V. Soong, one of China's most vigorous leaders in the 1930's. Under the aegis of two

Secretariat sections, the Health Organization and the Communications and Transit Organization, foreign experts were sent to China to render advice in many fields and to train Chinese to support and continue this work. Unfortunately the plan was never to grow as had been hoped and it soon became a victim of the tensions of the Sino-Japanese conflict which started with the Mukden incident of September 17–18, 1931. Many of the League responsibilities were soon dropped, and others were diverted to coping with the dangers of the epidemics being spread by the masses of Chinese refugees who were uprooted in the pervasive turmoil of that unhappy decade.

In addition to its work in China the League's Health Organization developed beneficial activities in a number of other areas. Immediately following the war Geneva was asked to help combat epidemics which had arisen in eastern Europe as a result of the dislocations created by the conflict. Governments were offered material and technical assistance and their various individual efforts were co-ordinated by a Temporary Epidemics Commission. Following this emergency experience the Health Organization turned its attention to efforts to prevent the recurrence of epidemic diseases. A Sanitary Conference was held in Warsaw in 1922 and a number of sanitary conventions were concluded between eastern European countries. A permanent reporting service was established which was designed to alert national agencies, ships at sea, and ports of call as to the movement of contagious diseases. Establishment of common standards soon became a substantial factor in the Health Organization's activities. This included the definition of agreed manufacturing criteria and the publication and recommendation of approved formulae for sera, vaccines, vitamins, hormones, and other medications. The Organization also endeavoured to obtain agreement on the standardization of morbidity and mortality statistics. It gave special attention to the methods of identification and treatment of a number of maladies of which the incidence was notably international in character such as malaria, tuberculosis, leprosy, and the venereal diseases. Finally, there were many projects which profited from the international exchange of health personnel.

The Financial Committee of the League of Nations also took early steps to put technical experts at the disposal of member states suffering from economic and financial difficulties. One of its first actions was to assist Austria when an almost complete economic collapse had brought the population of that country to the edge of starvation. Immediate aid was given to avert the impending famine and a large loan was advanced to the Austrian government with the stipulation that a long series of economic, financial, and administrative reforms must be implemented. Somewhat similar programmes were subsequently undertaken in Greece, Hungary, and Bulgaria.

Another useful beginning was that made by the Communications and Transit Organization of the League Secretariat which, considering the conditions of the time, compiled an impressive record of accomplishments. Conventions were proposed and ratified for safeguarding the freedom of shipment on inland waterways and railways, for the use of harbour facilities, for the transmission of electric energy, and for the development of water-power on international rivers.

In spite of these varied and useful activities the League obviously failed to develop an over-all, well-defined and coherent attitude towards the world-wide and basic problems of hunger, ignorance, and disease. Such efforts as were made to improve conditions were sporadic, piecemeal, and often incidental. For the most part they resulted from emergency needs or from the initiative and enthusiasm of individuals rather than from any established policy.

Nevertheless these early enterprises did foreshadow the spread of an idea and an ideal. Slowly it began to be realized by others than the so-called "impractical idealists" that in the ever-tightening integration of the modern world, poverty and wealth among nations could not indefinitely continue tranquilly or safely together. F. B. Walters, a former Deputy Secretary-General of the League and its most eminent historian, characterized this change in attitude as the beginning of a "renaissance of energy and initiative in the economic and social agencies." (F. P. Walters: *A History of the League of Nations, Volume II*, London, Oxford, 1952, pp. 750 ff.) For the first time international relations began, sporadically at least, to include a recognizable concern with the problems of the individual human being as well as with those of his government and of the nation's industrial and commercial interests. But unhappily these new concepts were beginning to flourish at the very time when the League as a whole was progressively losing all prospect of being able to control or even seriously influence the great issues of peace and war.

There was a single exception to this depressing recital. During the years just before the outbreak of the Second World War, one serious effort was made to organize and promote the work of the economic and social agencies of the League. This was the result, in part, of a deepening and spreading dissatisfaction with the practice of governments which approved proposals for social and economic reforms in words—especially in official orations at international conferences—but did little or nothing to implement them. It also arose from a growing realization, particularly within the Secretariat of the League, that the possibilities of material progress were being grossly neglected and that the gap between the possible and the actual conditions of human life was persistently widening rather than closing, especially for those in the under-developed countries. Largely on their own initiative, the Secretariat and various Committees of the League began extensive studies into living-standards and the possibilities of individual and community progress. Specific questions were investigated: agricultural production and prices; child welfare and education; housing and rents; the financing of public and private building and the provision of utilities; and many other questions relating to the conditions and problems of everyday life. (*Idem*, p. 752.)

One result of these enquiries was to bring under serious review what were, in official circles at least, new ideas on the strategy of world production and consumption. Attention began to be directed towards such questions as to whether it might not be better, in a world in which the majority of people could not attain adequate standards of nutrition, to try to foster programmes designed to increase consumption rather than to continue to concentrate on programmes aimed at limiting production. Might not increased food resources promote better health, and a prosperous agriculture create new demands for manufactured products, and thus bring about a higher level of employment for all?

These ideas, sparked in large measure by the remarkable pioneering work on problems of food and nutrition in Great Britain by Dr. John Boyd Orr (later a recipient of a Nobel Prize, appointed the first Director-General of the Food and Agriculture Organization, and elevated to the peerage) developed through the work of scientists and technicians and not through that of the political officials of the League. But in 1935 they did find a powerful champion in Stanley Bruce of Australia, who in the Sixteenth Assembly proposed that a general study be made of the question of nutrition in all its aspects: health, productivity, and as a component of the general economy. A committee was set up under the chairmanship of Lord Astor and their report on the *Relations of Nutrition to Health, Agriculture, and Economic Policy*, submitted in 1937, became a notable landmark in the field of international co-operation and mutual aid. The report endeavoured to create an active and enlightened public opinion as well as to provide governments with information and practical advice. Even in the disturbed conditions of its time a few of the recommendations of the report were adopted by a number of interested governments. While this report was being prepared, other expert groups were studying problems of housing, town planning, and conditions of rural life. The culmination of much of this work was to have been two great Conferences on Rural Life scheduled for late in 1939. They were among the first casualties of the Second World War.

In turning some of its attention to the economic and social problems of individuals and the nations in which they lived, the League was to that extent abandoning its previous position of being concerned almost exclusively with political issues. Growing recognition of its new interests resulted in benefits to the League itself which in a better climate and with more time might have had important consequences. Popular support began to increase; co-operative connections between international agencies began to multiply; a common front against ignorance, poverty, and disease began to appear as an eventual possibility.

A major aspect of the new work of the League was the fact that it was largely detached from official programmes of the Council and the Assembly. The beneficial results of this fact were so obvious that proposals that the economic and social activities of the organization should be made constitutionally independent began to be heard. Such an arrangement would have removed the most threatening weakness of the existing situation, namely, the always-present menace inherent in the veto power of the Council. The danger of this existing situation was that the work of the social and economic committees could be hampered or terminated out of hand by foreign ministers and diplomats who had no special knowledge of, and very often not even a meagre interest in, the kind of economic and social matters with which the Committees were designed to deal.

Another and universal element of weakness in all aspects of the work of the League of Nations was the ill-defined role of the United States, which participated in many of the expert organizations but not in the governing bodies of the League itself.

For these and related reasons some of the leading figures of the League, with Bruce again in the van, began to consider methods of bringing about a change in the manner of dealing with social and economic activities. The proponents of change, however, were divided among themselves. Some desired complete independence from the League, others argued for independence within the framework of the established organization. To judge between these opposing views a special Committee on the Development of International Co-operation in Economic and Social Affairs was appointed. This group, known from the name of its chairman as the Bruce Committee, produced a report which was the most significant document in the pre-war growth of the idea of interdependence and mutual aid.

The Bruce Report proposed the establishment of a Central Committee to take over the main functions of the Council in connection with the League's economic and social activities. Under its provisions the work would be financed by a separate budget and would form the subject of a separate annual report. In this way it was hoped that this important element of the League's reponsibilities would be brought "under supervision of the agency which should be both effective and representative," that the various aspects of the work would be better co-ordinated, and that "fresh efficiency and vigour" would be brought to the work itself. The proposal was so drafted as to provide also for states that were not members of the League to participate in this work. In spite of the outbreak of war, the report with certain amendments was approved by the Assembly on December 14, 1939.

There is no doubt that this initiative was encouraged and strengthened by the views of the then United States Secretary of State, Cordell Hull, who on February 2, 1939, had written to the Secretary-General of the League that:

> The League . . . has been responsible for the development of mutual exchange and discussion of ideas and methods to a greater extent and in more fields of humanitarian and scientific endeavour than any other organization in history.
>
> The United States Government looks forward to the development and expansion of the League's machinery for dealing with the problems in those fields and to the participation by all nations in active efforts to solve them. . . . It [the United States] will continue to collaborate in those activities and will consider in a sympathetic spirit means of making its collaboration more effective. (This letter is quoted in Martin Hill: The Economic and Financial Organization of the League of Nations, Washington, Carnegie Endowment for International Peace, 1946, p. 115 note. The author of this volume was the Secretary of the Bruce Committee and has, since its formation, been one of the most knowledgeable and astute of the senior officials of the United Nations Secretariat. He has been particularly charged with heavy responsibilities in the co-ordination of the social and economic activities of the United Nations and the Specialized Agencies.)

One effect of this letter, however, was to deal a death-blow to any persisting thought of the setting up of an economic and social organization separate from the League itself.

The work foreshadowed by the Bruce Committee was, of course, gravely interrupted by the outbreak of war in the autumn of 1939 and more particularly by the end of the "phony war" in the spring of 1940. Nevertheless, some thinking and planning continued along the lines that had developed in the last years of peace. This reached its culmination in a draft report prepared by the Economic Department of the League, Part I of which was issued in 1943 under the title The Transition from

War to Peace Economy. Part II followed in 1945. The progress that had been made in thinking about the problems of unequal development among the world's peoples was illustrated by the statement of the "objectives of economic policy," which was the most important feature of the report:

1/that *the fullest possible use is made of the resources of production, human and material, of the skill and enterprise of the individual, of the available scientific discoveries and inventions so as to attain and maintain in all countries a stable economy and rising standards of living;*

2/that, *in so far as possible, no man or woman able and willing to work should be unable to obtain employment for periods of time longer than is needed to transfer from one occupation to another or, when necessary, to acquire a new skill;*

3/that, *in the use of these productive resources, the provision of goods and services to meet the essential physiological needs of all classes of the population in food, clothing, house room and medical care is a prime consideration;*

4/that *society distribute, as far as possible, the risk to the individual resulting from interruption or reduction of earning power;*

5/that *the liberty of each individual to choose his own occupation is respected and promoted by equal educational opportunities;*

6/that *the liberty of each country to share in the markets of the world and thus to obtain access to the raw materials and manufactured goods bought and sold on these markets is promoted by the progressive removal of obstructions to trade; and*

7/that *the benefits of modern methods of production are made available to all peoples both by the progressive removal of obstructions to trade and by courageous international measures of reconstruction and development.*

This summary of objectives is a revealing indication of the distance that had been covered in the growing recognition of the moral responsibility of all governments, and particularly those of the major powers, for the general welfare of the human race.

Apart from the League itself, the outbreak of war also seriously curtailed the advisory services of the International Labour Organization. But from its temporary headquarters in Montreal, the ILO did some substantial and useful work on the compilation of social security and labour statistics in the Americas. After the war the organization began to offer technical assistance on a much wider scale and, gradually, in more effective forms. In 1948, it greatly increased the scope of its operations with a manpower programme covering aid in the organization of employment service, in vocational guidance and training, and in migration problems. Regional offices were set up in Asia and Latin America and training courses in various fields were offered at these centres. As funds were limited, these activities had to be performed for the most part by the permanent staff of the ILO, as and when they could be spared, and this restriction continued until the United Nations Expanded Programme of Technical Assistance was established in 1950.

Towards the end of the war and in the post-war period, the ILO was shortly joined by five other functional organizations, the newly-devised Specialized Agencies of the United Nations. Each of these from its inception began to offer in its particular field technical assistance, although it was not always so described, to applicant governments. In the order of their formation, these agencies were the Food and Agriculture Organization (FAO), the International Monetary Fund (IMF), the International Civil Aviation Organization (ICAO), the United Nations Educational, Scientific and Cultural Organization (UNESCO), and the World Health Organization (WHO). As in the case of the United Nations the early technical assistance activities of these agencies were financed from the regular budget of the organizations concerned. It was not long until in each organization the technical aid programme began to pre-empt a major part of the available funds.

The International Bank, in addition to offering advice in its specialized field, began almost immediately to assist governments in the over-all examination of the national economy, and to prepare comprehensive reports on general problems and their possible solutions. In the provision of this kind of inclusive examination of national needs the Bank was soon joined by the United Nations itself.

By 1951 the International Monetary Fund had supplied advisory missions to a score of member governments to assist in the solution of the fiscal and foreign exchange problems which are characteristic of many of the under-developed nations. The early work that was done in this and related fields was described by Professor Walter R. Sharp, whose study published in 1952 was the first detailed recording of the embryonic post-war efforts in the field of international aid. (Walter R. Sharp: *International Technical Assistance*, Chicago, Public Administration Service, 1952, p. 12 ff.)

From the beginning UNESCO provided equipment and technical advice in an effort to combat illiteracy; and ICAO gave widespread assistance in the establishment of air transport services and in the improvement of air safety standards and practices. But the growing volume of technical assistance provided by the Specialized Agencies prior to the start of the Expanded Programme is, perhaps, best illustrated by the work of the Food and Agriculture Organization and the World Health Organization.

As early as 1946, FAO began to send advisory missions to under-developed countries. Greece, Poland, Thailand, and Nicaragua were among the early recipients. Due to the limitations of the agency's regular budget resources, this aid consisted generally of brief visits by regular staff members or individual consultants. But in 1947, FAO reached an agreement with the United Nations Relief and Rehabilitation Administration, which was then reducing its scale of emergency operations, under which FAO received over $1 million to be used for direct advisory assistance to nine countries. With its regular budget thus supplemented, FAO began to provide its scientific and technical advisers for much longer periods than had previously been feasible and for the first time entered upon a fellowship programme as well. The terms *food and agriculture* in the FAO name have always been given a broad interpretation. In addition to covering farm products and animal husbandry, they have been interpreted to include such fields as fisheries, forestry, wood-processing and nutrition. FAO assisted in the study of problems of production, economics, and statistics in all these areas. Programmes were developed to help rid countries of animal diseases like rinder-pest and to reduce the danger of such tragedies as those caused by locusts. Help was given in making soil surveys, fertility studies, and in planning the agricultural aspects of land use and irrigation. Nutritionists aided in making dietary surveys and in developing new sources of food. The latter often included the contributions of fisheries experts who sought to develop fresh as well as salt water resources to increase the availability of proteins for the under-nourished masses of the poorer countries. The popularization of fish-farming and of new types of food production was of particular interest in this direction. FAO used advisory missions also to develop technical skills in local personnel by associating nationals of the recipient countries with the work of the foreign experts and by the establishment of training-centres in appropriate locations.

The World Health Organization also instituted a vigorous programme of field activities while it was under the control of its Temporary Commission. Under the inspirational, dynamic and wise leadership of the first Director General, Dr. Brock Chisholm, expert advice, the provision of fellowships, the collection of statistics, and the distribution of medical literature were soon being effectively organized. The First World Health Assembly directed the activities of this Organization to the control of malaria, tuberculosis, and venereal diseases and the fostering of maternal and child health, nutrition, and environmental sanitation. All of these activities had a direct relationship to the characteristic health problems of the less-developed regions. (World Health Organization, *Official Records of the World Health Organization, Nos. 16, 24, 330,* Geneva.) Despite the constraints imposed by its meagre budget, WHO was able in its first year to send demonstration teams in malaria control, and to provide fellowships in malariology to Greece, Yugoslavia, Pakistan, India, and a number of other countries. For the prevention or cure of tuberculosis WHO started a programme for mass immunization in Europe, the Near East, the Far East, and the Western Hemisphere. X-ray techniques were demonstarted and BCG vaccine manufacture was soon begun in India. Sanitary engineers, nurses and public health administrators were prominent among the many experts sent abroad. From the start the programmes of the Organization grew with phenomenal speed.

As has been shown, the legacies of the League of Nations in the realm of economic and social action, both in administrative planning and in the definition of ideals, were much more comprehensive than has usually been recognized. The relatively easy transition to the greatly expanded operations of the United Nations and its Specialized Agencies was due in large measure to the foundations laid in the waning years of the decade before the war. The United Nations Economic and Social Council in its form, powers and purposes was, in some measure at least, modelled on the Bruce Committee's proposals for a Central Committee for Economic and Social Questions. The Health Organization of the League developed into the post-war World Health Organization, and the League's Nutritional Committee into the Food and Agriculture Organization. The Committee on Intellectual Co-operation led more or less logically to the United Nations Educational, Scientific, and Cultural Organization—although the members of the Committee would certainly have been astonished by some of the more exotic undertakings of UNESCO!

The extent and the effect of the pre-war work in these important fields should not be over-estimated. It is true that much thought was given to economic and social problems and that a good deal of preliminary work was done. But for the most part the concepts were limited and the activity itself was sporadic and, by later standards, rudimentary. Above all, these aspects of the League's work were looked upon by those in authority in the League itself, and in the chancelleries at home, as being of minor importance. Few pre-war politicians and diplomats saw any great significance in foreign problems that were neither politics nor diplomacy. Action in relation to such things could be permitted as emergency projects or as friendly concessions to the rather queer enthusiasts who seemed to take them up, but they should not be allowed to impinge on the important aspects of international relations! Political debate and social diversions were usually found more attractive than the study of how human beings live and what could be done about it.

D · Problems and Progress at San Francisco

The slowly growing interest in international co-operation in the economic and social field that marked the pre-war period was given a powerful stimulant by the tragic but illuminating experiences of the years of world-wide conflict. The concept of mutual responsibility for the solution of international issues of this kind was generally recognized on the official level for the first time when the statesmen of the world met in San Francisco in April of 1945. They there faced a series of problems unprecedented in the history of mankind. Humanity had survived two world wars but the scars of conflict were everywhere apparent; within a single generation war and its attendant ills had brought death to tens of millions of human beings; devastation had visited many of the oldest, largest, and proudest cities of the world. To an extent never approached before, invention had become the mother of desolation!

The statesmen at San Francisco were confronted with difficulties far greater than the conventional problems of the traditional peace conference. A new factor had been introduced into human, and particularly into international, relations. A rising tide of determined discontent among the under-privileged persons and nations was threatening with disintegration many of the oldest and apparently most stable of political institutions. For the first time an almost universal rebellion against their conditions of life was sweeping over that great part of the human race that had always suffered and was still suffering from hunger, ignorance, disease and the many forms of injustice. The attitude of those in revolt against their lot was described long before by Don Quixote: "There are only two families in the world, the Haves and the Have-nots." The contrasting and intolerable conditions in which most human beings were condemned to live could be summarized as they were later on in the words of Dag Hammarskjold, Secretary-General of the United Nations, when he said that:

> . . . there were, on the one hand, those to whom good health was customary and for whom adequate facilities existed to provide attendance in disease; who could expect a life span of sixty-five or seventy years; who had opportunity for education and for attaining the magic power that goes with the knowledge of the written word; who were economically well-established and to whom hunger was sel-

dom known; who enjoyed political liberty and reasonable hope of justice under law.

There was, on the other hand, that much larger element of the human race whose members suffered chronically from disease and who could seldom expect to live beyond thirty years or thirty-five; who were illiterate and who were denied the other tools and values of education; to whom hunger, inadequate housing, and other economic and social ills were the common-place of life; and who, in many cases, were deprived of national independence and often of individual liberty and of consistent justice. Of over half the people in the world it could be said, to adapt the words of Thomas Hobbes, that their lives would almost inevitably be "poor, nasty, brutish, and short."

Conditions of this kind were not new. But what was new was that, for the first time, the majority of the people of the world had become convinced that the continuation of such circumstances was not inevitable. People could no longer be persuaded to believe that it was a rule of nature or a law of God that they should be born in misery and hasten to an early grave. They were no longer prepared to accept the hope of felicity in heaven as a substitute for happiness on earth. With a growing unanimity they were determined that something must be done! Their protests were beginning to make clear to everyone the dangerous truth of Havelock Ellis's definition of civilization as "a thin crust over a volcano of revolution."

By 1945 everyone everywhere knew that it was possible to enjoy material comfort and a reasonable measure of personal freedom in this life; in rapidly increasing numbers the poverty-stricken people and nations were becoming convinced that their unhappy condition was the result of a callous disregard by those whom fortune had more generously favoured. They were also coming to believe that, as Tolstoy once said, the wealthy man "will do almost anything for the poor man, anything but get off his back." The western world had sent out religious missionaries who had preached the gospel of the fatherhood of God and the brotherhood of man; political prophets who had expatiated on the glories of liberty and democracy; and commercial salesmen who had aroused desires for the products of industrial civilization. The moving picture, the illustrated press, the radio and increased personal contacts through improved means of transportation and communication, had carried these messages into even the most remote areas of human habitation.

By the end of the war, it was clear that the ideas and desires thus disseminated and popularized had been taken seriously by men and women everywhere. Rather than live in misery while waiting for happiness in a future life, they wanted freedom and comfort and pleasure here and now. The strength of this demand was being vividly illustrated by the colonial turmoil that was to result in the winning of political independence by over 600 million people in less than ten years. In the words of General Smuts, "The masses [were] on the trek." This psychological revolution had engulfed the whole of Asia and was soon spreading like a forest fire in Africa where, since the end of the war, a long list of new and independent nations were emerging to demand a less dismal life for their people in the world community.

To paraphrase the words of the late Dr. Bennett, first Administrator of the United States Point Four Programme, the more advanced countries by both intent and inadvertence had given the people of the under-developed areas a window into the twentieth century; now they must help them to find a door.

As has been indicated, it was soon made clear to the statesmen at San Francisco that the struggle for political independence was parallelled, within the under-developed nations, by an increasingly insistent demand for a more equitable distribution of the good things of life. Anger, envy, resentment and pain could not be assuaged by minor concessions of a political character. In the words of an intelligent though impecunious Jamaican, "Independence mek de people dance, but can't mek banana grow." Men and women wanted national freedom but they also wanted decent food and homes and health and opportunities for work and play. Independence was obviously not enough. Even after it was attained, inequalities in the distribution of comforts and privileges still remained —and in some cases became even more pronounced.

The demands of the leaders of the emerging countries of Asia and Africa for political independence and for practical help were supported at San Francisco by the more enlightened representatives of some of the great powers. These forces combined to persuade or to force the authors of the Charter to accord economic and social issues a position of equality with those of a political nature when the constitution of the new body was under negotiation. It is no secret that many of the more tradition-bound and conservative delegates to the San Francisco Conference fought against this trend. Many of the Europeans, in particular, took an overly cynical view of the whole thing, while the United States' delegation was split down the middle on this issue. The Canadians and the Scandinavians worked in general with the Asians and the Latin Americans for the new approach. Fortunately the campaign also had the very powerful support of enlightened public opinion in the United States, Britain and other countries and this, in the long run, proved decisive. It is noteworthy that eminent among those in the United States' delegation who fought the battle to establish and to give significant powers to the Economic and Social Council was Mr. Harper Sibley, who was President of the International Chamber of Commerce. His support was symptomatic of the changing attitude on such matters of the more sophisticated leaders of the business and financial community in many countries.

The battle of principle was won at San Francisco. The Covenant of the League of Nations had given the League a generalized authority to deal with any matter affecting the peace of the world. This presumably could have been interpreted to include economic and social conditions, and not just political matters, although until the Bruce Committee no very serious effort was ever made to utilize the Covenant in that way. But the Charter of the United Nations was clear and specific. Separate instruments were designed and detailed areas of responsibility were assigned to each. The Economic and Social Council, along with the Security Council, Trusteeship Council, the Secretariat and the International Court of Justice became one of the "principal organs" of the United Nations. The inclusion in the Charter of the Articles designed to provide help to all nations in their struggle for political, economic and social progress, provided the constitutional basis for the subsequent United Nations programmes of international technical and financial aid.

E · The New Obligations Imposed by the United Nations Charter

In comparison with the constitution of the League and with many other international papers there was surprisingly little that was ambiguous about the wording of the United Nations Charter. The purposes of the Organization are defined in Article One and they include the responsibility "to achieve international co-operation in solving international problems of an economic, social, cultural, or humanitarian character." This, it is to be noted, was thus defined as a responsibility of the whole organization, and not of the Economic and Social Council alone.

But, in addition to the well-intentioned statements of principle, the authors of the Charter decided that the United Nations should be provided with instruments and policies designed specifically to improve the social and material conditions of life in the less privileged areas of the globe. The most important of these instruments was the Economic and Social Council; the most significant statement of policy was that embodied in Ariticle 55 of the Charter by which all Member States pledged themselves:

> With the view to the creation of conditions of stability and wellbeing which are necessary for peaceful and friendly relations among

nations based on respect for the principle of equal rights and self-determination of peoples . . . [to promote]
(a) higher standards of living, full employment, and conditions of economic and social progress and development;
(b) solutions of international economic, social, health, and related problems; and international cultural and educational co-operation; and
(c) universal respect for, and observance of, human rights and fundamental freedoms for all without distinction as to race, sex, language, or religion.

And Article 56 embodied the definite undertaking whereby

All Members pledge themselves to take joint and separate action in co-operation with the Organization for the achievement of the purposes set forth in Article 55.

Here, indeed, was something new in human affairs. If this promise were taken seriously, humanity could never again revert to the standards characteristic of the international relationships of the past. Human beings were becoming as important as institutions.

F · Other International Aid Programmes

Before proceeding to a closer examination of the United Nations programmes of international aid it would be useful to review briefly what is now being done through other agencies, national and regional, and under public and private auspices. Of all these the work started and being carried on by the United States Government is much the most significant.

1/The Initiative of the United States

Although no one person or country can be credited with initiating the modern programmes of technical assistance, the United States has certainly played by far the largest part. More than sixty years ago the federal government in Washington inaugurated programmes for cultural, economic and technical co-operation among the nations of the Western Hemisphere (excluding Canada). Later the United States, although not a member of the League of Nations, encouraged the early initiatives being displayed by that organization in the field of international co-operation for economic and social progress. Following the Second World War, the United States was also the leader in urging the formation of the various

Specialized Agencies, and that country was and remains the major contributor of funds for their technical assistance operations.

The work of the Pan-American Union, founded in 1890, had resulted in the creation of several bodies designed to search for a solution to the pressing social and economic problems of the Western Hemisphere. Of these the Pan-American Sanitary Bureau (PASB) was the first and most distinguished. Formed in 1902, PASB is the oldest international health agency and it has performed valuable services in epidemiological reporting, malaria control, the combatting of such diseases as tuberculosis, yellow fever, and bubonic plague, and in providing leadership in the standardization of statistics, quarantine regulations, and sanitary codes. PASB co-operated closely with the Health Organization of the League of Nations and since the Second World War has become the operating agency for WHO in the Western Hemisphere.

In addition to PASB, there were several other specialized inter-American bodies which were strongly supported by the United States: a postal union, a highway confederation, an institute for child protection and an institute of geography and history.

In his inaugural speech of 1933, President Franklin D. Roosevelt had enunciated his "good neighbour" policy in these words:

> In the field of world policy I would dedicate this nation to the policy of the good neighbour—the neighbour who resolutely respects himself, and because he does so, respects the rights of others—the neighbour who respects his obligations and respects the sanctity of his agreements in and with a world of neighbours.

The Good Neighbour Policy quickly became associated with a policy of co-operative assistance directed primarily toward Latin America. Within a few short years it manifested itself in a variey of programmes involving governmental loans, private investment and technical co-operation in agriculture, health and educational projects. This aid, as Sumner Welles said, was "promised on the conviction that social progress and political stability in the hemisphere were contingent upon higher living standards, and the growth of true democracy was also contingent upon better nutrition, sanitation, education, and communications." (Quoted in Willard R. Espy: *Bold New Program*, New York, 1950, p. 68.)

The promulgation of the Good Neighbour Policy marked a major turning-point in United States attitudes toward international co-operation and this became even more evident after the formation in 1939 of the Interdepartmental Committee on Co-operation with American Republics which was designed to guide and co-ordinate the distribution of United

States aid. The name of this body was later changed to the Interdepartmental Committee on Scientific and Cultural Co-operation.

United States technical aid conducted through the Interdepartmental Committee started with a modest budget of $370,500 in 1940. By the end of its first decade, just before the new Point Four programme came into existence, the annual outlay was over $4 million. Over $26 million was spent in the ten years of this programme and more than 3,000 Latin Americans were brought to study and do research in the United States, while more than 1,200 American experts were assigned to technical missions abroad. (U.S. Department of State: *Point Four, Washington*, Government Printing Office, 1950, p. 130.) This was not, however, a unified programme of aid adequately planned to promote the growth of the economy of Latin America. Many of the approved projects were of individual value but were peripheral to the basic problems of the countries being assisted.

A companion technical assistance programme was that inaugurated by the Institute of Inter-American Affairs (IIAA). This agency was a product of two United States government-owned corporations set up under the jurisdiction of the Office of the Co-ordinator of Inter-American Affairs, which was itself an executive agency created in 1941. The purpose of the IIAA was to plan and administer technical programmes and projects in three fields: public health and sanitation, agriculture, and education. While the Institute also provided opportunities for Latin Americans to study in the United States, the real hallmark of its programme was the *servicio*. Essentially the servicio was an operational bureau established in the country being assisted and manned jointly by personnel of an IIAA mission and of the host government. The servicio was usually located within a national ministry but it enjoyed a semi-autonomous status and operated under a budget provided by both countries. The merit of this device, which was widely used in Latin America, lay chiefly in the fact that it ensured intimate daily contact and co-operation in dealing with the problems of national development between the United States experts and the personnel provided by the host country.

By the end of 1950, there were twenty-four servicios in operation staffed by 250 United States technicians, and with over 8,000 local employees. In addition, over 1,200 Latin Americans had been brought to the United States to study, while 7,500 more had received instruction or in-service training in their own country under IIAA auspices. The Institute itself estimated that 27,000,000 people had benefited from its programmes.

In theory the servicio device envisages the eventual withdrawal of the sponsoring country so that full responsibility will devolve upon the recipient government and its newly-trained personnel. Although the IIAA worked toward this end, in practice it seldom succeeded. There were many instances, as Professor Glick and others have pointed out, in which the director of the servicio and his American staff operated the programme as if it were entirely a United States venture. Moreover, IIAA operations suffered from a lack of adequate integration of its three programmes—education, health and sanitation, and agriculture. The Washington headquarters was organized around these three functional divisions and each recruited its technicians separately for their individual servicios. Programme planning based on a study of the total needs of the country was seldom practised and contacts between the IIAA technicians working in different servicios in the same country were usually infrequent. Contacts between representatives of Interdepartmental Committee technical missions and IIAA servicio personnel were even less common. While there was apparently little duplication in the United States programmes, there was equally little integration.

In Washington, toward the end of the 1940's, pressure for a reassessment of these programmes was growing on two fronts. The first arose from antagonisms at the administrative level on the basic question of programme organization. Were the specialist departments of government better equipped to give technical assistance, as through the Interdepartmental Committee, or should a special agency be set up for aid purposes, as was IIAA? Both the Department of State and the Bureau of the Budget became increasingly concerned as this debate continued. Relations were particularly strained between the Department of State and IIAA, the latter being accused of frequently ignoring established diplomatic channels. Various adjustments were proposed to alleviate these interagency conflicts, but the search for a solution was cut short by discussions taking place elsewhere in Washington.

The experience of the war and post-war years convinced many of those in positions of influence in the government that the time had come for an entirely new look at the whole scheme of technical assistance. The Atlantic Charter, drafted and handed to the press by Churchill, Roosevelt and King in August 1941, more as a propaganda stunt than as a serious programme for world development, had been received with quite unexpected approval and acclaim. To the surprise of its authors it was being taken seriously—and nowhere more so than in the under-developed countries. Robert Sherwood, whose knowledge of the circumstances in which it was prepared was as intimate as his description was precise said that to the Prime Ministers and the President it was "not much more than a publicity handout. Nevertheless the effect was cosmic and historic. The British learned that when you state a moral principle, you are stuck with it." Of course it was not only the British who could with profit learn this lesson. The Charter was taken seriously by men of goodwill, and of influence, in the United States, including not a few in Washington. After the end of the war the atmosphere it had helped to create, together with the arguments that had been advanced in San Francisco, resulted in President Truman's aides starting to work on plans to give greater recognition in United States foreign policy to the growing demand in the under-developed countries for economic progress.

The results of these studies became apparent in 1949, when President Truman challenged the economically and technically developed nations to mount a massive programme to share their scientific knowledge and their varied skills with the depressed nations of the world.

President Truman's inaugural address of January 1949 had an even greater impact on the international scene than had Franklin Roosevelt's "good neighbour" statements of sixteen years before. The President outlined four courses of action which would mark United States foreign policy in the coming years. The first three points committed the United States (1) to support the United Nations and the Specialized Agencies; (2) to continue programmes for general world recovery; and (3) to strengthen freedom-loving nations against aggression. It was the *fourth point*, however, that struck the imagination of the world. It read:

> Fourth, we must embark on a bold new programme for making the benefits of our scientific advances and industrial progress available for the improvement and growth of under-developed areas. . . . For the first time in history, humanity possesses the knowledge and skill to relieve the suffering of these people. . . . We should make available to peace-loving peoples the benefits of our store of technical knowledge in order to help them realize their aspirations for a better life. And in co-operation with other nations, we should foster capital investment in areas needing development. . . . We invite other countries to pool their technological resources in this undertaking. . . . This should be a co-operative enterprise in which all nations work together through the United Nations and its specialized agencies wherever practicable.

This challenge marked the beginning of a new stage in the history of international co-operation. It is true, as has been recorded, that a number of programmes were already being carried on by the United States, by the United Nations and by the Specialized Agencies. But the promise of the President's initiative foreshadowed a programme so enlarged in scope as to be new in substance.

Although the President had announced his policy, the administration had no specific plan ready for its implementation. Debate in the press, in Congress and in the White House itself continued for another eighteen months before a statute authorizing specific action was finally enacted. The debate over the Act for International Development began on the fundamental issue of whether the United States should in fact commit itself to co-operate with the peoples of the backward countries in the development of their economies and the raising of their standards of living. In the end the Congress gave an affirmative answer, basing its action on the belief that a programme of this sort would stimulate the growth of democratic practices, would expand mutually beneficial commerce, and would assist in promotion of world peace. The legislation wisely provided that financial and technical assistance would be handled by the same agency, thus making it possible for the United States to give good advice and at the same time to supply funds to enable the recipient of this advice to act upon it. This arrangement was one of the great advantages of the United States programmes as compared with those of the United Nations. The latter could provide advice but until much later had no funds to subsidize action.

Having approved the principle of the new policy, questions arose as to the kind of governmental organization that would be required to administer the programme and design the techniques that should be followed in its implementation.

In drafting the Act the members of Congress endeavoured to ensure that the programme would not become the instrument for a world-wide "dole" or for "make-work" projects in the less-developed countries. Two important provisions were inserted. In the first, the Point Four activities were defined as "technical co-operation," comprising "programmes for the international exchange of technical knowledge and skills" and for the provision of "surveys, demonstrations, training and similar projects."

The second provision vested a large measure of financial control over the programme in the Congress itself. Even though the legislation was intended to establish a continuing programme, the Congress required the President to return every year for new legislative authorizations and appropriations. Point Four, in effect, was made viable for only one fiscal year at a time. The problems created by this form of congressional control still confront the President today, in spite of some slight amelioration later obtained from Congress. Programmes such as those embodied in the Alliance for Progress and in the United States commitments to the United Nations are also handicapped in their long-range planning by being subject to the vagaries of the annual appropriation philosophy and procedures.

In spite of the general applause that had greeted the Point Four idea, the Act for International Development barely succeeded in obtaining senatorial approval. However, it was enacted and it set up a Technical Co-operation Administration under the State Department to carry out its purposes.

The many different departmental activities which TCA was expected to co-ordinate were sometimes discordant in their aims and equally divergent in practice. Some operating consistency was gradually being achieved under the strong leadership of TCA's first director, Dr. Henry G. Bennett, but his influence was terminated by his tragic, accidental death while he was in Iran in the course of an overseas tour of inspection, just a year after his appointment. Organizational and administrative problems have to varying degrees bedevilled the Point Four programmes ever since.

In 1951, Congress enacted the first Mutual Security Act which established a single agency designed to co-ordinate all United States foreign aid—whether technical, economic, or military.

When President Eisenhower came into office in 1953, still another agency was organized—the Foreign Operations Administration (FOA)—and the responsibilities for all economic and technical aid were transferred to it. Military aid, although administered in the Department of Defence, was made subject to the authority of FOA. This move sharply increased the real or alleged conviction of some critics that the technical assistance programmes of the United States were designed as a humanitarian cover for military activities. In certain countries all United States aid became suspect, and was denounced as a technique for the promotion of the political interests of the United States. The communist powers were particularly active in developing this theme and in describing Point Four as merely a new form of dollar diplomacy and as a disguise for new adventures in colonialism.

The life of FOA was short and, in general, unlamented; within a year it was dissolved by the Mutual Security Act of 1954. All military assistance responsibilities were restored to the Pentagon and the functions of economic aid and technical co-operation were given to a new body, the International Co-operation Administration (ICA). ICA was given a "semi-autonomous" position under the State Department where it was made subject to the views and programmes of the man responsible, under the President, for all aspects of United States foreign policy. Finally, President Kennedy again reorganized United States foreign aid under a fifth body, this time with the contrived label AID—the Agency for International Development. In the succeeding years its administrative standards have shown marked improvement.

Between 1950 and 1960 the wrangling over and repeated changes in the administrative arrangements for handling technical co-operation

inevitably had an adverse effect on the quality of the United States programmes. This was particularly true in the field where unified direction,
consistent and stable policies, and positive co-ordination were of great
importance. Under the conditions prevailing in Washington the field programmes inevitably suffered. The influence of the United States as an
example to the recipient governments was also adversely affected. Under
the International Co-operation Administration changes for the better
began to appear. United States Operations Missions (USOM) were established for each of the countries receiving aid and in these field offices
were combined the inter-related programmes of economic and technical
assistance. The Director of a USOM was charged with developing "country
plans" designed to make the most effective use of all United States assistance activities within the country concerned. In addition, the Director
was also to attempt to co-ordinate United States programmes with those
of the United Nations and with whichever of the Specialized Agencies
might be working in the same country.

The confused activities in Washington had a direct bearing on the
development of the United Nations programmes of technical assistance.
As will be shown in more detail later, plans for an expansion of the technical assistance work of the United Nations had been under consideration
for some time prior to President Truman's dramatic proposal in 1949. But
a major commitment by the United States was an essential factor if
these plans were to have any hope of implementation. In his initial proposals to Congress in connection with Point Four, President Truman had
included an item of $12 million for aid through the United Nations. But
the Act for International Development did not pass Congress until June
1950 and the first United Nations technical assistance pledging conference
could not usefully be convened therefore until after that time.

The United States legislation requiring annual congressional appropriations of technical assistance funds also constituted a continuing and
difficult problem for the United Nations administrators. The United
Nations operates on a calendar year, while the United States government
operates on a July–June schedule and there have been instances—in
1953 and 1954 for example—when Congress did not appropriate money
in time for United States representatives to give definite assurances
of support at the United Nations pledging conferences. The executive
branch of the United States Government has always given the impression that it would be willing to consider long-term commitments in connection with its pledges to the United Nations programmes, but any
effective steps have repeatedly been blocked in Congress.

It should of course be recognized that in spite of these procedural difficulties the United States has always provided by far the largest share of

the funds subscribed to the technical assistance programmes of the United Nations. In the beginning Washington gave over sixty per cent of the total. Subsequently this was reduced to about forty per cent and in some years, because of the failure of the other countries to provide their matching quotas, some of the money that the United States was prepared to provide was not forthcoming. The sardonic element in this disgraceful situation arose from the fact that the total amounts involved for most of the countries concerned were insignificant in relation to their other expenditures. In some cases individual countries would spend more on a single party or reception while the Assembly was in session, than would have paid their whole contribution to the Expanded Programme—a contribution which might be, and sometimes was, years in arrears.

Whatever may be said of some of its administrative arrangements, the value of the contribution of the United States not only to the programmes of the United Nations but to the whole scheme of mutual international aid can hardly be exaggerated. Not only has the United States provided more money but it has been the source of more leadership, more initiative, more imagination than any other country. In every aspect of the programmes—finance, personnel, ideas, facilities—the United States contribution has been as outstanding as it has been essential. Whatever measure of success has been achieved by mutual aid can be attributed in very large part to the generosity of the people and to the wisdom of the leaders of the United States.

2/The Colombo Plan

Apart from the technical assistance programmes developed by the United Nations and the United States, the complex of activities known as the Colombo Plan is perhaps the most significant contemporary undertaking of this kind.

After the end of the Second World War Great Britain's colonial empire began a rapid metamorphosis. A number of independent states emerged, some of them, but not all, retaining membership in the Commonwealth. In each case the British Government entered into joint arrangements with the government of the ex-colony, arrangements which were designed to assist in the economic and social progress of the new nation. Bilateral programmes were negotiated to take the place of the assistance originally given under colonial development legislation.

The Colombo Plan, devised to facilitate co-operation among, and to co-ordinate outside assistance to, the countries of south and southeast Asia (including others as well as the ex-British colonies), was one of the results of this willingness on the part of the British to aid the new nations.

The Colombo Plan originated in a meeting of the Commonwealth foreign ministers convened in Colombo, the capital of Ceylon, in January 1950. Representatives from Australia, Canada, Ceylon, India, New Zealand, Pakistan, the Union of South Africa and the United Kingdom, and observers from the colonial administrations of Borneo and Malaya, took part in the first meeting. After prolonged discussions the participating governments unanimously agreed to sponsor a six-year programme designed to raise living-standards for the quarter of the world's population that lives in the region from Indonesia to Pakistan. A Consultative Committee was formed to define the precise terms and procedures of the Plan and to set it in motion.

The Committee made two immediate decisions of basic importance. They proposed that the scale of Colombo Plan activities should be the aggregate of the development goals set out in the programmes prepared by the member nations; and they agreed that any acceptable plan of economic aid must be complemented by a substantial programme of technical assistance in order to prepare the people of the recipient countries to cope with the new world of specialized technology. In other words, the Colombo Plan was to supply both capital and technical advice.

As originally projected, the economic aid programme of the Colombo Plan would require $2 billion over the first six years and the technical assistance programme would involve the provision of $22.5 million during the first three years. One of the chief architects of the plan, Sir Percy Spender of Australia, later expressed the opinion that the technical assistance, despite the relatively small amount allotted to it, may have "returned more dividends than the other." (Sir Percy Spender: *The Colombo Plan*, Housing and Economic Development, Cambridge, Mass., Massachusetts Institute of Technology, 1955, pp. 14–20.) The four senior Commonwealth countries made small but useful initial pledges of support and these pledges have from time to time been renewed and considerably increased in size.

The Consultative Committee recognized from the beginning that additional support would have to be obtained and that active participation by the United States would be essential if a scheme of the projected magnitude was to be realized in practice. Approaches were made, a favourable response was received from Washington, and very shortly after its inauguration the United States became a partner in the Plan. In addition to the original members and the United States, other nations of the region soon began to participate. Thailand and the Indo-Chinese States joined almost immediately, while Burma, Indonesia, the Philippines, Malaya, Japan, Nepal, and the still-dependent British territories in the area enlisted soon afterwards. In 1965 a total of twenty-two governments were co-operating.

The member governments decided that it would be unnecessary and consequently wasteful to set up a large head-office staff to administer the plan. A small secretariat was installed in Colombo to act as a clearing-house for requests and as a centre for the maintenance of records. But no projects were designed or executed by this central body. The Colombo Plan is multi-lateral in that a number of nations have combined to provide aid, but it is bilateral in its actual operation. A project under this plan starts with a request from one government to another. It may go through the Colombo Secretariat or it may be addressed directly to the prospective donor state. When mutually agreed, the donor country simply deducts the cost of its aid from its pledge to the plan. At all stages the secretariat is kept informed but it has no more than advisory and record-keeping responsibilities. The principle of partnership, which should be basic in all technical and financial assistance, was particularly prominent in the Colombo Plan concept and a number of the less-developed member-nations were soon, in spite of their relative poverty, providing both capital and technical aid to other participants. Ceylon, Malaya and Singapore were among the earliest contributors and India provided many hundreds of opportunities for specialized training, some of which have been used by residents of Australia and New Zealand.

The record of expansion of the Colombo Plan activities can fairly be described as remarkable. At the meeting of the Consultation Committee in London in November 1964, it was reported that for the period from 1950, when the plan was started, until 1963, external assistance totalled $14,805 million, comprising external capital in the form of gifts or loans amounting to $14,370 million and technical assistance totalling $435 million. For the single year 1962–63, aid was $1,950 million. A considerable part of this aid is, of course, provided in the form of loans but the commercial soundness of some of these transactions is so questionable as to make them a bit difficult to distinguish from grants.

The Colombo Plan has developed certain characteristics in its programmes which distinguish it from either the United States or United Nations programmes. It has, for example, placed greater emphasis on training. That acute American observer, Rowland Egger, estimated in 1959 that whereas the United Nations ratio of trainees to experts was about 0.9 trainees to one expert, and the United States ratio about 1.3 trainees to one expert, the Colombo Plan trainees outnumber Colombo Plan experts by about seven to one. (Rowland Egger: *Financing Technical Co-operation*, Annals of the American Academy of Political and Social Science, 323, May, 1959, pp. 80–90.) One of the most important aspects of the Colombo Plan technique—an advantage shared by the Point Four programmes—is the close integration of financial and technical assistance. This stands in beneficial contrast to the programmes of the United Nations in which, as has already been indicated, the authority and responsibility for the two aspects of aid are largely separate. Their union in the Colombo Plan has greatly contributed to the considerable measure of success that it has achieved. The establishment of the United Nations' Special Fund has gone some way toward the remedying of this defect in the U.N. programmes. The recent amalgamation of the Special Fund and the Expanded Programme will carry this trend still farther.

In addition to their part in the Colombo Plan and in the other multilateral programmes, each of the older and wealthier countries of the Commonwealth devotes public funds to other schemes of international aid. The total sums involved are not insignificant and have been gradually enlarged. By 1965–66 Canada, for example, was planning total external assistance amounting to some $130–140 million. This does not include long-term financing under the Export Credits Insurance Act which in the fiscal year 1964–65 amounted to $76 million. (*Monthly Review*, Bank of Nova Scotia, June–July, 1965, p. 2.)

3/The British Colonial Development and Welfare Programme

Among the oldest of the technical assistance programmes is that carried on by the United Kingdom to stimulate social and economic development in the British colonies. As early as 1929 the first Colonial Development and Welfare Act was passed. Although modest by present standards, it allocated £1 million per annum for agricultural and industrial projects designed to promote economic progress in overseas territories. Second and third versions of the Act, passed in 1940 and 1945 respectively, increased the financial allotments to over £16 million annually. A significant aspect of this programme was the prominence given to the preparation of long-range (ten-year) development plans for the colonies, so that contributions of capital, equipment and personnel could be co-ordinated and long-range planning be effected. Almost one-half of the commitments made under this programme have gone for education of all types, including the training of administrators, and for scientific research. About one-third has gone into a variety of economic development schemes, including projects in agriculture, irrigation and drainage, soil conservation, fisheries, forestry, electric power generation and industrialization. A good deal of emphasis has been placed on attempts to diversify the economies of the colonial territories, many of which have been unhealthily dependent upon a single crop or on the exploitation of a single natural resource.

Agricultural diversification has been encouraged and new secondary processes have been introduced. Cottage industries have been promoted as has the increased use of local materials in manufacturing. Vocational training has been started or expanded and, when advanced training abroad is required, scholarships have been provided.

The colonial development legislation made little provision for meeting the need for large-scale capital investment, and as a contribution to the closing of this gap the Colonial Development Corporation was established in 1948. It was given the benefit of access to comparatively large resources of capital at low rates of interest. In addition to providing funds the Corporation was expected to ensure a greater measure of integrated planning in the programmes for investment in the overseas territories. It was also empowered to regulate profits and it was directed to encourage substantial domestic participation in local investment decisions. Within its clearly limited scope the Corporation has established a sound reputation for its handling of investments and for exercising a beneficent influence on such matters as labour practices, wage levels for native labour, the provision of social services to employees, and the training of large numbers of previously unskilled labourers.

4/The Special Commonwealth African Assistance Plan

Ten years after the Commonwealth Ministers made their important decision regarding technical assistance for the emerging nations of south and southeast Asia, a comparable decision was taken at a London meeting to set up a programme of aid to Commonwealth countries (and dependent territories) in Africa. This plan was initiated in September, 1960. The African programme is designed not only to expand Commonwealth bilateral aid for African states, but also to assist local governments to obtain increased aid from international organizations. One of the most important aspects of the work of the African Plan has been agreement on arrangements for the filling of executive and advisory posts of a technical and specialized nature in the African Commonwealth countries which have recently achieved independence, when suitable indigenous personnel are not locally available.

5/The Programmes of Other Metropolitan Countries

France began a programme of direct contributions to the economic development of its overseas territories as early as 1935 with a fifteen-year plan for the expenditure of eleven billion francs for such purposes. This plan was cut short by the Second World War but was resumed on a large scale following the liberation of the metropolitan area. Extensive financing was provided through two agencies (1) a Central Finance Office for

Overseas France (Caisse Centrale) and (2) an Investment Fund for Social and Economic Development (FIDES). In tropical Africa post-war French colonial policy concentrated on the extension of educational and health facilities. Housing, communications, irrigation and water-conservation programmes were given high priority. A number of scientific research institutes were also set up to seek additional or improved uses for domestic products as well as other new sources of income for the subject countries.

As the French colonies attained independent status, France continued to provide aid within the new constitutional context. A Fund for Aid and Co-operation was instituted in 1959 to give assistance to the new nations of the French community and especially to help them explore their resource potentials. French aid to tropical Africa, in all its forms, has now been running at about 100 million francs annually for some years.

While the French programmes have tended to concentrate on the ex-colonial states there has also been a slowly widening interest in other parts of the world. This has been most noticeable perhaps in Latin America where among other activities a great deal of assistance has been provided for the development and utilization of energy. In this the programme in Brazil has been outstanding.

The six members of the European Economic Community—the Common Market—also have set up a sizable fund to provide for the joint development of the overseas territories of France, Belgium, Italy and the Netherlands. A total of $581 million was earmarked for expenditure in the five years after 1958.

Technical assistance is also provided to African territories through the Commission for Co-operation South of the Sahara, which was organized by Belgium, France, Portugal and the United Kingdom, and includes as members Ghana, Liberia, Rhodesia and the Union of South Africa. The Commission operates several bureaus for co-ordinating technical assistance in such fields as soils utilization, rural economy, labour, education and disease-control.

Canada has from the start been close to the top of the list of contributors to the Expanded Programme of the United Nations and also to the Colombo Plan. The latter had received well over $500 million from Canada during its first fifteen years. Ottawa has also directed substantial contributions to other recipient governments that are experiencing special needs, particularly in Africa and the West Indies; and, although not a member, Canada began in 1965 to contribute to the work of the Inter-American Development Bank.

Denmark, Norway and Sweden have been most active in providing technical and economic assistance in a wide variety of forms. They participate in the Joint Scandinavian Project in Korea, which includes a major medical centre. Sweden has underwritten institutes of building technology in Ethiopia and Pakistan; Denmark has used its specialized experience in dairy farming to help organize experimental farms in India and has established excellent training-courses of various kinds in Copenhagen; and Norway, exploiting its wide knowledge of fishery techniques, has supplied equipment and technicians for a pilot project on the Travancore coast of India. This plan, in addition to providing training in modern fishing methods, is designed to assist in the organization of local co-operatives and in the development of health facilities for the fishermen. The Scandinavian countries have also established a number of semi-public funds which have provided money for a variety of beneficial projects in under-developed countries.

The Federal German Republic (West Germany) has, in recent years, also provided technical and other forms of developmental assistance in special cases. Besides co-operating with the other members in the Common Market undertakings, West Germany has given assistance to India, Pakistan, Indonesia, Yemen, Lebanon, Israel and other countries in Africa, Asia, and Latin America. Among the projects have been model agricultural developments in Turkey and Pakistan; vocational training institutes in Teheran and eighteen other centres in Iran; and a technological institute in New Delhi. The German programme in Turkey has been especially wide in coverage and high in quality.

Israel has for some years been engaged in the provision of various forms of technical assistance, especially to African countries and to Burma. This has been particularly beneficial in the case of countries needing help in the development of effective and economical plans for water utilization. Israel's successful experiences in the Negev made that country a natural source, through its TAHAL organization, of beneficial assistance to others with comparable problems. Road-building and shipping are other fields in which Israel has specialized, with marked benefit to the recipients of its aid.

There has been a significant recent change in the foreign aid programme of Japan. For understandable reasons Tokyo was a late entrant into this field and at first Japanese assistance was largely concentrated on projects likely to result in the promotion of Japanese exports. Indeed technical co-operation was included in the annual budget classification under the heading of export promotion. Tokyo has now however announced an intention to spend one per cent of its national income on the economic development of southeast Asia. This will take the form of direct and project loans rather than continue, as in the past, to be largely confined to a system of deferred payments for Japanese exports.

Activities of a comparable character, though on a generally more limited scale, could be recorded of a number of other countries. These, however, will suffice as illustrations of a process that is gradually growing in scope and importance.

6/Other Regional Assistance Programmes Under Multilateral Sponsorship

When the Organization of American States (OAS) was constituted out of the member states of the Pan-American Union in 1948, its charter pledged the mutual promotion of co-operative action toward social, economic and cultural development. Renewed attention to this article in its charter was attracted by President Truman's Point Four proposal in the following year. It was recognized that the United Nations programmes of technical assistance would fall far short of meeting the needs of the Latin American region and the OAS was urged to complement these activities by the development of special plans for promoting progress in the Western Hemisphere. When finally organized, the major activity of the OAS technical co-operation programme was the establishment of regional training-centres for nominees of the member states. Instruction at these centres is in the native tongue and the facilities are usually located in cultural and social environments that are familiar to the trainees. As such conditions are often absent in other programmes of technical assistance, the OAS centres have at least this one great advantage. Emphasis in these schools is placed on training at the operating level with special stress being placed on actual field experience. The OAS scheme is financed by voluntary contributions of member states with the United States pledging a fixed percentage. In this case the United States pledge is seventy per cent. Total contributions have amounted to slightly less than $2 million annually in recent years. Under the Alliance for Progress, if it survives Washington's new interpretation of the Monroe Doctrine, much more can be expected.

One of the earliest regional arrangements for international co-operation and mutual aid was the establishment of a Caribbean Commission which does not, however, offer direct technical assistance but acts only in a consultative and advisory capacity in dealing with problems common to that region. Its small secretariat, located in Trinidad, conducts studies and makes recommendations to member governments. The Commission performs an important function as a clearing-house for pertinent information relating to social and economic development and, particularly, in regard to the possibilities for technical assistance from bilateral and international sources.

An intergovernmental commission of a similar character was established in 1948 by six nations with dependencies in the South Pacific

Region. This South Pacific Commission, with the United States, France, Australia, New Zealand, the Netherlands and the United Kingdom as members, is concerned with the characteristic social, economic and welfare problems of the non-self-governing territories lying generally in the Pacific and south of the equator. Its activities closely parallel those of its Caribbean counterpart.

Technical co-operation is also practised by the members of the Conference of Independent African States, and amongst the members of the League of Arab States. The latter group has, in addition, formed its own fund to stimulate progress, modelled on the International Bank and known as the Arab Monetary Fund for Economic Development. Participating countries are the United Arab Republic, Saudi Arabia, Libya, Lebanon, Yemen and Jordan.

Several regional defence organizations, among them the Southeast Asia Treaty Organization and the Central Treaty Organization (for the Middle East), have inaugurated small technical and economic assistance programmes within the framework of their general activities.

Finally, reference should be made to the Inter-American Development Bank and particularly to the extensive technical assistance activities carried out through its Social Fund. This represents the kind of co-operative effort for the mutual good that should be much more widely practised.

7/Aid Programmes of the Communist Bloc Nations

The technical assistance schemes of the Soviet bloc are radically different from those of the non-communist countries. For the most part, the Soviet aid arrangements are embedded in credit agreements which the communist governments negotiate with carefully selected under-developed nations. As a result, technical assistance usually consists of the provision of experts in conjunction with some project concerning which an international contract has been made. Such schemes have included the Aswan Dam in Egypt, the Bhilai steel-works in India, a cement plant in Afghanistan and a sugar refinery in Indonesia. The Soviet bloc countries not only agree to construct the project and to supply equipment for it, but also undertake to train local personnel to operate the project when completed. This arrangement resembles many of the contracts negotiated by private firms operating from the non-communist countries.

Information regarding the size of the Soviet programmes and details as to their content are severely limited. What little factual material is available seems to indicate that communist aid was much smaller than that of the United States, or, in proportionate terms, than that provided by some of the lesser European or Commonwealth countries. However, evidence would seem to suggest that the scale of Soviet aid has been rapidly rising. Marshall Goldman has estimated that in recent years Russian aid to under-developed countries has constituted about the same percentage of its gross national product (0.4 per cent) as has aid from the United States. (Marshall I. Goldman: "How Effective is Soviet Foreign Aid?" *Challenge*, January 11, 1963, pp. 12–15.) An interesting aspect of this estimate is the fact that, until recently, the Soviet Union itself was considered under-developed—as, of course, it still is in certain respects. This fact taken in conjunction with extraordinary achievements of the U.S.S.R. in the last few years gives that country a special interest for the currently under-developed nations who are encouraged to believe that they too can achieve similarly rapid progress. How many of them would be prepared to make the same sacrifices is another question.

Until Stalin's death in 1954 Soviet aid was limited to countries of the communist bloc to which Russia supplied the ruble equivalent of something like $8 billion in credits and loans. Between 1954 and 1962 credits and grants extended to under-developed countries appear to have totalled the equivalent of just under $5 billion. In 1964 the scale of assistance rose to about $1.3 billion. Since these credits are of a long-term nature, the comparison of totals is likely to be misleading and it has been estimated that only about one-quarter of all the commitments to the under-developed countries has been drawn upon. Outside its own satellites the U.S.S.R. has given technical assistance to the United Arab Republic, Indonesia, India, Cuba, Afghanistan, and the Yemen. China is, of course, a special case and little reliable information is available. United Press International reported in August, 1965 that a recent British survey had indicated that over the past decade China had distributed aid amounting in value to somewhat more than one billion dollars. This was confined almost entirely to Asian and African nations. All told it is estimated that in 1963 there were about 14,000 communist technicians working abroad. A total of some 15–16,000 would probably be a reasonable estimate for 1965. (*Survey of International Development*, February 15, 1965, p. 4.)

Reference should also be made to the International Bank of Economic Co-operation which began operations in Moscow early in 1964. The aim of this institution is to facilitate an international division of labour in the communist world through the financing of communist trade. But as the capital of the new bank is limited to 300 million non-convertible rubles, its influence is not likely to be of any major significance until it obtains increased resources and greater liberty of action. Indeed, as critics have suggested, in the immediate future what the Soviet Union most needs is loans, not borrowers. However, the Bank does show the direction in which Russian intentions and hopes are pointing.

It is generally agreed that there are few strings attached to assistance given by the Soviet bloc, although the propaganda values of such aid are not, of course, overlooked. When work on a non-military project is complete, it is usually turned over immediately to local authorities. This applies to steel mills, public utilities, oil refineries, cement plants, irrigation projects, hotels and technological institutes, all of which the Soviet bloc have constructed at one time or another for under-developed countries. A notable example of success was the construction of the Bhilai steel mill in India. This mill was one of four that India hoped to build; Britain and West Germany had already contracted and started to build mills at Durgapor and Rourkela when Russia took on the Bhilai project. The Russians opened their mill first, built it at less cost, charged a lower rate of interest, used a larger proportion of domestic resources, and trained and used more Indian technicians.

There is general agreement that Soviet technicians who go abroad are fully qualified in their respective fields, although there is no evidence that they are all facile in the native language as would sometimes be inferred from the self-criticism applied to alleged weaknesses in the programmes of the democratic countries. The flawless Russians, who are depicted as invariably knowing the local languages and being trained in and adjusting to the local folk-ways, are the most unrealistic of the stereotypes in books like The Ugly American.

A final aspect of Soviet bloc assistance is the increasing emphasis being placed on the training of nationals from under-developed countries, in schools in the communist nations. In Czechoslovakia, for example, training-centres of considerable importance have been established in the famous resort towns of Carlsbad and Marienbad, where students from foreign nations are given language training followed by courses in their respective fields of technical interest. Much of the scholarship programme in the communist states is designed to train personnel to operate projects built with Soviet credits. In the case of the Bhilai steel works, for instance, several hundred Indian engineers and technicians were trained in Russia. But in other cases the Soviet bloc has chosen to concentrate its efforts on scholarships with no comparable explanation for this particular emphasis. The United Arab Republic and Algeria are two notable examples of countries in which this kind of concentration is to be observed. The usual explanation advanced by western critics for the Russian preference for the scholarship form of assistance is that the Soviet Union wishes to bring as many young men and women as possible to the Russian centres in order to expose them to ideological pressures. This may or may not be the real explanation. It is worth noting, however, that the current tendency in most other aid programmes is to reduce rather than to increase the emphasis on the scholarship technique.

By western standards the total number of scholarships given by the U.S.S.R. and its associates is still small. Foreign students in Russia, including those from the communist countries, almost certainly total less than one-third of those in either the United Kingdom or the United States at any one time.

8/International Aid Through Private Organizations

Technical assistance is very far from being confined to governmental or official agencies. In many parts of the world representatives of foreign private organizations—churches, foundations, societies of many kinds—are to be found carrying on programmes designed to improve the economic or social conditions under which the local people live. In most cases this work is financed by private contributions with little or no assistance from any public body.

Over the last century and a half a wide variety of religious organizations have sent out missionaries who have ventured into almost every corner of the earth. For the most part there have been representatives of Christian churches moved by the injunction of their Lord to go into the world and preach the gospel to every creature. Thus their cardinal objective was evangelism, the saving of souls. From the beginning, however, some of these devoted churchmen, appalled by the social conditions they encountered among the people they had come to convert, began to consider how they might help to alleviate the physical suffering by which they were surrounded. But the average missionary (and his church) did not consider such matters to be his primary responsibility. Moreover, with rare exceptions, neither the individuals nor their organizations had any training in the enigmatic processes of social and economic change. As a result, as Arthur H. Cole has pointed out in his illuminating article, "The Relations of Missionary Activity to Economic Development," until about the beginning of the Second World War many of the missionary efforts to improve local conditions were addressed primarily to the relief of immediate cases of individual suffering, to providing for the needs of the local mission itself, or to furnishing converts with a means of earning a living. (*Economic Development and Cultural Change*, Vol. 9, January, 1961, pp. 120–127.) It was not until the meeting of the International Missionary Council in Madras in 1938 that the churches stated officially, for the first time, that it was their duty to work for the development of an "adequate economic base" in the areas in which they were engaged. Without such action there would be doubts about "the welfare, and indeed the continuing existence of the churches."

Although official recognition of the obligation of the churches to be concerned with economic problems was long delayed there were, of course, a great many individuals who had recognized this duty at a much earlier date. It was difficult for a conscientious and sensitive man to live in comparative luxury in the midst of degrading and ubiquitous disease. When confronted with such circumstances many of the missionaries abandoned or at least modified their initial and almost exclusive concentration on the propagation of their faith. A series of famine years in mid-nineteenth-century China led many of the missionaries to study and then to instruct their flocks in more effective methods of cultivation. A missionary, Samuel Higginbotham, developed what was perhaps the first agricultural experimental station in India, in an attempt to help solve famine conditions in that country. The number of medical missionaries and missionaries with teaching and technical skills increased enormously during the first quarter of this century and until comparatively recently there were probably more missionaries than all other foreigners combined in the schools of such areas as India, Africa and even Latin America. Some of the developments initiated by missionaries had unexpected and lasting effects in other parts of the world. To take a minor example, Professor Cole attributes the large-scale production and use of feminine hair nets in the period 1908-25 to missionary activity in China. Belgian and English wives of missionaries originally offered local instruction in lace-making, which led to the spread of this skill and its exploitation by the entrepreneurs of Shanghai.

Missionary work still accounts for a substantial portion of non-governmental aid in under-developed countries. Today, however, the pattern is more highly organized with a tendency towards the creation of specialist agencies co-ordinating work among missions, churches and areas. The Agricultural Mission, Inc., for example, associated with the World Council of Churches, has established training-courses for rural leadership in Latin America, Asia and Africa. Many orders of the Roman Catholic Church have assistance programmes, an interesting example being the system of credit unions being fostered among the poverty-ridden farmers in the uplands of Peru. Other notable work is being done by the Unitarian Service Committee, by the Young Women's and Young Men's Christian Associations and by the American Friends Service Committee, among many others.

There are few poor countries in the world that do not have a project of some kind financed by a private foundation. The vast number and often very highly endowed organizations of this kind in the United States are particularly active in work overseas—with total expenditure running well over $40 million a year. Although the foreign commitments of some United States foundations go back as far as 1914, the scale of the present operations is a post-war phenomenon. The purposes and techniques of the foundation grants are highly diverse: some are aimed at the village level, others work directly with governments, and still others deal with established private institutions. But through the various undertakings runs a common thread: they are all concerned with development of human resources. They all share the desire to establish and strengthen institutions for the purpose of relieving present and prospective suffering, to increase individual and group competence, and to do these things by encouraging a maximum exercise of self-help. The Rockefeller, Ford, Kellogg and Carnegie Foundations are the largest contributors of this type of technical assistance. Smaller but highly significant organizations with more specialized concerns include the Near East Foundation and the Asia Foundation. In an increasing number of instances the various private agencies are co-ordinating their programmes to their mutual advantage—and to that of their clients. An interesting example of this kind of co-operation is found in the new International Rice Institute in the Philippines which was built with a grant from the Ford Foundation and is staffed by advisers from the Rockefeller Foundation.

A great many universities, particularly in the United States and Canada, have become direct participants in various aspects of international aid. In some cases this has been developed through the initiative of student organizations but the more usual procedure is for the project to be started and administered by the governors, trustees, or other responsible authorities. In 1960 there were 136 technical assistance programmes being carried out by United States universities. Many of them took the form of direct aid to or co-operation with universities in the host countries. The largest part of the work being done by United States universities, however, was financed by subsidies from AID and cannot, therefore, be accurately described as a private undertaking. This does not reduce its value and it greatly increases its dimensions. In 1962, for example, sixty-five United States universities were engaged on 107 contracts which would result in a total expenditure of over $100 million.

Finally, there are neary two hundred other voluntary organizations with a great diversity of interests and methods that are involved in the provision of technical assistance. Their variety is reflected in their names. Among them are such bodies as the American Foundation for Overseas Blind, the World Veterans Federation, the International Co-operatives Alliance, the International Federation of Housing and Town Planning, the Textile Institute, the World University Service and the International Chamber of Commerce.

It is impossible to calculate with any precision the total number of technical assistance programmes currently in operation. Some tentative estimates can be made, but they give only a general idea of the scope of these activities. First, there are at least sixteen separate programmes conducted within the United Nations family—the United Nations itself, the Specialized Agencies, the Special Fund for Economic Development and the International Development Association. Second, amongst single government programmes, there are at least twenty-five countries that extend technical assistance under bilateral agreements. This figure does not include those countries, many of them still under-developed, that supply technicians only through regional or general international programmes. Third, there already exist at least twenty-three intergovernmental arrangements such as the Colombo Plan and the OAS scheme for the dispensing of technical assistance on a regional basis. Fourth, there are more than 165 voluntary agencies of many kinds which conduct regular programmes of technical assistance. Many more organizations than this carry on some limited version of technical assistance through the provision of fellowships, or the supply of such things as technical literature, advice and tools, but no accurate or official record exists of their operations. Mr. A. G. Mezerik, from whose studies many of the figures are taken, probably did more research on this subject than anyone else but he was far from satisfied that his listings were complete. (A. G. Mezerik: *Technical Assistance for Economic Development*, New York, International Review Service, 1959, pp. 39–49.)

The number of individuals, private organizations and governments engaged in one or more of the manifold forms of technical aid is not, of course, of vital importance. Some of the agencies are operating on a very small scale, and in many cases their operations are intermittent and sometimes badly chosen. The really significant fact is that the field is now recognized as an essential area of continuing concern, that the number of participants is constantly increasing, that some beneficial results are beginning to accrue, and that every government in the world is now aware that no national policy can be considered realistic that fails to embody provisions for the giving of aid, the receipt of aid, or both.

CHAPTER FIVE

The United Nations Programmes of Technical Assistance

A · Unique Factors in the United Nations Programmes

In most of the examples of technical assistance and other forms of international aid to which the last chapter referred, the programmes were the result of accident or of an independent and unrelated initiative devised by an individual, an organization, or a government, to meet some specific and immediate need. This was, in general, true of the activities of the League of Nations and of the earlier Specialized Agencies as well as of the work of individual governments and of many foundations, missionary societies and other private organizations.

It was not until the establishment of the United Nations that this kind of activity became a fully accepted and permanent feature of the international scene. Then, for the first time in history, a central mechanism was set up to develop consistent, formalized, inclusive programmes designed to provide for the transmission of knowledge from any part of the world in which it existed to any other part in which it was needed. Moreover, as has been pointed out by a distinguished American student of these matters, the creation of the new machinery moved the knotted problems of the under-developed nations for the first time "to the centre of the world stage." (Robert Asher: *Economic Co-operation under United Nations Auspices*, in *International Organization*, 12. Summer, 1958, pp. 288–302.) These changes constitute the unique contribution of the aid programmes of the United Nations.

The United Nations is, of course, in a singularly favourable position to provide help to the poorer and more backward nations—nations whose need is often only matched by the sensitivity of their leaders. It is much easier for such countries and such leaders to accept aid from an international organization in which their governments are recognized, officially at least, as equal members, than it is to take such assistance from a single donor power. As Sir John Maud has said, multilateral "aid lacks the taste of patronage which may seem sour" to the recipients, particularly

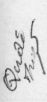

in the case of states that have only recently achieved nationhood after a long period of colonial rule. (Maud, *op cit.*, p. 8.) This is especially true of countries that require assistance in such sensitive areas as public administration or national financial policy. It is these considerations that give the multilateral United Nations programmes their most obvious advantage over the bilateral arrangements.

Through the United Nations, not only can any country draw upon the common store of scientific and technical knowledge available anywhere in the world, but it can obtain the desired assistance through a programme that is by its essential nature divorced from all political and military connotations. The recipients can thus avoid the conditions and restrictions sometimes placed upon the aid that is offered, for example, by the protagonists in the "cold war," by the political nature of many of the bilateral agreements, or by the limited membership of regional arrangements.

In this connection it is important to note that all the organizations participating in the United Nations programmes are committed to the avoidance of any preferences or limitations that are based on political or economic structure, on race, or on religion, when extending technical assistance.

United Nations programmes lay particular stress on the completely voluntary nature of their aid. By constitutional mandate their technical assistance is provided only on request by, and in full agreement with, the governments concerned. The prospective recipients define the nature and scope of the problems involved and specify the kinds of services required. In all cases, the country receiving assistance retains the last word in deciding whether it will utilize an expert, agree to the establishment of a training-centre, or avail itself of a fellowship. This authority extends to such things as the right to refuse, without explanation, to accept a particular nominee, or to decline a fellowship if the country in which it is to be utilized is for any reason thought to be inappropriate. Anti-communist countries, for example, sometimes reject Soviet experts or fellowships in the u.s.s.r.; Arab countries will not at present accept Israeli experts. The United Nations does attempt to obtain agreement on the principle that when an expert has become a member of the United Nations staff he is, for the time being, an international civil servant whose previous national character is temporarily suspended. As such he should be acceptable to any country. In practice, however, human nature being what it is, this principle cannot always be insisted upon in practice. This subordination of the United Nations programmes to wishes of the recipient governments imposes in theory and to some extent in practice severe restrictions on the participating organizations, and in some cases the results have been unfortunate. On balance, however, and taking all considerations into account, the policy is probably beneficial. In any case, no other procedure would be politically possible.

A major factor in confirming the pre-eminent acceptability of the United Nations programmes is their ability to draw upon the technical assistance resources of the whole world, whereas the resources available under other programmes are normally confined to national, or at most regional, personnel and facilities. While a few countries such as the United States, Great Britain and the Soviet Union are able to provide most of the techniques and materials that are needed in the under-developed countries, even they on occasion find difficulty in providing the highly specialized skills that are required to meet some of the special problems of the applicant states. Sometimes, moreover, an intimate past experience of actual living conditions in an undeveloped community is of very great value to a technical assistance expert and to his new clients. as David Owen, as Chairman of the United Nations Technical Assistance Board, has pointed out, "Frequently, a problem will yield more readily to the attack of an expert informed by experience and understanding of life in a country whose circumstances are not dissimilar from those in his homeland." (David Owen: *The United Nations Expanded Programme of Technical Assistance—A Multilateral Approach*, Annals of the American Academy of Political and Social Science, 323, May, 1959, pp. 25–32.) The United Nations technical assistance programmes have provided many and valuable opportunities for under-developed countries which are possessed of certain specialized experience to help others that lack such qualifications. Both psychologically and practically, the contributions made by experts from economically under-developed countries have proved to be a most valuable component of these programmes.

In addition to providing an unequalled field for the recruitment of experts, the United Nations and the Specialized Agencies also take advantage of their world-wide network of resources to strengthen their procedures of fellowship-placement. Study facilities have been available in many countries: industrial workers from Turkey and Yugoslavia have been trained in England, Germany and France; young scientists from Africa and the Middle East have taken advantage of excellent research facilities in Indian technological institutes; a centre for the training of Arab teachers of the blind has been established in Egypt; and aviation ground-crews from all over Latin America have been trained in Mexico City at a school sponsored by the International Civil Aviation Organization.

When a social or economic problem is global in scope, it is usually desirable that it be dealt with on a global basis. Here the United Nations (or a Specialized Agency) is likely to be the most appropriate body to organize a programme of international co-operation for its solution. Thus, the United Nations and the Specialized Agencies have been accepted as the most effective instruments for dealing with such matters as the reduction of the traffic in narcotics and other harmful drugs, the control of communicable diseases, the development of international postal and telegraph services, and the promotion of maximum safety provisions as well as efficiency in international civil aviation. These activities are of concern to all peoples and have generally been supported without political considerations being allowed to interfere. It must of course be recognized that some governments, and this is perhaps most true in the case of certain countries that have been concerned with the traffic in drugs, have been so influenced by selfish and malevolent domestic interests that they have hindered rather than helped the international efforts to improve services or abate evils.

The great fund of knowledge and experience gradually being acquired by the United Nations and the Specialized Agencies can be expected in the future to play an increasingly significant role in dealing with conundrums of national development. With the progress of modern science and technology tending more and more to make the nations of the world interdependent, the arguments in support of a world-wide and unified attack on the common problems of under-development become increasingly persuasive.

B · The Slow Beginning

When the San Francisco Conference recommended international action to promote social and economic progress, there was little practical precedent and virtually no accepted body of theory as to how this might be accomplished. However, from both the partially-developed and the grossly under-developed countries alike, demands for aid were rapidly increasing in urgency and number. In the first few years of international activity there was a good deal of experimentation : frequent mistakes were made and many delays occurred. The resulting dissatisfaction and criticism were shared by members of the United Nations Secretariat and Secretary-General Trygve Lie himself admitted that he was "uncomfortably aware of the somewhat slow start made by the Economic and Social Council" in the formative years after 1945. (Trygve Lie: *In the Cause of Peace*, New York, 1954, p. 143.)

Despite the lack of any proven techniques or of any established theories as to the most effective way to promote development in a backward country, it was apparent from the beginning that the provision of technical advice and of operational and investment capital would both be essential components of any successful programme.

Capital being hard to procure, the early aid activities of the United Nations soon began to concentrate on the furnishing of technical and scientific advice and the whole effort was soon given the shorthand label of "technical assistance." Technical assistance can be simply defined as the provision of advice, the organization of training facilities, and the designing and operation of demonstration programmes, based on the experience of the more advanced countries in the application of scientific knowledge and successful administrative techniques to the solution of economic and social problems. The principal devices used to dispense this aid include the provision of technical literature; the recruitment of individual experts or groups of experts; the organization of seminars or conferences to bring together the experienced and inexperienced for the explanation of needs and the exchange of ideas; the granting of fellowships to assist persons from under-developed countries to gain technical instruction abroad; and the development of demonstration programmes and the establishment of pilot projects to give opportunities for on-the-spot training, guidance and experience to local personnel.

It was in 1946 that the United Nations budget for the first time included an item to allow the Secretariat to provide technical, scientific, or administrative assistance to any member government that should request it. Within six years the United Nations had expanded its funds to finance the exchange of specialized knowledge among the nations of the world from $400,000 to (if allocations to the United Nations Specialized Agencies are included) over $20 million; by 1965, the technical assistance budget had grown to over $50 million. In comparison with the enormity of the needs of the under-developed countries the early expenditure was, of course, totally inadequate. However, a start had been made and the technical assistance programmes soon became, as they remain today, by far the most popular activity of the United Nations and the Specialized Agencies. Their objectives are almost universally commended, and their records, financially limited as they have been, have stirred the imagination of much of the world. It was probably true, as Dr. Myrdal said in 1951, that the United Nations programmes were based on "the most talked-about twenty million dollars in the world." Most of the talk—at that time and since—has been eulogistic; very often, in fact, far more laudatory than the size and achievements of the programme could possibly justify. Some of the delegates to the United Nations seem to have acted on the principle that if they praised the programme with sufficient oratorical fervour it would be unnecessary for their governments to make any financial sacrifices in its support. It is as depressing as it is disgraceful that more than one national delegation has seen nothing incongruous in spending ten to fifteen thousand dollars on a cocktail party or reception in a New York hotel, in the same week that their governments pledged half that sum as the maximum contribution they could possibly afford to make to a year's programme of technical assistance through the United Nations. Similar displays of bad taste have become more rather than less common in recent years and those responsible for such public exhibitions of social irresponsibility apparently still fail to recognize that they subject themselves and their governments to far more scorn than their hospitality (the acceptance of which in any case is generally considered a duty rather than a pleasure) could possibly assuage. Any national delegation that should take the astonishing initiative of informing the General Assembly that it planned to omit its customary annual reception, in order to devote the money thus saved to increasing its contribution to the funds available for technical assistance, would gain far more in respect and friendship than would be evoked by a dozen parties. The shock of such a practical example of sensitivity and of common sense might, of course, prove fatal to some of the more conventional members of other delegations.

Although the United Nations programme was, from the first, generously and sometimes even extravagantly praised, it encountered a good many procedural and substantive difficulties and these resulted from time to time in vigorous criticism of its administrative practices, its allocation of funds, and other aspects of its operations.

In some cases this criticism had a clear political motivation. For example, the Soviet Union and other communist powers refused at first to take any part in the new programme, describing it as merely a disguised form of "dollar diplomacy" designed to give the western powers, and particularly the United States, effective control over the economic and political policies of the under-developed countries. They also labelled it a form of "neo-colonialism" and advised the poorer countries to avoid involvement if they wished to gain or to retain their independence. But by 1953 the Soviet Union was forced to recognize the great and rapidly increasing popularity of the new programme and in that year, for the first time, began to make contributions to technical assistance funds.

Other countries criticized the administration of the programme because they felt that their own nationals were not assigned an adequate role in its implementation. France, in particular, and in accordance with its characteristic practice in the painful years of its relative decline, was insistent in demanding a greater share in the management of the programme and an increase in the number of French experts and facilities employed.

But in addition to these specialized complaints it was natural and proper that there should be a continuing critical approach to the operation of any programme that was new, that was designed to be universal in scope, and the functioning of which was complicated by the participation of many more or less independent agencies.

In view of its dimensions and of its unavoidably complex organizational arrangements, it was inevitable that the programme should be slow in starting and should be beset by administrative and operational difficulties. It took some time to get the machinery for such a programme into operation. As a first step it was necessary for the General Assembly to adopt resolutions authorizing the introduction of the various methods of aid and providing the funds to give the authorizations substance. So in a series of resolutions, beginning in 1946, the Assembly began to lay the legal foundation for the several forms of technical assistance.

As in all its activities the United Nations had to be careful to avoid impinging on the traditional rights of the Specialized Agencies, and its technical assistance operations from the first were limited to those fields not covered by the terms of reference of the related organizations. Thus the first of the Assembly resolutions only authorized the development, on a temporary and experimental basis, of "advisory social welfare services." The first expenditures from this vote, which were made in 1947, totalled just over $400,000 and it was not until the fourth session of the General Assembly in 1949 that the arrangements for these services were placed on a continuing basis. Although the resolution then approved authorized the provision of aid in the general area of social welfare, the United Nations officials had to be most careful to avoid anything that dealt directly with problems of health, which was primarily the responsibility of the World Health Organization, or with education, in which priority naturally was claimed by UNESCO.

In the field of economic development, the Assembly did not take action until its third session in 1948. Resolution 200 (III) then authorized the rendering of technical assistance through the provision of internationally recruited experts or teams of experts, facilities for training, and aid in procuring and installing equipment and supplies designed to foster economic progress. However, the approved expenditures reached less than $200,000 in 1949, and only slightly more than double that in the following year. Here again the United Nations Secretariat had to omit from the scope of its responsibilities the whole range of agriculture, over which the Food and Agriculture Organization claimed exclusive jurisdiction.

The third field of technical assistance recognized by the United Nations was public administration. By Resolution 246 (III), approved at the 1948 session, the Assembly allowed budgetary appropriations to be made for fellowships and scholarships for civil servants to study abroad, for group training projects in the under-developed countries, and for the distribution of technical information on comparative administrative practices. No actual expenditures were made for technical assistance in public administration until 1950, and then only $89,000 was used for this purpose. In public administration the United Nations was not restricted by competing agency claims as there was no specialized agency with any major responsibility or outstanding experience in this field.

Thus the somewhat optimistic phrases used by the framers of the Charter began to be translated into something like significant action only after the lapse of about four years. Even then, the annual expenditures still totalled little more than one million dollars. In part, the meagreness of funds can be attributed to the fact that money for technical assistance had to come from the general-purpose funds of the United Nations, and requests for budgetary allocations for this activity had, therefore, to compete with many other demands.

Because of the source of its revenues, the early technical assistance activity which was financed in this way came to be known as the "United Nations Regular Programme," to distinguish it from the subsequent "Expanded Programme" which was to be financed by special and voluntary contributions.

The United Nations Regular Programme of technical assistance was at first organized and administered by the Departments of Social Affairs and Economic Affairs of the Secretariat.

While the United Nations was gradually getting itself organized, most of the Specialized Agencies were also beginning to develop technical assistance activities of their own. Although their programmes were based on their common recognition of the almost universal need, and were stimulated by the same kind of insistent appeals for help, the aid plans of the United Nations and of the Specialized Agencies were from the beginning kept administratively separate and independent. To a regrettable extent this remains true today.

The first major turning-point in the history of United Nations technical assistance came during the third session of the General Assembly in 1948, when, after making provision for aid in public administration and economic development, the delegations joined in urging ECOSOC to give consideration to a general expansion and intensification of its technical assistance activities (Resolution 198 (III)). A still more important event occurred shortly thereafter, when, as has already been described,

President Truman, in his inaugural address in February, 1949, announced the willingness of the United States to embark on a "bold new programme" designed to make its resources of technical and scientific knowledge available to all nations that desired such help, and at the same time urged other developed and prosperous nations to join in this effort to meet the growing number of appeals for aid.

The soon-famous "Point Four" of President Truman's address greatly stimulated interest and activity in the whole range of technical assistance. The response, verbally at least, was as approving as it was widespread and instantaneous. It was followed at the eighth session of ECOSOC later in the spring by the introduction by the United States delegate of a resolution calling upon the Secretary-General to prepare a plan, in conjunction with the heads of the Specialized Agencies, for expanding the "Regular" technical assistance activities of the agencies and the United Nations. A group of staff experts drawn from all the prospective participants and under the leadership of David Owen and David Weintraub of the United Nations Secretariat, was organized to prepare a draft scheme. On May 18, 1949 their report was presented and Secretary-General Lie, who seldom acted without prior assurance of support, gave it emphatic endorsement. ECOSOC received the report at its August session where it was at once greeted with great enthusiasm by the representatives of the less-developed countries and with rather resigned approval by the governments of the more affluent states.

At the same time the Council adopted a resolution defining the principles on which the new programme should operate and describing the machinery that would be required. This ECOSOC resolution, number 222 (IX), became and has since remained the basic legislation of the new programme. In November, 1949 the General Assembly in Resolution 304 (IV) ratified the action of the Council and thus the United Nations Expanded Programme of Technical Assistance (EPTA) came into existence.

The resolutions instituting the Expanded Programme, although passed quickly in comparison with most actions requiring international agreement, were not enacted without debate. In the discussions in the Council, in the General Assembly and in the governing bodies of the Specialized Agencies, questions were raised as to the character of the programme, as to its "cold war" implications, as to the methods by which it should be organized and operated, and as to the means by which it should be financed. In some cases only interim solutions were reached and certain issues were to come up again and again in subsequent years.

As the limitations imposed on the Expanded Programme became clear, many of the under-developed countries began to express grave disappointment. They had hoped and even expected that the United Nations would inaugurate a massive international programme for economic development, which would provide financial as well as technical aid. Among many others, India, Brazil, Lebanon, Peru, and Turkey expressed deep regret that the plans for the Expanded Programme did not include provisions for meeting the capital needs of the poorer countries. Financial assistance would still be available only through bilateral grants, which in many cases might be expected to have political or even military implications, or through the International Bank, which at that time was known to be operating on the strictest banking principles—which meant in practice that its activities were hardly distinguishable from those of the most conservative commercial institutions. In the original ECOSOC debate on the Expanded Programme, the United States delegate stated that while his country was anxious to broaden the scope of United Nations aid, it was not prepared to provide large-scale financial assistance through the United Nations. This attitude was not hard to understand in view of the difficulties the Truman administration was having in getting Congress to accept an expansion of its own aid activities. But as the United States was expected to be the major contributor to the Expanded Programme, the other well-to-do nations had a plausible excuse, if not a sound reason, to place similar limitations on their own contributions. The disappointment of the poorer countries was not difficult to understand.

The initial attitude of the communist states has already been described and the Soviet bloc representatives in ECOSOC abstained from voting on the resolution to set up the Expanded Programme. Nor did they attend the first conference called in 1950 to receive financial subscriptions to the Programme.

The establishment of the Expanded Programme raised many issues relating to its form of organization and methods of administration as well as to its scale and its provisions for financing. The most contentious issue concerned the relationship of the Specialized Agencies to the United Nations. There was an extended argument among the staff experts assembled to prepare the over-all plan, as to whether the United Nations itself should control the Programme and its funds or whether the money and responsibility for its use should be divided in advance among all the participating agencies. Indeed, the whole debate on the larger question of the organization of the economic and social activities of the United Nations was reopened at this time. Secretary-General Lie proposed that a new body be set up within the United Nations Secretariat to be charged with full administrative responsibility for the entire Expanded Programme. It was not suggested that the proposed new organ would duplicate the work of the Specialized Agencies. Rather it would itself directly employ experts in fields not covered by the existing agencies but, for the rest, farm out projects and programmes to the appropriate organizations, at the same time transferring the necessary funds. Such an arrangement would facilitate planning and would ensure that assistance activities in each recipient country would be integrated and rationally co-ordinated. It would also mean a significant saving in headquarters administrative costs.

This proposal was strongly resisted by all the agencies. They felt that its acceptance would be a threat to their independence and would reduce their responsibilities. After a prolonged and vigorous debate the question was settled with virtually no concession to the wise and reasonable suggestions of the Secretary-General. The fact that the membership of the governing bodies of the various organizations was drawn from the same national administrations was not enough to ensure the acceptance of the sensible plan for a single operational authority. Agency patriotism was too strong to be overcome. In consequence it was decided to apportion the funds of the Expanded Programme among the Specialized Agencies and to the United Nations according to an arbitrary formula. The United Nations would set up its own operating agency to cover only those fields not specifically allocated to one or other of the Specialized Agencies. Decisions as to the use of the funds were left to the governing bodies of the agencies, subject only to the principles laid down by ECOSOC in its omnibus resolution. Thus, from the very beginning the procedures on which the programme was to operate were such as to make it inevitable that there would be inefficiency and duplication in administration, that there would be only a most reluctant approach to the idea of co-ordination in planning assistance to applicant countries, and that the various agencies would in fact compete for clients. The freedom of choice by recipient governments was also to be drastically restricted by the prior allocation of arbitrary amounts of money to the various operating organizations.

The experts appointed to draft plans for the Expanded Programme had suggested that initial operations should be envisaged on a scale of about $85 million per annum, but when ECOSOC considered the experts' report in the fall of 1949, the United States representative was instructed to deflate this optimistic concept. In part because of a realistic understanding of what the United States Congress would be likely to support, in part because it was obvious that the needy countries would not at the outset have a sufficient number of well-considered requests ready to present, and in part because it was believed that there would be an actual shortage of experts and training facilities available, Assistant Secretary of State Willard Thorp was instructed to inform ECOSOC that it was doubtful whether more than $25 million could be wisely spent during the first year.

In the event even this sum proved to be a heavy over-estimate. Sensible, carefully designed requests were slow to come in, the operating organizations were not ready to go into immediate and effective action, and experts were at first difficult to find and slow to get into the field. During the first year and a half only one-third of the available $20 million was spent. Before long, of course, this paradoxical situation was overcome and the participating agencies were faced with a "crisis of success" in which solid, well-prepared and fully justified requests far surpassed the limits established by the restricted availability of funds.

To meet the anticipated financial requirements of the programme, the Council had decided to convene a Technical Assistance Conference late in 1949 but congressional delays in the United States resulted in this being postponed until June, 1950. When it was eventually convened it was an oratorical success, but pledges totalling only $20,035,578 were forthcoming. This sum, moreover, was to be spread over a period of eighteen months.

Many of the delegates to the 1950 conference, most notably perhaps Señor Santa Cruz of Chile and General Carlos Romulo of the Philippines, expressed the hope that although the Expanded Programme would have to start on a limited budget, the scale of its support would soon increase to permit the mounting of a more serious attack on the problems of poverty, disease, ignorance and hunger. The sum of $100 million was frequently and favourably mentioned—usually by representatives of prospective recipients. It was, of course, clear that obvious and immediate needs would justify expenditures on that scale—if the initial planning and administrative problems could be solved. However, having once started on a miserly scale (in relation to the dimensions of the task) it proved impossible, even after most of the operational problems had been largely overcome, to raise the level of the programme to the shining goals that had originally been envisaged. In the first five years the contributions and the resulting expenditures moved only slowly upwards— as the following figures show :

YEAR	PLEDGED	EXPENDED
	$	$
1950–51	20,035,578	6,436,000
1952	18,797,232	22,968,000
1953	22,320,725	22,810,000
1954	25,020,589	19,465,000
1955	27,882,907	25,405,222

Four major reasons largely explain this hesitant beginning.

In the first place, it was necessary for the participating agencies to organize themselves internally to handle their tasks efficiently. In certain cases this has not even yet been fully achieved. Within the United Nations Secretariat a completely new unit, the Technical Assistance Administration, had to be created to manage the United Nations' own part of the programme. Competent personnel had to be recruited for the headquarters staffs of all participants, and effective techniques of technical assistance had to be improvised, applied and the early results evaluated. Finally new machinery had to be designed and instituted in an effort to bring some measure of co-ordination into the activities of the various participating agencies.

The problem of obtaining suitable experts in sufficient numbers proved in the beginning to be much more difficult than most of the authors of the programme had originally anticipated. This has always been a major problem, because in the selection of experts it is necessary to find men and women who are not only technically competent, but who also have the qualities of character and personality that make them suitable for the responsible duties they must shoulder and the sensitive relationships in which they must participate. It is not only the quality of the technical advice that must be considered; the way in which it is provided is at least equally important in dealing with under-developed countries.

The third difficulty arose from the inability of some governments to convince themselves that there were no political or economic strings attached to the offers of help from the United Nations organizations. Some people in some governments found it impossible to believe that the United Nations could be trusted, even when bearing gifts. Among these skeptical and suspicious officials the communist critics found their most receptive audience.

A final reason for the slow start was the fact that many governments —and particularly those most in need of help—either did not know what to ask for, or did not know how to formulate and present their requests. Nor were the agencies themselves always in a position to be definite and confident in their advice to the countries they were trying to aid. Very little was known, by anyone, about the intricate and complicated process of development planning. It sometimes took months of hard and diplomatic negotiation to reach agreement about the real requirements of a country, and then to work out with the government an accurate and convincing justification for its requests. One of the most characteristic difficulties of inexperienced governments is their failure to recognize the true nature of their own most pressing needs.

C · The Basic Legislation and its Principles

As has been stated, the basic legislation upon which the United Nations Expanded Programme of Technical Assistance was established is found in Resolution 222 (IX) of the Economic and Social Council. The pertinent paragraphs of this Resolution reads as follows.

The Economic and Social Council,

> Being impressed *with the significant contribution to economic development that can be made by an expansion of the international interchange of technical knowledge through international cooperation among countries;*

> Believing *that a sound international programme of this character must combine and make use of the experience of many nations, with different social patterns and cultural traditions and at different stages of development, so as to facilitate progress in the less advanced countries and to help solve their technical and economic problems...*

> Recommends *that the General Assembly approve the draft resolution ... which provides for an expanded programme of technical assistance for economic development of under-developed countries.*

This recommendation, passed by the Council on August 14–15, 1949 and approved by the General Assembly on November 16, 1949, was supplemented by a series of "Principles" of which the following is the basic statement:

> *The participating organizations should, in extending technical assistance for economic development of under-developed countries:*

> 1/*Regard it as a primary objective to help those countries to strengthen their national economies through the development of their industries and agriculture, with a view to promoting their economic and political independence in the spirit of the Charter of the United Nations, and to ensure the attainment of higher levels of economic and social welfare for their populations;*

In addition to the basic proposals, a message by the Secretary-General which accompanied the approved resolution set out certain conditions which requesting governments would be required to accept. First, applicant countries normally must *assume responsibility for a substantial part of the costs of technical services with which they are provided, at least that part which can be paid in their own currencies.*

Furthermore, they are expected to

give full and prompt consideration to the technical advice they receive as a result of their co-operation with the participating organizations in response to the requests they have initiated;
undertake to maintain or set up as soon as practicable such governmental co-ordination machinery as may be needed. . . .
undertake the sustained efforts required for economic development, including continuing support and progressive assumption of financial responsibility for the administration of projects initiated at their request under international auspices; . . .

Governments requesting assistance are also obliged to provide all relevant information for which they may be asked, including information on all assistance received or requested from other sources. Then they are expected to agree to publish any suitable material concerning the results of technical missions in order to build up a fund of recorded experience that may help other countries in the same or similar predicaments.

There has been a rather surprising measure of adherence to these principles which have from the first been generally recognized as a constant and essential aspect of the operational responsibility of those in charge of the Expanded Programme. The wisdom of the authors has been amply demonstrated by experience. The principles protect the recipient countries but they also make demands upon them; they guide the participating agencies yet allow reasonable freedom of action.

Having decided that the Expanded Programme would not be centralized in and administered by the United Nations (or any other single body) the responsible governments found themselves faced with the necessity of devising some scheme that would prevent such a diffusion, duplication and contradiction of efforts as would stultify the whole operation. To meet this problem a rather elaborate machinery was created to legislate for, and to review the administration of, the new programme.

D · The United Nations Machinery for Technical Assistance

The General Assembly is, of course, the final authority on all questions of policy relating to technical assistance, as on most other United Nations matters. The number, complexity and importance of the problems brought before the Assembly make it impossible for its members to give detailed

FIGURE 2: STRUCTURE OF UNITED NATIONS EXPANDED
PROGRAMME OF TECHNICAL ASSISTANCE

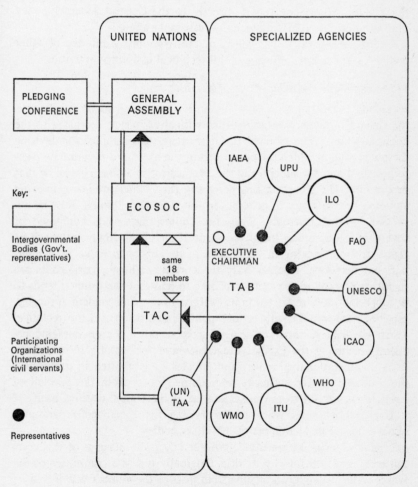

Source: Sixth Report of the Technical Assistance Board, 1957;
United Nations Document E/2965, E/TAC/REP/97.

examination to each. In practice, therefore, most of the Assembly work is distributed among its seven standing committees, of which three have responsibilities in the field of technical assistance. These three are the Second Committee (Economic and Financial), the Third Committee (Social, Humanitarian, and Cultural), and the Fifth Committee (Administrative and Budgetary Questions). The last is the Assembly's watch-dog on United Nations finances and administration. As these are committees of the whole and as they report directly to the General Assembly, they play an important role in all technical assistance affairs.

Under the general responsibility of the Assembly, a number of other bodies have a major influence on all technical assistance activities.

1 / The Economic and Social Council (ECOSOC)

As technical assistance is essentially an economic and social programme, the General Assembly, in accordance with the Charter, delegated to the Economic and Social Council the immediate responsibility for devising the policies upon which the operations of the Expanded Programme were to be based and for supervising the administrative units engaged in that programme. The policy-making powers of the Council are far from being supreme or complete. In general, decisions by the Council must be approved by the Assembly. Since the United Nations is composed of sovereign states, and as the government of each is narrowly jealous of its rights and not lacking in confidence in its ability to make wise international decisions, whereas only the current eighteen participants are members of ECOSOC, it is not surprising to find that the Council tends to be more and more restricted in its exercise of any independent authority, especially in matters with serious policy implications. In the technical assistance field it carries a general responsibility for encouraging co-operation among the executive agencies and for making recommendations on operational practices and policies. It is assisted in performing this function by its authority to require reports from the Specialized Agencies as well as from the Secretariat of the United Nations itself.

To assist it in its work of supervising the Expanded Programme, ECOSOC has created a number of subsidiary bodies.

a/ *The Technical Assistance Committee* (TAC) The purpose of this committee is made obvious by its title. Originally it was a committee of the whole with just eighteen members but in 1956 the number was increased to twenty-four. Of these, eighteen represent the member nations currently on ECOSOC and six represent other member states of the United Nations or the Specialized Agencies that have an important interest in the Expanded Programme. This committee exercises a general supervision: it examines the activities undertaken and the progress made; it receives reports on the disbursement of funds and reviews working relationships among the participating agencies; and it reports its findings and makes recommendations to ECOSOC.*

b/ The Administrative Committee on Co-ordination (ACC) As is not unnatural in an organization with so many and such diverse activities, co-ordination is one of the holiest words in the lexicon of the United Nations family of agencies—as failure in its practice is one of its most besetting sins. In the earliest days of the United Nations ECOSOC had recommended, and the Assembly had agreed, that there should be:

> . . . *a standing committee of administrative officers consisting of [the Secretary-General] as Chairman, and the corresponding officers of the Specialized Agencies for the purpose of taking all appropriate steps, under the leadership of the Secretary-General, to ensure the fullest and most effective implementation of the agreements entered into between the United Nations and the Specialized Agencies.*

Thus the ACC was born. It had been functioning—rather ineffectively—for nearly four years when the Expanded Programme of Technical Assistance was inaugurated. Its task was to foster co-operation between the dozen or so independent and international United Nations entities in all the fields in which their interests, activities or ambitions overlapped.

c/ The Technical Assistance Board (TAB) In 1949, in its basic resolution establishing the Expanded Programme, ECOSOC requested the ACC to set up a Technical Assistance Board (TAB) to facilitate co-operation among the participating agencies, to interpret policy at the operational level, and to exercise general administrative control over the utilization of funds. It was provided that the board would be presided over by the Secretary-General and would include the Directors-General of the participating Specialized Agencies. The board was authorized to recruit a small secretariat and meetings were normally held three or four times a year, generally in New York or Geneva. In practice, as so often happens in such cases, the Secretary-General soon delegated his authority, and the Assistant Secretary-General for Economic Affairs, Mr. David Owen, became the *de facto* chairman of TAB. When the Secretary-General stopped attending the meetings the Directors-General of the Specialized Agencies followed

---

* *Following the amalgamation of the Expanded Programme and the U.N. Special Fund in 1966, TAC and the governing council of the Fund were replaced by the 37-member governing council of the new "U.N. Development Programme." At the same time TAB (see below) and the Fund's consultative board were fused in the "Inter-agency Consultative Board for the U.N. Development Programme."*

suit and the board meetings were soon delegated to senior, but not necessarily very influential, members of the agency staffs. These changes were
detrimental to the work of the board which, lacking from the start all
power of coercion was now losing its powers of persuasion as well. In
an effort to raise its status, ECOSOC in 1953 established the full-time post
of Executive Chairman and Mr. Owen was appointed thereto.

These actions created a somewhat anomalous situation. Although the
Technical Assistance Board was established by the Administrative Committee on Co-ordination, it reports not to the ACC but to the Technical
Assistance Committee. The views of the ACC in regard to the actions of
the board are made known in reports to ECOSOC. Similarly, while the
Executive Chairman of the board is appointed by the Secretary-General
with the concurrence of the appropriate members of ACC, he is responsible to ECOSOC. But he is also responsible to the Secretary-General, as
the latter, having the power of appointment, has equally the power of
termination. Thus a measure of confusion is inherent in the basic
organization.

It is worth noting that ECOSOC assigned to the Technical Assistance
Board the additional duty of working toward an effective co-operative
relationship between the various participants in the Expanded Programme and those organizations outside the United Nations family,
including the bilateral agencies, the multi-national groups such as the
Colombo Plan, and the larger foundations and other private agencies
which engage in programmes of international aid.

2/The Technical Assistance Administration (TAA)

Even before the inauguration of the Expanded Programme it became
apparent that some new organizational arrangements would have to be
made if the United Nations Secretariat was to perform its proper role
in the new scheme. The Department of Economic Affairs and the Department of Social Affairs were not equipped to manage an operational programme of the dimensions that were now envisaged. As a result the
Secretary-General on August 1, 1950 set up the Technical Assistance
Administration (TAA) as a department of the Secretariat. A more detailed
examination of this department will be presented later. Here it will be
sufficient to point out that the new department, except in the field of
public administration, was to be exclusively an operational unit, drawing
its technical support from other departments. In public administration,
as no other department of the Secretariat was staffed to deal with this
responsibility, the substantive as well as the operational duties were
centred in TAA.

As in the case of the Technical Assistance Board the theoretical position of the new department was somewhat unusual if not, in fact, unique. In the first place, it was a department of the Secretariat on equal terms with all other departments. At the same time it took part in the work of the Technical Assistance Board, its delegate representing the United Nations as the other members represented their respective agencies. Yet, in the beginning, the Board was under the chairmanship of the Secretary-General of the United Nations. Thus, it was possible to have the mildly anomalous situation of the Secretary-General presiding over a board of which he was, in the person of his subordinate officer, also a member.

3/The Specialized Agencies of the United Nations

Eleven members of the United Nations family have participated in the Expanded Programme; ten of these were Specialized Agencies, the eleventh was the United Nations itself (the Technical Assistance Administration from 1950 to 1959; thereafter the Bureau of Technical Assistance Operations). The agencies are : the International Labour Organization, the World Health Organization, the Food and Agriculture Organization, the United Nations Educational, Scientific, and Cultural Organization, the International Civil Aviation Organization, the International Atomic Energy Agency, the Universal Postal Union, the International Telecommunications Union, the World Meteorological Organization and the Inter-Governmental Maritime Consultative Organization. (See *Figure 2.*) The International Bank for Reconstruction and Development, and the International Monetary Fund have also participated in a minor way through the attendance of observers at the meetings of the Technical Assistance Board.

The fields of activity of the ten Specialized Agencies are generally revealed in their titles. However, the objective of the Expanded Programme was to promote over-all economic development, and certain essential fields were not covered by the terms of reference of the agencies. These the United Nations had to fill, otherwise public administration and many aspects of social welfare and economic development would have been omitted from the scope of the aid that the Expanded Programme could offer to applicant governments.

While the United Nations and the other agencies may each be said to have had a primary focus of activity, it was inevitable that their joint frontiers would in places be vague and ill-defined. Hence the necessity for consultation and the desirability of creating some effective means of co-ordination. The actual practice of co-ordination was, however, made more difficult by the fact that the headquarters of the agencies were dispersed in seven different cities and on two continents. The United Nations was in New York, ICAO in Montreal, FAO in Rome, UNESCO in Paris, WHO, ILO, UPU and WMO in Geneva, IAEA in Vienna, IMCO in London. The associated bodies, the International Bank for Reconstruction and Development and the International Monetary Fund, have their head-quarters in Washington. This dispersal made it impossible for senior officials of the organizations to maintain effective personal contacts. The independence of the Specialized Agencies was also underlined by the fact that in addition to each having its own policy-making and opera-tional staff, each agency had its own governing body. Membership in the latter varied somewhat from agency to agency, and very often the same national government sent different representatives to the different inter-national organizations—and not infrequently with conflicting instruc-tions.

From the beginning, the organizations engaged in the Expanded Pro-gramme received assistance from a wide variety of agencies associated more or less directly with the United Nations family, or activated by similar ideals. Within the United Nations orbit itself, the most prominent are the regional economic commissions, various functional commissions of ECOSOC, and the substantive departments of the Secretariat.

4/The Regional Economic Commissions

The regional economic commissions have gradually developed into semi-independent organs concerned with promoting programmes of development within their respective geographical areas—Africa, Asia and the Far East, Europe, Latin America. Their headquarters are respec-tively in Addis Ababa, Bangkok, Geneva and Santiago. In view of their basic purposes it is natural that they should have stimulated and helped to guide technical assistance projects in the areas they serve. In some instances, they have joined with agencies of the Expanded Programme in sponsoring specific projects. In others, they have brought together a number of governments in a search for a solution to problems of common concern—as in the project for the development of the power, naviga-tion, fisheries, and irrigation resources of the Mekong River in southeast Asia. They have set up programmes for study and training in fields of significance to their regional interests, as, for example, the training-centre for resource-development economists in Santiago, Chile. Co-operation between the regional commissions and the various agencies participating in the Expanded Programme has varied from time to time and from agency to agency. The closest relationship, as was perhaps natural, has been that with the United Nations itself.

5/The Functional Commissions of ECOSOC

A number of substantive commissions were established in the early days of the United Nations and were placed under the general supervision of ECOSOC. These commissions have on a number of occasions sought to emphasize the importance of giving technical assistance for the solution of certain general problems such as population, human rights, statistics, or the status of women.

In a few cases the functional commissions have pushed their particular panaceas with a persistency and even urgency that has been embarrassing to the United Nations or to the agency most directly concerned. This has been especially true in those cases in which the recipient countries are not greatly interested in the subject which the particular commission concerned believes to be of great importance.

The substantive departments of the United Nations Secretariat work very closely with the functional commissions and as a result they sometimes combine to suggest important problems to the solution of which technical assistance may be able to contribute. The Department of Economic and Social Affairs has the direct responsibility of providing substantive back-stopping for the United Nations' own technical assistance operations, in which role it has occasionally disagreed with the approach used by the operating agency.

From what has just been written and from an examination of the chart in *Figure 2*, it will be seen that TAA and other participating agencies were enmeshed in a highly complicated external administrative apparatus. It was certainly not the original intention of those who initiated the Expanded Programme that it should be weighted with so burdensome a load of machinery. The complications were brought about by the decision to make existing agencies full partners in the programme and to divide the available funds amongst them, rather than to confine the whole responsibility for programme design and administration to a single unit. Once this decision was made it became necessary, if the programme was not to disintegrate into a series of unrelated and fragmented activities, to set up an organizational framework that would, or could, be used to impose at least some measure of co-ordination on the various participants, and to provide at least some hope that the various projects of the independent agencies would be integrated to the advantage of the countries being served.

E · Operational Problems and Programming Procedures

Starting with very little in the way of established techniques or knowledge of effective working-procedures, the participants in the Expanded Programme were forced to invent, contrive, and experiment before anything like an agreed and generally accepted system of operation could be developed.

1 / Agency Programming

In the early stages of the Expanded Programme of Technical Assistance, the participating organizations encountered many practical difficulties in trying (some of them perhaps not trying very hard) to live within the terms of reference set down by ECOSOC. In spite of the Council decision that the kind of technical assistance to be given in each case "shall be decided by the Government concerned," from 1950 to 1955 the initiative in diagnosing a country's needs, and in prescribing the appropriate kind of technical aid, was usually taken by the agencies rather than by the applicant governments. This "agency programming" procedure arose in part at least from a paternalistic belief on the part of most agency officials (1) that the knowledge required for economic development must be sought outside the under-developed areas; (2) that the governments of the poorer countries could seldom be expected to identify accurately their own needs; and (3) that international agencies with experience in development techniques must be better able than anyone else to propose practical programmes and establish valid priorities for the governments of the countries in need of assistance. In spite of the fact that these assumptions violated its own clearly stated principles, ECOSOC indicated at least a partial acceptance of this view when, in order to dodge a number of other problems, it adopted a formula dividing the available funds among the major agencies in accordance with an agreed scale. In the early years of EPTA the money secured through the annual pledging conferences was distributed as follows:

AGENCY	PER CENT
FAO	29
UNTAA	23*
WHO	22
UNESCO	14
ILO	11
ICAO	1

* In the early years TAA also looked after requests submitted through WMO, ITU and UPU.

Governments of the under-developed countries were then encouraged to submit requests to the participating agencies or to the Technical Assistance Board, with the understanding that in making requests they would not insist upon their own estimates of the urgency and importance of their various needs, but would adhere in general to the percentages established by ECOSOC for the different agencies. As a result, the early emphasis in the programme was placed on agricultural, industrial, social and public-health projects.

One effect of this procedure was that each agency was in a more or less protected position and could decide, within the limit of its funds, how to divide its aid among countries, and within each country among specific projects in its allotted field. This apparent freedom of action was to some extent restricted by the agreement that no agency would make a final commitment to meet a specific request until all the other participating organizations had been circularized and given an opportunity to comment on the value of the proposed project. Any of the participants (or the Executive Secretary of the Technical Assistance Board) could then ask for joint consideration of the proposal if it was felt to be important to the over-all programme or to infringe on the territory of another organization.

An "important" request was one that was likely to produce more than an average impact because of its magnitude, cost, duration, the extent of its ramifications, or the possibility that it might encounter special difficulties in implementation. Requests of this nature were reviewed by the board as a whole and the necessary compromises or adjustments were usually effected.

This method of agency programming was unsatisfactory in at least two ways. In practice it placed the final authority as to the need for or the character of technical assistance in the hands of the staffs of the international agencies, rather than in those of the governments concerned. It is true that on some occasions this resulted in the avoidance of mistakes, or in the undertaking of valuable projects that would otherwise have been neglected, but the agencies were not always right. In any case it violated the basic principle of the Expanded Programme. Psychologically the result was often detrimental as the attitude of the governments was adversely affected by the constant insistence on the superiority of agency opinions.

The second weakness in the procedure arose from the fact that the Technical Assistance Board had no real authority and in fact did little more than provide a false façade of integration to cover independent action by the participating agencies. The year 1950 was not ended before criticism began.

True to the traditions of bureaucratic rule and contrary to the patent facts, some of the Directors-General and other senior officers of the Specialized Agencies denied that any serious fault was being found with their activities. At a meeting of the Technical Assistance Board in Paris, at which Secretary-General Trygve Lie himself presided in the spring of 1951, it was agreed by all present, except the representatives of the United Nations itself, that, in the words of the head of FAO, "there is nothing wrong with the Programme and no one says there is." Fortunately, officers at a somewhat lower level were better informed and were already giving thought to ways in which the situation might be improved.

The goal of the Expanded Programme was not intended to be the random improvement of technical skills or the promotion of a haphazard set of unrelated projects. Its purpose was to stimulate indigenous processes of economic growth and to give the citizens of the countries concerned consistent guidance and training in methods of promoting their own material and social progress. To achieve those ends, it was apparent that individual projects and training-plans should be seen in perspective as parts of a general scheme. Yet within a year after the Expanded Programme began, it sometimes seemed that the chief reason for undertaking a particular project was not the fact that the applicant government had placed it high on its list of priorities, but merely that a particular agency had money available and was willing to finance it. The system, moreover, strengthened the natural tendency for an agency to use hard-sell or high-pressure tactics to increase its volume of requests in order to keep its staff busy and to impress its supporters with the popularity and importance of its particular programmes. Thus the practice of agency programming was leading directly away from the concept that the work of the Expanded Programme should become, in each country, a well-integrated undertaking. In fact, in this early period, it could not be said that any of the recipient countries was being helped to establish a consolidated or well-thought-out development programme, or even a closely-ordered group of programmes. Professor Philip M. Glick, a careful student of this and related problems, summed up the rapidly rising criticism of the situation when he wrote that the Expanded Programme in its early stages was "but a miscellaneous congeries of scattered and unrelated projects, many of them too trivial to contribute significantly to social or economic development." (Philip M. Glick: *The Administration of Technical Assistance*, Chicago, 1957, p. 257.)

Arthur Goldschmidt, one of the authors of the Expanded Programme and from its inception a very senior participant in the technical assistance activities of the United Nations, indentified the more important weaknesses which arose from this control of programming by the agencies rather than by the governments. There was first, he said, the fact that the international agencies were themselves too new to the job of dispensing technical assistance and their staffs too small and too inexperienced to frame with wisdom and guide with success the kind of programmes required for the economic development of the countries in need of aid. Second, there was the natural sensitivity of recipient countries to any suggestion, even when politely or indirectly expressed, of outside superiority or criticism. Local officials often entertained doubts as to the objectivity of foreign advisers, no matter what their country of origin or what agency they served. Finally, Mr. Goldschmidt recognized the general inadequacy of the current knowledge of the processes of economic growth and development, as well as the variety of circumstances and conditions which made impossible the discovery or invention of a single formula which could everywhere be successfully applied. (Goldschmidt: *Programme Planning and Development*, Annals of the American Academy of Political and Social Science, 323, May, 1959, pp. 50–58.)

Thus it soon became clear that the grave frailty of its elaborate coordinating machinery constituted a serious defect in the arrangements for the implementation of the Expanded Programme. It is true that almost from the beginning the handicap imposed on the Technical Assistance Board by the automatic apportionment of funds was modified to a minor extent by agreement that thirty per cent of the second ten million dollars of available funds would be retained by TAB to be used for special schemes or for supplementary grants to unfinished agency projects. But here also some of the agencies made it very clear that they would expect to receive their proportionate shares even of these reserved funds. As a result and to avoid trouble and inevitable charges of favouritism, the board in practice allocated this extra money almost exactly in proportion to the original agency percentages.

In the second programme year (1952), further changes were introduced and, with ECOSOC approval, automatic distribution was limited to the first ten million dollars and the whole of the balance was given to TAB "with a view to assuring the development of well-balanced and coordinated country and regional technical assistance programmes." But despite the renewed emphasis placed by ECOSOC on the programming responsibility of the recipient governments rather than the agencies, and despite the revised distribution arrangement, little difference was noticeable in the final results. For the reasons already given and as Table 2 indicates, the initial percentages continued to influence the ultimate allocations by TAB.

TABLE 2

Automatic Allocation of Expanded Programme Funds and Actual
Allocations to Participating Agencies 1950–55

Agency	Percentage for Automatic Allocation	Percentage of Total Project Costs Received by Agencies				
		1950–51	1952	1953	1954	1955
FAO	29	33	26	27	25	31
UNTAA	23	16	24	24	25	23
WHO	22	22	20	20	21	18
UNESCO	14	18	16	13	13	13
ILO	11	5	9	11	12	11
ICAO	1	6	5	5	4	4
Total	100	100	100	100	100	100

The composition of the Technical Assistance Board made any real independence of decision and action most improbable. The Specialized Agencies had fought hard and successfully to establish their independence and it would have been unreasonable to expect that they would surrender to TAB what they had denied to the United Nations. Moreover, it had been agreed at the beginning that the board must act with unanimity and this rule made any significant variation from the established allocations almost impossible. There was, and to a somewhat lesser extent still is, only too much truth in the statement that TAB was "almost a patent device to cause the maximum amount of trouble in spending small sums of money." (Andrew Shonfield, quoted in Blelloch: "Making Multilateralism Work" in *Venture*, Sept., 1964, p. 29.) Only governmental representatives acting through the Technical Assistance Committee and the Council itself could alter this situation. But for several years these delegates also took the easy way, and having spoken warmly in favour of giving real authority to TAB, did little to establish or maintain it.

The members of the Technical Assistance Board suffered from the further handicap of having in many cases very little knowledge of conditions in the field. In some cases they had never participated in a practical field assignment. This seriously limited the board's function of evaluation and review. Adequate criteria for judging proposed projects were lacking and the board had often to content itself with a superficial examination of proposals, with trying to eliminate any obvious overlapping, and with refusing to support the occasional project that was quite clearly without merit.

Pressures, designed to bring about a practical recognition of the fact that proper planning of projects in the recipient countries was a duty that must be faced, gradually mounted both within and outside the board. It was reluctantly recognized that if proper programme procedures were to be achieved, the authority of TAB as an independent body, and not just as a periodic meeting-place of agency delegates, would have to be established.

Between 1952 and 1954 several useful and ultimately significant changes were effected. The rule of unanimity was dropped in favour of decisions by majority vote—although in practice this procedure was almost never used. The post of Executive Secretary was abolished, and the incumbent was appointed by the Secretary-General, with the concurrence of the Directors-General of the Specialized Agencies, as the Executive Chairman of the board. Provision was also made for a small but permanent secretariat. The new chairman was given the power to refer any issues which he could not himself resolve to the Technical Assistance Committee for decision. And finally the stature of TAB was further enhanced by the placing of all resident representatives in the field under the board's supervision.

The post of resident representative had been invented by the United Nations Technical Assistance Administration in the hope that such an official might prove effective in supervising and improving the quality of the department's own activities in the countries in which TAA was working. It was hoped that these more or less permanent field supervisors might become sufficiently influential to bring at least a small measure of co-ordination to the work of the often very mixed group of experts to be found in the recipient countries. It was the original intention that these supervisors would report to the Secretary-General, through the Director-General of TAA. In the initial stages some did submit reports in this way, but as the usefulness of the post became recognized and as the number of resident representatives increased, some were instructed to report to TAB, and still others to the agency that had the most substantial field group at work in the country concerned. This diffusion of authority arose in large measure from the demands of the Specialized Agencies, who saw in the appointment of permanent TAB representatives the threat of the eventual subordination of their experts to board control. This recalcitrance did not readily break down, and as late as 1956, in spite of pressure from the Technical Assistance Committee and of criticism from outside observers, some agencies were still resisting the exercise of any real responsibility by the resident representatives. But even the most obdurate opponents gradually came to recognize that better co-ordination in the field was essential if really effective programming was to be achieved. It was also seen that the resident representative could be a useful channel of information on the nature of requests for assistance and on the character, quality and dimensions of existing United Nations—and other—programmes. By September, 1952 the fifteen resident representatives then in the field, in such countries as Haiti, Indonesia, Iran, Afghanistan, Colombia and Burma, had been placed under the direct authority of the Chairman of TAB. Their, and his, influence was beginning to grow.

A more detailed description of the increasing role of the resident representative in the programming process will be found below.

In spite of these organizational changes, the years 1950–54 saw only limited progress toward the goal of the proper planning of technical assistance programmes at the country level. Agency "salesmen" were still competing for clients for their special services. Governments were still being encouraged to submit requests directly to the participating agencies, with the result that the countries concerned often found themselves involved in a combination of unrelated and sometimes conflicting projects. Moreover, as the programmes were often negotiated in a great hurry, under headquarters pressure to get in ahead of some competing organization, the project plans were sometimes as vague in outline as they were imprecise in detail. There was little conception, in many of the requesting countries, of the number and types of specialists required, of the desirable length of stay, and of the timing, priority and inter-relationship of their duties. The advice of the agencies sometimes added to, rather than resolved these difficulties.

A heavy share of the responsibility for this situation rested with the participating organizations, for the real decision to accept requests and to commit resources lay with them. Moreover, had they been willing (or perhaps it would be fairer to say, had they been permitted by their governing bodies) to reduce their local loyalties and to join in a more effective programme of co-operation in both the design and the execution of integrated plans, there would have been an immediate and significant improvement in the general situation.

But the governments that provided the funds and designed the machinery for the Expanded Programme—and especially those represented on ECOSOC—were most gravely at fault. They knew what was going on but did little to stop it. Their representatives talked critically in the corridors but talked platitudes in the conference rooms. They hinted but did not command.

Weakness and incoherence in the Technical Assistance Committee, in ECOSOC, and in the committees of the General Assembly that dealt with technical assistance, were the result, in part at least, of continuing controversies in the various national capitals. Here the officials in the Departments of Agriculture, Health, Education, Industry and others were fighting within the national services the battles of their particular interests and of their respective friends in FAO, WHO, UNESCO, TAA and the other international organizations. A similar kind of competition was being waged in some of the donor countries between proponents of the bilateral and those of the multilateral programmes.

It is fortunate that this sort of competition was much less marked among the experts who were on assignments in the field. These men and women were usually so absorbed in their responsibilities, and so anxious to assist the people of the country in which they were working, that they tended to welcome any other participant no matter what organization he represented or what his area of expertise. Serious organizational rivalry was almost exclusively a headquarters and governmental disease.

These conditions explain some part of the inefficiency which marked the early days of the Expanded Programme. The partial failure which they caused, and reflected, stimulated constant debate and resulted, in 1954, in major changes in the direction of what came to be known as "country programming."

2/Country Programming

As has repeatedly been emphasized, the basic ECOSOC Resolution stated that the recipient countries themselves should decide on the kind of technical assistance to be provided by the participating organizations. However, although the practice varied somewhat from country to country, it was not until 1954, over four years after the start of the programme, that the recipient governments began, in general, to exert a major influence on the content and form of the aid they received under EPTA. In January of that year the French delegation finally screwed up enough courage to submit to the Technical Assistance Committee proposals which, if accepted, would have the effect of terminating the process of automatic allocations to the agencies, and of vesting the responsibility for the allocation of funds in TAB. The weaknesses of agency programming have already been summarized, but the following quotation from the "French proposals" will illustrate the quality of the argument in TAC:

> When the funds are distributed among several participating organizations, i.e. among projects of different kinds, in proportions fixed in advance, it can scarcely be expected that the comprehensive programme will, except by remarkable coincidence, in the end repre-

sent the sum of the country programmes which would be drawn up
on the basis of each government's needs and preferences. . . .
There is good reason to believe that the present system of the auto-
matic allocation of funds induces governments to request or prompts
them to accept services which, while they are undoubtedly by no
means useless, do not conform to the priority which these govern-
ments establish, or might establish, in connection with their country
programme. (United Nations Document E/TAC/32, January 11, 1954,
and E/TAC/32 Add. 1, March 22, 1954.)

After a prolonged and rather vigorous debate, the French proposals
were accepted in principle and embodied in part in an ECOSOC ruling in
July, 1954 that programmes should be drawn up by the governments
concerned, in consultation with TAB's resident representatives. This change
was approved by the General Assembly at its session in the fall of that
year. While this action established a new procedure for the allocation
of funds, it constituted only a partial step in the direction of country
programming.

The role of TAB itself had also to be enlarged if the ideas underlying the
proposals of the French delegation were to become effective in practice.
This was accomplished as the result of recommendations made by the
Assembly's powerful Advisory Committee on Administrative and Budgetary Questions. As far back as October, 1953, this committee had been
requested by the General Assembly to study the administrative procedures
of the Technical Assistance Board. Its report, issued in June, 1954 (United
Nations Document A/2661, June 25, 1954), coincided with the ECOSOC
debates on the French proposals. The committee proposed and the
Assembly later agreed that TAB should be given authority over Expanded
Programme funds and that this responsibility should be ensured by maintaining a "clear and direct line of authority from the Secretary-General"
to the Executive Chairman of TAB. At the same time that TAB's authority
over programme operations was thus being strengthened by the Assembly,
the Advisory Committee on Co-ordination, with the Secretary-General as
chairman, was given direct responsibility for the conduct of the Expanded
Programme. In April, 1955, ACC announced that the Secretary-General
would thereafter be charged with ensuring that TAB policies and actions
were in accord with the directives of TAC. (United Nations Document
E/2728, April 28, 1955.) With the acceptance of the ACC report of 1955,
the administrative structure of the Expanded Programme assumed the
general characteristics that it still retains.

In 1954 the Technical Assistance Board started the policy of working
out target figures to indicate the probable size of the funds likely to be

FIGURE 3:   PROCEDURE FOR PLANNING AND
DEVELOPING THE ANNUAL COUNTRY PROGRAMME

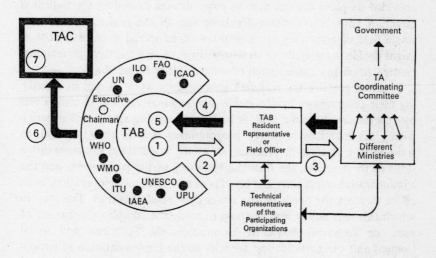

October–April	1	(a) TAB establishes global planning target for the field programme on the basis of estimated contributions.
		(b) TAB formulates target figures for country and regional programmes.
May	2	Target figures communicated to governments via TAB resident representatives.
May–June	3	Representatives of participating agencies negotiate projects with government ministries; resident representative assists in and coordinates programming discussions with government's Technical Assistance Committee, which assigns priorities and consolidates country programme within target figure.
July	4	Governments transmit programme requests to TAB via resident representatives, with copies to participating agencies.
August	5	TAB secretariat examines and consolidates government requests in the light of participating agencies' cost estimates.
October	6	TAB recommends over-all programme to Technical Assistance Committee.
November	7	TAC reviews and approves the over-all programme and authorizes allocations of funds for its implementation to the participating agencies in proportion to their earmarked shares in the over-all programme.

(After U.N., Technical Assistance Board, 1958.)

made available to each interested government. Thereafter, except for the honouring of agency commitments carried over from the previous year, the government in theory at least could design its own programme, provided its plans did not involve expenditures exceeding the indicated target. A government might decide to use all the available funds in a single field of assistance, or it might wish to spread it more widely; it might decide to concentrate on scholarships, or on experts, or on training-centres, or on any combination of these or other forms of aid.

In actual practice the recipient governments were assisted in organizing their programmes by the resident representatives, and in some cases by experts already in the field, or by local or visiting agents of the participating organizations. Country programming was in principle and, to some extent at least in practice, an effort to combine the substantive skills of the agencies, the financial resources of the programme, and the administrative constraints and benefits of international co-operation, in an effort to meet the needs of the under-developed countries. The way in which this new policy was designed to apply the complex mechanism of TAB, the Technical Assistance Committee, the Economic and Social Council and the participating agencies to the implementation of nationally drafted programmes, is admirably described in a brochure prepared in 1959 by M. Maurice Milhaud, who was for many years Chief of the Geneva Office of the TAA. (Milhaud: *The Expanded Programme of Technical Assistance for Economically Under-Developed Countries*, UNTAA, MTAO/12/59/a, Geneva, March, 1959.) As had been intended and hoped, the focus of this new activity gradually became more and more concentrated in the Technical Assistance Board.

Prior to 1954 the Technical Assistance Board had started its annual programming procedure in March by making an assumption as to the probable total amount of money that would be available for Expanded Programme activities during the subsequent calendar year. It then "earmarked" a certain sum for each of the participating agencies. The ECOSOC legislation provided that each agency should be guaranteed that it would not receive less than eighty-five per cent of its previous year's allocation—barring of course any greater decrease in over-all funds. Each of the participating agencies then proceeded to divide its share of estimated funds among requesting countries on the basis of requests already received, programmes under way, and convincing indications of need.

These procedures obviously made any general application of the country programming principle quite impossible. A government might, for example, wish to spend all its allocation on health projects, or on public administration, or on agricultural development, but because of the initial allocation of funds to the separate agencies this became almost impossible.

Each agency felt itself entitled to maintain its position in each country and only the toughest of governments could resist this agency pressure.

The new programming process adopted after the reforms of 1954 was described in some detail in the TAB Report for 1957 (see also *Figure 3*):

The first steps for preparing the programme were taken in March when global planning targets were fixed by TAB on the basis of preliminary estimates of the financial resources expected to be available in the following year. Individual planning targets were then fixed for the recipient countries along with a target covering all regional and inter-regional projects. Working out appropriate country targets was no easy task, especially when the needs were large and resources were limited. Nevertheless, the Board sought to give due weight to such factors as the needs of the countries as indicated by the Governments, the relative urgency of such needs as between different countries, size of population, per capita income, the quantum of assistance received from other sources, levels of programmes in previous years under EPTA, and the extent of commitments for projects already in operation. The primary objective before the Board was to obtain an equitable distribution of the limited resources to meet the more urgent needs in different countries.

The country planning targets so established were communicated to the Governments concerned early in April. The preparation of individual country programme-requests involved intensive consultation and negotiation over a four-month period from April to July, between recipient Governments, Participating Organizations and TAB officers. This no doubt helped ensure that the requests as finally submitted by the Governments reflected the priority needs of their own developmental programmes. The individual programme requests were then given a technical review by the Participating Organizations and consolidated in the TAB secretariat. The draft programme as it emerged from this exercise was considered by the Board at its October session and, after necessary adjustments, was submitted to TAC with a recommendation for approval.

The programme recommended by the Board was reviewed and approved by the Technical Assistance Committee at its session held in November. (United Nations Technical Assistance Committee, Annual Report of the Technical Assistance Board for 1957, 1958, p. 9.)

When TAC and ECOSOC approval had been obtained, the Board started the actual allocation procedures in January.

In defiance of the hopes aroused by the approval of the French proposals in 1954, there was no immediate departure from the proportionate distribution of funds among the participating organizations that had prevailed under the agency programming procedure. This was because the different agencies were generally successful in persuading recipient governments to maintain about the same level of agency requests as had been established under the earlier procedure. However, from this time forward any failure to use its own judgement and follow its own wishes was the responsibility of the government concerned.

In addition to its basic or "Category I" approved programme each country was encouraged to present a list of "Category II" projects which were also submitted for approval to TAB. This list was designed to constitute a backlog which could be drawn upon to provide projects to utilize any unused funds that might result from delays in the execution of "Category I" projects, or from an unanticipated increase in the scale of contributions.

To meet special or emergency needs that might arise in the course of the year, the Executive Chairman of TAB was empowered to allocate money from a Working Capital and Reserve Fund up to a total of not more than five per cent of the approved programme. In making these allocations the Chairman was expected to consult with the appropriate agencies and he was naturally under constant and heavy pressure to keep his special allocations closely in line with the conventional standard for each agency. As a result, the Chairman's allocations soon became, in effect, just a small supplement to each of the agency programmes.

The principles involved in the practice of country programming were also extended to apply, in theory at least, to projects undertaken for the benefit of several countries in the same geographic areas, or, in other words, to *regional programming*. As the term suggests, these projects involve the concerted development of an area comprising more than one country or territory. For example, in the case of the comprehensive project designed to co-ordinate power, fisheries, irrigation, navigation and flood-control plans in the Mekong Valley, four different countries are involved. This kind of approach was found to be particularly valuable in promoting joint projects of a research and planning nature. Programmes for the control of diseases such as yaws, malaria and trachoma, of foot-and-mouth disease among animals, and of pests such as locusts, to be effective must often be planned on a regional basis. And for obvious reasons, such projects as training-centres, demonstrations, seminars, and study tours frequently profit from a regional approach. In fact, more than half the funds spent on regional activities in any year have normally gone to projects concerned with such training activities as the Civil Aviation Training Centre in Mexico City, the Higher Institution of

Nursing in Alexandria, and the Regional Railway Training Centre in Pakistan.

Among the more recent developments in regional co-operation has been the programme for economic integration in the five Central American republics. This is a concerted effort to strengthen the regional economy through the rationalization of area activities in labour, finance, industry, transport and communications. And in the Middle East the governments of Iran, Turkey and Pakistan have united to promote joint projects for their mutual benefit.

In the Expanded Programme the rule at first was that not more than ten per cent of the total available funds would be allocated to regional projects. This was raised to twelve per cent in 1958.

As in the case of individual country projects, regional programmes had to be based on requests from the governments concerned. But in the case of the latter, it was even less likely than in the case of country requests that the action would be taken solely on the initiative of the governments concerned. Regional requests usually originated in the minds of the staff of a technical assistance agency, either within or outside the United Nations family.

In spite of the considerable progress that had been made, TAB was still faced with the normal and persistent problem of maintaining an adequate flexibility in the programming procedures. Difficulties continued to occur for both recipient and contributing governments because insufficient time was available for the preparation of projects, for the recruitment of experts, for the placement of fellows, and for the acquisition of supplies and equipment. Very often the result of inadequate planning or initial administrative delays resulted in the assignments of experts or the terms of fellowships having to be extended beyond the periods originally planned, with consequent disruptions in other projects. In an attempt to meet these problems a two-year programming procedure was introduced in 1961 and it has done something to improve the situation. It has given the assisting organizations more time to devote to the recruitment of experts and to making arrangements for the reception of fellows. At the same time the recipient governments and the participating organizations have benefited by having more freedom to refine their proposals and to take full advantage of the benefits inherent in longer-term projects. Two-year programming, moreover, has resulted in a considerable saving in the amount of time that used to be spent in the annual negotiations between agencies and governments. Provision for financing on the basis of two-year periods has also had a markedly beneficial effect because, of all activities, technical assistance needs time to be effective. Even the biennial planning and financing is so short as to be inconsistent with the essentially long-term nature of technical assistance. Both present needs and future prospects make a further extension of the permissible programming period a most desirable amendment.

3/The Expanded Role of the Resident Representative

Reference has already been made to the appointment of resident representatives and some indication has been given of why the post was invented. As time passed and experience accumulated it became clear that the scheme was a sound one. Although originally appointed by the Technical Assistance Administration it became obvious that if the resident representative was to produce maximum results and exploit his opportunities to the full, he should represent all the agencies and be responsible not to one operational organization but to the Technical Assistance Board. The duties of the incumbent as they eventually evolved were to represent the board before the host government and to help co-ordinate the planning and execution of the EPTA projects. Within this general framework, the resident representative found himself engaged on a wide variety of tasks. Some of these were specifically prescribed but many were the result of the initiative, imagination and energy of the resident representative himself. Personal initiative was an essential quality because of the great diversity in the situations and problems that were likely to be encountered. This was especially important because the resident representatives (unlike the country director of a United States Operations Mission) did not head an organized group, nor was he supported by a large staff.

From the beginning, the decision as to whether or not a resident representative should be appointed to a specified country was influenced by the size of the national programme and, of course, by the wishes of the government concerned. In a few cases, as experience accumulated, resident representatives have been accredited to more than one country in the same area as, for example, in the case of the five nations of Central America. Appointments have normally been for a period of not less than two years. When a country's programme has been too small to justify a senior appointment, the Technical Assistance Board has sometimes provided a part-time liaison officer or a resident correspondent, to perform some of the simpler duties of a resident representative.

The most important responsibility of the resident representative has, from the beginning, been to assist the government and the agencies in the preparation of the annual programme of requests. Not later than April of each year the government is notified through the resident representative of its prospective allocation. It is then expected that he will co-ordinate the ensuing consultations between the field representatives of the participating organizations and the relevant government departments, or the government's Technical Assistance Co-ordinating Committee, if such a body exists. By mid-July, the government transmits its programme requests, through the resident representative, to TAB headquarters. It is the representative's duty to ensure that the requests are in a form that can be readily understood and evaluated by the officers of the board. In some cases, when dealing with an inexperienced government or when his personal influence is unusually strong, the resident representative may have a major role in the actual drafting of the country's presentation. In most of the recipient countries, as experience accumulates the annual programming procedure gradually becomes a less regorous task. A former and highly competent resident representative in Pakistan reported in 1959 that the situation was becoming almost static with many projects extending over several years and limited funds inhibiting the introduction of many new and potentially valuable schemes. "Moreover," he concluded, "there is little actual shifting of technical assistance from one government department (or United Nations Agency) to another, and the *status quo* percentage comes to be jealously safeguarded by each government department or United Nations Agency as something each 'possesses.' " (Huntingdon Gilchrist: "Technical Assistance from the United Nations—As Seen in Pakistan," *International Organization* 13, Fall, 1959, pp. 505–519.)

One of the important duties of the resident representative is to try to ensure that the visiting experts receive adequate supporting services from the government they are sent to aid. He is expected to help them get established and oriented and to remove difficulties that would prevent the effective performance of their duties. Attendance to such details as housing, office space, secretarial services, transportation, and translation are common problems. In the early days of the Expanded Programme it was frequently found that the government departments had made no adequate preparation to receive and utilize the abilities of the experts for whom they had themselves asked. Very often no counterpart personnel had been assigned, no budgetary provision had been made, and no money was available to meet the local costs of the expert. An even more difficult situation was likely to arise when in the interval between the presentation of the request for specialized assistance and the actual arrival of the approved expert, political developments had resulted in the establishment of a new government with different interests as well as different personnel.

The resident representative is in a strategic position to assist in promoting inter-agency co-ordination among the various bilateral as well as the United Nations sources of aid. Through informal contacts and through knowledge gained in the annual country programming process, he will understand the signal importance of friendly co-operation between those engaged on the United Nations programmes and those working on aid projects under other, public or private, auspices. A good deal of progress in this direction has been made and today many projects are undertaken jointly, or at least with a sympathetic awareness of each other's activities.

In recent years the United Nations has also used the influence and knowledge of the representatives to assist in the execution of two of its newer activities—the Special Fund that was set up to supply capital grants for large-scale training institutes, for basic surveys, and for other pre-investment activities, and the United Nations scheme for the supply of operational and executive personnel known as OPEX. Resident representatives have also become closely involved in a steadily increasing number and range of duties on behalf of such organizations as UNICEF, the World Bank, the International Monetary Fund, and the Office of the High Commissioner for Refugees.

Utilization of the services of the resident representatives began in a serious way following the criticism of the behaviour of the agencies participating in the Expanded Programme and the consequent introduction of policy reforms in 1954. It was too much to expect that there would be immediate and complete acceptance of the new directives and in fact some of the participants were slow and reluctant in giving up their independent practices. But the situation gradually improved and by 1964 TAB had established seventy-two offices in the field from which over eighty-five countries and territories were served by resident representatives or functionaries with comparable duties.

In the light of the heavy responsibilities he must carry and of the great diversity in the nature of the obstacles he must overcome, it is not surprising that the United Nations has had difficulty in finding suitable persons to fill the resident representative posts. To be successful in his assigned role the incumbent's qualities must be such that he will be accepted by and can deal effectively with the many divisions of the government to which he is accredited. His success or failure can perhaps best be judged by the degree to which he is voluntarily consulted and to which his advice is finally accepted by the government, and by the agency or agencies concerned, when important programme decisions are to be made. As that careful observer, Dr. Glick, has said, it is his duty

> . . . to give the host government technical assistance on how to request technical assistance, how to use it, how to get more out of it,

and how to guide and control it. For doing this, however, there is no "recipe." The Representative must know the host country as intimately and as broadly as it is possible for one man to do, and he must know the resources available to the Expanded Programme. (Glick, *op. cit.*, p. 283.)

Even more difficult than this, in the beginning at least, was the task of gaining the confidence and arranging for the co-operation of the more independently inclined—or more suspicious—of the participating agencies.

In the preceding paragraphs the resident representatives have been referred to in a generalized way as being of masculine gender. This practice is justified because while women have in a number of instances held the posts of Deputy and Assistant Resident Representative there have only been two appointments to the full position. Of these the first was Miss Joan Anstie who, after serving as Assistant in Colombia and Officer-in-charge in Uruguay, was appointed to the difficult and important post of Resident Representative in Bolivia. It is probable that there will be very few opportunities of this kind and that discrimination against women will indefinitely continue. Governments in most parts of the world are hesitant about accepting such nominees: some would not receive them under any circumstances. The nomination of a Barbara Ward or an Eleanor Hinder would, of course, be a compliment to any country but the number of such women is extremely limited and those who could be found would almost certainly be engaged in other and probably even more important tasks.

In view of the critical references to some of the attitudes and activities of the Specialized Agencies that have been made in this chapter, it is essential to stress that many of the difficulties that were encountered were practically inevitable after the basic decision to disperse the control of the Expanded Programme had been taken. That decision made competition unavoidable and created a situation in which organizational loyalty became an enforced virtue. Indeed, had it not been for the good sense and the sincere dedication of many of the agency representatives to their task of helping governments and people in need, the situation might easily have become far worse than it did. The whole Programme owes a great debt not only to the high intelligence, but also to the real determination to co-operate in a good cause, of people like Dr. Gustavo Martinez Cabañas (U.N.), Sir Herbert Broadley (FAO), Dr. Brock Chisholm and Dr. P. M. Dorolle (WHO), Dr. Malcolm Adeseshiah (UNESCO), E. R. Marlin (ICAO) and David Morse and D. Yalden-Thomson (ILO). The contribution that these men made to the development of the international programmes cannot easily be exaggerated and should never be forgotten.

4/The Relationship to Other Aid Programmes

Those concerned with the United Nations technical assistance programmes have made repeated and sensible efforts to establish close and affirmative working relationships between the Expanded Programme and other regional, national or private activities of a related character. At its 1957 session in Geneva, the Technical Assistance Committee noted with approval that increasing attention was being given to the development of joint measures designed to promote co-operation among the rapidly expanding number and variety of sources of technical aid. In earlier years, emphasis had necessarily been placed on efforts to eliminate the grosser evils of overlapping and duplication. But this was clearly not enough and the United Nations has increasingly taken it upon itself to seek a higher level of positive co-ordination among the various programmes. The resident representatives, and the expert personnel of the participating organizations, have consistently been urged to study not only the full range of the needs but also the quality and the size of the sources of aid available to the countries in which they serve. They have been encouraged to establish the closest possible working relationships with representatives of other programmes, both in the planning and in the actual provision and implementation of assistance.

The United Nations has also strongly supported plans for the creation and operation of co-ordinating machinery within the recipient countries, in the hope that the governments themselves will participate in the rationalization of the work in this field. The failure of many of the recipient governments to establish such internal controls is clear evidence of the widespread need for help in public administration. It has been difficult, however, for the United Nations to be insistent that governments recognize and remedy this condition, when it has been only too evident that at least part of the problem has been created by the fact that the various United Nations and other organizations have themselves contributed to internal disorder by their own concentration on the competitive selling of their respective services.

Fortunately a good deal of progress toward administrative efficiency has been achieved both by the governments and by the various assistance agencies. Today, over thirty per cent of the Expanded Programme projects enjoy the direct participation of, or close co-operation with, two or more of the other programmes—bilateral or multilateral—of international assistance. Interesting examples of this trend have been a fisheries project in India (in which Norway, the United States, and FAO have combined their efforts); a multiple-purpose river-valley development in the

Cauca region of Colombia (U.N., FAO, and the United States); a radio communications scheme to link East and West Pakistan (ITU, Australia and the United Kingdom); a programme of agricultural extension and mechanization in Iraq (FAO and the United States); assistance to the Cambodian Royal School of Medicine (WHO and France); assistance to the Academy of Civil Aviation in Indonesia (ICAO and the Colombo Plan); and arrangements made in Turkey between the United Nations, the United States, the United Kingdom, the Federal Republic of Germany, and the Netherlands, to exchange lists of persons accepted for fellowships in order to avoid duplication and the playing-off of one agency against another. This kind of collaboration in the handling of fellowships and scholarships should, of course, be routine practice in every country in which more than one agency is engaged. Some progress is being made but it needs to be greatly extended.

Examples of co-operative effort have also involved private foundations. For example, a United Nations clerical training-centre in Egypt was assisted by the Ford Foundation; in the Philippines, FAO experts designed a forest products research institute to be established and equipped by the United States, the Colombo Plan, and the Rockefeller Foundation; and in Ceylon, the Central Institute of Industrial and Scientific Research obtained its director and chief engineer from the United Nations, the International Bank recruited a technical librarian from Canada, equipment was provided by the United Kingdom and the United States, and books were supplied by the Asia Foundation.

One of the most widely known and most extensive examples of co-ordination of technical assistance is the already noted project for the development of the Mekong River valley. In its final form this imaginative, enormous and complicated programme was largely the result of the industry, intelligence and determination of a distinguished Indian administrator, C. V. Narasimhan, who was the Executive Secretary of ECAFE until he was appointed, in effect as Chef de Cabinet to the Secretary-General of the United Nations, in 1961. As a result of his persuasive insistence, and the active support of TAA (and later of some of the Specialized Agencies) and of the staff of ECAFE itself, a co-ordinating committee of the four riparian countries, Cambodia, Laos. Thailand and Vietnam, was set up. This committee still administers the project, which is now receiving assistance from the Expanded Programme as well as direct contributions from Australia, Canada, France, Japan, New Zealand, the United Kingdom and the United States. The object is to harness the waters of this great river for a number of useful purposes: to furnish power for industrialization; to control flooding to help prevent disease and destruction; to divert water for irrigation; to increase the fisheries potential; to improve stream-flow for navigation. At present the river is of meagre value and most of the people within its valley live at a subsistence level. The potentially fertile, but as yet arid, soils produce only one poor crop of rice a year. For five months in each twelve the land and the people are idle. Navigation is spotty and uncertain, the fisheries are undeveloped, the great power potential lies dormant, and floods bring recurrent disaster. The scheme will take twenty years to complete and will cost almost a billion dollars. Without the kind of co-operation that has been established, the river would lie unharnessed into an indefinite but certainly far-distant future. It is to be hoped that the present abominable war in Vietnam does not destroy the programme.*

As a result of the introduction of country programming, there has been a slow and spotty but recognizable increase in the quality of the work accomplished by government departments or agencies in the recipient countries. Faced by the problems inherent in the new procedure, governments were almost compelled to create machinery for channelling and screening their requirements and for establishing priorities. Nearly all the countries receiving assistance under the Expanded Programme have now made at least a beginning on the rationalization of their own procedures. In most instances, the same national organizational unit that handles the United Nations programmes is also made responsible for scrutinizing departmental proposals involving other sources of external aid. This development is of particular value because, as additional governments have become recipients of direct assistance, advance consultation and co-ordination have become more difficult as they have become more essential.

5/The Place of the "Regular" Technical Assistance Programmes

The Expanded Programme is, of course, the most important of the United Nations undertakings in technical assistance. It is, moreover, the exemplar that sets the tone and establishes standards for other activities of related kinds. But the "Regular" technical assistance programmes of the agencies in the United Nations family, while limited in size are by no means insignificant. There is a great variation among the participating organizations, but in over-all dollar volume the Regular Programmes constitute about thirty per cent of the Expanded Programme. Fortunately, there has been a growing trend toward the integration of the two, so

---

* The current conflict has already seriously delayed the programme. The prospect of early progress is becoming more and more dubious.

that instead of tending to duplicate activities they complement, support, and strengthen each other.

The size, nature, and purpose of the Regular Programmes vary considerably among the Specialized Agencies. The regular budgets of FAO, ICAO, ITU, and WMO make no specific provision for technical assistance under that name, although this is a semantic rather than a factual variation. In the regular budget of ILO, a relatively small amount is earmarked for aid to governments. But the United Nations, UNESCO, WHO and the International Atomic Energy Agency include substantial allocations in their regular budgets for technical assistance of various kinds. In fact, both WHO and IAEA spend more money for aid from their regular budgets than they do under the Expanded Programme. As is pointed out in the 1957 Report of the Technical Assistance Board, most of the Regular Programmes have their own *raison d'être*; they developed within a framework of policies and directives of the legislative bodies of the respective agencies and their purposes are specifically related to the basic agency goals.

In the case of certain agencies it is sometimes difficult to distinguish clearly between the work done under the ordinary budget and that performed under the Expanded Programme. Some organizations administer both programmes together, using the same staff and the same facilities, and attempts to separate the two would be both artificial and generally pointless. Projects are sometimes transferred from one programme to another, and some activities are financed in part and simultaneously by each.

In certain cases the two programmes play complementary roles. For example, in the United Nations Regular Programmes emphasis is usually placed on the collection, analysis, and dissemination of statistical data, on surveys of various types, and on research, experimental and pilot projects. Work of this kind is often an essential pre-condition for the provision of effective technical assistance and thus prepares the way for help under the Expanded Programme. Conversely, problems are sometimes highlighted through activities of the Expanded Programme and thus suggest useful directions in which research and investigation can be pursued under regular financing.

In some cases also the Regular Programmes enable a participating organization to undertake activities which are not permitted under the procedures that have had to be established to control the EPTA projects. In the case of ILO, for example, even its very small regular budget permits urgent missions to be undertaken at short notice, a step that cannot easily be arranged within the normal rules of the Expanded Programme. The Regular Programmes also allow technical assistance to be given to countries, such as the more developed nations of Europe, that are ordinarily thought of as being ineligible under EPTA. Secretary-General Hammarskjold, for example, was astonished and troubled to discover, when he first came to the United Nations, that Sweden was obtaining aid under the Regular Technical Assistance Programme of the United Nations in the person of a casework social welfare expert from Canada. His immediate reaction was to consider this an improper use of funds that should be exclusively reserved for help to backward countries. It was only after a good deal of debate that he later—and then with some reluctance —became reconciled to the idea of a limited amount of United Nations money being used to assist a highly developed state like Sweden to meet special problems.

Another difference between the two programmes is the fact that under the regular budget technical assistance can often be planned on a long-range basis. This is somewhat less significant since the introduction of biennial budgeting under EPTA in 1961, but there are still many instances in which it is desirable to make commitments for a period longer than two years. The Regular Programmes can be used in such cases because they do not depend upon voluntary pledges, which are subject to unexpected fluctuations, but derive their funds from budgets that are provided from the normal and comparatively stable assessments made by the various agencies upon their constituent states.

Of all the members of the United Nations family, the World Health Organization carries on the most extensive Regular Programme of technical assistance. This sometimes runs to as much as thirty per cent higher than the amount WHO disburses under EPTA and when the special programme for malaria eradication is included, WHO's Regular activities are nearly double those under the latter. In addition to the malaria control projects which cover over three-quarters of a billion people, WHO dispenses a full range of technical assistance through its regular budget allocations—fellowships, expert advisers, conferences, statistical standardization, disease eradication. In a recent year, for example, the organization awarded 1,041 Regular Programme fellowships, three times as many as those awarded in its Expanded Programme operations. In the same year 480 expert advisers were sent abroad to seventy-four different countries; and an inter-regional conference of Mediterranean countries was held to discuss the organization and financing of community water supplies. In other years, conferences were held in conjunction with projects to control yaws, leprosy, bilharziasis, and influenza.* WHO's remarkable

---

* Its great failure is its inability to gain the approval of its governing body for an assault on the population problem.

record of achievement was largely due to the imaginative, inspiring, as well as practical, leadership of its first Director-General, the Canadian, Dr. Brock Chisholm.

The United Nations itself has the second largest Regular Programme of technical assistance, running to over two million dollars annually. As has already been recorded, this programme, operated by the Bureau of Technical Assistance Operations, covers activities in the fields of economic development, social welfare, public administration and advisory services in the field of human rights. Since 1959, moreover, the Regular Programme has also included allocations for the OPEX operations. In general, the United Nations applies the same rules, principles, and procedures in its work under the Regular and the Expanded Programmes, and the same staff is used without distinction. Regular Programme funds are frequently and beneficially used to meet requests that could not easily be accommodated under the country totals of the Expanded Programme, especially in the case of urgent requests from newly independent nations. It is also used to provide expert advice and for training of counterpart personnel for employment on Expanded Programme projects.

The International Atomic Energy Agency (IAEA) joined the United Nations family in 1958 and began immediately to provide technical assistance under both its regular budget and through EPTA. Obligations incurred under the Regular Programme of IAEA have been the larger of the two. The agency, which is authorized to consider requests for aid to research projects or for the development of atomic energy for peaceful purposes, provides technical assistance through the provision of advisory services and training in such matters as the exploration and survey of nuclear needs; planning and programming; library and documentation services; ore prospecting and mining; fabrication and processing of nuclear fuels; nuclear research centres; nuclear reactors, use of radioisotopes; health and safety; and the disposal of atomic wastes. Much of this could not be done if the agency were limited to its allocations under the Expanded Programme. An exchange programme under which IAEA provides for the interchange of scientists and professors to assist governments and universities in organizing and conducting courses on the development of research programmes is also noteworthy among the agency's regular budget activities.

UNESCO carries on a sizable regular programme (about one million dollars annually) in which priorities are given to projects ineligible or difficult to introduce under EPTA, including such matters as scientific research in problems of the arid lands, the mutual appreciation of eastern and western cultural values, and studies of the scientific approach to the improvement of living standards.

The International Labour Organization allocates only about $100,000 of its regular budget for technical assistance activities.

ICAO provides a number of short-term missions of experts on air navigation, air transport statistics, freight and passenger handling, and national air laws, from its own staff, although this is not formally described as technical assistance.

ITU's normal activities are generally limited to the collection and distribution of technical documentation designed to keep member states abreast of the latest developments in the field of telecommunications.

WMO gives considerable attention to the supplying of comprehensive reports on the current state of knowledge in the various aspects of meteorology. In the case of WMO as in that of ITU their activities are directly relevant to projects carried out under the Expanded Programme.

In the realm of agriculture and nutrition FAO offers direct help from its permanent staff in response to governmental requests, although this is not officially listed as technical assistance.

F · The Expanded Programme's First Fifteen Years

On December 19, 1961 the General Assembly dedicated the 1960's as the "United Nations Development Decade." Member states and their peoples were urged to intensify their efforts during this period to advance measures designed "to accelerate progress towards self-sustaining growth of the economy of the individual nations and their social advancement." It is appropriate, therefore, to review what was done during the first ten years of the Expanded Programme, 1950–1960, and the start that has been made on the work of the development decade.

The experience in technical assistance obtained by the United Nations during the 1950's and early 1960's helped to promote new concepts of international solidarity in a number of different ways. Most important of all, perhaps, was the slowly dawning realization in some of the developing countries that immense efforts and real sacrifices, including radical departures from tradition, combined with drastic social and economic reforms, would be part of the price they would have to pay for any significant improvement in their standards of living. But few, even among the governments that accepted the idea, showed any real determination in taking the hard but essential decisions that were obviously required.

On the side of the donors, the first fifteen years were marked by a slowly increasing recognition by many countries that the giving of assistance to those in need should be considered a normal part of a nation's duty. And although the increase was very slow in coming, there was also a gradual rise in the proportion of national incomes being allocated to international aid. This was reflected, among other ways, by the expansion of the World Bank's capital and its increased rate of lending, by the creation of the United Nations Special Fund, by the establishment of the International Development Association and the International Finance Corporation.

Perhaps more auspicious for the future than these changes was the tardily widening recognition of the need for development planning, and the even more gradual refinement of planning techniques. This progress was due in part at least to the country programming procedures instituted under EPTA and it brought great satisfaction to those, particularly in the United Nations Secretariat and in the public services of such countries as Canada, Chile, France, India, Israel, the U.S.A., the U.S.S.R. and Yugoslavia, who had joined in forcing the acceptance of that procedure against the opposition of some elements in some of the Specialized Agencies.

The experience of these fifteen years also brought a more widespread realization of the importance of the human factor in economic development. This resulted in new approaches to education and training, to community development, to public administration, and to the problems of nutrition and the eradication of disease, which made it possible for the latent human resources of the now developing countries to be more effectively employed. If these changes had been accompanied by a serious and responsible approach to the problem of sky-rocketing populations the hopes for future progress would now be infinitely brighter and far more solidly justified than in fact they are. But the dead weight of custom, of tradition, and of religious intransigence has not yet been lifted. Before the Expanded Programme began, the problem of the developing countries was viewed essentially as one of increasing the supply of food and other basic necessities; a decade and a half later it is generally recognized that the real problems are the checking of population growth and the promotion of the capacity of nations to produce. Perhaps by the end of the '60's it will have become clear that neither an increased capacity to produce, nor any conceivable increase in production itself, will solve humanity's problems as long as unrestricted procreation continues to add to the sum of human needs and to impede most efforts to meet them.

It is also worth recording that in the general field of international aid there has been a great increase in regional co-operation, a change to which the work done under the Expanded Programme has made an important contribution. It is not impossible that the slowly-widening practice of co-operation on economic issues may eventually be reflected in a growing experience of political harmony.

Finally, reference should be made to the advantages that resulted from the continued presence in the Technical Assistance Committee of ECOSOC and in the Second Committee of the General Assembly of a few men of particular competence, of unusual devotion and of exceptional intelligence and experience. Representatives like Bannier of the Netherlands, Stanovnik of Yugoslavia, Grez of Chile, Lind of Sweden, Svec of Czechoslovakia, Kotschnig of the United States, Wershof and Hadwen of Canada, made outstanding contributions to the sensible development and guidance of the Expanded Programme. Perhaps the most important contributor during the first two or three years was the remarkably competent representative of France, M. Philippe de Seynes. M. de Seynes was subsequently appointed by Secretary-General Hammarskjold to head the Department of Economic Affairs of the United Nations Secretariat and in that post has provided stimulating leadership in all aspects of economic assistance.

A summary register of the organizational progress of the Expanded Programme from its beginning in July, 1950, to the end of the year 1965, will contribute to a clearer understanding of the nature of the advances that have been recorded. In the pages that follow these changes are collated under such headings as methods, fields of activity, geographical range, number of participants and financial resources.

1 / Methods and Scale of Activities

Technical assistance provided under the Expanded Programme is often summed up as consisting of "experts, fellowships, equipment and supplies." However, by the end of the period under review a wide diversity of techniques for dispensing aid was being employed. These included such things as training institutions, pilot and demonstration projects, regional training-centres, topical seminars, the provision of technical literature, and group study tours. In each of these the services of experts as leaders, instructors, or demonstrators are normally employed. In many cases they provide training opportunities for fellows and they use supplies and equipment for teaching or demonstration purposes. Thus, technical assistance projects range all the way from a single expert spending a few weeks or months to advise on the solution of some specific technical problem, or a single fellow studying a particular administrative technique, or the supply of equipment for a pilot plant, to large regional training-centres combining many forms of assistance and operating over a number of years. By 1965 all these forms of assistance were recognized as valuable components of any large programme of external aid. It is unlikely that any of them will be abandoned or that they will be supplemented by any very radical innovations.

A total of over $450 million, not including the administrative and operational costs of the participating agencies and TAB, was spent for technical assistance projects by the various organizations participating in the Expanded Programme during its first fifteen years. A statistical summary covering all activities during these years was published by the Technical Assistance Board in May, 1965. This presented the following record:

FINANCIAL SUPPORT/the equivalent of $456.6 million pledged by a total of 108 countries, plus $22 million in local cost contributions by recipient Governments and substantial further amounts in supporting services, facilities and capital investment.

TOTAL EXPENDITURES/the equivalent of $457 million, consisting of $376 million in project costs and $81 million in administrative and operational services costs.

GEOGRAPHICAL DISTRIBUTION/150 countries and territories in five main regions: Africa, where 20.3 per cent of direct project costs was spent; Asia and the Far East (32.6 per cent); Europe (6.3 per cent); Latin America (24.1 per cent); and the Middle East (13.6 per cent); to which must be added inter-regional projects absorbing 2.9 per cent.

COUNTRY AND REGIONAL/country projects, $323 million, or 85.8 per cent of total project costs; regional and inter-regional projects, $53 million, or 14.2 per cent.

CATEGORIES OF EXPENDITURE/$276 million (60 per cent) on expert assistance; $36 million (8 per cent) on equipment; $64 million (14 per cent) on fellowships; administrative and operational costs, $81 million (18 per cent).

NUMBER OF EXPERT MAN-YEARS/32,000, spent by 13,000 men and women of 90 different nationalities.

NUMBER OF FELLOWSHIP AWARDS/31,000, granted to trainees from 165 different countries and territories and taken in 126 different host countries.

During a typical year the programme recruited more than a thousand men and women from eighty or more countries. Their assignments covered service in one or more of over 125 countries or territories around the world, where they remained, on the average, about eight months. The wide distribution of the countries of origin of the experts was a matter of increasing satisfaction in a programme described as one of mutual aid. In the early years of the Expanded Programme, a disproportionate number of experts came from a few of the most highly developed countries. In 1950–51, for example, three countries, the United States, the United Kingdom, and France provided over fifty per cent of the experts. But by 1963, the proportion from these three countries was only thirty-one per cent, while slightly over twenty per cent were recruited from nations which were themselves in receipt of technical assistance. As early as 1958, for example, India received 146 experts but provided 109 for service in other countries; Argentina received 52 and provided 30; and Mexico received 25 while contributing 30.

By 1964 fellowship awards had been made for many kinds of training —from on-the-job experience in industrial enterprises to long-term research in the graduate faculties of leading universities. During the period under review the number of fellowships annually awarded showed a considerable volatility, much more than did other components of the Programme. For example, less than 1,200 were awarded in 1953 as compared with over 3,800 in 1962. In some instances these variations resulted from the fact that fellowships were an increasing part of Regular Programmes of the participating agencies, thus reducing this element of pressure on the Expanded Programme.

A useful aspect of the fellowship programme was the assistance to counterpart personnel, men and women assigned by under-developed countries to work with the international experts and subsequently sent to acquire further training abroad in the hope that on their return they would be able to continue the work already under way. As a result of early experience, an increasing effort was made to ensure that fellowships constituted an integral part of some broader technical assistance project, thus recording mutual advantages in promoting economic development.

Fellowships and study grants under the Expanded Programme fell generally into one of four categories. First, special study and observation visits were organized on a group basis for applicants from a number of countries, thus providing the participants with an opportunity to gain first-hand experience of the techniques and processes employed in other areas, and to make useful professional contacts. In this category there was, for example, a study tour arranged for electric-power experts from India, Indonesia, Japan, Pakistan and Thailand, which visited projects in seven countries—Czechoslovakia, France, West Germany, Sweden, United Kingdom, United States and U.S.S.R. A second category of training awards involved practical instruction given in workshops, laboratories, factories, or on farms, thus providing opportunities through which specific technical skills could be acquired. An ILO programme for worker-trainees was a particularly noteworthy example of this type of fellowship. By the end of 1959 more than 1,500 workers and foremen had been sent to gain knowledge and experience in modern plants in foreign countries. The third type of fellowship (or scholarship) consisted of awards made for regular study in recognized institutions of learning in which conventional academic courses were followed. And finally, there were the training courses, seminars, and other kinds of special projects organized by, or with the co-operation of, the participating organizations. Regional training-centres and seminars played an important role in providing training at comparatively low cost and in surroundings akin to those with which the trainees were already acquainted. In 1957, a typical year in this period, there were nine regional training-centres in operation, and four seminars and two study tours were organized; in all, 1,144 fellows participated.

As experience accumulated, there developed among the more acute observers of the Programme a gradually hardening conviction that the value of fellowships for study abroad had been over-estimated. Not only were there continuing difficulties in ensuring the selection of the most satisfactory candidates,* but the number of those who were trained abroad and who subsequently were reluctant to return home, or who were unhappy when they did return, was seriously eroding the confidence of both governments and agencies in the value of this form of aid. In many cases, moreover, the government which had applied for the fellowship failed to make effective use of the incumbent when he did return to his own country. And finally there was an increasing doubt as to the average value of a year or two abroad as an element in the training process. Taking all things into consideration the Executive Chairman of TAB, and other responsible officers, after a few years of somewhat disappointing experience, began to encourage a shift in emphasis away from the fellowship solution.

Equipment and supplies of a total value of nearly $36 million were provided by the Expanded Programme between the years 1950 and 1964. Although the yearly total fluctuated considerably, this part of the Programme was a gradually increasing factor. There was, of course, heavy pressure on TAB and the agencies to supply capital goods, often under

---

* The number of government nominees who turned out to be the sons or nephews of ministers, or otherwise "well-connected," was statistically astonishing. So also was the percentage of applicants who indicated that their intellectual needs could be satisfied only by a year or two in Paris!

circumstances which created doubts as to how, and by whom, they would be used. All of the money available to the Expanded Programme could easily have been dispensed in this way if the rules, and those who enforced them, had permitted.

Purchases of some equipment and supplies were made from many countries (sometimes from as many as fifty in a single year). In every case the amount was small and items purchased had, under the rules, to form part of a broader technical assistance project. Generally they were used in research and survey work, demonstration programmes, pilot projects, or training institutions. Typical examples in a single year (1957) were the geological equipment for a phosphate production project in Jordan; electronic machines for an Indian Statistical Institute; civil aviation supplies for an ICAO training-school in Indonesia; meteorological equipment for Libya and Ecuador; and teaching and demonstration supplies for the environmental sanitation projects in Formosa, Indonesia, Yemen, and Lebanon.

The usefulness of equipment provided in this way is indicated by the many instances in which governments bought additional supplies themselves or arranged for its local manufacture, following experience with that provided by the Expanded Programme. In Chile, for example, the State Technical University in 1959 spent more than four times as much as the agency to purchase equipment of the type supplied for a laboratory improvement project supervised by a UNESCO expert. In Libya, the small-tools section of a farm mechanization project developed a simple plough for local use that is now being manufactured within that country. In general, it can be said that sensible use was made of supplies and equipment provided under the Expanded Programme, although there were a few cases in which there was inadequate utilization. Effective use can generally be assured if the provision of equipment is carefully co-ordinated with the work of related experts.

Fortunately there were not many cases of misuse such as that of the residents of a rural area of Afghanistan who, after thousands of years during which they were acquainted only with the knife and the sickle decided, when they were introduced by FAO to the scythe, to use the fine new blades for weapons rather than tools.

2/Fields of Assistance

Technical assistance under the Expanded Programme covered a very wide range of subjects. By 1959 the Technical Assistance Board was using forty-nine different classifications which were still not sufficient to describe the full variety of its activities. Table 3, in which the direct project costs have been summarized under ten major headings, gives a broad idea of the proportion of money spent in different fields during the decade from 1953 to 1963. It can be seen that out of total expenditures of just over $306 million, the largest share, or twenty-three per cent, went to services in the field of agricultural production, and that this was followed by expenditures on health services. These and the other allocations have remained fairly constant throughout the history of the programme.

TABLE 3

The Distribution of Field Project Costs* by Major Fields
of Activity, 1953–1963

(thousands of U.S. dollars)	Amount $	Per Cent
I. Assisting governments in the formulation and implementation of development plans—basic surveys of resources and building up of administrative services	44,321	14
II. Development of public utilities—power, transport, and communications	25,005	8
III. Industrial production and mining	23,358	8
IV. Agricultural production	69,190	22
V. Auxiliary services to industry and agriculture	23,827	8
VI. Health Services	52,571	17
VII. Education	33,876	11
VIII. Community Development	29,213	7
IX. Other Social Services	11,570	4
X. Atomic Energy	2,263	less than 1
Total	306,194	100

Although the various headings used in the table are generally self-explanatory it is perhaps useful to follow the example of the Technical Assistance Board in providing a brief description of each.

I/*Assisting governments in the formulation and implementation of development plans—basic surveys of resources and building up of administrative services.* This includes all assistance provided to governments in basic economic surveys, covering such subjects as natural resources, manpower, and meteorology; in the various fields of statistics, including agri-

* *"Field Project Costs" do not exactly correspond to the classification, "Field Programme Costs," used elsewhere, due to the inclusion of local costs in the former.*

culture, labour, health, and education; in the preparation of economic development plans; and in improving public administration, including the training of administrative personnel. In one or more of these activities most of EPTA's participating organizations took part. In recent years a steadily increasing emphasis has been placed on activities of this character.

II/*Development of public utilities—power, transport and communications.* This included assistance for the discovery, estimation and development of power resources, production, transmission and distribution planning, telecommunications, civil aviation, and sea and land transport.

III/*Industrial production and mining.* Activities under this heading included advice on the development of factory-based manufacturing, aid to the processing and mining industries, changes designed to increase industrial productivity, and the development of small-scale or cottage industries. In spite of their repeated verbal expressions of interest in plans for industrialization, the applicant countries did not make any very significant allocations of funds for assistance of this kind. Nor were the already industrialized countries concerned to encourage such allocations. Eventually, because industrialization is so basic to economic progress, the General Assembly took the matter into its own hands and in December, 1965 approved a resolution setting up within the U.N. an agency to promote industrialization with an executive director and a full-time permanent secretariat.

IV/*Agricultural production.* This category covered services intended to increase the production of food and other crops; to rationalize the use of available land and water resources; and to improve forest, fisheries and livestock production. It also embraced the storage, marketing, and distribution of agricultural commodities.

V/*Auxiliary services to industry and agriculture.* Projects for vocational training and technical education, for developing co-operative organizations of different types, and for promoting international and domestic trade, are comprised within this classification.

VI/*Health services.* This title encompassed assistance provided to governments for the control of communicable diseases, for the strengthening of national health services, and for the training of medical and auxiliary health staff. Work on environmental sanitation, health education, and statistical services are also important components of this grouping.

VII/*Education.* Under this heading came all assistance to governments in organizing and expanding their primary and secondary education systems; improving the methods as well as strengthening the institutions of teacher training; introducing better methods of teaching science; developing efficient and economic methods for the production of textbooks to meet local needs, and the use of audio-visual aids and broadcasting services; and in the promotion of pure and applied research, together with the establishment of scientific documentation centres to make the results of research available.

VIII/*Community development*. This covered assistance to governments in fundamental education, agricultural extension, home economics and nutrition as well as community projects in general. In these activities the United Nations, ILO, FAO, UNESCO, and WHO all participated.

IX/*Other Social Services*. Activities in the field included assistance in town planning and housing, in drafting and administering labour legislation designed to improve working conditions, in regulating industrial relations, in developing plans for social security; and in devising other methods of promoting social welfare.

X/*Atomic Energy*. This was added in 1961 and comprised aid in the development of knowledge of the potential of nuclear energy for many aspects of peaceful progress.

3/Geographical Distribution

During the first fifteen years of the Expanded Programme, 163 countries and territories requested and received technical assistance. The majority of countries aided were those with an estimated annual per capita income of less than the local equivalent of $200.

By the end of the 1950's, over 100 countries and territories were receiving aid each year. In 1963 the total was 123; by 1965 it was over 140. Included each year were certain countries that participated in regional or inter-regional programmes, although without individual programmes of their own.

The regional distribution of expenditures showed certain significant changes over the period. As was to be expected the major change was the increasing proportion of costs incurred in African countries. This rise was chiefly due to larger programmes that were required to meet the needs of the newly independent nations of the region. The total expenditure in these countries rose from $442,000 in 1950–51 to $29,525,000 in the two-year period of 1963–64.

Somewhat similar circumstances operated to increase the share of expenditures allocated to Asia and the Far East. Cambodia, Laos, Malaya, and Viet Nam, for example, received technical assistance amounting to $185,000 in 1954, but $1,375,000 in 1963.

The shifts in the geographical distribution of technical assistance were made possible in part by the use of contingency allocations from TAB's Working Capital and Reserve Fund, and in part by a relative decline in expenditures in the Middle East and of the allocations to regional and inter-regional projects.

The geographical distribution of project costs by different fields of activity showed only small fluctuations in the period under review. In general, agricultural production and health services had the largest share of programme costs in each region; while the categories with the smallest share were those comprised under the headings of other social services and community development. Some minor but interesting variations between regions did, however, occur. These were due to differences in the prevailing level of development and to contradictory attitudes toward development planning among the governments of the different regions, or to both. In Latin America, for example, a relatively higher proportion of technical assistance expenditures went into the formulation of development plans and the strengthening of administrative services. In Africa, a relatively small proportion was devoted to public utilities projects. In Europe, health services were not as important a part of technical assistance as auxiliary services to industry and agriculture.

4/The Financial Record

The growth of the substantive coverage of the Expanded Programme between 1950 and 1963 and the extension of its activities to a widening range of countries, was made possible by a slow, but generally consistent increase in its financial resources. Annual pledges grew from $18.8 million in 1952, the first regular twelve-month period, to $50.6 million in 1964. The number of contributing governments increased from 54 in 1950 to 86 in 1958 and to 108 in 1964. By the end of 1959, the total of all contributions had reached $233.9 million and by 1964 this had increased to $456.6 million (*Table 4*).

During this period the general record of the payment of pledged contributions was not unsatisfactory, although certain years were disappointing. But by the end of the first decade, the Expanded Programme could boast a collection record of over 98 per cent of the amounts pledged. However, the Technical Assistance Board in 1963 still reported cumulative arrears of just over five million dollars. Current payments on pledges for individual years ranged as low as 79 per cent in 1957 and as high as 94.8 per cent in 1956 and although this is a reasonable record as such things go in international programmes, the fluctuations did cause the curtailment of certain projects in some years. It also, on occasion, necessitated the making of piecemeal adjustments in the approved programme with the result that some of the benefits of advance planning were jeopardized or lost.

TABLE 4

Contributions Pledged by Governments to the Expanded
Programme, 1950–1963.

Year	Number of Contributors	Amount Contributed (U.S. Dollars)	Per cent Increase Over Previous Year
1950–51	54	20,035,600	—
1952	65	18,797,200	—6.2
1953	69	22,320,700	18.7
1954	73	25,021,000	12.1
1955	70	27,626,700	10.6
1956	77	28,829,100	4.2
1957	84	30,813,400	6.9
1958	80	31,048,400	0.8
1959	83	29,420,000	—5.2
1960	85	34,023,400	15.6
1961	91	42,408,500	24.7
1962	92	45,438,600	7.1
1963	105	50,506,800	11.2
1964	108	50,316,000	—0.4
Total 1950–1965	108	456,600,000	

Source: TAB, *Technical Assistance Newsletter*, July, 1963, Table V A. and *15 Years and 150,000 Skills*—ECOSOC, May 10, 1965, p. 65.

The United States was by far the largest single contributor to the technical assistance programme, as it is to the cost of most other United Nations activities. However, its share of the contributions to the Expanded Programme fell progressively from over sixty per cent in the first years to forty per cent at the end of the first decade. By congressional decision the United States cannot now provide more than forty per cent of the total contributions. Despite this declining proportion, the U.S. contribution of nearly $22 million in 1963 was almost six times greater than that of the next largest contributor, the United Kingdom. The twelve major contributing nations in 1963 are shown in Table 5. As was appropriate and as might be expected, the more highly industrialized countries dominate this list, but it is significant that India, with an extremely low per capita national income, is also included.

If comparisons are made on the basis of the population of the contributing countries—i.e. dollars of contributions per capita—significant changes appear in the list. At the head of the second tabulation are the three Scandinavian countries, followed by the Netherlands and Switzerland. All of these countries are well-developed, but none of them is large in population. The United States is sixth on this list, with a rate of contribution to the Expanded Programme of less than one-third that of Denmark. France, Japan, and the U.S.S.R. do not appear at all. The really significant feature of this table is the fact that even the most generous donor government gives a sum that costs just over forty cents per person a year. It can hardly be seriously suggested that the price of two or three cups of coffee each, once a year, is a cause of hardship to the citizens of these fortunate nations. Yet the complaints that emanate from some of the critics of the United Nations in these countries rather more than suggest that they are being seriously impoverished by their donations to the United Nations programmes of international aid.

TABLE 5

Major Contributing Nations to the Expanded Programme, 1963.

Twelve Major Contributors in Total (U.S. dollars)		Twelve Major Contributors in Per Capita Terms (U.S. cents)	
United States	21,772,000	Denmark	40.8
United Kingdom	3,750,000	Norway	27.1
West Germany	2,650,000	Sweden	26.6
Canada	2,150,000	Netherlands	15.2
Sweden	2,010,000	Switzerland	14.5
U.S.S.R.	2,000,000	United States	11.7
Denmark	1,882,000	Canada	11.6
France	1,852,000	New Zealand	11.2
Netherlands	1,790,000	United Kingdom	7.1
Norway	980,000	Australia	7.0
Italy	900,000	Belgium	6.8
India	850,000	West Germany	4.7

Source: TAB, *Technical Assistance Newsletter*, July 1963, Table V, B, C and United Nations General Assembly: *Report on the Pledging Conference of the Expanded Programme of Technical Assistance and the Special Fund*, United Nations, New York, 1963.

The use of TAB's Working Capital and Reserve Fund, which reached a total of $12 million in 1963, has been of considerable value in helping to overcome the difficulties created by fluctuations in yearly contributions to and collections for the Expanded Programme. For example, at the end of 1958, when the programme for 1959 was approved by the Technical Assistance Committee, there was a substantial gap between the estimate of the cost of the programme and the resources expected to become available for its implementation. Accordingly the Executive Chairman of TAB was authorized to withdraw $1.5 million from the Fund in order to avoid serious cuts in the programme.

Expenditures under the Expanded Programme fall into four categories (1) *Field programme costs* or *project costs* are the expenditures incurred in paying for expert services, providing fellowships, conducting seminars, organizing demonstration projects and supplying equipment. These costs amounted to $326.1 million, or eighty-two per cent of all expenditures made during the period under review. (2) *Agency administrative costs* are the expenditures incurred by each of the nine participating agencies in processing requests, recruitment, and other general administrative needs arising from their participation in the Expanded Programme. The ten-year total of this component was $13.8 million and accounted for six per cent of total expenditures.*

During the later years of the period the direct administrative costs of the agencies were consistently below the ten-year average. In some agencies these costs reached a level of about five per cent which could properly be considered to be exceptionally low for an activity of this kind. (In the last two years of its existence the administrative ratio of the Technical Assistance Administration of the United Nations was just over four per cent. (3) *Indirect project costs* or *operational services costs* of the agencies are expenditures incurred in the process of servicing experts and fellows and in delivering equipment. Transportation, substantive backing and research at headquarters, translation services, etc., are typical expenditures in this category, which totalled $17.1 million between 1950 and 1959, or 7.8 per cent of the total. Under constant pressure from the General Assembly and ECOSOC for economies in administration, these costs, as well as those directly incurred by the agencies, declined, in combination, to just over thirteen per cent in 1959. (4) Both headquarters and field offices expenditures are included in the *Technical Assistance Board costs*. For the thirteen years, TAB costs totalled $24 million, or six per cent of all costs. The ratio of these costs to the other three is naturally

---

* *After 1959, Agency Administrative Costs were reported in combination with Indirect Project Costs.*

rising with the expanding role of TAB and especially of the resident representatives in the yearly planning procedures.

The following table indicates how the various participating agencies shared in the total volume of expenditures for the Expanded Programme during the 1950–1963 period:

TABLE 6

Participating Organizations' Share of Total Programme Costs
1950–1963

Organization	Expenditures (Millions of U.S. dollars)	Per cent of Total
UNTAA a	83.2	21
ITU } b	4.2	1
WMO }	4.4	1
ILO	37.8	9
FAO	100.4	24
WHO	66.8	17
UNESCO	58.0	15
ICAO	15.9	4
IAEA	3.3	1
UPU	0.1	less than 1%
TAB	24.0	6
Total	398.1	100

Sources: Table 4, Annex.

Notes: a. After January, 1959 UNTAA was superseded by the Bureau of Technical Assistance Operations of the United Nations Department of Economic and Social Affairs.

b. Between 1950 and 1955, expenditures of ITU and WMO were administered by UNTAA and included in the latter's total.

A final aspect of the Expanded Programme's financial record is the assessment of host governments for the local costs of maintaining experts in the field. Under ECOSOC Resolution 470 (XV), passed in 1953, arrangements were approved under which recipient governments are required to contribute to the local living allowances of experts a flat sum calculated on the basis of fifty per cent of an estimated daily subsistence. The Technical Assistance Board thereafter set rates for each country based on the relative cost of living and these rates were multiplied by the number of man-days served by the experts. The host country could choose to provide lodging in kind, and if this were done it was given an eighty per cent credit against its share of the assessment. Assessments are initially based on estimates, made by TAB, of the number of man-days included in the approved Category I Programme for the country concerned. The plan called for the payments of assessments in advance. Credits would then be given when the number of expert man-days actually spent in the country was determined. A considerable number of governments failed to meet these requirements, and by the end of 1963 there were local cost obligations outstanding for the previous years totalling $560,000. This amount has been steadily growing (it stood at less than $400,000 a year earlier), thus causing some concern in TAB as delays in assessment payments necessitated resort to the Working Capital and Reserve Fund for cash advances to the participating organizations.

CHAPTER SIX

The Technical Assistance Administration of the United Nations

A · The Case History of an Operational Agency

The history of the department of the United Nations Secretariat known as the Technical Assistance Administration reflects so many of the problems and the experiences, both encouraging and frustrating, of all the organizations that have participated in programmes of international aid, that it provides an illuminating case history of such bodies. For that reason its story is worth reviewing in some detail, even though it may in part repeat what has already been written.

By the middle of the year 1950, the United Nations was operating two programmes of technical assistance. It was participating in an involved and complex administrative machine created to handle an activity world-wide in scope, immensely varied in character, but relatively small in financial dimensions. When the Expanded Programme had become a reality, it was recognized by Secretary-General Lie and his senior assistants that the Secretariat's Departments of Social and Economic Affairs, with their primarily research-oriented staffs, could not be expected to handle the new programme's complicated and extensive operational problems as satisfactorily as they had been able to manage the much smaller Regular Programme. Therefore, in order to meet the new responsibilities with greater assurance, the Secretary-General on August 1, 1950, set up the Technical Assistance Administration (TAA) as a department of the United Nations Secretariat. The new department was designed to be an operational unit only, except in the field of public administration in which it was also given responsibility for substantive (that is, theoretical or research) activities. Otherwise its research and analytical needs were to be met by the co-operative assistance of the other departments and to a lesser degree, of the U.N.'s regional Economic Commissions.

The experience of the Technical Assistance Administration as a separate and distinct agency in the field of international co-operation was strenuous, exciting, but short. Less than a decade after its inception, TAA was abolished and on February 1, 1959, its functions were transferred to two bureaus, one of them immediately and the other subsequently incorporated in what was by that time the amalgamated Department of Economic and Social Affairs. But its life, despite its brevity, was a full one. It covered most of the first decade of the Expanded Programme with its drama and frustrations, its failures and its successes. Thus TAA's history reflects and records most of the significant elements of that important period in the development of a new approach to the solution of the age-old problems of human suffering and distress. Its chronicles illustrate how the task of providing technical assistance is defined and how an international agency can be organized to perform the duties that such a task entails; its story helps to provide an understanding of the nature and extent of the practical problems that arise in the course of such an operation. The compact case history of this organization also usefully illuminates the general problems of administration in a multi-national organization, problems that are becoming increasingly grave as the number, variety and importance of such agencies increase.

B · Administrative Problems in a United Nations Setting

The scope and role of the Technical Assistance Administration were basically determined by the nature of the United Nations itself, and in particular by the fact that the United Nations is a voluntary association of independent states, the nature and extent of their association being defined in a detailed charter. As the Charter particularly prohibits any invasion of the domestic jurisdiction of member states, the technical assistance programmes had, of necessity, to be developed on the basis of voluntary requests received from countries in search of aid. It was impossible for the United Nations to impose assistance no matter how apparent, how urgent and how specific its officers might consider the need to be. The United Nations cannot prohibit national self-injury—unless it involves immediate danger to world peace.

Decisions taken by the governing bodies of the United Nations and of the Specialized Agencies manifest themselves in resolutions, not laws. The result in far too many cases is a weak, and often an ambiguous, directive for administrative staffs to follow. Moreover, executive leadership in the United Nations family of organizations does not stem from the various governing bodies but from appointed, non-political executives —from the Secretary-General of the United Nations or from the Director-General of a Specialized Agency. As a result, the channel of authority and communication between policy-makers and administrators is sometimes twisted and is almost always unclear.

In the case of the United Nations, the administrative officers receive policy direction either from the Secretary-General himself or through the Secretary-General, from a variety of sources including the General Assembly, the various councils and a changing but steadily increasing complex of commissions, boards and committees. When to this is added the complications inevitably resulting from the mandatory recruitment of an international staff of widely varying backgrounds, and the assignment to that staff of an almost unequalled diversity of functions and responsibilities, the difficulty facing the administrators who seek to put together an efficient operating agency with clear terms of reference and following established principles of procedure, must be experienced to be fully understood.

The definition and execution of policy is somewhat less difficult in most other international organizations that it is in the United Nations. The Specialized Agencies, for example, have the great advantage of limited areas of technical competence within which to operate and around which to mobilize staff. Their goals can be more readily stated in terms that are likely to be familiar to technical experts in the respective fields.* Moreover, the delegates to the governing bodies of the Specialized Agencies are usually practitioners in their various areas of competence and thus there can develop what Peter Lengyel has described as a distinctive "professional camaraderie" (see Peter Lengyel: "Some Trends in International Civil Service," *International Organization*, 13, Fall 1959, pp. 520–537) between the secretariat staff and the members of the delegations.

The responsibilities of the United Nations, on the other hand, cover a much wider range of subjects and its secretariat in consequence reflects a far greater diversity of interests and skills. Dealing with such varied matters as human rights, the maintenance of peace, industrialization, administrative techniques, the solution of political difficulties, and the resolution of social and economic problems, the staff of the United Nations operates in sensitive areas in which passion, prejudice and the

---

* *This is less true in the case of* UNESCO *than in that of the other Specialized Agencies because* UNESCO *operates, for the most part, in areas in which there are few absolute standards and few unquestioned canons of true and false, right and wrong, success and failure. In agriculture, in meteorology, in aviation, even in medicine, it is relatively easy to test the theories and practices of the expert and to distinguish him from the impostor. In education and in cultural matters generally, the line between the sage and the charlatan is much less easy to define. The situation in* UNESCO *is further complicated by the fact that this agency deals with subject matters in which almost everyone believes himself to be fully competent to appraise and judge. Because few conclusive tests can be applied this delusion is seldom corrected.*

conviction of infallibility are likely to be the rule rather than the exception.

It was with problems that tended to arouse much of this vanity and emotion that the Technical Assistance Administration had from the beginning to contend.

C · The Early Years of TAA

When the Technical Assistance Administration was established in 1950, its initial organization consisted of forty persons of varying staff grades who were transferred to the new unit chiefly from the Departments of Social Affairs and of Economic Affairs. Almost without exception, these pioneers had volunteered to work in the new department because of their belief in the importance as well as the intrinsic interest of the United Nations programmes of international aid. Moreover, the remarkable group of senior officers of the parent departments, Mr. David Owen (United Kingdom), Mr. Henri Laugier (France), Mr. David Weintraub (U.S.A.), Miss Julia Henderson (U.S.A.), Mrs. Alva Myrdal (Sweden) and others, were deeply concerned with the new venture and encouraged some of their best officials to volunteer for service with the embryo unit. For these reasons the quality of the TAA staff was from the beginning high.

In distributing functions under the Expanded Programme, the General Assembly and the Economic and Social Council assigned to TAA certain reasonably well-defined responsibilities in the fields of economic development, social welfare, and public administration. But the Administration was also given the additional duty of providing aid in every sphere of activity not specifically or inferentially covered by a Specialized Agency. The Technical Assistance Administration, and the substantive departments of the Secretariat working with it, were thus to be the residual legatees of the whole Expanded Programme.

In public administration TAA had the exclusive franchise; its responsibility was substantive as well as operational. In its other areas—economic development and social welfare—the Administration's field of operation was somewhat restricted by the fact that various Specialized Agencies had duties that also fell under these headings. The Food and Agriculture Organization, for example, works within the field of economic development; the World Health Organization and UNESCO similarly deal with problems that are obviously a part of social welfare. The World Bank and the International Monetary Fund are also called upon to aid governments in the definition and solution of economic or financial problems.

From the beginning, TAA's operational character was strongly emphasized both by the Secretary-General and by its own leaders. Except in public administration, it relied heavily on the other departments of the Secretariat for the research and analytical services required to ensure the high quality of United Nations aid. TAA was responsible for providing headquarters support and facilities for field projects. It was directly engaged in the recruitment of expert advisers, the organization of missions, the awarding of fellowships, and the management of seminars, workshops, conferences, pilot plants and demonstration projects. In carrying out these tasks, which might cover fields as disparate as industrialization and child welfare, or national budgetary practices and penal reform, the Administration would naturally be expected to enlist the best help obtainable in any branch of the Secretariat.* Fortunately, highly competent personnel was available in a wide variety of technical and professional fields. Nonetheless, this division of labour was not without its difficulties. These difficulties were not lessened by the eventual incorporation of TAA in the Department of Economic and Social Affairs.

The decision to establish a separate administrative unit for technical assistance had developed in part because the idea made organizational sense in itself, and in part as a compromise solution for difficulties that had already arisen. In the first years of the Regular Programme, the Department of Economic Affairs and the Department of Social Affairs had each built up its own set of interests, loyalties, and procedures. The officers of the Department of Social Affairs in particular, and not without reason, were afraid that their concern with problems of welfare might be subordinated to the immediate economic objectives of their colleagues in the Department of Economic Affairs. The latter tended to feel that any really significant progress in welfare must wait upon economic development and that for the time being a preponderant part of the available resources should therefore be concentrated on the latter objective.

Support for the proposal to create a separate department which could make more or less independent decisions as to priorities among the various kinds of aid, gained special favour because of these growing internal tensions. It was also felt that the duties of the substantive departments of the Secretariat could not be satisfactorily handled if the work of their officials was constantly interrupted or harried by the necessity of intense concentration on the importunate demands of day-to-day administrative operations. It was not helpful to interrupt a piece of serious research in order to check on an expert's luggage allowance or to spend

---

* The UN was also asked from time to time to assist governments in such esoteric and unacceptable projects as the creation of an army and navy.

days in trying to locate a fellow who had unaccountably disappeared. The two kinds of activity were fundamentally incompatible.

Finally it was felt that a separate entity would bring real advantages because it would facilitate the establishment and maintenance of satisfactory relations with the Specialized Agencies by creation of a distinctive image of the United Nations in the sphere of technical assistance. Secretary-General Lie believed in the "functional" approach to international co-operation and he was convinced that this could best be fostered by the organization of a special operating unit within the Secretariat. (Trygve Lie: *In the Cause of Peace*, New York, 1954, p. 145.) He was afraid that without a strong and separate department highly committed to its own programme, the work of the United Nations in technical assistance might easily be over-shadowed by that of the Specialized Agencies. This he believed would be as politically unfortunate as it would be operationally unwise.

The organizational environment into which the Technical Assistance Administration was launched was not such as to encourage the belief that the new department would have an easy or a long life. In spite of great goodwill at the top, the rank and file personnel of other departments could naturally be expected to seek to protect their vested interests and to be fearful of administrative empire-building by a new operational, and to some extent an overlapping, agency in their midst. The established and independent Specialized Agencies, which were in any event apprehensive in their attitude towards what they considered to be the expanding power of the United Nations, were certain to be critical of a body with such widespread responsibilities as those assigned to TAA. It was also apparent that heavy governmental demands would be made on the new Administration because of the rather extravagant hopes that were entertained for the success of the Expanded Programme and because of the certainty that these hopes would, in some measure at least, be disappointed. For the new programme was an undertaking on which many eloquent words were being expended, but for which there was little practical precedent, and from which quick, radical and conspicuous achievements were as impatiently anticipated as they were inherently improbable.

All of this was recognized from the beginning by the staff of the new organization. It served to strengthen the determination to succeed which had already been aroused by the challenge of the opportunities which were explicit in this new adventure in international co-operation, applied intelligence and goodwill.

From the original staff of forty, TAA grew to over one hundred within a year; by that time it had settled into the performance of the following duties:

1/*The provision of fellowships and scholarships to persons from under-developed areas, to enable the holders to learn at first hand the methods and policies employed in countries that had achieved effective progress in the selected fields of interest;*

2/*The organization of seminars, conferences, and demonstration projects within under-developed countries, thus making available on the spot the fruits of foreign research and experience;*

3/*The contribution of technical literature and, under controlled conditions, limited quantities of equipment and supplies for the instruction and use of officials or specialists within the recipient states; and, most important of all,*

4/*The discovery, selection, nomination, recruitment and subsequent servicing of individual experts or of groups of experts to proceed to appellant countries and to work with local personnel in attempting to solve the difficulties which characterize, and in many cases are responsible for, the under-development of the nations concerned.*

5/*The conduct of research and other substantive duties in the field of public administration.*

The staff seconded to and recruited by TAA soon reflected a wide geographical distribution, an important consideration in United Nations personnel policy and above all in the technical assistance operations. The nine very able senior officers below the Director-General (who was from Canada) came, in order of seniority, from Mexico (Gustavo Martinez Cabañas), the United States (Arthur Goldschmidt), the United Kingdom (George Cadbury), Belgium (Charles Fonck), the Netherlands (Hubertus Van Mook), India (D. Ghosh), France (Maurice Milhaud), Australia (Gordon Menzies), and Brazil (Benedicto Silva). In all, twenty-seven nationalities were represented in the fifty-two persons of officer (non-clerical) grade. Staff experience was not quite as diverse as was the geographical distribution, as most of the senior officers were professional administrators. This was understandable and appropriate as the scope of TAA's activities was so broad that the Administration could not hope to employ within its own ranks an array of talent commensurate with the variety of requests for assistance which it was soon receiving. Moreover, as has been stated, TAA was expected to utilize, and did habitually use, the staff resources of the two substantive departments of the Secretariat. Its own special need, therefore, was for men and women who could operate quickly and successfully in the realm of organizational and administrative problems.

The Technical Assistance Administration's responsibilities were defined by the fact that it served countries distributed widely over the earth and requiring aid in a great variety of fields and in a wide diversity of forms. Thus an internal division of duties based either on *geography* (Asia, Latin America, etc.), or on *subject matter* (child welfare, industrialization, civil service reform, and so on), or on *function* (seminars, fellowships, expert missions, etc.), would have been possible and arguments in favour of each arrangement were reviewed at the organizational stage. Although each would have presented its own complexities, any one of these schemes might have been expected to operate with reasonable efficiency.

Adopted in its pure form the *geographical* organization would, as indicated, have involved the creation of four or five divisions within TAA, each designed to serve countries in its assigned area by providing fellowships, seminars, training and demonstration centres, technical information, and expert advice, with the consequent fragmentation of each of the functional transactions. Such a geographical form would also have required the development of small servicing branches for reporting, assessment, and implementation within each geographical division, not to mention separate lines of communication with the Departments of Economic Affairs and Social Affairs. Finally, it would have required the assignment to each area office of one or more experts in public administration (since substantive backing in this subject was nowhere else available in the Secretariat). This would have had the advantage of ensuring a co-ordinated and centralized control of all the technical assistance work being done by the United Nations. But it would also have resulted in an excessive degree of elaboration and a significant increase in the size of TAA. The result would have been, in some measure, inefficient and uneconomic.

A rather similar, although perhaps somewhat less complex, result would have been produced by an organizational arrangement based exclusively and precisely on the *substantive fields* with which TAA was concerned. The great advantage in this arrangement would have been the rapid accumulation by the members of the different units of a high degree of experience in dealing with the subject matter assigned to each. But in each of the three areas of interest—economic development, social welfare, and public administration—this would also have involved the creation of small sections to deal respectively with fellowships, seminars, information and expert advice. These again might have had to be broken down by geographic areas, and the result once more would have been excessive cost and operational complications.

In view of these considerations it was decided in the early days of TAA that a *functional* arrangement (with one minor variation) would provide the simplest and most effective structure. It was arranged that the Ad-

FIGURE 4: ORGANIZATION OF TECHNICAL ASSISTANCE ADMINISTRATION 1950

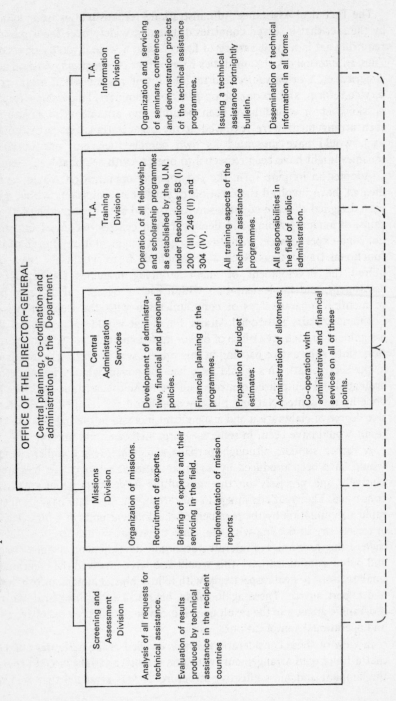

OFFICE OF THE DIRECTOR-GENERAL
Central planning, co-ordination and administration of the Department

Screening and Assessment Division

Analysis of all requests for technical assistance.

Evaluation of results produced by technical assistance in the recipient countries

Missions Division

Organization of missions.

Recruitment of experts.

Briefing of experts and their servicing in the field.

Implementation of mission reports.

Central Administration Services

Development of administrative, financial and personnel policies.

Financial planning of the programmes.

Preparation of budget estimates.

Administration of allotments.

Co-operation with administrative and financial services on all of these points.

T.A. Training Division

Operation of all fellowship and scholarship programmes as established by the U.N. under Resolutions 58 (I) 200 (III) 246 (II) and 304 (IV).

All training aspects of the technical assistance programmes.

All responsibilities in the field of public administration.

T.A. Information Division

Organization and servicing of seminars, conferences and demonstration projects of the technical assistance programmes.

Issuing a technical assistance fortnightly bulletin.

Dissemination of technical information in all forms.

ministration should have a Training Division dealing with fellowships and scholarships for all countries and in all three substantive areas; a Missions Division that would handle all problems related to the supplying and servicing of experts; an Information Division (later Special Projects) that would organize all seminars, conferences, demonstration projects, and related activities; and, finally, a Screening and Assessment Division to analyse requests and to process reports from experts and fellows (*see Fig 4*). Public administration activities were handled initially by the Training Division, but in 1951 this was changed and thereafter they were dealt with by a unit designed for that specific purpose and which combined research and operational activities.

The form of organization thus set up in 1950 lasted with only the one minor modification until the end of 1952. During this time it operated with a modest, but less than wholly satisfactory measure of efficiency and it was not free of external criticism. Some members of other Secretariat units with which TAA worked accused it of being "too formalistic" in its methods and the General Assembly's Advisory Committee on Administrative and Budgetary Questions was critical of what it considered to be the complexity of the Administration's machinery. Although these particular criticisms were perhaps of doubtful validity, it was agreed within the Administration that changes were required if the maximum service was to be provided at minimum cost. In 1952, therefore, it was decided that the whole structure should be reviewed in the light of two years' experience and that basic changes should at least be considered. A number of interesting conclusions resulted from this exercise in self-examination.

D · Operational Problems

The first and perhaps the major reason for the operational weakness of the original organization of TAA had soon been identified. The scheme, as designed, would probably have worked quite satisfactorily in a national administration in which all the participants were trained in the same tradition and acted from consistent and common motives. Such persons would have found it possible to maintain their individual responsibilities without insistence on the excessive use of hierarchical channels and formal procedures. But in the early stages of an international organization with a widely diversified staff, the protection of personal positions and the defence of familiar practices and procedures is almost certain to take on an exaggerated importance.

This was the case in TAA. The wide variations in the background and viewpoint of the men and women who constituted the initial staff resulted in a somewhat rigid adherence to formal and mechanical procedures that would have made the efficient operation of any organizational scheme a difficult achievement. Instead of walking across the hall, or settling minor problems by a quick word on the office telephone, the more frequent practice in the early experience of TAA (as of the United Nations Secretariat as a whole) was the preparation of memoranda, each of which would take the better part of a day to move each way. Such punctilious communications, moreover, made compromise difficult, and emphasized individual rights and positions instead of facilitating the quiet and sensible meeting of minds that is the basis of good operational practice. Indeed, it is somewhat incongruous that excessive adherence to ritual, a weakness that is often criticized in the public services of under-developed countries, should have been found also in the international agency designated to help solve the administrative problems faced by the governments of such countries.

The situation was further complicated by the avidity with which many members of the secretariat adopted the (largely American) system of committees and conferences. Few items of business seemed too small to justify the appointment of a committee or the calling of a meeting. On such occasions, moreover, because of national and other sensitivities, it was not safe to omit anyone with even a meagre claim to participation. It seemed to be equally important that unusually detailed minutes should be taken and that each participant's contribution should be permanently recorded to his or her satisfaction. As a result, a wholly unreasonable amount of staff time was likely to be devoted to joint meditation and to the embalming of unimportant views. The proverbial definition of a committee as a group of men that keeps minutes but wastes hours was often applicable to the early days of the Secretariat of the United Nations, and of TAA.

At first, attempts were made to overcome these difficulties by discussions with, and appeals to, members of the TAA staff, and there is no doubt that real efforts were made by many of those concerned to change their habits and adjust themselves to a new environment and new procedures. But the strength of old habits and the novel conditions of the new international organization combined to make the speedy adoption of a more relaxed but more efficient system very difficult to achieve. It soon became apparent that the organizational scheme would have to be simplified still further if it was to expedite rather than delay the activities of the technical assistance programmes with which the members of the staff were so intimately and so sincerely concerned.

Another complicating element in the early work of the Administration was the fact that the financial and personnel policies of the Secretariat as a whole had been applied without modification to the work of TAA, in spite of the fact that many of the Administration's activities were quite different both in form and substance from most of the duties of the remainder of the Secretariat. The TAA was an executive agency engaged in day-to-day operational problems and was not, except in public administration, a substantive or research organization. Eventually, certain modifications and exceptions in the customary United Nations practices had to be introduced for TAA's benefit, including—after a prolonged and somewhat heated debate—a radical but obviously sensible change in the absurd registry and filing system, which was one of the major failures in the original secretariat design. But all of this took time and it delayed the early achievement of the desired measure of efficiency.

Before examining the eventual solution of its organizational difficulties, it would be appropriate to notice certain other aspects of the administrative problems with which the responsible officers of TAA had to contend.

Among the first and most difficult was that resulting from the political necessity of maintaining a reasonable and defensible (two qualities which are not necessarily identical) distribution of posts both at headquarters and among the experts selected for external service, in terms of nationality, geography, and language. With regard to the Secretariat as a whole, the Secretary-General is directed by the charter to give due regard "to the importance of recruiting the staff on as wide a geographical basis as possible." In carrying out this policy, the Secretary-General uses as a rough guide for the establishment of national quotas the comparative scale of the contributions made by member governments to the regular United Nations budget. This is not, of course, a Procrustean system that allocates posts precisely in accordance with an absolute standard. Nor does it apply in any very significant manner to staffing in the stenographic or junior clerical categories where, for the purpose of economy, the principle of local recruitment normally obtains. This last fact explains, in part at least, the preponderance of United States citizens among the Secretariat personnel. (An incidental result of these rules is the heavy demand for secretaries and clerks from the French-speaking areas of Canada.)

The general United Nations policy of national distribution of appointments was adopted and applied, as far as it was practicable to do so, to the staffing of the Technical Assistance Administration. There were, of course, definite limits to its applicability in this unit. Although the whole programme of technical assistance is based on the conviction that every country has something to contribute to the general body of experience, knowledge and principle, and that every country has something to learn, it is quite obvious that in the realms of economic development, social welfare, and public administration the people of the more advanced nations will inevitably have a disproportionately large contribution to make. Technical assistance, in this sense, is one field in which the Marxian slogan "from each according to his abilities; to each according to his needs" should, theoretically, be acceptable as a basis of operating policy. But even here, in practice, national and racial sentiment made some deviation from a purely objective standard inevitable and indeed, for political reasons, desirable. The "skeleton keys of compromise" are, and must be, standard equipment for officials of the United Nations—except in matters of basic principle.

Concern for the rule of geographical distribution of posts within the Administration and in the selection of experts for assignments abroad, inevitably added a conflicting and delaying factor in the execution of the whole programme of technical assistance. If it had been possible to concentrate recruitment efforts within a few of the more highly developed nations, the whole operation would have been greatly simplified. On the other hand, such a concentration would have meant the loss of much of the operational flexibility and of many of the psychological values that have resulted from the practice of universal recruitment. It would have reduced the sense of partnership that is such a valuable element in the concept of mutual aid.

While countries in an advanced stage of development provided the larger proportion of the staff of TAA and of the body of experts sent into the field, in both categories there was more than a token adherence to the policy of geographic distribution. Reference has already been made to the fact that the ten senior officials of TAA in its formative years came from ten different countries. Among the 6,000 experts sent to the field between 1950 and 1959 more than seventy nations were represented. The results of this personnel policy definitely slowed down recruitment, but the internationalization of the programme was not allowed to lower its quality and in many instances it made the United Nations services more acceptable to the recipient countries.

Another problem of recruitment, at least in the early years of the Expanded Programme, was the relatively uncertain tenure of United Nations assignments in the headquarters Secretariat. Under Secretary-General Hammarskjold (after 1953), however, a major effort was made to emphasize the element of permanency in such appointments.* The old "indeterminate" contracts which were the nearest approximation of permanent engagements were abolished, with the result that it became possible for competent and devoted officials to enlist in the service of the United Nations with reasonable assurance of continuing employment. This problem was normally limited to headquarters staff, since experts' contracts were usually for a specific term, varying in most cases from three months to two years. More recently, efforts have been made to arrange for the enlistment of competent and experienced experts for a series of assignments covering an extended period of service. However, the typical expert does not contemplate a permanent career in the United Nations, but enlists for a particular task with limited responsibility and an equally limited commitment of time.

Finally, it is also important in any discussion of administrative difficulties to understand both the obligations and the expectations of those who enlist for service with the United Nations.

First, salaries in the Secretariat are based on comparable rates in the New York area. To most people in most countries these rates seem unduly generous. This impression is likely to be modified, however, when the pay scale is compared with the extraordinary cost of living in one of the most expensive areas in the United States, and especially in those parts of New York City and its suburbs in which staff members would normally expect to reside. Nevertheless, it is probably fair to conclude that members of the Secretariat, in the middle grades in particular, are provided for with at least reasonable liberality, although this was more true when the rates were first established than it was after the drastic increases in the cost of living in the middle and late nineteen-fifties. The position of members of the Secretariat is considerably improved, of course, by the granting of various perquisites in the form of generous superannuation, low-cost insurance, group medical services, and ample leave. The leave arrangements, which amount to six weeks in every year, with home leave for all non-Americans, supplemented by travel time every second year, are of almost unexampled and quite unnecessary generosity.

The obligations imposed upon every person who joins the staff of the Secretariat, or who enlists for duty abroad as a United Nations expert, are illustrated in the following oath:

---

* Later on Hammarskjold attempted to popularize the idea of having governments second suitable personnel from their own services to the United Nations for specific periods—usually two years. This had a number of obvious advantages but if adopted too widely would have had a serious effect on the quality of a service which depends heavily on experience.

*I solemnly swear (undertake, affirm, promise) to exercise in all loyal-
ty, discretion, and conscience the functions entrusted to me as a
member of the international service of the United Nations, to discharge those functions and regulate my conduct with the interests of
the United Nations only in view, and not to seek or accept instruc-
tions in regard to the performance of my duties from any government or other authority external to the Organization.*

Thus the incumbent of a United Nations post, for the period of such duty,
undertakes to give his primary devotion to the international body. Within his new relationship he should cease to demand or to enjoy the right
of intervention on his behalf by the representatives of his national
government. The degree to which this principle has been applied in practice has varied from individual to individual, from country to country,
and from time to time. Some governments have scrupulously and consistently avoided interference with the recruitment policies of the
Secretary-General, with questions of promotion or of assignment within
the Secretariat, or with the exercise of objective judgement by the
Secretary-General and by the Bureau of Personnel in the selection of
experts to serve either at headquarters or abroad. Certain governments,
however, have been notorious for the frequency and insistence with which
they have intervened in attempts to ensure "adequate" representation and
"suitable" status for their nationals. Among those that have been the
least demanding—for reasons that have been variously interpreted—have
been the communist countries; among the most blatant offenders against
the recognized principles have been such "western" governments as
France, Belgium and the United States. The behaviour of the Scandinavian
and Commonwealth countries, except India, has been almost uniformly
good.

Among the members of the United Nations Secretariat, a very large
proportion from the beginning have taken seriously their terms of service
and have striven conscientiously both to maintain the objectivity and
impartiality that should mark the international civil servant and to base
their personal expectations on a reasonable estimation of the quality of
their services. Unfortunately, this scrupulous attitude has not been universal and the Secretary-General, on more than one occasion, has spoken
in vigorous terms about the way in which national influences have been
invoked to promote the careers of ambitious individuals. The attempt to
substitute influence for industry, pressure for performance, is not unknown in other organizations, but it is particularly deplorable in an
international body devoted to the promotion of the ideals of human
progress and welfare. Here, if anywhere, sound principles should be

maintained, and an honest example be demonstrated in practice.

Within the specialized field of technical assistance a generally nice regard for the canons of personal and official rectitude is of unusual importance. Members of the headquarters staff and experts in the field alike are charged with problems of vital concern to the nations they have been asked to help and any deviation from the ideals of objective service could produce lamentable repercussions. Thus, in TAA from the beginning, the selection both of staff for service in the Secretariat and of experts for foreign assignments, had to be undertaken with most meticulous care.

This review of the relationship between governments and their nationals who are serving the United Nations should not be concluded without a brief reference to the attempts made in the mid-fifties by some elements in the United States Government to control the recruitment and to decide on the retention or dismissal of United States citizens by the Secretary-General of the United Nations. This problem arose—not only in the United Nations itself but in certain of the Specialized Agencies as well —during the dismal years of the McCarthy-ite hysteria in the United States. The witch-hunting tactics inspired by the Wisconsin senator were actually carried into the Secretariat buildings in New York by agents of the Federal Bureau of Investigation and of other United States organizations who ferreted through the building in search of evidence against citizens suspected of subversion. Friends and associates of those under suspicion were questioned in detail as to the personal habits and ideological views of the suspects and of other U.N. officials. So intimidating was the general atmosphere that it took a certain amount of courage for members of the staff to refuse to co-operate in this wholly improper procedure.

Secretary-General Lie's public statements in regard to these matters were unexceptionable, but behind the scenes he co-operated with the United States officials by agreeing to a system under which no United States citizens were hired without prior clearance provided through the State Department in Washington. Much less defensible was his action in forcing the resignation of certain members of the staff against whom no charges had been made, but who had incurred the animosity of the McCarthy investigators by refusing to give evidence against their friends or associates. The Secretary-General put it to at least one very senior member of his staff, against whom there was no charge of any description, that he should resign because his retention was making it more difficult to maintain good relations with the United States. He agreed that the staff member's record was without blemish, that he was indeed an exceptionally able and a thoroughly loyal official, but added that if the officer was really concerned for the good of the organization he would resign. Finally he followed his persuasion by saying that the American pressure was so great that if the officer did not resign he would have to be discharged. The resignation was forthcoming and the United Nations lost one of its ablest officials.

After the election of Dag Hammarskjold to the post of Secretary-General in 1953, the situation rapidly improved. Without any great fanfare, but in unmistakable terms, the new Secretary-General made it plain that no further interrogations were to be carried on in the Secretariat offices and that no members of the staff would be dismissed at the demand of any government unless proof of misbehaviour was first adduced.

The complaints of the head of the United States permanent delegation were of no avail. The new Secretary-General, who in any case entertained only a most limited regard for Henry Cabot Lodge Jr., was not to be moved. Thereafter the morale of the United Nations Secretariat rapidly improved and it was not long before relations with the United States returned to normal.

It took somewhat longer for a similar improvement to be effected in some of the Specialized Agencies. In others the staffs were more successfully protected from the beginning. This was particularly true of the World Health Organization whose Director General Dr. Brock Chisholm, by any standard one of the most distinguished international figures of his generation, was quite unmoved by the gross discourtesy, the threats and the attempted bullying by Mr. Lodge.

In addition to the general problems that affected all units of the United Nations Secretariat, the work of the Technical Assistance Administration faced certain distinctive issues that arose from its special duties and responsibilities. Among the most important of these was the task of ensuring that the original requests from applicant governments were both clear and within the terms of reference of the Administration. In some cases the degree of under-development in a particular country was clearly evidenced by the form or substance of its requests for aid. Early in the Programme especially, certain governments simply did not know what to ask for, nor how to prepare and present their appeals. One of the major tasks of the Administration, therefore, was to assist such governments in the evaluation of their needs and in the submission of their proposals in such a way that they would be formally acceptable and would have a reasonable hope of producing useful results. The working out of detailed job descriptions and the identification of the precise type of specialist who could best fill the national need was an important step in the same complicated and vital process.

The selection of personally suitable experts to represent the United

Nations in providing assistance to applicant countries was undoubtedly TAA's most important single responsibility. Obviously, the success of most technical assistance programmes depended on the number and quality of the specialists recruited to participate in it. On the average, over six hundred highly qualified men and women had to be selected, briefed, placed in the field and serviced during each of TAA's nine years. To be fully acceptable to the recipient governments, the persons thus selected to carry the knowledge of the scientific, industrialized, socially progressive world to the under-developed nations, had to belong to a very special category. They had to be individuals of distinguished reputation for their scientific or academic qualifications, for their practical accomplishments, and for their professional standing. Anyone less qualified had to be considered incompetent to give the kind of service required. On more than one occasion, a requesting government refused the services of a highly capable nominee simply because he was not already known to them as a person of outstanding ability and distinguished achievement.

Among the United Nations agencies there was a growing tendency during the 1950's to believe that too much stress could be placed on the public reputation or official position of potential experts. In many instances, it was felt that equally competent people might be found among those to whom full public recognition had not yet been accorded, who were brilliant men, but still "on the way up." More than one delegation in the General Assembly, and especially that of Sweden, pleaded the case for the younger, less widely known recruit. But recipient governments were hard to convince, and the agencies, which were building their reputations on the quality of their appointees, were also hesitant to take chances with such men and women. Sometimes it almost seemed that grey hair or baldness were essential qualifications for field assignments in technical assistance.

In addition to technical competence, the United Nations expert must be a person endowed with unusual human qualities. In most instances he will be dealing on matters of exceptional importance with senior members of a national public service, men who, in general, are likely to be sensitive, critical, and perhaps even a little suspicious. Any suggestion of impatience, any indication of a feeling of racial, social or intellectual superiority, or any assumption of personal authority on the part of the United Nations adviser, could be instantly fatal to the success of his mission.

The case of a senior Indian official, who on the advice of Mr. Nehru himself was sent to an important post in Jakarta, illustrated this danger. This official got into the unfortunate habit of lecturing the Indonesian officials and even members of the government, in much the way he had dealt with his subordinates in the public service of his Indian state. He criticized the state of the public buildings and objected to the habits of the Indonesian legislators, who wore hats and smoked in their legislative chamber. Within a year he had to be recalled. Similarly a Belgian expert who was alleged (it was never finally proven) to have referred to the people of the North African country in which he was stationed as "niggers," had obviously to be dropped from the service of the United Nations.

TAA could do comparatively little, financially, to tempt the potential expert. Salaries were reasonably attractive in comparison with those in government or academic service, even in Canada or the United States. But they were often meagre in relation to what the expert could earn at home in business or in the more remunerative professions. More than one competent professional gave up an assured income of over $100,000 a year to work for TAA at about one-tenth of that sum. Except for resident representatives, or heads of missions, the maximum paid was usually about $1000 a month, tax-free, plus subsistence in part or in whole. More frequently the figure was within the $600 to $900 range.

As a result of the high qualifications demanded and the limited financial rewards obtainable, the only really persuasive arguments that could be used with most of the prospective experts were, first, the interest of the task; second, the prestige of service as a representative of the United Nations; and third, the human needs of the people to be assisted. Such an approach was likely to be successful only when the businessman, the professional or scientific expert, or the administrator, was also a person of broad human interests, and infused with some measure of the true missionary spirit. This combination, in the acquisitive society of the modern industrialized state, is not by any means common. Nevertheless, it represents the kind of person required in the field of international technical assistance. Any other type, regardless of his specialized qualifications, would almost inevitably fail. Hence, an increased salary range might have been dangerously unwise if it had been set high enough to tempt those primarily interested in money.

Still another aspect of the recruitment problem lay in the particular attitude of certain governments or groups of governments. It was always impracticable, for example, to send a Jewish expert to one of the Arab States, or, except in special circumstances, a citizen of the Netherlands to Indonesia. It was also vitally important to avoid the nomination of a group of experts of a single nationality to aid a single recipient country as, for example, to propose a mission that was predominantly composed of United States citizens to a Latin American state. Any such arrangement would *prima facie* be unacceptable to the recipient government and would give further ammunition to those few governments that professed to see the technical assistance programmes merely as a disguised form of economic imperialism.

In addition to the identification of individuals who were technically competent, personally suitable, nationally or racially acceptable, and, finally, available, there were other difficulties to overcome in the recruitment of a technical assistance expert. The candidate had to be physically capable of enduring the circumstances of life in the country in which he was being asked to serve. In some cases these could be notably severe; in none were they likely to be really easy. Disease was always a threat; dysentery was almost a part of the contract. Good transport and communications were likely, at best, to be intermittent. Food was often strange and not always appetizing. The climate in many of the underdeveloped areas was far from salubrious; the customs alien; the usual services inadequate or lacking; and the language strange. As R. D. Cleghorn, a Canadian teacher on assignment in Africa, described it,

> There is nothing romantic, exciting, or very ego-satisfying about this task. It is hot, sapping, frustrating, and never-ending work. The language barrier and poor plant facilities sometimes appear to be more than one can cope with. But the job is there. It is a big job. And it is educational.
>
> One feels, as he sweats and talks himself into a state of wet weakness, that among the dark and intent faces confronting him are those of future administrators, perhaps a future Education Minister. Here, this is no idle dream. Here, education is still for the fortunate few. And they shall be the leaders.

Very often, also, the prospective expert had to consider the effect of life in the country in which he was being asked to work on his wife and family—or to be reconciled to leaving them for a long period at home. Of course, there were also compensations—travel, new experiences, new beauties of nature, and above all, for the man or woman truly interested in the task, new intellectual problems and new friends.

A vital step in the processing of the expert was the submission of the nomination for the approval of the recipient government. This often was, and still is, a source of considerable difficulty. Because of unsatisfactory arrangements for internal clearance, approval may be so delayed that in the meanwhile the expert will have changed his mind, or may be faced with altered personal circumstances which make him no longer available. Experts of the quality described are hard to find at any time, but for most of the 1950's, with the economies of most western nations functioning at a quickened tempo, the domestic demand for men and women of competence was high, the salaries tempting, and the opportunities wide. There was a seller's market for intelligence and ability. This made it doubly difficult to obtain specialists of the essential quality in the requisite numbers.

On the whole, the quality of the experts recruited by the United Nations (and the Specialized Agencies) has been remarkably high. Few informed observers would dispute the conclusion that no other comparable body has maintained a standard that has been so consistently superior. It is true that there were failures and incompetents. The expert in Iran who ran off with a camel-driver's wife did not add to the prestige of the United Nations—and didn't finish his job. Nor did the adviser to the Government of Paraguay who kept his white Cadillac parked in front of his temporary house in one of the most poverty-stricken capitals in the world. Nor did the phoney British naval captain, whose forged credentials fooled all concerned, who ran up unpaid bills for luxurious services all over the country of his assignment, who threatened the President (in person) with a suit for damages because a local mongrel had enjoyed a successful romance with the Captain's prize (bulldog) bitch, and who when fired by TAA borrowed enough money from the governor of a British colony to return home in the luxury to which he had become accustomed. (When the Government of the United Kingdom put him in jail he wrote protesting letters to the *Times* as well as to the Secretary-General of the United Nations.) But these cases were so infrequent that they could almost be enjoyed. Far more numerous have been the many experts of unquestioned talent, character and reputation who have sacrificed time, comfort and income to the advantage, sometimes the repeated advantage, of countries in need of aid.

A final and onerous responsibility of TAA was created by its type of operation, which necessarily involved the processing of a great volume of reports from experts in the field, and from fellows and scholars. Some five thousand of these could be expected to arrive in the course of a typical year. Each had to be studied, analysed, and, in suitable cases, recommendations had to be implemented. No report could be disregarded. The work on a report might involve the attention of one man for half an hour or the efforts of various divisions of the Secretariat, intermittently, for weeks or months. Apart from the immediate administrative problems thus presented, there was the obvious necessity of drawing from these reports a series of general conclusions on the technical assistance activities of TAA as a whole. This process of generalization was important for the assessment of the current programme and as the basis for decisions as to future policies and procedures.

The work of TAA was further complicated by the number and com-

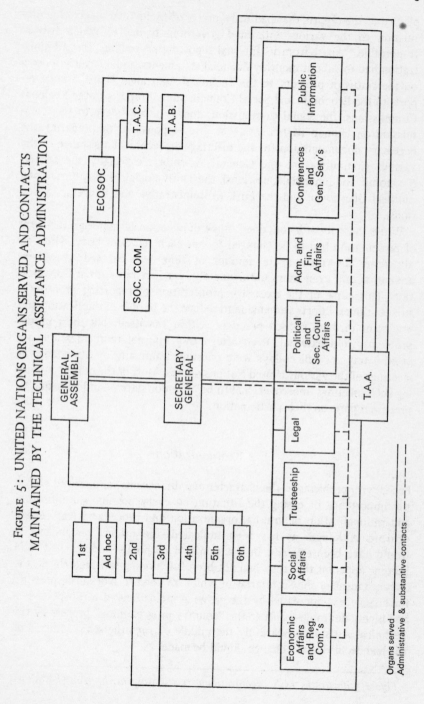

FIGURE 5: UNITED NATIONS ORGANS SERVED AND CONTACTS MAINTAINED BY THE TECHNICAL ASSISTANCE ADMINISTRATION

Organs served
Administrative & substantive contacts — — — — —

plexity of the reports that had to be prepared by its own officers for submission to the various interested governing bodies to which it was responsible.* Apart from its internal reporting procedures, the Administration had to submit monthly financial statements, and quarterly reports on the status of projects, to the Technical Assistance Board; annual reports to the Economic and Social Council; annual reports to the Regional Commissions, the Social Commission, and at a later stage to the Commission on Human Rights. TAA was also responsible for preparing the necessary documentation for the meetings on technical assistance of the various Committees of the General Assembly, especially the Second (Economic and Financial Questions), the Third (Social, Humanitarian and Cultural Questions), and the Fifth (Administrative and Budgetary Questions).

While these reports contained much duplication of material, the form of presentation had to be changed to suit each recipient body. Thus, an altogether disproportionate amount of time was devoted to self-examination and even more unfortunately, yet inevitably, to self-justification. This curse of the excessive proliferation of reporting procedures still continues. Efforts were made to reduce the burden of duplication and argument through revised practices within TAA itself, but most of the problems were external. Even after TAA's internal reorganization, approximately 260 officer-days were consumed annually by attendance at meetings of the various United Nations organs. Most of the officers attending such meetings, moreover, had to be of senior status—and they had to prepare reports on their participation.

E · Reorganization

Faced with problems of the character and dimensions summarized above, the importance of easing the situation by every possible simplification and rationalization of internal organization and procedures was clearly evident. Although, as has been indicated, the original arrangements would have been effective in a national or corporate body, it had soon become apparent that they had not been functioning satisfactorily in the circumstances of the Secretariat in which TAA had to work. The pressure for change was increased by the growing indications of a prospective— and highly desirable—shift to the "country programming" process by the Technical Assistance Board. By the middle of 1952 the senior officers of TAA had decided that a change should be made.

---

* Figure 5 illustrates TAA's organizational relationship in the United Nations.

Before the end of the year a new plan had been devised which placed all programme activities in one division. Within the division were three geographic units, each of which was made responsible for the whole programme in the social and economic fields—expert services, fellowships, seminars, conferences, workshops and so on. The geographic units were Asia and the Far East; Europe, the Middle East and Africa; and Latin America. All public administration activities, including those of a research and substantive character, were consolidated in a second division. The two divisions were held together, and given policy and administrative guidance, by a strong central office consisting of the Director-General, the Deputy Director-General, the Executive Officer, and a programme control (statistical, recording, and checking) unit. (See Figure 6.)

Although no rearrangement of staff and procedures could solve all administrative problems, the reorganization achieved many of the purposes for which it was designed. The change facilitated, and was in turn aided by, a growing mutual acquaintance and a rising sense of unity among the members of the TAA staff. These improved personal relationships combined with the new organizational arrangements made possible a considerable simplification of departmental methods and procedures. The number of formal communications was greatly reduced, the need for frequent committee meetings with large numbers of participants was decreased, more direct and effective control was established over all departmental activities, and a more accurate and current record of programme developments became feasible.

As a result of these changes it became practical to reduce the number of administrative personnel in spite of a rapidly rising scale of operations. The ratio of administrative to operational expenses was soon reduced to less than six per cent and the efficacy of the new arrangement continued to prove its value over the succeeding years. Before TAA was dissolved in 1959, its administrative expenses were reduced to just over four per cent. By that time, according to those charged with the scrutiny of such matters, the overhead costs of TAA were the lowest in the family of United Nations agencies. It was, of course, far below the ratio of administrative expenses in the foreign aid programme of the United States.*

To understand the significance of the organizational arrangements, the nature and volume of the work performed by the different units of the Administration is worth review.

---

* In an examination conducted in 1953 it was found that the per capita cost of recruiting experts for the Point Four Programme was to that of TAA as 19 to 4.

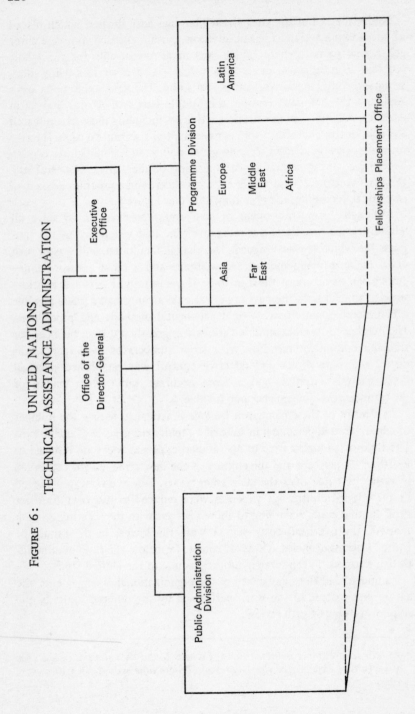

FIGURE 6:   UNITED NATIONS
TECHNICAL ASSISTANCE ADMINISTRATION

The Director-General's Office was responsible for the establishment and the interpretation of policy and for the central direction and co-ordination of TAA activities. It made major administrative decisions, maintained a strict programme control procedure, and was responsible for external representation and contacts. Governmental requests, which were the raw material of the TAA operations, came first to this office. On the average in the course of a year, over eight hundred requests for expert help were received. Through the services of highly competent Executive Officers (Mr. Van Wijk of the Netherlands, succeeded by Mr. Goodkind of the U.S.A.), the Director-General and the Deputy Director-General maintained direct control of personnel and of the domestic operations at the Administration's headquarters. The Executive Officer was also responsible for the preparation of the annual budget estimates to be submitted to the Secretary-General and, with his approval, to the Advisory Committee and the Fifth Committee of the General Assembly. This officer dealt with a staff of about 150 persons in New York. A very efficient programme control section (under Mrs. P. Ross Kidd of Canada) was set up in the Director-General's Office. This centre kept complete and immediate records of every request received from an applicant government and of its subsequent history within TAA. As a result, instant answers could be provided to any question about the work of the Administration. The Director-General and the Deputy Director-General maintained personal contact with or arranged for representation before the General Assembly, ECOSOC, the Technical Assistance Committee, the Technical Assistance Board, the Specialized Agencies, the national and bilateral agencies, and non-governmental organizations of many kinds. These activities, together with the preparation of reports and papers for submission to these bodies, required a good deal of travel and consumed a regrettable part of the time of the officers concerned. Much of this paperwork was of only marginal value for the proper legislative control of the technical assistance programmes, but as it was demanded by the governing bodies concerned, TAA (and other similar organizations) had no alternative but to comply.

The Programme Division (under Mr. Arthur Goldschmidt of the United States), working in close collaboration with the Department of Economic and Social Affairs and with the secretariats of the Regional Economic Commissions, was responsible for planning, scheduling, organizing the substantive management of, and administering the technical assistance programmes in the economic and social fields. On projects calling for the provision of experts, seminars, or demonstration and training-centres, the Division was responsible for the handling of the project from the clarification and assessment of the request, through all stages of implementation, to the review and physical processing of final reports. In the case of fellowships the division, acting in co-operation with the Public Administration Division and the substantive departments of the Secretariat, arranged for the selection and guidance of the successful candidates. Each award involved the study of all competing nominations, the announcement of the award, the arrangement of placement and training facilities, the provision of travel documents, the payment of stipends, the review of interim and final reports, and the follow-up on the subsequent history of the fellow or scholar in his own country. Fellowship awards under the Regular and Expanded Programmes varied from a low of about 350 to a high of about 950 per year.

The Programme Division also administered the TAA office in Geneva. The function of that office (under the able direction of Mr. Maurice Milhaud of France), was to brief experts recruited in Europe, to place and brief fellows and, under the Regular Programme, to administer a scheme of social welfare assistance and exchange of personnel among European countries.

As has been indicated, the Division was divided into three geographical units, for each of which an area office was organized at headquarters. These area offices, in addition to being responsible for the strictly operational aspects of the programme, maintained contact with the active departments of the Secretariat to ensure the proper briefing and servicing of experts. The operational duties included the selection of experts and field personnel, making arrangements for their briefing and travel, checking on operating conditions in the recipient country, and dealing with the solving of problems on the termination of service. In the case of requests for equipment, the area offices obtained the necessary specifications and arranged for the purchases to be made through the established United Nations channels. Direct relations with recipient governments were maintained by these offices, chiefly through the resident representatives, or through the permanent national delegations at the United Nations. On both substantive and administrative matters the area office was the sole channel of communication between headquarters and experts in the field. This avoided the confusion that inevitably results from the use of multiple channels and ensured that field correspondence was conducted by head office personnel who soon became familiar with field conditions and personally concerned with the welfare of field personnel. Arrangements were also made to have senior headquarters staff given the experience of assignments in the field and by 1959 almost every senior member of the staff had held at least one post abroad.

The Public Administration Division (initially under the distinguished leadership of Hubertus Van Mook of the Netherlands and subsequently under the equally able direction of S. B. Bapat, India, and F. J. Tickner, United Kingdom), was directly responsible for TAA's activities in its special sphere. Because of its substantive responsibilities in public administration this was perhaps the most vital as it was the most unique of TAA's responsibilities. In consequence it deserves particular attention.

It is probably quite safe to say that there is no other large organization in the world in which so much emphasis has been placed on administration as is the case in the Secretariat of the United Nations. This has been due in part to the immediately difficult problems of organization and operation in the Secretariat itself, in part to the personal views of Secretary-General Hammarskjold as to the importance of administration, and in part to the great number of requests for aid in this field that have been addressed to the United Nations. In connection with the last factor it was obviously important that if the United Nations was to act as mentor and guide to countries in need of administrative aid, the organization itself should set a good example.

Parenthetically it might be observed that in view of the importance attached to administration it has been rather astonishing that, although the United Nations Secretariat and its procedures have been under almost constant review and although that body has undergone a long series of reorganizations, the United Nations' own Public Administration Division, which has included some of the world's leading theoreticians and most practised administrators (such men as Bapat, Emmerich, Tickner and Van Mook), has seldom been used for advice or counsel on Secretariat problems. Instead, these tasks have from time to time been assigned to senior officials temporarily without other employment (whose competence and experience in administration have greatly varied), or quick decisions have been taken on the advice of other officials whose original appointments and normal duties had no reference to such responsibilities. As might have been expected there have been some rather whimsical results.

As organized in TAA the Public Administration Division consisted of three small units—one for research and conferences; one for the Western Hemisphere; and one for the Eastern Hemisphere. Operational and substantive duties were divided among all three. The two area units were responsible for experts and training-centres, and worked with the Programme Division in integrating projects for public administration with country programmes, and in maintaining an appropriate geographical distribution of projects.

The division itself undertook the briefing of public administration experts in New York before they went into the field, and a similar service was performed for the division by the TAA office in Geneva. It was also the task of the division to review reports of experts prior to their submission to governments and the Programme and Public Administration Divisions worked together on the selection of candidates for fellowships and scholarships in public administration. Finally, the division supervised the assignment and subsequent distribution of studies undertaken for the United Nations by the International Institute of Administrative Sciences in Brussels, which had a contract to supply technical materials in its special fields of expertise.

Reviewing TAA's record of activities during the 1950's, the organization's story can be statistically summarized in this way. An annual average of over 800 requests for experts and 1,500 requests for fellowships was handled. A central staff of less than 200 persons serviced, on the average, (a) over 600 experts recruited from some 55 different countries and working in over 65 recipient states; (b) over 600 fellows or scholars selected from 70 countries and being trained in more than 40 host areas; (c) 20 to 25 seminars, training or demonstration centres, or continuing institutes. In carrying out these duties the Administration in a typical year handled funds totalling over $7,000,000, processed nearly 1,000 final and 4,000 interim reports from fellows, scholars, or experts, and received mail at a per capita rate eight times higher than the average for the Secretariat as a whole. During this period just under one-third of all mail received at or dispatched from the United Nations headquarters was dealt with by TAA, although its staff was less than one-fifteenth of the total.

F · Amalgamation with the Department of Economic and Social Affairs

To complete the story of TAA it is necessary to record the way in which its life as a separate department of the Secretariat was concluded. The tale is not without drama as it includes an account of the only instance in which the Assembly (through its committees) decisively defeated the Secretary-General on an issue of a character which would normally have been left to his own administrative discretion.

The organization of the United Nations Secretariat is almost exclusively dependent on the judgement of the Secretary-General. He could be over-ruled as to the composition and form of the establishment by the General Assembly acting on the advice of the Advisory Committee on Administrative and Budgetary Questions but, except for placing limitations on funds and numbers, this power is most unlikely to be employed.

Internally, the Secretary-General is faced with the competing claims of a great variety of interests and activities and of those who espouse them. Externally, he must be aware of the demands generated by the rapidly changing political, economic, and cultural setting in which the United Nations operates. It is his duty to decide among the many pressures to which he is subjected and to mobilize the resources of the Secretariat to meet the demands which he considers most important, as well as those that he must accept—regardless of his personal judgement—because of decisions taken by the General Assembly or the various councils.

The essence of Trygve Lie's approach to the post of Secretary-General can be gleaned from the following statement in the published record of his seven years in office.

> The group of Assistant Secretaries-General was to be my official "cabinet", available for advice on all matters—not least on questions related to their respective "home areas". I delegated them broad administrative authority from the beginning. (Trygve Lie, op. cit., p. 51.)

Mr. Lie's Assistant Secretaries-General were few in number (seven or eight) and each headed a major department of the Secretariat. These also included the Director-General of TAA. Below them was a level of Directors of principal bureaus or of divisions of these departments. The Directors were described as being "co-ordinate with rather than subordinate to" their department heads. However, a real gulf existed between these two ranks, despite the lip-service paid to their alleged equivalence. Lie devised this rather implausible arrangement as a means of spreading responsibility while at the same time restricting the number of his immediate advisers. The nominal equality of status also allowed him to point to a wide geographical distribution of major Secretariat posts. It is noteworthy that just before his resignation, the first Secretary-General was entertaining the idea of reducing the number of Assistant Secretaries-General who reported directly to him to three, plus the Director-General of TAA.* Within this administrative structure he felt free to attend personally to the pressing matters of peace and security—Palestine, Kashmir, Korea—that so dominated the first few years of the United Nations.

In Trygve Lie's views on technical assistance as on other matters, he favoured the creation of strong functional bodies.

> International co-operation gains added force if it can be kept functional; the pragmatic approach can go farther than the bureaucratic. (Trygve Lie, op. cit., p. 145.)

---

* The Director-General had from the beginning been given Assistant Secretary-General's status and emoluments.

It was for this reason that he argued for the unquestioned primacy of the United Nations among the international agencies. It was for this reason, among others, that he had stressed the desirability of centralizing control of the Expanded Programme within the United Nations. This suggestion he put forward on two occasions, first during the discussions leading to the establishment of the new Programme, and again during the crisis over the powers of the Technical Assistance Board in connection with the "country programming" issue. From the standpoint of operational efficiency he was unquestionably right. He had a far clearer view of the problems that would be created by the decision to maintain the independence of the various Specialized Agencies in this field than did most other observers.

Dag Hammarskjold agreed with his predecessor in believing that the United Nations should hold the primary position among the international agencies, but by the time he came into office the issue had been settled insofar as the technical assistance programmes were concerned. He could and did argue for a more powerful role for TAB, but the hope of establishing a single administrative body for the Expanded Programme had by then been recognized as impracticable.

The major difference between the two views of the Secretary-General's Office lay in the greater degree to which Hammarskjold brought the resources of the Secretariat under his own direct control. Whereas Trygve Lie had less than ten officers reporting to him the number was eventually raised by Hammarskjold to over twenty.

Dag Hammarskjold was unquestionably one of the most remarkable and most enigmatic men of his generation. Coming to the post of Secretary-General without warning and without specialized knowledge of many of the most important problems the United Nations would have to meet in the succeeding years, he established for himself and for the post of Secretary-General an influence and prestige that constituted the most significant development in the functional history of the United Nations during his time. His intellectual capacity, his negotiating ability, his personal integrity and distinction made him a force that could not be disregarded on international issues. Not the least of his capacities was his ability to engage in hard, constant, all-absorbing and almost unremitting labour. The simple physical strain of his engagement on United Nations duties would alone have been beyond the capacity of most men. But until his tragic death Dag Hammarskjold survived the pressures with apparently undiminished vigour and continued his daily routine of negotiation, study, and administrative oversight with only the most occasional intermissions.

In addition to the political responsibilities assigned to the Secretary-

General in the United Nations Charter and those acquired through the new dimensions given to the post by Dag Hammarskjold himself, the Secretary-General was responsible for the organization and administration of the Secretariat. On the complexity of this task it is unnecessary to elaborate; it is sufficient to recall that it involved control over a staff of more than 4,000 persons drawn from 70-odd countries, scattered over the world in dozens of missions, offices, commissions and individual assignments; five official languages; and an organizational structure inherited largely from the complex models of war-time Washington. The proper oversight and operation of this machinery would be more than a full-time task for an administrator of the highest capacity and widest experience.

There was more than a little justification for the repeated Russian complaint that the administrative duties of the Secretariat were so heavy that they should receive the constant and undivided attention of the Secretary-General. The fact that the Soviet complaint became persistent only after Mr. Hammarskjold began to extend the political responsibilities of his office in ways that Moscow disapproved, did not lessen the validity of their basic criticism. There is, in fact, a convincing argument to be made in favour of the proposal for the appointment of a Deputy Secretary-General and for the assignment to him of most of the administrative duties now directly performed by the Secretary-General himself. No other organizational decision would do so much—assuming the selection of a first-class administrator for the second post—to improve the operational record of the United Nations Secretariat. The present standard is by no means wholly unsatisfactory but, given the exceptional personal quality of a large proportion of the staff, it should be outstandingly good.

Hammarskjold had practically no administrative experience. Whether or not he had the qualities that would have made a good administrator is doubtful, but no one will ever know. Deeply and constantly involved as he was in political issues of the gravest importance and urgency, he had no real opportunity to prove his executive capacity. He cast some doubts on his potential ability as an administrator by trying to deal with almost everything himself. Nor did he display any remarkable talent in the selection of his immediate assistants and staff. Dag Hammarskjold was much more successful in the choice and marshalling of ideas than of men.

In his first year in office, Hammarskjold began a reorganization of the Secretariat at the senior level. He requested and received the permission of the Ninth General Assembly (Autumn 1945) to terminate the "double echelon" of Assistant Secretaries-General and Principal Directors. They were replaced, where possible, with a single level consisting of "Under-Secretaries and officers of equivalent rank," * or a total of seventeen senior officers reporting directly to him. (See United Nations Document A/C. 5/728, November 7, 1957.) A number of more junior officials also took their orders directly from the Secretary-General. A related move was the amalgamation of the Social Affairs Department and Economic Affairs Department in the summer of 1954. From his statement to ECOSOC regarding this merger, an insight can be gained into Hammarskjold's view of how the Secretariat should operate:

> I look toward a shift of emphasis away from certain of the existing information services and clearing-house activities; a more limited framework for the prosecution of certain work requested of the Secretariat in order to bring it within the proper sphere of the Secretariat's competence: the reconsideration of certain low-priority projects by the organs concerned; the recognition of the full responsibilities of the Specialized Agencies for particular tasks clearly within their mandate. . . .
>
> These changes are designed to ensure closer integration of social and economic activities, stronger policy direction, greater coherence in internal programming, more logical grouping of functions and responsibilities, simplification of lines of authority, and staff economy. (United Nations Document E/2598, May 13, 1954).

He added at the same time that there seemed to be an advantage in maintaining a separate Technical Assistance Administration.

For several years, starting in 1951, when TAA was but a year old, the General Assembly's Advisory Committee on Administrative and Budgetary Questions had been advocating the consolidation of the then-independent Departments of Economic Affairs and Social Affairs, and TAA. In its report to the General Assembly after the first year's operation of the Expanded Programme, the committee raised the following questions:

> 1/whether the continued operation of the Departments of Economic Affairs and Social Affairs is administratively sound and economical in view of the establishment of the Technical Assistance Administration; and

---

* This concept of equal status for two officers, one of whom in normal practice necessarily reported to the other—as well as to the Secretary-General—was derived from the Secretary-General's Swedish experience. Apparently it works well in that country, which must be interpreted as proof of some peculiar capacity inherent in the Swedes that is not shared by others.

2/*whether an effective co-ordination of the activities of the three units as a whole can really be achieved within the existing structure.* (United Nations Document A/1853, 1951.)

During his incumbency, Secretary-General Lie agreed to the amalgamation of the two substantive departments. He maintained, however, that technical assistance operations would be hampered rather than made more efficient by being consolidated with units of a quite different character and of a contrasting pattern of activities.

In succeeding years the arguments in the Advisory Committee for the amalgamation of TAA with the Department of Economic and Social Affairs continued, although they seemed to find little support in the Fifth Committee or other committees of the Assembly. Moreover, it was known that within the Advisory Committee itself there were some grave doubts as to the desirability of the proposal. The member from the U.S.S.R. was the most ardent advocate of amalgamation but his arguments in the Fifth Committee, of which he was also a member, were so extravagant in their forecast of possible savings, and so sweeping in their advocacy of changes in the whole scheme of technical assistance, that he harmed rather than strengthened his case. He argued, for example, that the regional economic commissions should take on most of the responsibility for technical assistance. This idea was anathema to most delegations because it was recognized that such an arrangement would result in these regional agencies becoming pressure groups for their respective constituents. It was also felt that to assign operational responsibility for technical assistance programmes to these physically scattered and research-oriented bodies would divorce them from effective Assembly and ECOSOC control, and at the same time place upon them duties that they had little competence to perform. Among other absurdities, an arrangement of this kind would have meant either the confining of expert recruitment for regional service to the region itself, or else the creation of large recruitment units in each regional commission to carry on its world-wide search for experts.

A more apparently logical argument for amalgamation came from the United Kingdom representatives whose arguments were characteristically echoed by the Australians. They insisted that any amalgamation would be a good thing because it would result in economy in posts and administrative expenses. While this was not necessarily true the argument had at least a superficial plausibility.

Although the Assembly showed no enthusiasm for the proposal to amalgamate TAA with Economic and Social Affairs, the Advisory Committee continued to press the idea on the Secretary-General. In its 1954 report, the committee stated that it "trusts that within two years the Technical Assistance Administration will be amalgamated with Economic and Social Affairs." Again in the spring of 1955 the committee declared that it was waiting with anticipation for "the Secretary-General's report on how the Technical Assistance Administration might be amalgamated."

Within the Secretariat also there were advocates of amalgamation, particularly, as was to be expected, among some of the membership of the substantive departments servicing TAA. To what degree this was the result of reasoned conviction and to what extent it reflected the obvious and far from surprising desire of some members of the research departments to increase their personal or departmental responsibilities, is a matter of opinion; undoubtedly both influences were at work.

Another factor contributing to the pressure for change was the continuing debate between the Advisory Committee and the Secretary-General over his proposals for the reorganization of the Secretariat at its senior level. TAA was an important point of issue in this contention, for it incorporated a "double echelon" of Director-General and Deputy Director-General, and both now held the rank of Under-Secretary. At this time the Advisory Committee was espousing two somewhat contradictory views on the reorganization: one deplored the existing system and sought simpler lines of authority with fewer Under-Secretaries reporting directly to the Secretary-General. But at the same time that the committee was advocating the amalgamation of TAA in part to reduce the number of senior posts, it was actively arguing for a wider geographical distribution of top-level assignments in the United Nations service!

The Secretary-General was, of course, fully aware of the arguments for amalgamation that were being advanced both in the Secretariat itself and in the Advisory Committee. But he was not quickly persuaded. In November, 1955 he reported to the Fifth Committee:

After renewed deliberation, I have reached the conclusion that, for the time being at least, a formal merger of TAA with the recently reorganized Department of Economic and Social Affairs would offer little, if any, advantage in terms of either administrative economy or, more importantly, of the more efficient and expeditious prosecution of technical assistance programmes.

I am convinced, on the contrary, that any arrangement that would result in greatly enlarging the already extensive and complex responsibilities carried on by the Department of Economic and Social Affairs would be bound to create difficulties and delays to the detri-

ment of technical assistance activities. (United Nations Document A/3050, December 2, 1955.)

The Secretary-General sought to divert the pressure by recognizing a need for greater "integration" of the activities of the two units. To this end, he proposed to implement the recommendations of a survey group (four senior members of the Secretary-General's own executive staff) that had been appointed to study the whole question. The survey group had suggested that greater integration could be achieved through an "out-posting" of some of TAA's headquarters staff to the offices of the regional economic commissions (which were maintained by the substantive department). This, the Secretary-General held, would enable both units to be brought into closer relationship on field operations.

The response of the Advisory Committee was to report to the Fifth Committee that they recommended against the out-posting of TAA personnel. Their grounds for dissent were that this might "parallel Economic and Social Affairs activities and that recipient countries might still wish to deal with top TAA [Headquarters] officers" as they now did. (United Nations Document A/3050, December 2, 1955.) Moreover, they noted in their report that they were "still inclined to believe that the normal arrangement should be a merger of TAA with Economic and Social Affairs." The Secretary-General, during the debate in the Fifth Committee, said, in reply to this criticism, that

> *His proposals went far to meet the Advisory Committee's concern for the integration of the programme within the Department of Economic and Social Affairs. The recommendations reflected the need for the improved use of over-all resources of the Secretariat in the Technical Assistance Programme and for a clear definition of Headquarters responsibilities. The substantive Departments should give TAA much more help than had hitherto been the case: that could best be done, not by duplicating resources, but by distributing the workload throughout the competent parts of the Secretariat.* (United Nations Document A/C.5/SR.524, December 8, 1955.)

After a good deal of debate the Fifth Committee gave limited approval to the proposed decentralizing of the TAA staff and recommended that the scheme be critically evaluated after a year's experience. The debate, however, for the first time evoked some forcible statements in opposition to the Advisory Committee's stand on amalgamation. Some of the underdeveloped countries, being convinced that they were receiving effective service from TAA, instructed their representatives to enter the battle on the side of the Secretary-General. Specifically, they supported the Secretary-General's proposal for the out-posting of TAA personnel, which they were confident would not disturb the harmonious relations prevailing between TAA and the under-developed nations.

The strongest supporters of amalgamation were still the countries of the Soviet bloc; they continued to believe that a merger would result in considerable economies, although they failed to adduce any concrete evidence in support of this belief.

The Eleventh General Assembly in the autumn of 1956 received a report from the Secretary-General indicating that the experimental out-posting of TAA personnel could not be evaluated on the basis of the limited results so far experienced. Permission was granted to continue it for another year.

By November 1957, the Secretary-General had made up his mind that amalgamation would be less disruptive than the continuing public debate on the issue. There is little doubt that he came to this conclusion reluctantly and that if it had not been for the repeated insistence of the Advisory Committee he would have been glad to drop the whole idea. He was opposed to amalgamation but he thought that it was unlikely to do any great harm, and it would stop the argument. He was not prepared, however, to go the whole way at once. In a report on the Budget Estimates and Organization of the Secretariat at the Senior Level to the Fifth Committee he announced his acceptance of the idea, in principle, in the following words:

> So far I have advised the General Assembly to postpone the consideration of an amalgamation of the Technical Assistance Administration and the Department of Economic and Social Affairs. In an arrangement intended to provide a more lasting organizational frame-work for activities of the Organization, I consider that strong reasons of principle and logic exist for an early integration of the technical assistance activities within the United Nations Secretariat with the Department of Economic and Social Affairs; in view of the many and important practical considerations involved, the matter will require further study. (United Nations Document A/C.5/728, November 7, 1957.)

In support of his new position the Secretary-General also suggested that there would be an advantage in having the number of departments in the Secretariat correspond to the number of councils; that it was "logical" that there should be concentrated in a single department all the elements necessary to serve a particular council to which the department would be directly responsible—i.e., the Department of Economic and Social Affairs, with TAA incorporated, to ECOSOC.

It is noteworthy that the amalgamation decision was made in conjunction with over-all proposals for the reorganization of the Secretariat's senior level of officers. With the dissolution of TAA, two of the five Under-Secretary posts which Hammarskjold hoped to delete from the rolls would be accounted for. But the "reasons of logic and principle" of which he spoke here, and several times later, were never elaborated in detail. The "practical considerations" for delaying action which Hammarskjold mentioned in the last sentence of his quotation likewise were not spelled out, but were understood to relate to the disposition of the two senior officers of TAA. (Both officials had offered their personal resignations if these would in any way be helpful.) But the Secretary-General hoped to use the Director-General to launch the proposed International Civil Service scheme (OPEX), and this project had not yet been approved. Elimination of the Deputy Director-General's position posed the problem of losing a "Latin American post" in the Secretariat, and this would be hotly debated. Moreover, the incumbent, Dr. Gustavo Martinez Cabañas, was one of the most influential and popular members of the Secretariat and would be very hard indeed to replace if he should resign following the amalgamation to which he was known to be strongly opposed.

In accordance with the normal procedure the Advisory Committee received, to review for the Fifth Committee of the General Assembly, the Secretary-General's paper in which he committed himself to eventual amalgamation. In its report to the latter the Advisory Committee confined itself to noting receipt of the Secretary-General's promise and adding that

... while it appreciates the practical aspects of the question [the Committee] hopes that the Secretary-General will be able early in 1958 to formulate plans and, as soon as practicable thereafter, achieve full integration of the arrangements in question.

The views of the senior officers of TAA itself were set out in carefully restrained representations to the Secretary-General. Both political and administrative arguments against the abolition of TAA were summarized in their submissions.

On the political side it was pointed out that in the eight years of its existence, TAA had established particularly intimate and cordial relationships with the governments with which it had been working. The submergence of TAA would inevitably have an adverse effect on these relationships and it would, in addition, be interpreted as a down-grading of technical assistance as a function of the United Nations. Administratively, the work done by TAA, being almost wholly operational in character, could not be easily or beneficially merged with the research and substantive activities of the Department of Economic and Social Affairs; it required a different type of personnel and was performed at a different tempo. Mr. Hammarskjold was reminded that he had himself pointed out that amalgamation would "create difficulties and delays to the detriment of technical assistance activities" because the Department of Economic and Social Affairs was so large and was already engaged on very complex responsibilities. The Secretary-General had also repeatedly informed the Fifth Committee that amalgamation would not result in any appreciable financial savings.* It would probably create difficulties, temporarily at least, with the regional economic commissions with which TAA had worked out mutually agreeable methods of co-operation, while the commissions' relations with the Department of Economic and Social Affairs were, traditionally, much less harmonious. Amalgamation would also lower the level of contacts with governments, would adversely affect the carefully nurtured esprit de corps of the present staff, and would be unlikely to result in any closer or more concordant relationship with the staff of Economic and Social Affairs than already existed.

It was well known in the Secretariat that an exceedingly close, effective and co-operative relationship did now exist between TAA and most parts of ESA. Indeed the co-operation between TAA and, for example, the fiscal division and many of the Social Affairs units, was already much closer, more amicable, and more mutually helpful than that existing between various components of ESA itself.

The reports of the Advisory Committee and of the Secretary-General, both advocating amalgamation, were received by the Assembly's Fifth Committee. Meetings covering two days, December 10–11, 1957, concentrated almost exclusively on the question of the proposed merger, although the meetings had initially been convened to consider the wider question of the general reorganization of the Secretariat's senior posts. A vigorous debate took place. Having been warned of what was to be proposed, in part by their general acquaintance with Secretariat matters; in part as a result of the inept lobbying by officials from the Secretary-General's office and by one or two of the more irresponsible junior members of the staff of the Department of Economic and Social Affairs; in part by the activities of a senior officer of TAA who, having presented his resignation to the Secretary-General, felt free to express his views; and finally, by a badly drafted paper on the subject circulated in the Secre-

---

* *The Director-General of TAA noted in a memorandum to the Secretary-General that amalgamation would save the difference between his salary and that of a director but doubted that any other significant economy would result. He twice offered to resign if this would in any way assist in reaching a solution to the problem.*

tary-General's name, many of the members of the committee came to the debate prepared to examine the proposal with jaundiced eyes.

It was, of course, clear to everyone who had followed the debate over the years that the Secretary-General was not enthusiastic about amalgamation nor was he intellectually convinced. He was giving in to external and internal pressures because he did not feel very strongly on the subject and was prepared to sacrifice his own views on this issue in order to put an end to a tiresome controversy, and in the hope of gaining support on other, and in his view more important, issues. Unwisely he left the preparation of his case for the Fifth Committee to aides who knew little about the technical assistance programmes and who were not in sufficiently close touch with the departments concerned to obtain and develop the knowledge they should have had to establish a plausible case. When eventually the Secretary-General himself presented his arguments for amalgamation to the Fifth Committee, he lacked the knowledgeable and sophisticated support that would have helped him to avoid the difficulties he encountered.

As the officer charged with the organization and administration of the Secretariat, the Secretary-General was not constitutionally required to seek formal approval for such a step as the amalgamation of two departments. But as Hammarskjold had previously explained his reasons for keeping the departments separate, and as the issue had become a matter of concern to governments as well as to the organizations directly involved, he felt that it was incumbent upon him to place the matter before the committee and to record the grounds for his radical change of position.

As was to be expected, the argument against amalgamation and for the continued independence of TAA was led by representatives of the under-developed countries. The main points in their case were (1) that if Economic and Social Affairs with its existing work-load was already the most heavily burdened department in the Secretariat as the Secretary-General and others had stated, it was unreasonable to add further to its responsibilities; (2) that it was unwise in principle to amalgamate two units with essentially dissimilar functions; (3) that the Secretary-General had repeatedly said that no significant savings in funds or in the number of posts would result from the proposed change; (4) that the whole technical assistance programme would be down-graded by the abolition of the independent department and its submergence in another; and (5) that TAA had performed its duties in an exemplary manner and had established intimate and effective relationships with governments, all of which would be placed in jeopardy if the Administration were abolished. (United Nations Document A/C.5/SR.641, 642, December 12, 13, 1957.)

The proponents of amalgamation, primarily members of the Soviet bloc, stressed the greater efficiency to be gained by the centralization of control, and the financial savings which would result from the elimination of a vast number of posts which (contrary to the Secretary-General's explicit statements) they still believed the merger would make possible. Certain of the advanced countries, notably Sweden and the United Kingdom, also seemed to favour the merger on the general grounds that any amalgamation should result in a reduction in the number of personnel, but when they had assessed the prevailing temper of the committee they decided to be discreet rather than resolute. A motion to postpone any decision for consideration at a subsequent session of the Assembly was introduced. This motion was, in reality, a recommendation against amalgamation but it was put in the chosen form to avoid a head-on clash with the Secretary-General and with the Advisory Committee. The motion was passed by a vote of 45 to 2, with 16 abstentions. As a result, for the first and only time in the experience of the United Nations, a proposal by the Secretary-General on an organizational problem that was constitutionally within his own prerogative, and which he had actively espoused, was shelved by action of the General Assembly.

Following the Assembly's decision to defer action on the merger, the officers of TAA put forward a proposal which they considered would both maintain the identity and independence of the Administration and yet provide the Secretary-General with a means of solving the problem on his chosen basis of "logic and principle." This suggestion was to move the Public Administration Division with its substantive activities out of TAA so that the latter could confine itself exclusively to operational functions. This would rationalize the whole organizational arrangement by eliminating any mixture of functions in a single department.

The TAA proposal would undoubtedly have gone some way towards satisfying those delegations that supported the idea of amalgamation, and would have been acceptable to those who were opposed. It would also have been logical and readily defensible on the basis of principle, and be thus in accord with the Secretary-General's declared philosophy. However, Hammarskjold was a proud and sensitive man and the rebuff he had received in 1957 had not been easily accepted. He was now in no mood to compromise on this issue. For the next round he laid his plans with far greater care.

During the intervening year the Secretary-General took a direct personal interest in the preparation of his case. A great deal of lobbying with influential delegations was organized but it was carried out, on this occasion, by the Secretary-General himself. He also arranged support for his case by using two more or less unemployed under-secretaries—a Russian and an Englishman—to review the situation and prepare a report advocating amalgamation.* The report which they presented to the Secretary-General was, on the most favourable interpretation, a most disingenuous document but it enabled the Secretary-General to claim that two very senior officials had reported in favour of his proposals.

In October 1958 the Secretary-General informed the Fifth Committee that "the time has come for the establishment of a unified department." (United Nations Document A/C.5/752, October 16, 1958.) As in preparing for the debate he had left little to his immediate aides, so in the committee he himself appeared to present his case and to argue that the course he advocated would reduce the administrative machinery, diminish the volume of correspondence, decrease the amount of time spent in attending meetings, and make substantive staff more readily available for field assignments. He also made concessions. He denied that his proposal would in any way submerge the technical assistance activities of the United Nations and promised that a "clearly identifiable entity" would be preserved under a Commissioner of Technical Assistance. The steps involved in effecting the change-over would be as follows: (1) the functions of the Department of Economic and Social Affairs would be combined with those of the Technical Assistance Administration, but would not include the work of the Public Administration Division; (2) a new unit for public administration would be headed by an Under-Secretary, and a new Commissioner of Technical Assistance (economic and social matters) would also have the rank of Under-Secretary; (3) a unit concerned with Technical Assistance Operations (to be called TAO) would be established within the Department of Economic and Social Affairs, and it would be headed by a Director under the Commissioner; and (4) a Planning Board consisting of senior officers of the enlarged department would be established to co-ordinate policy for technical assistance.

---

* *The quality of this report can be estimated when it is understood (a) that neither of the under-secretaries had any previous knowledge of technical assistance, (b) that the Briton had only a limited experience and the Russian none in administration, (c) that they did not discuss the problem they were supposed to be studying with the responsible officers of TAA, nor —in spite of promises to do so—did they show their report to these officers, (d) that their ignorance of the way in which technical assistance was organized as between the United Nations and the Specialized Agencies was so complete that they actually proposed that the Technical Assistance Board should also be included in the proposed amalgamation, and (e) that their political understanding was of such a quality that they even suggested that UNICEF might also be incorporated in ESA.*

It will be observed that in outlining these proposals, which were obviously designed to meet some of the criticisms of his earlier plan for amalgamation, the Secretary-General abandoned finally any attempt to effect any saving in senior personnel. In place of a Director-General and a Deputy Director-General, the new plans provided for a Commissioner for Technical Assistance, a Director, and an Under-Secretary for Public Administration. It is true that the last named was intended as a temporary arrangement to continue only until some special plans of the Secretary-General in the public administration realm were piloted through the Economic and Social Council and the General Assembly, but this was not explained to the members of the Fifth Committee. And in the end, when this post of Under-Secretary was abolished, a new post of Director was established. The fact is that amalgamation did not, either immediately or eventually, result in any recognizable reduction in costs or personnel.

This time the Secretary-General had done his preparatory work well. The whole weight of his office and his personal prestige were brought to bear. He demanded, and received, promises of support from each of the major powers and they in turn put pressure on the others. It was well, for his cause, that these steps were taken. Anything less would have resulted in another defeat because the majority of the countries concerned were still at heart strongly opposed to his plans. However, the Advisory Committee, recalling its earlier advocacy of amalgamation, and disregarding the Secretary-General's reiteration that no savings in personnel or money were to be anticipated, was willing to go along with the new proposals. The Fifth Committee, perhaps rather frightened by its own temerity in denying the Secretary-General's requests in the previous year now, with obvious misgivings and a marked lack of enthusiasm, acquiesced. The vote was 33 to 0, but there were 26 abstentions.

On January 31, 1959, after almost nine years of effective operation, the Technical Assistance Administration was abolished.

In its ultimate result the amalgamation of TAA with the Department of Economic and Social Affairs was not particularly important. There is much truth in Pope's line "Whate'er is best administered is best." Competent officials could do a satisfactory job under either the old or the new dispensation. Psychologically the arrangement with an independent TAA had certain definite advantages which were lost when it disappeared. The technical assistance activities of the United Nations are not now as clearly identifiable as was previously the case, and the public administration function has suffered badly since it also has now been incorporated in the already swollen Department of Economic and Social Affairs. But under the present Under-Secretary (the exceedingly able and devoted

TABLE 7

Distribution of Programme Costs Expended by the
Technical Assistance Administration, 1950–1958

(*Thousands of U.S. dollars*)

| | OPERATING COSTS | | | | | | ADMINISTRATIVE COSTS | | TOTAL | |
| | Project Costs | | Operational Costs | | Total | | | | | |
	Amount	%	Amount	%	Amount	%	Amount	%	Amount	%
July 1950–Dec. 1951	732	61.1	295	24.7	1,027	85.8	170	14.2	1,197	100.0
1952	4,524	83.3	576	10.6	5,100	93.9	332	6.1	5,432	100.0
1953	4,215	79.8	724	13.7	4,939	93.5	341	6.5	5,280[1]	100.0
1954	3,844	82.6	565	12.1	4,409	94.7	245	5.3	4,654[1]	100.0
1955	4,982	86.6	532	9.2	5,514	95.8	239	4.2	5,753[1]	100.0
1956	6,199	87.0	636	9.0	6,835	96.0	287	4.0	7,122	100.0
1957	5,686	85.4	655	9.8	6,341	95.2	318	4.8	6,659	100.0
1958	6,010	85.7	680	9.7	6,690	95.4	326	4.6	7,016	100.0
Total	36,192	83.9	4,663	10.9	40,855	94.8	2,158	5.2	43,113	100.0

Source: *Annual Report of* TAB, 1956, 1958.
Note: [1] Includes costs of ITU and WMO

TABLE 8

Project Costs by Type of Assistance Dispensed by the Technical Assistance Administration
Under the Expanded Programme, 1950–56

(*Thousands of U.S. dollars*)

	Expert Services		Fellowships		Equipment/Supplies		Total	
	Amount	%	Amount	%	Amount	%	Amount	%
July 1950–Dec. 1951	484	66.1	224	30.6	24	3.3	732	100.0
1952	2,367	52.3	1,836	40.6	321	7.1	4,524	100.0
1953	3,286	78.0	643	15.2	286	6.8	4,215[1]	100.0
1954	3,127	81.3	467	12.2	250	6.5	3,844[1]	100.0
1955	3,631	72.9	1,216	24.4	135	2.7	4,982[1]	100.0
1956	3,861	57.4	1,847	27.5	1,014	15.1	6,722[1]	100.0

Source: Annual Report of TAB, 1956.

Note: [1] Includes costs of ITU and WMO

TABLE 9

Experts Engaged by the Technical Assistance Administration Under the
Expanded and Regular Programmes 1952–58

	1952	1953	1954	1955	1956	1957	1958	Total
Expanded Programme	343	389	366	457	465	516	524	3,060
Regular Programme	108	105	132	107	168	226	158	1,004
Total	451	494	498	564	633	742	682	4,064

Source: Official Records of ECOSOC, 1952, 1953, 1954, 1955; Annual Report of TAB, 1956, 1957, 1958.

TABLE 10

Fellowships Awarded by the Technical Assistance Administration Under the
Expanded and Regular Programmes, 1952–1958

	1952	1953	1954	1955	1956	1957	1958	Total
Expanded Programme	443	436	165	517	632	430	554	3,177
Regular Programme	286	191	175	286	308	288	244	1,778
Total	729	627	340	803	940	718	798	4,955

Source: Same as Table 9.

Philippe de Seynes of France) there is a continuing and slowly expanding programme of technical assistance, especially in relation to the newly
independent states of Africa. Looking back, amalgamation can be seen
as having been, on balance, unnecessary and confusing, but not a major
calamity. It saved no money, did nothing to improve the service, but
did no very significant harm.

CHAPTER SEVEN

The Present Programmes and the Future Needs

Before proceeding to a consideration of future needs and prospects it may be useful to draw up in summary form an assessment of the situation that has resulted from the developments outlined in the preceding chapters.

As matters stand in the mid-sixties an under-developed country in need of external aid to strengthen its economy, to improve its administrative techniques or to help its people to move towards a more decent and more hopeful life, is faced with a wide array of agencies and of programmes from which to choose. Although the total quantity of aid is inadequate and some of it inappropriate, there is no lack of variety in kind, or of channels through which help may be sought. And with all its shortcomings, to have brought about within a period of about a quarter of a century an almost universal acceptance of the philosophy of general responsibility for the welfare of all peoples is a very remarkable and a wholly unique achievement in the history of international relations.

From the beginning of the present era during which international assistance has been accepted as a natural and indeed an imperative component of national policies, there has been a widespread, continuous and very proper questioning of the methods employed, as well as of the scope and direction of the various aid programmes. The importance of finding satisfactory answers to the problems of content and of form is increased by the steadily and rapidly rising pressure for more and more aid from those countries that have now become accustomed to look for this kind of support for their national development projects.

At the same time many of the donor countries, being continually importuned to increase their contributions, show strong signs of becoming less and less satisfied with the degree to which their past assistance has been appreciated. Nor are they satisfied with the extent to which their aid has produced beneficial changes in the countries that they have helped. In many cases they attribute this failure to inexcusable errors of omission or commission on the part of the recipient governments or peoples. Donors are also showing increased skepticism toward the thesis that if only more were given much better results would accrue. There is in many cases a very sincere concern both with the methods by which aid is provided and the use to which it is put. Before agreeing to a vast extension of the scope of assistance, there is an increasing desire to be assured that both its form and its utilization will be improved. This new disillusionment is perhaps more widespread in the United States than in any other country and it is undoubtedly associated with the recent relapse into an isolationist attitude by many of the people of that country. But this is not by any means the whole explanation. In other countries as well there has been a growing concern with the failure of the aid programmes to produce the expected results, and an increasing desire to ascertain the causes of this lack of success.

It is for these reasons that it is important to take a careful look at the scope and diversity of the present programmes before going on to consider what objectives should be accepted for the future character and dimensions of international aid.

It would be useful to begin by reviewing what is presently being done. Much of what follows has been covered before but to facilitate its assessment it is repeated here in brief and related form.

A · A Summary of the Present Programmes

In 1966, technical assistance is made available to under-developed countries through four basic types of programme: 1/ those operated by international organizations within the United Nations family; 2/ those organized by individual nations on a bilateral basis; 3/ those administered by regional bodies, as in the case of the Colombo Plan or the Alliance for Progress; and 4/ those developed by private and voluntary organizations. Because of frequent changes, and as has already been pointed out (in Chapter Four), it is impossible to calculate precisely the number of technical assistance programmes in operation at any one time. Moreover, there is a considerable amount of overlapping in the sources of funds and in the personnel involved in these programmes. It is possible, however, to make a tentative estimate of the numbers involved and at the same time to indicate, in a general way, the scope of their activities.

Of the more than twenty-five countries that provide technical assistance under bilateral agreements most if not all contribute also to the various United Nations programmes. Of the twenty-three or more inter-governmental arrangements for dispensing technical assistance within designated areas of the world some are based on political alliances, some on historic relationships, and some are open to all countries that choose to join. Among the more than 165 well-established voluntary agencies of various kinds which conduct regular programmes, and the many other organizations and even individuals who carry on limited versions of technical assistance there are, of course, extreme variations in size and coverage as well as in character.

Because of the difficulty of obtaining accurate information about the aid programmes of the u.s.s.r., China and the communist bloc countries, no allowance has been made in the foregoing brief survey for the participation of those countries—although there is no doubt that the programmes are both continuous and extensive.

As has already been recorded, some of the current programmes ante-date the United Nations, British and United States efforts in technical assistance. Some, like the work of church missions, gave technical assistance long before it had become a defined and self-conscious task and before it had been given that name. In general, it can be said that these national and group programmes did not take on a consistent form until the announcement of Point Four in 1949 and the inauguration of the Expanded Programme in 1950. Furthermore, the now generally adopted methods of technical assistance were worked out and formalized only after a good many years of trial and error. Today they can be divided into three major classifications.

These categories have been usefully defined by Gustav Papanek (Gustav F. Papanek: "Framing a Development Programme," *International Conciliation*, 527, March 1960, pp. 307–372) in a way that can be summarized as follows:

The first is assistance in the carrying out of a specific operation by the provision of expert advice, directed toward the solution of an immediate and concrete problem. The second type is based on assistance through the teaching or training of individuals or groups as the method of transferring knowledge. Assistance in the establishment of viable institutions to perform technical functions on a continuing basis is the third basic method covered by Papanek's definitions.

The categories of aid are not, of course, independent of one another and many technical assistance projects combine two or all three in varying proportions. A knowledge of the three techniques is basic to an understanding of the possibilities inherent in the whole scheme of international aid. A review of how each operates will contribute to an informed evaluation of what is currently being done.

Assistance in the carrying out of a specific operation usually means the provision of an outside expert to advise on the direct performance of some technical task. This kind of aid becomes necessary when either there is no local personnel trained in the particular operation, or when the local technicians have encountered difficulties which they cannot surmount. The kinds of tasks for which outside experts are recruited are of an infinite variety. In some cases the problems can be solved by an individual, while in others a group of experts may be required. As an example of the former may be cited the case of a steel-rolling mill in Pakistan, which was plagued by continuing difficulties in operation. The United Nations was able to provide a Yugoslav technician who during a visit of about four months succeeded in identifying and removing the "bugs," with the result that output was quickly increased by some fifty-four per cent. Groups of experts have provided technical aid which has made possible the construction of electrical generating-stations and of adequately designed and equipped airports. Other illustrations include the work done by a single specialist sent by FAO to help villagers in the rural areas of the Sudan to develop an adequate water supply, and by a doctor sent by WHO to help eradicate yaws in Thailand. An experienced technician was sent by the United Nations to advise the government of Ceylon on the construction of low-cost housing, and an engineer sent by the Colombo Plan directed the building of an important dam in India. Typical examples of work done through the provision of teams of experts can be found in the surveys of national economic resources as a basis for the formulation of comprehensive development plans which have been carried out under the auspices of the United Nations or of the World Bank.

This kind of direct participation by outside experts in development projects often includes provision for the training of local individuals as a part of the programme. In fact, it is a rather unusual project that lacks this component and most technical assistance agreements specifically provide for the appointment of counterpart personnel by the host country. Such persons are almost certain to receive at least some measure of training by osmosis, if not by more active intent. Assistance on a particular project may also involve the supply of equipment as in the case of machinery provided by UNICEF to a DDT factory in Yugoslavia, the installation by the OAS of laboratory equipment in a university in Brazil, or the distribution of scientific and technical literature by UNESCO through a centre established in Mexico City.

Technical assistance in teaching or training means the provision of opportunities for the nationals of an under-developed country to acquire the knowledge or techniques necessary to perform work previously done (or yet to be done) by experts imported from abroad. This may be accomplished through individuals or groups; it may be implemented in the recipient country itself or may require foreign study by those being trained. There are few aspects of human knowledge, from medicine to agriculture to social defence, that have not been included in such training projects. When training is done locally a selection can be made from a variety of procedures. The essential element is the recruitment of a foreign expert who can provide the required instruction. This may be a visiting professor sent by the United States AID programme to a university in Turkey, or an instructor from the United Nations for a housing research centre in Indonesia, or a doctor from WHO sent to a health demonstration project in El Salvador. Regional training-centres of a permanent nature have also been established in many areas and for a wide variety of purposes and in these instruction is provided for successive groups of students.

Technical seminars, conferences and workshops are other widely used devices for the transfer of knowledge and the exchange of experience.

Fellowships for study abroad constitute the most widely used component of this second form of international aid. They are in fact the oldest as well as perhaps the most characteristic form of technical assistance. As already noted, the United Nations and the Specialized Agencies award over two thousand fellowships in an average year, in the course of their Regular and Expanded Programme operations. It is estimated that countries outside the Soviet bloc offer about one hundred thousand educational opportunities each year to foreign students and trainees while the communist countries according to recent calculations have been training something over fifteen thousand foreign fellows or scholars each year in the recent past.

In the bilateral programmes, overseas training normally means the acceptance of an invitation to study only in the country which offers the fellowship. In the facilities provided by the United Nations organizations, and in the case of some of the regional programmes, there is a wider field of selection. For example, an engineer from Nigeria interested in rural land development was recently awarded a fellowship by the United Nations to study the Israeli experiences in this field; an Indonesian student was awarded a fellowship through the Colombo Plan to study tropical medicine in India; and having been awarded a fellowship by OAS, a Colombian town planner was enabled to study the successful low-cost housing programme of Puerto Rico.

Aid in the establishment of permanent organizations is sometimes referred to as "institution-building," as its aim is to create and firmly establish agencies that will play a continuing role in the process of modernization in the countries in which they are set up. This form of assistance goes beyond just the solution of an immediate problem or the provision of temporary training opportunities, although it often involves some elements of each. The factors of permanence and of close integration in the social economy of the nation are the distinguishing features of an organization of this kind. Illustrations of this type of aid are of many kinds, including such things as international organizations in the field of telecommunications, the establishment of the governing body for a customs union, and the development in Cairo of a publishing agency to produce Arabic books in Braille.

An ICAO project in Iran provides another good example of aid in institution-building. In response to a request from the Iranian government, the International Civil Aviation Organization agreed to send an expert in air transportation to assist Iranian Airways in improving their organizational arrangements and simultaneously to supply a team of experts to train personnel of the Iranian Department of Civil Aviation in the operation of ground facilities and services. The prime object of this mission was not just the immediate training of personnel or the short-term improvement of airline operations, but rather to develop an organization capable of functioning on its own in the modern world of air transport. Another example is the work done by a number of experts assigned by the United Nations and FAO to organize agricultural marketing and credit co-operatives in a number of under-developed countries. The servicio, the well-known and widely practised device of institution-building used by United States programmes to develop local skills in the administration of economic development programmes through joint management by United States and domestic personnel, is another illustration of this principle at work. The negotiation of inter-university contracts under which a university in a developed country works directly with a university in an under-developed nation to improve the research and educational and administrative practices in the latter, is also an example of this kind of technical assistance.

Among the most important and most widely practised programmes of institution-building are those concerned with the improvement of administration in the under-developed countries. Mr. Willard Thorp, one of the earliest exponents and administrators of technical assistance programmes in the United States, described the situation both accurately and succinctly when he said in 1950 that "an under-developed country often has an under-developed government." (Willard L. Thorp: *Practical Problems of Point Four*, Annals of the American Academy of Political and Social Science, 314, July 1950.) Experience since this was written would certainly justify an even stronger assertion today. It is difficult to think of an under-developed country anywhere in the world that has anything that could possibly be described as a really competent adminis- tration. Israel, and perhaps the Sudan, Jamaica (under Mr. Manley) and Costa Rica, or at a somewhat different level, Mexico and India, come nearer than most others to being exceptions to this rule.

It has already been emphasized that under the conditions of rapid social and economic change which are required in the poorer countries if they are to experience sustained growth, the lack of an efficient and honest public administration comes near to being a fatal handicap. The development and successful implementation of plans for economic pro- gress and social welfare require machinery for planning, regulation, and management. Moreover, because of the emphasis on state aid and active participation in economic development that characterizes so many of the under-developed countries, the dangers resulting from a shortage of com- petent administrative personnel in government service must be heavily underlined. The newly emerging countries need not only to reorganize and to improve the administrative machinery that now exists, but they must also create new departments and agencies to deal with the ex- panding demands of independence and growth.

The United Nations has tried to meet this critical need by establishing a broad programme of technical assistance in public administration. It provides experts to give advice on subjects ranging from budgetary pro- cedures to personnel management. Fellowships are awarded for overseas study by civil servants; conferences and workshops are held in various regions of the under-developed world; and technical literature dealing specifically with the administrative problems of these countries is dis- tributed by the United Nations through the International Institute of Administrative Sciences in Brussels. In addition, the United Nations has helped to establish and support eleven regional training institutes in public administration located in Brazil, Turkey, Egypt, Costa Rica, Burma, Argentina, Libya, Sudan, Iran, Nepal and Ethiopia. These public adminis- tration programmes have been growing in scale to such an extent that they now account for more than fifteen per cent of the total annual expenditures of the United Nations on technical assistance.

Before leaving this general discussion reference should also be made to such organizational initiatives as that of the European Economic Com- munity Commission which up to January 21, 1965 had provided nearly $40 million for assistance to eighteen African nations which are associated with the European Common Market. The commission, under the Yaounde Convention of June 1, 1964, has accepted a target of about $730 million to be provided for this purpose over a period of five years.

B · Certain Specialized Activities

As the nineteen-fifties moved toward a close, four new projects which both broadened and gave more substance to the concepts of international assistance emerged within the framework of the United Nations family. In their order of appearance they were 1/ the OPEX Programme to provide governments with senior administrative personnel to perform operational and executive functions within, and as members of, the public services of the countries concerned; 2/ the United Nations Special Fund to provide grants for pre-investment projects basic to economic development; 3/ the International Development Association designed to offer flexible or non-conventional loans for development purposes and 4/ the International Finance Corporation. The directions taken by these new programmes were similar to those previously explored by the Technical Assistance Board and by those who had been trying to gain support for the establishment of a large United Nations fund for economic development, and while they could not be said to be adequate either in design or in size to meet the obvious and steadily increasing need, they did mark a signal advance on what had been done before. However, unless they are endowed with greater financial resources and operated under more flexible and generous conditions than are possible at present, they are likely to fall short even of the more realistic expectations of those responsible for their original designs. But they are of sufficient importance to justify in each case a brief individual review.

1/ The Opex Programme

Reference has already been made to the new concept of technical assistance in administration originally developed in 1950 by the United Nations Mission to Bolivia (page 62). In 1956 in an address at McGill University Secretary-General Hammarskjold, having adopted this idea as his own, made a concrete proposal for the creation of an international corps of experts in administration, from which individuals could be recruited to provide the kind of high-level and high-quality service that was so glaring a need in the less-developed countries. His proposal at first varied from that of the Bolivian scheme in that it embodied a co-operative element, with a permanent panel of international civil servants from which individuals could be seconded to under-developed countries. At the same time nationals from the countries being assisted would be seconded for training in the service of the United Nations itself. After further consultation with his own staff, with member states and with the Specialized Agencies, however, it was decided to return to the original Bolivian idea and to concentrate on the provision of a service that would, on request, provide appropriate and specially-recruited personnel to operate as members of the public service in the applicant countries.

Under the OPEX scheme, which is operated by the United Nations Secretariat, experts in any field of professional competence, including those covered by the Specialized Agencies, may be appointed at the request of any government that recognizes a deficiency in its administrative procedures or substantive capacity and that decides to take advantage of this service to work toward a solution of its problems. The OPEX expert is recruited by the United Nations and then enters the service of the requesting government. He is paid the same salary a national of the host country would receive in the same post. The United Nations supplements this salary by an amount necessary to bring the expert's income into line with that paid to United Nations personnel recruited for the more conventional advisory services abroad.

There is a fundamental difference between an advisory expert and an expert nominated under the OPEX scheme. The former is charged with the responsibility of giving advice to the government that has requested his services on what should be done to solve an identified problem, and on how it should be done. At this point his duty ends although in practice, of course, many individuals, at the request of the government concerned, may in fact do much more than this suggests. But if he does so it is on an informal basis and as a result of the personal relationship he has established with the government to which he has been providing advice. The OPEX expert on the contrary becomes an integral member of the national civil service. In theory at least he is governed by all civil service rules and conventions. He may be reprimanded, penalized or fired at the will of the government. Alternatively, of course, he may be commended, his duties may be enlarged, or he may be promoted to a more important post.

The advisory expert, moreover, is a direct employee of the United Nations and is responsible to no one else; the OPEX expert, while he has a protective contract with the United Nations is, in fact as well as in name, an employee of the government by which he has been appointed. A major element in most of the OPEX assignments is the responsibility placed on the expert to train local personnel to take his place, or to occupy a similar post, as soon as possible. All OPEX appointments are initially for one year, but it is assumed that at least a second year will be necessary if his training function is to succeed and if his general influence on the administrative activities of the public service is to be effective.

Initial progress in gaining acceptance for the OPEX idea was exceptionally slow. Not only the communist countries but many of the "half-developed" states, led in this case by Mexico, professed to see in the idea the incipient danger of a new form of colonialism. The fact that OPEX aid could only be given in response to a national request and that the incumbent could at any time be dismissed by the government in whose service he had enlisted did not seem, to those who adopted this view, to be adequate protection. That the campaign against OPEX was not just another illustration of the hostility of some of the communist and ex-colonial powers to any serious expansion of the United Nations programmes, was made clear by the fact that its most articulate and effective exponent was Dr. Victor Urquidi of Mexico, a man who was normally as strong a supporter of technical assistance as he was eloquent in debate. But most of the opposition came from the communists and from some of the colonial and ex-colonial powers who seemed to fear that if the United Nations entered this field on any significant scale, the newly independent nations might seek administrative help through the international organization rather than from the governments of the metropolitan powers from whom they had obtained their independence, but who still sought to supply them with personnel and policy guidance. The most vociferous and the least influential of these opponents was Portugal. The British, French, Belgians and others did not seek to prohibit the programme, but merely to delay its introduction and to limit its scope. The less than lukewarm temper of the Conservative Government of Great Britain was an illustration of this attitude. David Blelloch described the situation in this way:

> When the Secretary-General of the United Nations asked ECOSOC for authority to establish the Bolivian plan (OPEX) on a more general and systemic basis, Lord John Hope, speaking as United Kingdom delegate, "noted that it was no part of the function of the United Nations to act as any kind of international government, or even to plan for government on an international scale. It should never remotely consider assuming responsibility for the general direction, economic or social, of any nation or region. Countries must plan for themselves and aim to raise standards of living chiefly through their own efforts. . . . The function of the United Nations is to provide a forum for international discussion of problems, common to many, and a channel through which help and advice can be sought on request. These are principles to which my Government attaches great importance. I felt that I must emphasize them again because of the suggestion of the Secretary-General . . . that some kind of career service under international responsibility might be established, which

would provide officials to work in administrations of under-developed countries. This suggestion raises grave doubts in our minds, for several reasons. But I mention it here because it could lead to a degree of control of the policies of under-developed countries. It is not a direction in which we should like to see the United Nations move."

This soapy stuff is one of those typically disingenuous statements which British official delegates so often seem to consider appropriate for international audiences, and which earn them such an unenviable reputation for cheap and blatant insincerity. It is so obvious that Lord John Hope could not possibly have thought that Mr. Hammerskjold's modest proposal might "lead to a degree of control of the policies of under-developed countries." And Lord Hope must have known that his own Government had, only a few weeks before he made his speech, issued a statement of policy (Cmd. 9768) proclaiming its intention "to recruit people with the necessary qualifications for secondment to overseas governments," both inside and outside the Commonwealth. Was this a move towards "assuming responsibility for the general direction, economic or social, of any nation or region"? And could any British Government imagine for a moment that the Governments of any under-developed countries would prefer to have administrators "seconded" to them by itself rather than sponsored by the United Nations? So long as the Governments of important countries can take such a flippant attitude towards the technical activities of the international organisations there can be little hope that those activities will ever be effective.
(David Blelloch: *Aid for Development*, London 1958, p. 39.)

In spite of the opposition and after repeated and lengthy debates in ECOSOC and in the committees of the General Assembly, in which Bolivia and other under-developed countries took a prominent and affirmative part, the General Assembly in November, 1958 approved Resolution 1256 (XIII) sanctioning, on an experimental basis, a programme to provide "operative, executive and administrative personnel" to countries requesting aid of this kind. From this time on the future of the OPEX programme was assured.

In 1959 a special allocation of $200,000 was granted to the new United Nations Office of Public Administration (now the Division for Public Administration) on the understanding that not more than twenty-five OPEX appointments would be made during the financial year. Over one hundred requests were received in the first year from thirty countries, but because those in charge of the programme were being very careful to make no mistakes that would prejudice the whole programme, only eleven appointments were in fact made. The Assembly voted a continuation of the experiments for 1960 and increased the funds to $300,000. A total of thirty OPEX experts were assigned in that year. Among the early appointments as OPEX experts were a Director of Industrial Management for Afghanistan, a Manager of the National Bank of Nepal, and a Director of Fisheries Operations for South Vietnam.

The success of the first two years led the Economic and Social Council to recommend that OPEX be placed on a continuing basis and by Resolution 1530 (XV) the General Assembly made OPEX a permanent programme with an appropriation of $850,000 for 1961. Since that time there has been a steady growth both in the number of requests and of appointments. The service is no longer a subject of active dispute. The opinion of informed observers of the experiment has been well expressed by David Blelloch:

> This new departure in the field of international technical co-operation seems to be of quite outstanding importance, potentially at least, and it is greatly to be hoped that the UN and the specialized agencies will publish, at the earliest possible moment, a frank and thorough evaluation of the results achieved. If the scheme is successful it could develop into one of the most useful and significant forms of aid supplied by the UN family of agencies. Colonialism is dead—no people, whatever stage of development it may have reached, will in the world of today willingly submit to foreign domination. On the other hand, many of the countries which have won independence since modern empires began to decay do not possess the administrative cadres of experience required in order to ensure rapid modernization and industrialization. That they should increasingly rely on the UN to provide them with key officials, capable of exercizing authority without incurring the suspicion of serving any foreign interest, is already one of the most convincing justifications of the UN's existence, and is at the same time one of the most important steps we are likely to witness towards the emergence of one co-operative world community. (David Blelloch: Technical Co-operation and the Development Decade, London, 1964, p. 19.)

2/ The Special Fund

The same session of the General Assembly that approved the OPEX Programme, also gave assent in Resolution 1240 (XIII) to the establishment of the Special Fund. The Fund officially began operation on January 1, 1959 under the direction of Paul G. Hoffman, whose distinguished service in the administration of the Marshall Plan was as widely known as it was universally respected. The basic responsibility of the Fund is to finance the kind of pre-investment surveys, feasibility studies, and the establishment of research and training facilities that are required to encourage the subsequent provision of public or private capital for development projects. The Fund's fields of particular interest are industry, agriculture, transport and communications, building and housing, health, education, statistics, and public administration. Projects qualifying for assistance must fall within one of two broad classifications. The first is those that are designed to bring about a better utilization of natural or physical resources, such as geological and river-basin surveys, general and comprehensive resource evaluations, feasibility studies in relation to particularly promising projects, and the establishment of research institutes for industry and agriculture. The second category includes the creation of institutes for the purpose of training personnel to ensure a better utilization of human resources, and the establishment of vocational schools and advanced technological institutes.

The Special Fund is capitalized through contributions of member states of the United Nations and other well-disposed governments, as is the Expanded Programme. In its first year contributions totalled less than $26 million; and the first year's programme included 44 projects in 50 countries. By 1966, the level of contributions had risen to almost $100 million. A study completed in January, 1964 recorded 421 projects implemented in 130 low-income countries and territories at a total cost to the Fund of $374 million. A valuable aspect of the programme is illustrated by the fact that the recipient countries had contributed $545 million towards the costs of the same projects. A recent study of the first twelve of the Fund's pre-investment surveys disclosed that these surveys had been followed by $520 million of foreign and $236 million of domestic investment on a variety of power, transportation, communications and mining projects.

Although the Fund's resources are received on a yearly basis, grants are made for schemes that may take several years to complete. Projects are executed, whenever possible, through the United Nations or one of the Specialized Agencies, but they may also be contracted out to other agencies, to private firms, or to individual experts. In addition to its Managing Director, Paul G. Hoffman, and his senior and very able assistant Mr. Myer Cohen, the Fund is directed by a Governing Council appointed by ECOSOC, which in turn has the assistance and advice of a Consultative Committee consisting of the Secretary-General, the President of the World Bank, and the Chairman of TAB. (See footnote p. 157.)

Concentrating as it does on relatively large projects which also may involve considerable expenditures for equipment, the Special Fund carried United Nations assistance one useful step forward. In its first year, the average cost of projects to which the Fund contributed was $1,700,000, but as its rules require a maximum of self-help on the part of recipients, an average of over one-half of the cost of the initial projects was paid by the governments which were being assisted. Most of the first projects were surveys of natural resources: minerals, soils, ground water and so on. Among the projects involving the establishment of training and research agencies were such instances as a marine resources institute in Peru, a regional labour institute in India, and a technical university in Turkey.

The Special Fund uses a variety of criteria to judge the value of projects for which its help is requested. Above all it insists that projects fall within a framework of some consistent economic policy, that they involve an element of urgency, and that provision is made to ensure that the assistance provided will result in sustained subsequent action.

The Fund also endeavours to choose projects which will have early and tangible results and which will be likely to attract and facilitate new capital investment from both the public and private sectors of the national economy concerned.

In the case of assistance provided to research and training institutes, support is limited to five years and the amount of aid diminishes in each of the last three years. This arrangement makes it necessary that a thorough appraisal of the project should be undertaken by the Fund and the recipient in order to ensure that the size of the new institution will be kept within such limits as the government can sustain after aid from the Fund is terminated.

Under its present management the whole approach of the Special Fund is business-like and realistic, yet imaginative enough to ensure that there shall be no failure to recognize real opportunities and needs in the under-developed countries. The Fund is performing a useful service in providing the preliminary information and facilities which are essential if any significant increase in capital investments in the under-developed areas is to be both encouraged and realistically anticipated.

The recent amalgamation of the Special Fund and the Expanded Programme should have beneficial results as both are operational in character. Advice and material aid may now be more effectively combined. In January 1966 the new council approved 82 projects costing over $250 million.

3/The International Development Association

In part as a sop to those who during the 1950's were persisting in their demands for grants and for "soft" loans through a proposed Special United Nations Fund for Economic Development (SUNFED), and in part as a result of the pressures for something in the nature of an international development authority, the International Development Association came into operation in November, 1960. The declared purpose of the Association was to finance development projects through long-term loans granted at low interest rates and repayable in whole or in part in local currencies. The Association was affiliated with the World Bank by which it is managed, and it is financed by subscriptions from members of the Bank. But it is designed to do many things that the Bank itself will not undertake.* The latter acquires funds in the private capital market and it must therefore confine its activities to projects that will not adversely affect its general credit standing. Moreover, the Bank is prohibited from equity financing and its loans require the guarantees of governments or of central banks. The new Association therefore was designed to finance a wider range of projects than the World Bank is in a position to support, including projects that are not in themselves revenue-producing or directly profitable. The Association's basic stipulation is that the projects it is asked to finance shall be of "high developmental priority." If that criterion is met, the current loaning policy of the IDA is both generous and liberal: fifty-year terms, ten years of grace for payments on principal, and interest at only ¾ of 1 per cent.

If all the members of the Bank were to join the Association, its total capital would be $1 billion, to be made available over five years. By January, 1961 thirty-seven members had subscribed the equivalent of $852 million, of which the United States contributed one-third.

The Association gives assistance only in under-developed areas and only to its own members. It may provide financing to a government, to a political subdivision such as a province or a state, to a private or public entity in the territories of a member, or to a public international or regional organization.

The International Development Association represents an important step forward in international assistance but it suffers from the same

---

* It should be recorded that as a result of decisions taken at the annual meeting of the World Bank, held in Washington in September, 1965 there has been a remarkable liberalization of Bank policies. It has now been accepted that agriculture and education are basic to development and that Bank funds may properly be expended in these fields. It was also agreed that the Bank would intensify its concern with industrial development.

quantitative shortcoming that afflicts all similar and related activities. The present capitalization, at best $1 billion over five years, is too little even to come near to closing the gap that Hoffman estimated to be $2 billion yearly. If IDA is not expanded to fill this gap, there will be a steadily increasing demand for some other agency to meet the need. The fact that the Association's aid is confined to countries that are members of the Bank sets another and very important limit to its value as an instrument of economic progress.

4/ The International Finance Corporation

A recently-established institution closely affiliated with the World Bank is the International Finance Corporation, which was set up in 1956. Its purpose, like that of the IDA, is to promote economic development by joining with private investors and private management in promoting productive enterprises. Its activities are carried on without governmental direction or guarantees. Unfortunately the scope of its transactions was at the start so restricted as to limit severely the value of its contribution to the development programmes.

Mr. George D. Woods, who holds the presidency not only of the World Bank but of the IDA and the International Finance Corporation as well, argued persuasively in 1965 that the terms of the Articles of Agreement between the Bank and the IFC should be amended to permit the Bank to make loans to the Corporation, within limits, for re-lending to private enterprise without governmental guarantees. With the increased resources that such loans would make available, the IFC could make much larger commitments in individual transactions than was then possible. It would also be able to provide financing in the form of direct loans without equity features. This argument was accepted in 1966 and it is now possible for the IFC to borrow from the Bank up to an amount equal to four times IFC's paid-up capital from governments. The result of this change should be a marked increase in aid to programmes for industrial development.

5/ Other Activities

Among the many other developments that contribute to the general progress being made in the field of international aid during the 1960's, there are a number that deserve special attention, such, for example, as the initiative taken by the Norwegian trade unions in collecting funds for special aid purposes, and the useful programme developed by the government of the Netherlands to provide "junior assistant experts" to act as aides to advisory personnel sent out by the United Nations. The work that Israel is doing in the new states of Africa is of direct benefit to the contributing government as well as to the many recipients. A considerable variety of Canadian programmes of international aid are now being brought into an increasingly useful co-ordination under the active and imaginative leadership of the Overseas Institute established in Ottawa.

Perhaps the most significant as well as the largest of these new initiatives is that of the Peace Corps, organized under governmental auspices in the United States. This body offers a valuable outlet for the energy and the idealism of the youth of the nation and provides the recipient governments with a worthwhile measure of assistance in a wide variety of forms. It provides a ready answer to the question so often addressed by young and active men and women, who want to help those less fortunate than themselves and their compatriots, to leaders in the national and international programmes: "But what can I myself do?" By 1965 over 12,500 Americans had found at least a partial answer to that question by volunteering for service overseas in the Peace Corps.*

An even earlier example of the same kind of thing is found in its British counterpart known unimaginatively as Voluntary Service Overseas. In this case, however, the initiative came from, and the work is still primarily dependent upon, a number of non-official agencies, although government support is now being provided on a rising scale. Starting in 1958 with eighteen people sent to two or three countries in Africa, by 1964 it had 482 volunteers in some fifty-six different territories. Because they describe so well what is being done by the participants in many organizations in many countries, the words of a distinguished journalist, Patrick O'Donovan of the *Observer*, in writing about Voluntary Service Overseas are worth quoting:

> . . . *Voluntary Service Overseas . . . was the first of its sort and it justifies the sort of civilised pride that has taken the place of Imperial pride.*
> . . . *It depends on the enthusiasm of dedicated people. It avoids all political commitments. . . .*
> *Its aims are almost wholly altruistic. . . .*
> *It simply sets out to tap the bottomless reservoir of the idealism and energy of the young. . . .*
> *It is impossible to predict quite what the work will be. A volunteer is likely to end up teaching in a small Indian town with a negro headmaster, or a Sarawak school with a reed roof or at a Uganda*

---

* *Of whom over 8,500 had had actual experience abroad.*

mission. A sixth former, still fresh to classroom discipline, will him-self be exerting it, teaching English perhaps, running games, organis-ing the school play, the Scouts and the YMCA. An ex-apprentice will be teaching bricklaying, mending the Bishop's jeep, going on long expeditions through . . . jungle. A graduate will be teaching his sub-ject to people longing for the only magic that can change them.

And for all of them, the work outside the classroom, the talking, the laughing, the larking about, is at least as important.

Applicants . . . are not taught to argue about politics or neo-colonial-ism. They are told to keep out of local politics, to be themselves, to listen. They appear to be far better at this than their elders. There have been no ugly incidents and virtually no failures. . . .

Before concluding this review such other agencies as the Inter-American Development Bank, the Atlantic Development Group for Latin America, and the important Asian Development Bank should at least be named among the bodies that can be and to some extent at least are being used to assist the economic progress of the under-developed countries.

But in spite of the many agencies and the vast number of people who in the mid-sixties are working, planning, and sacrificing; in spite of the real progress that has been made by governments; and in spite of the achievements that have been recorded by international organizations of many kinds, it is still lamentably true that only a beginning has been made toward solving the contrast of luxury and poverty among nations. That more will have to be done, and done more effectively, if the world is not to degenerate into the kind of perpetual turmoil, kept in bounds only by force, that is the inevitable and natural result of a grossly unequal distribution of the good things of life, is apparent to anyone with eyes to see, ears to hear, with a brain to understand and a heart to care.

C · An Estimate of Present and Prospective Needs

Having reviewed the scope and diversity of the current programmes, it is illuminating to consider the extent and character of the needs these programmes are designed to meet.

All the technical assistance activities that have been described above involve an annual expenditure of somewhat less than $500 million. This money is piped into the field through over two hundred separate channels under an equal number of separate controls. In spite of a great deal of sanguine talk about co-ordination there is, in fact, only a meagre degree of effective co-operation in practice. The work of the Technical Assis-tance Board under the direction of the Economic and Social Council of the United Nations is the only really solid achievement of any magnitude that has been accomplished in this domain.

Detractors of the current efforts to assist the backward nations are critical of both the over-all size of the present programmes and of the complex administrative arrangements which depend on so many agencies and operate such a cumbrous and Rube Goldbergish machine to produce so small a product in applied assistance. The problems of size and of method are closely related, for any considerable expansion of the resources available for technical assistance would certainly and quite justly be accompanied by demands for reform in the organizational arrangements for its disbursement.

Before any definite conclusions in regard to the desirable dimensions of the resources required for aid programmes can be confidently accepted, a great deal more study must be devoted to the recognizable needs of the under-developed countries, and to their ability to utilize additional funds effectively, as well as to the techniques for the acquisition and distribution of such sums.

At the outset it must, of course, be recognized that no easily defined and precise estimate can be made of the financial resources that would be needed to satisfy all the sound and sensible requirements of the under-developed countries for technical and related forms of aid. Even the most expert observers could not be expected to agree on the details and scale of aid required by even one country, much less of 140 or more. The dimensions of the present programmes were initially established more by the political vagaries of the developed countries, and by the individual initiatives of a wide variety of persons and organizations, than by any serious calculation of the over-all requirements for the economic development of the depressed areas of the world. And although the present programmes have expanded remarkably over the years since the end of the Second World War, the reasons for this expansion have not been a careful assessment of actual needs, but have been simply the widespread recognition that not enough was being done to meet even the most obvious and pressing needs. No reliable theory and no accurate and acceptable yardstick have yet been devised to define and measure the national or regional requirements for aid—and none is likely to be invented. Certainly, at present the under-developed countries with their under-developed governments are among the least likely to assess their own needs correctly. It is, however, reasonable to assume that further experience combined with a continuance of the current widespread study of this problem will result in some improvement in the measurement of existing and prospective requirements.

The best that can be done at present is to put together a rather crude estimate of the probable magnitude of the financial demands that will be presented over the next decade to the more important of the technical and economic assistance programmes now in operation. For such an over-all assessment there are two useful sources. The first is found in the forecast of future needs of the United Nations Expanded Programme which are prepared from time to time by the Technical Assistance Board. The second is the estimate of over-all investment needs of the under-developed countries in the nineteen-sixties made by Paul G. Hoffman, Managing Director of the United Nations Special Fund. (Paul G. Hoffman: *One Hundred Countries One and One Quarter Billion People*, Washington: Lasker Foundation, 1960.)

The various programmes of the United States comprise, in total, a much larger contribution to the general effort to assist the needy nations than anything that is done by other countries, and is more significant—in size at least—than what is being done by the United Nations itself. But the United States programmes are so dependent on the changes and chances of national policy as interpreted by different administrations, and as permitted by the exigencies of congressional politics, that there is in Washington only a minimum concentration on forward planning either by estimating of prospective needs or by provision for the pro-gressive expansion of available funds to meet anticipated demands.

Almost ten years ago, the U.N. Technical Assistance Board took a cau-tious "forward look" at the probable financial requirements of the Ex-panded Programme. (*A Forward Look*, Report of the Technical Assistance Board of ECOSOC, United Nations Document E/2885, May 1956). At the time about $25 million were being spent annually on projects under that Programme and the members of TAB estimated that the minimum required would be an increase to $50 million annually "over the next few years." (Five years earlier the proponents of the Expanded Pro-gramme had talked of immediate operations at the $50 million level and of an early rise to $100 million annually.) In 1954 TAB estimated that even $50 million would "do no more than enable the participating organiza-tions to maintain the momentum of present activities . . . and to meet the more urgent requests of newcomers (including a growing number of formerly dependent countries)." More than the "few years" have passed and the present scale of project expenditures under the Expanded Pro-gramme has only recently exceeded the $50 million minimum.

In its report under reference the board noted three reasons for the fact that the resources of the Programme were falling short of current requirements. First, needs arising out of continuing projects and urgent new requests were already exceeding target figures by $3 million, or over ten per cent. Second, there was a widespread feeling that a greater measure of equity in the allocation of Programme resources should be achieved. This would require that more attention be given to such questions as the size of population, level of per capita income, and conditions of health and education. Even to meet the most obviously desirable adjustments, if actual reductions in the programmes of certain countries were to be avoided, would mean increasing yearly allocations by some $8 million. It was clear that many countries were not receiving their "fair share" and this situation could not be remedied in any significant degree unless the total of available resources could be expanded. Finally, experience had already shown that as colonial territories became independent, their demands for aid from international organizations were at once increased. If current target figures were not to be reduced and if any serious effort was to be made to meet these new demands, an increase of "several million dollars" would be required.

These observations are no less pertinent today. The review of the work of the first fifteen years presented by the Executive Chairman of the Technical Assistance Board in 1965 is almost identical in argument, philosophy, fact and spirit ("15 years and 150,000 skills"—U.N. Document E/TAC/103, May 10, 1965). This interesting summary of the work of the Expanded Programme ends predictably with a section called "A Long Way to Go." The contributors to the Expanded Programme have increased its resources only enough to meet the target of $50 million that was considered by TAB to be essential almost a decade ago. Even this amount provides just enough money to keep pace with the volume of requests of the limited types being considered when it was first requested. It has never been thought of as being enough to allow the kind of development of the Programme that a stronger and more equitably distributed fund would make possible, and that the clearly recognizable needs require.

There has always been a wide range of valuable projects that can be considered by the Expanded Programme only if very much larger resources are made available to it. This is, of course, equally true of the bilateral or regional programmes that constitute so large a part of the total effort. The most vital of the areas in which progress should be made are to be found in the logical, and urgently solicited extension of work already in progress. Of special importance is a widening of the limited attention that has been given by the various programmes to basic surveys of the human, water and land resources which are badly needed in almost all of the under-developed countries. Without the kind of data they provide, no confident and dependable planning of development programmes is possible. Such surveys demand the combined skills of many persons, most of them of a type not normally available in under-developed countries. They also require money, expensive equipment and relatively long periods of time if they are to be satisfactorily completed. Some of the money required for these purposes can be supplied by the Special Fund as it contributes directly to its purpose of providing pre-investment information of the most important kind. But much more assistance of a preliminary and of a continuing rather than a pre-investment nature, is urgently required.

The dimension of the monetary needs of the technical aid programmes is dependent in part on what is done in the way of financial assistance to the under-developed nations. Any substantial increase in financial aid would immediately be reflected by a great increase in the demand for technical assistance. Later, as local training-centres and universities begin to produce results, as the personnel of the local economic and commercial institutions begin to gain experience, the requirements for expert advice from abroad can be expected to decline. Any such decline, however, is, in most of the developing countries, still a longe distance in the future.

Reference has already been made (Chapter Three) to Paul Hoffman's proposal in 1960 that the developed countries of the world should adopt as their goal for the nineteen-sixties the doubling of the annual per capita rate of economic growth in the 100 most under-developed countries and territories (not including China). This would mean an increase in the per capita economic growth rate to an average of two per cent annually, and a rise in per capita annual income from an average of $100 to an average of $125. Even this modest proposal, he estimated, would require an additional three billion dollars yearly beyond the present four billion dollars of governmental and private capital that is flowing into under-developed countries each year. Of the additional three billion dollars, he believed that two-thirds would have to come from governmental sources and the remainder would represent the expected increase in the scale of private investment.

It is estimated that technical assistance and related programmes of all kinds were using funds at a rate approaching $400 million a year by the end of 1960 (see Table 11). This amounted to a little under ten per cent of the total annual flow of capital into under-developed countries. If it is assumed that Hoffman's capital investment objectives are achieved and that in 1970 technical assistance funds will be required in the same proportion as before, the result would be a required expansion of $300 million a year in the funds available for technical assistance programmes. If it is further assumed that international, bilateral, regional and voluntary agency programmes would maintain the same proportion and relationship to each other, the following picture of technical assistance would emerge :

TABLE 11

Summary of Annual Expenditures for All Technical Assistance
Programmes and Estimated Needs to 1970 under the Hoffman Plan:

	1960		1970		Increase
	Amount	%	Amount	%	Amount
	(Estimated Expenditures—Millions U.S. Dollars)				
International Programmes:					
U.N. Expanded Programme	32	8.6	58	8.6	26
U.N. Family Regular Programmes	14	3.8	25	3.8	11
U.N. Special Fund	50	13.5	91	13.5	41
Bilateral Programmes:	230	61.5	415	61.5	185
Regional Programmes:	4	1.1	7	1.1	3
Voluntary Agencies:	43	11.5	77	11.5	34
Total Expenditures	373	100.0	673	100.0	300

Many critics have emphasized that to expand the financial base of technical assistance programmes is not by itself an answer to the problems facing the developed and the under-developed countries alike. Some kind of greater coherence in the machinery for purveying such aid to the under-developed countries must be achieved. Harlan Cleveland, who was until recently United States Assistant Secretary of State for United Nations Affairs (now United States Ambassador to NATO) and one of the most active supporters as well as one of the wisest critics of international aid in all its forms, has pointed out that "As things now stand, the leaders of an under-developed country will normally deal with a minimum of sixteen and often with more than twenty different agencies. . . ." (Harlan Cleveland: "The Fits and Starts of Foreign Aid," *The Reporter*, April 16, 1959.) The result is not only an administrative burden on the governments of these countries, but it also contributes to excessive competition among the various agencies and to a waste of skilled manpower, both local and imported.

A different, but related, criticism is that which argues that technical assistance is not itself likely to engender a pattern of cumulative growth in an under-developed country. Even if technical assistance funds are greatly increased, they must be accompanied by massive doses of investment capital if they are to be really effective. (See for example, Robert E. Asher: "Economic Co-operation Under U.N. Auspices," *International*

Organization, 12, Summer 1958, 288–302.) If an under-developed country —or any country—is to raise its average annual per capita income, it must increase the output by its workers on the farm and in the factory. In the under-developed country this will normally mean the acquisition of new techniques and new investment in power-plants, factories, roads, harbours, the development of natural resources, the improvement of agriculture and the training of technical personnel. In developed countries large amounts of investment capital can be obtained from domestic savings. But this is extremely difficult in under-developed countries because the bare subsistence needs of the people take almost everything that they earn. As has repeatedly been emphasized, the enormous growth of the population in these countries makes the problem very much more difficult because it means the division of the already meagre income among a constantly increasing number of people.

Another tremendous handicap has been the impatient but understandable determination of many people in the under-developed nations to obtain an *immediate* improvement in their standards of living. They are not prepared to wait, to make present sacrifices for future gain. This is particularly true of the ex-colonial peoples who during their struggles for independence were often misled into thinking that political independence would result naturally and immediately in a better way of life. When, subsequent to gaining their political freedom, they found that they were still as poor, still as likely to be ill, still as far as ever (or even farther than ever) from the many good things they had been promised or had imagined, their disappointment was only equalled by the vehemence and the persistence of their demands for redress. As a result many of the governments in the under-developed countries have been forced in self-defence into trying to satisfy the expectations of their peoples by diverting to consumptive and entertainment purposes the monies that might otherwise have gone into capital goods to the lasting benefit of the national economy. In other cases governments, for example that of Indonesia, have attempted to distract the attention of their people by embarking on a belligerent or grandiose foreign policy. In the long run, of course, even a military victory is a poor substitute for a full stomach. In still other cases, in many countries in Latin America for example, governments have introduced social legislation which if carried out effectively would strain the resources of a country at a far higher level of economic development. Most of this legislation is not in fact implemented but it illustrates the force of the popular demand.

People in the under-developed nations today are determined to vault over the stage in national development that was marked in England and other industrial nations by the appalling cruelties of the early days of the industrial revolution. It would be easier for the governments of the poorer countries to demand present sacrifices from their people if the latter did not have before them the constant evidence that at least some of their compatriots—and very often those who are known to control the government—are leading anything but spartan or ascetic lives. Gross and conspicuous extravagance are nowhere more evident than in many of the poorest countries in the world.

Bedevilled by circumstances such as these, many of the under-developed countries must borrow the money they cannot or will not supply themselves if they are to make a serious start on programmes of economic development. This is particularly true when such governments face the necessity of meeting the costs of non-self-liquidating projects such as schools, hospitals, roads and sanitation systems. The transfer of technical knowledge and skills must, therefore, if it is to accomplish real and lasting benefits, be integrated with the provision of investment capital. The present aid programmes have, on the whole, done very little in this direction. The United States has done more than any other participant in tying together the two forms of assistance. The Colombo Plan, on its much more limited scale, has moved in the same direction. The United Nations, even with the Special Fund, has so far been able to do comparatively little.

The argument for the integration of financial and technical assistance, and the case for a more consolidated and coherent structure for disbursing international aid, converged in and were illustrated by Sir Robert Jackson's proposal for an International Development Authority. In this plan a single agency would combine all the present United Nations programmes of technical assistance together with a "soft loan" lending agency. (Commander Sir Robert G. A. Jackson: *The Case for an International Development Authority*, Syracuse, Syracuse University Press, 1959.) With these combined responsibilities the Authority could serve as a co-ordinator of both capital and technical assistance programmes. It would, moreover, be in a favourable position to decide what combination of the various forms of aid would be most effective in any specific case. In contrast to the past practice of the World Bank, the Authority would provide capital, in loans and grants, on the basis of approved national development programmes involving facilities and services that might be difficult to justify on purely financial grounds. Under this arrangement, moreover, loans might be repaid in the borrower's own currency.

Sir Robert's Authority would be established under the United Nations and its membership would consist of all governments subscribing funds. Each would be assigned voting rights according to the size of its contribution. Management would be under a strong executive staff very much as in the case of the World Bank. Capital requirements of the Authority were proposed as about $25 billion, to "be used gradually over the years." The extent of yearly operations has never been clearly indicated, but it would probably compare to Hoffman's $3 billion. The Specialized Agencies and the United Nations' own technical assistance operations would not be abolished under this scheme but in Harlan Cleveland's words would revert to performing functions as "research centres and as promoters of scientific collaboration on a world-wide basis. . . ." Finally, it was proposed that the Authority should organize its field work on an evaluation of country and regional needs, rather than by functions as is customary at present.

The case for the Authority has yet to receive substantial backing. It runs counter, of course, to the many vested interests in the Specialized Agencies, the United Nations, and, not least, in the governments of the more-developed countries. Even the Labour Government in Britain has indicated through Mrs. Barbara Castle, the first head of the new Ministry of Overseas Development, who is generally sympathetic to the principle of international aid, that at least for the present it is not prepared, or perhaps it would be better to say, is not in a position, to support such an initiative.

Although no widespread attempt has been made to gain official support for the programme even in principle, the proposed Authority has had a somewhat more sympathetic hearing than was the case of the aborted Special United Nations Fund for Economic Development (SUNFED) which was alternately opposed, postponed and deflected for over a decade by the wealthier countries, led by the United States and the United Kingdom. The SUNFED plan was for the creation of a capital investment fund from which grants and loans would be made to countries in need. In this case also it was proposed that loans might be repaid in local currencies. The Fund would have been controlled by the General Assembly, a provision that was viewed with particular hostility by the countries that would have been expected to become the major contributors but who could have been readily outvoted in that legislative body. Washington and London argued that this would have given a controlling voice to the have-not countries and to the Soviet bloc which would be likely to result in irresponsible decisions as to the size, terms and recipients of the funds dispersed. That there was much justice in this criticism cannot be denied. But it was equally undeniable that had the major powers shown any willingness to approve in principle the idea of such a fund adequate safeguards could have been devised.

It is unlikely that a proposal as radical as that embodied in the International Development Authority will gain general acceptance, sensible as it may be. It will be remembered that when Secretary-General Lie proposed the establishment of a centralized control over the Expanded Programme he met with no success. Today it would also be argued that great improvements have occurred in the administration of the Expanded Programme, that the amalgamation of EPTA and the Special Fund has improved the situation still further, and that the leadership of the Technical Assistance Board has introduced at least a substantial measure of co-ordination into the technical assistance activities of the United Nations and the Specialized Agencies.

While the country programming procedures practised by the Expanded Programme cannot be said to be perfect, they go much further toward rationalizing technical assistance efforts than the practices of most bilateral programmes. It would, of course, make a tremendous improvement if the same nations that complain of the inefficiency in the Expanded Programme would consent to co-operate more fully in field operations, would refrain from political manoeuvring to gain their own ends within the United Nations and the Specialized Agencies, and would make a larger share of their technical assistance funds available to the Expanded Programme.*

From this brief review of the scope and diversity of the programmes of international aid, as they have now developed, it can be seen that there are few areas of social and economic life to which technical assistance is not appropriate, and to which it has not already begun to be applied. The fact is, that there is not today a single under-developed country or territory that has not been a recipient of some form of technical assistance from one or more donors. Significant and valuable as these developments have been, however, it is obvious that the progress that has been achieved in the recipient countries is infinitesimal in comparison with the need that still exists. Over all the efforts that have been made there still looms the shadow of a steadily and rapidly increasing number of human beings who are hungry, illiterate and angrily discontented. In some countries the national economy has not only failed to progress but has actually deteriorated since the end of the Second World War.

Speaking in Toronto in February, 1964, the then British Prime Minister Sir Alexander Douglas-Home said, "It is quite clear that the problem of problems in the years ahead is the disparity of wealth between the rich nations and the poor." He went on to suggest that the prosperous nations that run the world may soon be facing a new 1789 unless in this generation they can enable "the poor and discontented to see the prize before them of the fullness of life." As Sir Alex, when Foreign Minister, had been

---

* *It may be significant that in December 1965 the* U N. *General Assembly set up a committee to "make new efforts with a view to reaching a large measure of agreement" on legislation for a "U.N. Capital Development Fund."*

noted for the evident relish with which he had disparaged the technical
assistance programmes of the United Nations, it must be assumed that
with wider responsibilities he had come to a more favourable view of
the task that those programmes were designed to perform. Whatever
the explanation of the change, there are few informed observers who
would fail to support his more recent judgement. That the world is faced
with a rapidly developing crisis is becoming every day more apparent.

An earlier and more convincing observer of the world's problems, the
late Adlai Stevenson, put the situation in this way in an address to the
Economic and Social Council on July 9, 1965:

> We meet here in Geneva at the mid-point of the Year of International
> Co-operation and the mid-point of the Decade of Development. Let
> us be neither cynical nor despondent about the gap between these
> brave titles and the fact that at the moment, our world community
> is in fact chiefly notable for minimal co-operation and very lopsided
> development.
>
> Let's face it: We are nowhere near conquering world poverty.
> None of us—neither the weak nor the strong, the poor nor the rich,
> the new nations nor the old—have yet taken seriously enough the con-
> trast between the abundance of our opportunities and the scarcity
> of our actions to grasp them. It is good that the rich are getting richer
> —that is what economic development is for. But it is bad that despite
> our considerable efforts in the first half of this decade, the poor are
> still poor—and progressing more slowly than present day society can
> tolerate. What shall we do to improve the trend during the next five
> years? . . . There are clear and present tasks for the developing coun-
> tries in doing what they know is necessary to their own economic
> growth and social progress. There are tasks, equally clear and equally
> present, for the industrialized countries. And there are tasks—a
> growing number of much larger tasks—for United Nations organi-
> zations themselves. . . .
>
> We travel together, passengers on a little space ship, dependent on
> its vulnerable reserves of air and soil; all committed for our safety
> to its security and peace; preserved from annihilation only by the
> care, the work, and I will say the love we give our fragile craft. We
> cannot maintain it half fortunate, half miserable, half confident, half
> despairing, half slave—to the ancient enemies of man—half free in
> a liberation of resources undreamed of until this day. No craft, no
> crew can travel safely with such vast contradictions. On their reso-
> lution depends the survival of us all.

CHAPTER EIGHT

The Prospects for the Future — I

A · *The Situation in 1965*

There are few places and no governments in Asia, Africa or Latin America that have not been affected and influenced in some measure by the assistance programmes of the United Nations and the Specialized Agencies. These programmes have touched the daily lives of countless children, women and men in the poorer countries throughout the world. Millions of people are alive who would now be dead if it had not been for the work of the international organizations.

And it is, of course, true that even more people have been helped by the bilateral programmes of the United States and other countries.

Nevertheless, and in spite of the fact that eighty per cent of the time, personnel and money of the United Nations and its agencies is now devoted to economic, social and administrative co-operation with governments in need of aid, and in spite of the fact that the bilateral programmes are being maintained and in some cases increased, there are today hundreds of millions more people living in misery and frustration than was the case when this work was expanded into a major activity fifteen years ago. In spite of the rather impressive total that comes from adding together the results of all the programmes of technical and economic assistance—international, regional, national, and private—it continues to be true that the gap between the rich and the poor countries is still widening, and that the number of people needing help is steadily, and rapidly, increasing.

Twenty years after the end of the most destructive war in human history, and in a period of almost unexampled turmoil and discontent in the less-developed countries, but of rapidly spreading affluence in their wealthier neighbours, the best that can be said about the efforts being made to foster human progress through programmes of mutual aid is:

1/*that the governments of the world have recognized, in words at least, the fact of their interdependence and the responsibility of* the more fortunate countries, primarily in their own continuing interest, to aid those who cannot solve their problems by their own efforts alone;

2/that a start has been made to organize and operate a series of programmes designed to bring the assistance of technical knowledge, of financial resources, and of personal and official encouragement, to the governments and peoples who badly need such help;

3/that the methods by which help can be provided are being refined and improved, and

4/that the scale of assistance is slowly rising.

If this is the situation after fifteen years' effort it is obvious that major changes of scale, technique or both are required if the new processes of international co-operation for mutual aid are to make the kind of impact that is necessary if solutions are to be found for the massive problems by which the people of the world are afflicted. It is obvious to all those who have any acquaintance with the situation that if the essential changes are to be brought about this will require action within the recipient countries, in the policies of the donor governments, and in the management of the programmes of the national and of the international agencies.* A summary of some of the more important changes that must be sought may help to clarify the situation and at the same time to re-emphasize the objectives that must be achieved.

B · What the Recipient Countries Can Do

The core of the problem is in the under-developed countries themselves. No matter how much goodwill and generally beneficial self-interest is displayed by the governments of the more fortunate nations, and no matter how far generosity and the recognition of that self-interest may increase the financial and other contributions of donor countries, only the most meagre progress can be anticipated unless the recipient countries do much more than they have ever done before to assist themselves. They must be prepared for a vastly increased expenditure of thought, toil and suffering if even their minimum objectives are to be attained. The austere road of progress cannot be travelled in a Rolls-Royce. Among the many ways in which the under-developed nations can increase the effectiveness of their own participation are the following:

---

* That there is no clear and exact line of distinction between donor and recipient governments has repeatedly been noted and should be kept in mind in considering what follows.

1 1/*Population Control*

Very few of the countries in need of assistance are making any serious effort to reduce the appalling speed with which their populations are increasing. Yet this is the most obvious as it is the most dangerous element among the infinitely complex problems they face. It can be taken as axiomatic that few of the under-developed countries whose populations are increasing by over two per cent per annum can have any real hope of social and economic progress. Yet failing such progress major catastrophes will result. It is only necessary to look at the obscene slums of Bogota or Colombo or Cairo, or at the village life of India and Peru, to realize that violent explosions cannot be long postponed. No inheritance of social custom, no prevalence of religious taboos, should be allowed to inhibit remedial action—action which should be taken instantly if tragic calamities are to be avoided. India has begun to break the bonds of custom, Puerto Rico has faced the religious issue and beaten down the clerical opposition. Other governments must do the same or soon face the inevitable and disastrous results. In the past it has been permissible to leave birth control to the individual, which meant, in effect, that its possibilities were understood and its practice extensively applied only by the wealthier and the better-educated members of the community. Until very recently in the history of national communities, there has been no example of a conscious effort to spread the knowledge of contraceptive practices by governmental action. The time has now come when this official abstention not only should, but must, be ended. Education in birth control is today vastly more important than training in the maintenance of health.

2/*Social Reform*

Any significant degree of economic progress in a previously under-developed country will inevitably be accompanied by major structural change. This in turn will create and itself constitute a serious social revolution. When a country begins to climb the steep path of economic development, as Dr. Hans Singer has said,

> there is bound to be a shift away from subsistence production to-
> wards market production; from agriculture towards industry; from
> village life to urban life; from communities based on status to com-
> munities based on function; etc. No economist was hard-boiled
> enough to close his eyes to the fact that these changes—so easily
> set down on paper—involve serious social problems of transition
> and adjustment, many personal tragedies, much tension and unhap-

*piness, and that they carry with them the seeds of social conflict
and disruption.* (Hans Singer: *Problems of Social Planning and Social
Development,* unpublished paper, 1964.)

Among the most obvious problems that must be faced by many of the
less-developed countries today is the fact that little real and certainly no
early economic progress can be expected in those under-developed countries in which entrenched oligarchies successfully refuse to make any
significant sacrifice of privilege for the national good. In comparing the
various countries there would seem to be, outside the communist areas,
an almost direct relationship between the degree of concentration of
economic and political power and the immaturity of the national economy. The report prepared by the group of experts appointed by the United
Nations in 1950 to advise on the problems of the under-developed
countries summarized the situation created by such oligarchic rule in
these words:

> *In our judgement, there are a number of under-developed countries
> where the concentration of economic and political power in the
> hands of a small class, whose main interest is the preservation of
> its own wealth and privileges, rules out the prospect of much econo-
> mic progress, until a social revolution has effected a shift in the
> distribution of income and power.* (United Nations: *Measures for
> the Economic Development of Under-Developed Countries,* New
> York, 1951, p. 51.)

When eighty per cent of the land is held by ten per cent of the people;
when government posts, lucrative business opportunities and professional careers are open only, except in rare instances, to members of a
restricted ruling class; when men of wealth habitually escape taxation;
when the incompetence of administrative practices is only equalled by
the corruption in which they are immersed, and, even worse, when assistance provided by other countries or by international organizations is
diverted to the benefit of local individuals or groups, no amount of foreign
aid is likely to produce significantly beneficial results. Moreover, the
people and the governments that provide the aid will inevitably become
disillusioned and lose interest to the extent that it becomes apparent
that their assistance is being improperly used. When an imaginative, enlightened and generous programme such as that embodied in the Alliance
for Progress in Latin America encounters conditions of this kind it is
almost certain to fail in its major objectives, as has recently been demonstrated in Brazil. Incidentally, the Alliance would have one less obstacle
to overcome, if there was less talk in Washington of the necessity of

the Latin American nations accepting the American way of life if they are to receive the promised help. Fortunately the United States member of the advisory committee appointed to guide the programme did not suffer from this preoccupation. Such men as Mr. Harvey Perloff and others who share his sensitive and intelligent approach are among the major assets of the programme. On the other hand recent indications in Guatemala and elsewhere, that Washington is likely to put down any revolutionary or reform effort in Latin America that enlists, or can be alleged to have enlisted, communist support (as of course all such movements will), makes the future outlook in that part of the world even less hopeful than in the past.

When the national resources of a country can be exploited in such a way as to permit the profits to be immediately expatriated, the nation and its people reap little benefit. The fact that the exploiters may themselves be nationals of the nation thus despoiled is immaterial. As was pointed out in an earlier chapter the Patiños were Bolivians but this was no advantage to their native land as every boliviano they could screw out of their mines and miners was immediately deposited in Paris or London, in Switzerland or Canada. As Gunnar Myrdal has well said, the ruling oligarchies "are often all out for economic development in a narrow sense but would want to see it happen without changes in the social structure within which they are privileged." (Gunnar Myrdal: *An International Economy*, p. 168.) Except in limited and special circumstances this cannot happen.

The history of political conflict, revolution, corruption and social turmoil that marked the beginnings of modern economic progress in the presently highly-developed nations should not be forgotten in considering current conditions in the backward countries. The obstacles to social and economic change were smaller in seventeenth- and eighteenth-century Europe than they are in most of the under-developed countries today. Yet vast social upheavals had to take place and swamps of blood had to be shed in the eighteenth and nineteenth centuries before the national communities of Europe and America could really "take off" into the industrialization phase of development. Grim experiences are almost inevitably ahead for many of the countries that are now striving to break the bonds of stagnation and despotic control. Countries in which conditions of entrenched privilege are allowed to continue unabated can anticipate little general benefit from the United Nations or other programmes of international aid.

Another aspect of the same problem of the influence of powerful vested interests in the recipient country is illustrated by the following excerpt from a recent TAB report:

not even strong government support can always assure the success of a technical assistance project, when it runs counter to strong national sentiment or "vested interests." The Food and Agriculture Organization (FAO) has done a great deal of successful work to improve the working conditions and the economic standards of small scale fishermen in about thirty countries. One of these projects, however, turned out badly when the owners of the big fishing fleets opposed the organization of a co-operative which would have permitted some of the fishermen to own their own boats and to escape from the inevitability of inadequate wages. In another part of the world, an attempt to improve the utilization of forest resources ran into public indifference, which tolerated an uncontrolled and destructive exploitation of rich timber lands. And again, in another region, an attempt to organize better care for lepers was slowed down, despite the strong support of the Minister of Health; the basic weakness was a lack of interest on the part of the local medical services in the treatment of leprosy and insufficient authority to assure a follow-up of the expert's recommendations and demonstrations. (U.N. Technical Assistance Newsletter, Issue No. 53, May 1959.)

With the spread of knowledge, tempers have been rising in most of the poorer areas of the world, and this has had the result in some cases of frightening governments—and the ruling cliques that control the governments—into reluctant, but usually closely limited measures of reform. This process should be encouraged by pressure from outside, as has been done in certain instances by both Washington and London. More frequently, however, outside influences have taken the easier and temporarily more convenient and profitable line of propping up—through subsidies, bribes, and, sometimes, military support—the very elements that are most hostile to serious plans for social progress. Moreover, when the inevitable revolution does break out, and the ruling clique raises the cry of communism, the temptation in the leading capitals is to support the group in power. This has been particularly true in recent years in Washington, where the fear of communism has taken on quite irrational, even pathological, dimensions. In view of the fact that revolution is almost certain during the next few decades in most of the countries of Latin America, the re-interpretation of the Monroe Doctrine by President Johnson at the time of the Dominican crisis in 1965 raises serious questions as to how essential reforms can be effected.

In many cases and as a last resort, nothing short of revolution will offer any hope of breaking the shell of reaction and stagnation that encompasses so great a part of the contemporary world. In such circumstances this too should be welcomed, not condemned. In the words of Thomas Jefferson, "rebellion to tyrants is obedience to God." But to justify itself and to offer hope to its people an upheaval of this kind must aim at a social revolution and not merely a transfer of political authority within the same establishment. A change of exploiters is just a change in the façade of misgovernment. Drastic social reform is an essential element in any plans for economic development. Otherwise it may well continue to be true in many countries today as Plato's Phaedrus said it was in the Mediterranean 2,400 years ago, that when there is "a change in government the poor change nothing but their masters."

3/Organizational Reform

There has been a great variation in the skill with which the recipient countries have organized themselves to procure and to utilize the assistance they have required. In some cases—Yugoslavia, Israel, India, Sudan, for example—the internal arrangements for the identification of needs, the development of requests, the reception of experts, and the final application of external aid, have been handled in a reasonably well-designed procedure that encourages the hope that, unless other conditions make progress impossible, the anticipated and desired benefits may be expected to ensue. But these are exceptions. In most recipient countries it is still unhappily true that one branch of the government often does not know what another is doing; that requests for aid are often the result of departmental haggling and pressures, with the ultimate applications mainly reflecting individual influence or political compromise rather than the objective assessment of national needs; that the abilities of expert advisers are incompetently employed and their proposals disregarded or misapplied; that counterpart personnel are either not appointed at all, are personally inadequate, or are ineffectively utilized; and that efforts are made to use fellowships and scholarships for personal rather than for national purposes.

The losses suffered by a country that allows internal disorganization of this kind to continue have been repeatedly brought to the attention of the governments concerned, but the number of cases in which improvement is still required is disappointingly large.

Basic to all aspects of organizational reform in the under-developed states is adherence to the concept of central planning. Even the most ardent opponent of governmental planning in his own advanced country (except of course when the planning can be directed to his own advantage) becomes a "planner" when he is sent out as a technical assistance expert to aid in the search for a solution to the problems of an under-developed nation.

Whether the preparation and supervision of a national development programme is undertaken by the government itself or by the government with the assistance of a planning board or some comparable agency, is relatively unimportant. But the value of the practice of central planning is now almost everywhere accepted. It is only by this technique that new knowledge can be applied in a concentrated manner, and that some measure of compensation can be provided for the traditional absence of an experienced commercial and entrepreneurial class. In many cases it is only by the exercise of governmental initiative that a hopeful effort can be exerted to speed the processes of economic growth.

This does not, of course, mean that the central government should itself try to do everything that needs to be done. Indeed the success of a government in modernizing and developing the national economy can be judged in part by the degree to which it succeeds in encouraging the growth and efficient participation in that dynamic process by local authorities, private organizations and competent individuals. But for the most effective results all this should be within the framework of certain basic policies designed, and when necessary supervised, by the central authority for the general good.

In this connection reference should be made to a stimulating article in the admirable journal published by the Society for International Development, in which Robert L. Oshins outlined a series of proposals which emphasized and illustrated the desirability of increasing the partici-pation of private agencies, organizations and corporations in the receipt and use of foreign aid, and more particularly of the participation of such bodies in the provision of aid. (*International Development Review*, December, 1963.) The "people-to-people and organization-to-organiza-tion" approach could certainly be used much more widely and more profitably than is now being done. This kind of thing, of course, is much more difficult to organize at the recipient end than among the donor countries. And it would be quite impracticable as a working process for the United Nations programmes, which by definition must operate through governmental channels. Nevertheless, Mr. Oshins' ideas de-serve serious consideration; and to the extent that they can be brought into effective use both donors and recipients should greatly profit. Such pro-grammes, however, can never take the place of governmental action nor could they greatly reduce the need for competent central guidance and control in the recipient country.

It is sometimes argued that the expansion of governmental responsibilities carries with it the dangers inherent in the establishment of a totalitarian society. On this, as on so many other matters, Dr. Myrdal has provided succinct and persuasive comment:

> I believe that a considerable amount of central planning and state direction is quite compatible with democracy and a free society; I do not believe that the advanced countries, because they give ever greater scope for planning and state direction, are moving towards a society with less personal freedom and less democratic participation: quite the contrary. I find no example in history where democracy has been lost because of too much planning and state intervention, but plenty of examples of the contrary. (Myrdal, op. cit. p. 211.)

Paul Hoffman, who earlier in his distinguished career was a most successful practitioner in the free-enterprise/rugged-individualist milieu of the United States, has drawn attention to one of the problems faced by those who believe in planning by government bodies, in the following words:

> International development programmes suffered in the 1950's from an ill-defined but often deep-felt prejudice against anything that involved "planning." For many years the concept of government planning was suspect domestically in the United States and this attitude rubbed off into international planning efforts. (Paul G. Hoffman: World Without Want, p. 120.)

It is of the very greatest importance that this prejudice should be overcome. Fortunately this change is rapidly taking place.

In a recent article in the Fund and Bank Review Mr. Albert Waterston, a member of the development advisory service of the World Bank, clearly summarized the present situation in these sentences:

> The spread of development planning has . . . been stimulated by Western countries providing loans and grants. . . .
> The worldwide acceptance of planning as a means of achieving national development objectives has made academic the doctrinal debate about whether a country should plan. For most countries the question now is how to plan. There are still those who equate planning with socialism or with central controls harmful to freedom and private enterprise but these are "a dwindling band." Sir Arthur Lewis' assertion that "we are all planners now" may have been premature when first published in 1949, but it is not likely to be seriously disputed today.
> (Albert Waterston: "A Postwar Prodigy: Development Planning," The Fund and Bank Review, March 1965, pp. 1, 7–8.)

4/Concentration of Effort

In addition to the reform of organizational arrangements within the applicant countries, a vast improvement in the quality of external aid could be achieved if governments would reduce the present degree of fragmentation and dilution in their country programmes. There are far too many cases in which governments include requests for help in peripheral areas of only marginal value with a consequent reduction in the help that might otherwise be supplied for the solution of problems of more fundamental importance. It makes little sense to ask for aid in devising a code of social security, when the national economy is in such a primitive condition, or in such a state of disrepair, that it cannot conceivably support the expenditure that the implementation of such a code would entail. Or to ask for assistance in the setting up of a system of dental clinics when what is most needed is a clean water supply. Or to seek help in the establishment of a school of music when, as Professor P. M. S. Blackett has pointed out, many hundreds of millions of people are less modern in their dealing with their sewage than were many communities 5,000 years ago. (P. M. S. Blackett, television programme, Canadian Broadcasting Corporation, June 7, 1964.) Those in charge of planning national programmes should be encouraged to identify the basic factors which are inhibiting economic and social progress and to focus all available resources in an attack on these critical points. As Clausewitz said of war, the real attack should be directed at the centre of the enemy's strength.

Although much has been written about the vital importance of industrialization as an essential factor in any programme of national development, this importance is not always reflected in the plans prepared for submission to the international aid programmes. Very often, in fact, requests for assistance are diverted to meet much less important needs. There was some truth in what Oscar Wilde once said, that "industry is the root of all ugliness," although this is not nearly as accurate today as it was in the nineteenth century. There can be no debate, however, about the assertion that no nation can solve the problem of economic stability and progress without the development of its industrial potential. The plan is to set up a centre for the promotion of industrialization studies and projects in association with the Secretariat of the United Nations underlines the importance of this subject.

An essential element in any country's programme for economic and social development that is to have any real hope of success is the emphasis that must be placed on education in its many aspects. Such fundamental absurdities as the case of the poverty-stricken and economically torpid country that until a short time ago had seven universities of which 90 per cent of the graduates were lawyers, while it lacked even one techni- cal school or agricultural training-centre, cannot be allowed to continue if there is to be any valid hope of general progress. Of course, as David Blelloch has pointed out, the present situation is influenced by the fact that in the under-developed country a lawyer can usually go into politics or otherwise manage to scrape a living, while a trained agronomist probably could not. But in many countries the exclusive stress that is still placed on philosophic studies means, in effect, a comparable down- grading of the technical education that the situation urgently demands. The hypnotic lure of the white collar is as prevalent as it is pernicious.

In this connection Harlan Cleveland, whose views have been or will be frequently quoted elsewhere in this book, has aptly said that the real "measure of education is not only excellence but relevance." (Harlan Cleveland, address at the College of the Virgin Islands, St. Thomas, April 10, 1964.) An example of how relevance can be avoided was cited by Dr. Thomas Balogh who pointed out that the only college in one Central American country gave instruction in Latin and Greek, but not in economics.

Literacy by itself is not enough. As the distinguished Mexican econo- mist Dr. Victor Urquidi has said,

> The appalling illiteracy rate of most Latin American countries ap- pears even worse when the countless number of uneducated literates is considered. Only a small fraction of primary school age children ever conclude their elementary education, for lack of facilities and teachers in rural areas, insufficient school buildings in the cities and, usually, because of family poverty. There is considerable doubt as to the quality and methods of teaching. Secondary schools, technical institutes and universities are attended by but a few, mostly from well to do classes. Adult workers' educational programmes and train- ing schemes are of limited scope. Although great strides have been made in the past by some countries, even in these cases it has been difficult enough not to lose ground, let alone to progress, since in the last decade urbanization, declining death rates and a growing realiza- tion of the value of education have put heavy pressure on existing public and private educational services. (Victor L. Urquidi: Two Years of the Alliance for Progress, Inter-American Economic Affairs, Vol. 17, No. 4, Spring 1964, p. 27.)

The national importance of teaching people to read and to write has also been emphasized by Dr. Myrdal :

Something tremendously vital to his spiritual integration into the nation and into the world happens to the peasant when he can read the names of the streets as he goes to town and when he can start to make out the syllables in the local newspaper—especially if the process goes further and he also obtains easy access to reading material that is of personal importance to him. All other education—in government, health, more rational methods of production, etc.— becomes relatively hopeless without this basic condition of literacy. To start on a national development programme while leaving the population largely illiterate seems to me to be futile. (Myrdal, op. cit., p. 186.)

A most significant component among the educational requirements of the economically backward countries is the need for institutionalized training, and for research services to support programmes of industrialization and the introduction of new agricultural techniques. For these purposes training and research centres must be established and the activities of existing universities and colleges both widened and strengthened.

One of the most urgent requirements of almost all of the less-developed countries is the training of indigenous groups of experts in the more important branches of science. In Africa, for example, the average number of scientists per million of population is about twenty, whereas in European countries the corresponding figures range from five hundred to two thousand. The vital importance of this weakness in the national equipment of the African countries has not gone unrecognized. In a conference in Lagos convened by UNESCO and the Economic Commission for Africa in August 1964, twenty-nine nations from that continent unanimously decided to institute a crash programme to raise the number of African scientists to two hundred per million of the population by 1980. This would mean the training of about 60,000 scientists in fifteen years. These new indigenous experts, moreover, will be expected to concentrate on those sciences which are likely to be of the greatest direct value in the development of African resources and not to go whoring after the nuclear and other esoteric temptations that only the most advanced and wealthiest powers should pursue. A similar recognition of the importance of this kind of education would be of equal value in many other parts of the under-developed regions.

Another aspect of the vital need for adequately trained leadership has also been identified by Mr. Cleveland. This is the importance of education in administration.

Among the scholars who think hard about development, there is by now a clear consensus on one point at least: The central bottleneck

> to rapid development is people—many special people specially trained to do special things; and a critical few people with enough education in complexity to govern and manage the special people—in Paul Appleby's delightful phrase, "to make a mesh of things." So we can begin with an agreed proposition that whatever else is involved—education is the centre of the development process—everywhere, at every stage of growth, and for as far as we can see into the future. (Harlan Cleveland, idem.)

The need for technical training, all the way from the use of the simplest tools to that of the most sophisticated applications of science, is so important as to be almost axiomatic. But there are still many places in which it is not recognized. Yet any significant and sustained national progress is impossible without a widespread impact of such training.

In this connection it is important to recognize the value of specialized training in the handling of certain problems that are usually thought of as being of concern only to the more highly-industrialized states. Among these are the difficulties created by the increasingly rapid growth of urban communities in many of the under-developed countries. To meet these issues, education in the discovery and application of new methods of town planning and related activities is a matter of deepening concern.

In a broader sense governments must be prepared to make an all-out effort to educate their people to accept changes in many ancient, pervasive and unquestioned customs, practices and beliefs. So long, for example, as local communities cannot be persuaded, because it is the home of a local deity, to allow the draining of a malarial swamp which for generations has poisoned the water supply and infected every neighbouring family, no real progress can be rationally expected.

It is true that many of the philosophic and cultural traditions of some of the countries that are economically under-developed have great and lasting value. It is equally true that any effort to force the acceptance by such countries of an unmodified American or European "way of life" would be both a sterile and a dangerous exercise. It is nevertheless true that many of the traditional habits and beliefs that prevail in the under-developed areas are detrimental to plans for economic or social progress. Some philosophies will have to be abandoned, some social institutions will have to be changed, some domestic and commercial practices will have to be modified or totally renounced, some religious convictions will have to be surrendered, and the comfort of many old antipathies will have to be relinquished, if progress is to be made.

The history of development seems clearly to show that the creation of a strong nation-state is a prerequisite to sustained advance. Only in this way can national integration involving what are all-too-often hostile communities now divided by religion, race or caste, be achieved. So long as vicious antagonisms of this kind remain, the essential concentration on the development of a viable national economy will be delayed if not precluded.

Such radical and painful changes, if they are to be effected in any reasonable period of time, will require a vigorous educational initiative by the governments that are seriously and intelligently concerned with the welfare of their peoples—or with their own survival. That real progress can be made when governments devote themselves resolutely to this task can be seen in what has been done in Mexico and in certain other parts of Latin America, in Yugoslavia, and in the slowly disintegrating barriers of caste under the influence of Gandhi, Nehru and their followers in India. But an enormous range of problems still exists and far too little is being done to remove them.

The difficulty of effecting the essential changes cannot easily be exaggerated. It is clear that only a lively hope of escape from almost intolerable misery can provide an adequate incentive. Today the misery exists; the hope can be provided. But only if those who rule in the poorer countries are themselves prepared to act with far greater determination than most of them have ever before displayed.

5/Encouragement of Foreign Investment

While there is now a general willingness to accept the right of a national government to establish rules which will protect its own interests against foreign exploitation and, specifically, to nationalize such basic industries as power and railways, there is an increasing recognition of the importance of a clearly stated, objectively applied (and not too onerous) investment code to encourage foreign capital to participate in the development and beneficial utilization of the resources of an under-developed country. The principles set out in the many post-war treaties of "Friendship, Commerce and Navigation" between the United States and other countries (for example the bell-wether case of Uruguay) constitute an excellent example of the kind of policy that might well be more widely copied. So far similar arrangements have been initiated by Germany, Switzerland, and on a lesser scale by Japan, the Netherlands and the United Kingdom. In the same connection the Organization for Economic Co-operation and Development has prepared a serviceable draft convention on the Protection of Foreign Property, which could usefully be adopted by all countries. This draft convention embodies the concept of a new international arbitral tribunal for the rapid and just settlement of disputes between governments and investors. A somewhat similar draft, prepared by the International Bank, was approved at its Tokyo Conference in 1964. It is to be hoped that something of this kind will soon be formally adopted and widely used.

The importance of encouraging foreign investment under reasonably designed and mutually acceptable rules of this nature can hardly be exaggerated. As things stand, there are many obstacles to such investment. This is evidenced by the fact that in recent years the private capital component has declined as a proportion of the total flow of financial resources into under-developed countries. There is moreover a regrettable though understandable tendency to rely more and more on export credit guarantees in the selection of areas and projects for investment. While it is encouraging that an increasing number of governments is entering the export credit field, the declining attractiveness of poorer countries as areas of unguaranteed investment is a disturbing fact. Moreover, a large proportion of what investment is taking place is confined to the extractive industries rather than finding its way into the generally more beneficial areas of secondary manufacturing.

Capital is available on the free markets of the world in enormous quantities. David Horowitz, Governor of the Bank of Israel, has estimated that "fixed-interest debentures and bonds are issued at a rate of $35 billion per annum on the financial markets of the industrialized countries." At the U.N. Conference on Trade and Development held in Geneva in 1964 he went on in his closing address to point out that:

> The bridge between the developing nations and these capital markets cannot be constructed by free competition of the developing nations with the highly-industrialized nations on these markets. Such resources can be tapped for the developing nations only by a combination of intergovernmental aid with commercial transactions.

> Relatively small amounts provided by the rich nations of the world on a governmental and multilateral basis could act as an ignition spark with regard to these resources and generate a vast transfer of capital. This multiplier effect can be achieved by a relatively small subsidy overcoming the gap between what the developing nations could pay in interest and the rates on the free markets, and by an international guarantee. This guarantee will never become effective if the operation is successful, as it should be, and the developing nations are launched on the road to self-sustaining growth. (David Horowitz: "The International Welfare Community," International Development Review, December 1964, p. 9.)

Vastly increased access to these sources of capital is essential if the poorer countries are ever to rise from their poverty.

The factors that tend to discourage investment in many of the under-developed countries do not need much elaboration. Costs are often inflated because of inadequate transport and communication facilities, skilled management and labour personnel is lacking or relatively expensive, both local and external markets are usually limited, but, above all, the thing that will continue to inhibit essential foreign investment in the poorer countries is the kind of uncertainty and the implicit threat of expropriation and loss which exists in so many parts of the world today.

The importance to the less-developed countries of private investment from foreign sources must be much more widely recognized if progress is to be beneficially accelerated. Valuable, indeed essential, as are the contributions of such public international agencies as the United Nations Special Fund, the Alliance for Progress, and the International Bank for Reconstruction and Development, especially for initial and "pump-priming" purposes, it is certainly true that in the long run as David Rockefeller, President of the Chase Manhattan Bank, has vigorously argued, that a most important contribution must be made by the "programme of loans, investments and financial counselling which are the concern of the commercial banks." (David Rockefeller: "Creative Banking and the World Economy," *International Development Review*, June 1964, p. 3.) Such banks bring in outside capital but they also join with indigenous financial institutions to mobilize local funds and put them to work in starting new and expanding existing businesses. In many cases they do not confine themselves to ordinary commercial loans but make direct equity investments and investment loans.

In the same article Mr. Rockefeller also pointed to the private development bank as

> *a new and potentially promising field. . . . These banks which aim at promoting as well as financing ventures have become a valuable tool in broadening the economies of the poorer nations. . . . One of the most heartening aspects of the spread of these private development banks is the major impetus they give small and medium sized industries. They reflect a growing awareness on the part of the developing nations that steel mills and hydro-electric plants by themselves are not sufficient. Secondary industries are equally necessary and, in some cases in the early stages of development, more appropriate to stimulate economic growth. (Ibid, p. 4.)*

It would be encouraging if more of the leading bankers in the highly developed countries showed evidence of sharing Mr. Rockefeller's enlightened conviction that their "place on history's canvas may well be judged by how satisfactorily we measure up to those new demands, and by the degree to which we can relate ourselves to the hopes of people beyond our borders." (*Ibid*, p. 5.)

It is of course axiomatic that in the long run the greater part of the capital essential for the progress of the economy of an under-developed country will have to be supplied by the domestic savings of the nationals of that country. This will involve sacrifice and require patience—two commodities that are everywhere in short supply.

But in the earliest stages of national progress, carefully planned injections of foreign capital are one essential element in any hopeful plan of development. One of the great problems, of course, is the selection of the right projects for the most beneficial ultilization of such funds. This is true whether the external capital comes from public or private sources although, because of the greater variety of projects for which appeals are made to public agencies, the difficulties of selection are enhanced in this sector. Nevertheless as Gunnar Myrdal has pointed out :

A substantial inflow of capital from the advanced countries is an almost necessary precondition in most under-developed countries if they are to witness a rapid rate of economic development; the social and political dangers inherent in their failure should also be borne in mind. In spite of the limitations to their absorptive capacity—which, viewed from another angle, are nothing else than their staggering difficulties in initiating and sustaining economic development—there is no doubt in my mind that if the advanced countries approached this problem with the same seriousness and zeal which they ordinarily devote to their own affairs, not to speak of their attitudes to defence and national security, they would not fail to find productive outlets for a considerably increased stream of capital for the under-developed countries. (Myrdal, *op. cit.*, p. 214.)

No inflow of foreign capital will be of permanent benefit unless it has the effect of increasing the productive capacity of the recipient state. If foreign funds are allowed to be used for consumptive purposes they may have an effect that will be of temporary benefit—but they are unlikely to have any lasting value. Here the necessity of sacrifice will arise and the real problem will be to devise a procedure by which the people concerned can be persuaded to meet this ordeal without abandoning the practices of democracy and without suffering the full measure of human torment that accompanied the economic transformation and development of the now wealthy countries in the early days of the industrial revolution.

Before leaving the subject of foreign investment it would be appropriate to add a word on the general subject of profit. To those whose experience has been in the public sector of the economy, where service is the ideal and profits tend to be considered almost immoral, there is a tendency to overlook the value of the profit motive as a stimulant in an under-developed society. Yet the encouragement of profit-making, by both private and public organizations, combined with a tax system designed to foster re-investment, can be of tremendous value to a country that is trying to accelerate the accumulation and active use of investment capital. The examples of Russia and Japan are cases in point.

6/Other Desirable Changes

In addition to the major fields in which countries in receipt of international assistance could make a greatly improved contribution to their own welfare, there are a number of smaller areas in which beneficial changes could profitably be introduced. One illustration is the need for a more careful selection among the various forms of aid. There is, for example, an increasingly clear recognition of the fact that the provision of scholarships and fellowships for study abroad has been overdone, that much of the money and effort thus expended would almost certainly have produced more significant results if employed in other ways. After fifteen years' experience in his responsible post in the technical assistance programmes of the United Nations and its Specialized Agencies David Owen wrote in 1964,

> I think we should take a hard look at that all-too-popular prescription —the offer of fellowships and scholarships in foreign parts. I would venture the sweeping judgement that there are now far too many such offers, and that the extraordinary international body-snatching competition which is still in progress in Africa and elsewhere today may be doing far more harm than good. Our first aim should be to expand, strengthen and sustain local training and research institutions in the developing countries themselves. There will remain plenty of room for selective scholarships and fellowships carefully designed to meet specific needs. (David Owen : Fifteen Years of Technical Assistance, United Nations, 1964, p. 11.)

While it is true that some of the early weaknesses of the scholarship programme—poor selection of candidates including gross examples of nepotism, unsatisfactory servicing, improper post-scholarship employment—have been greatly reduced, it is also true that the number of cases in which beneficial results can be demonstrated is so low as to cause increasing concern. Governments should give very critical scrutiny to every fellowship or scholarship proposal to ensure that the candidate is suitable, the course of study appropriate and the arrangements for subsequent employment such as to ensure some real prospect of national benefit.

Recipient governments would also profit themselves as well as the experts they secure if they would pay greater attention to the provision of better facilities to enable the experts to do their jobs effectively. Above all, there should be a substantial improvement in the number and the quality of the counterpart personnel assigned to work with and to assist in the application of the advice provided by, the foreign consultants. The situation in this regard is much more satisfactory than used to be the case but a good deal more could still advantageously be done.

A great increase in the use of operational and executive personnel provided by the United Nations under the OPEX programme could be expected to bring results of exceptional value to governments and countries wise enough to make substantial use of this kind of technical aid. No other form of assistance can have such a direct, intimate, and immediate effect at the vital points of the national economy of a state determined to progress.

Increased use should also be made of the "Funds in Trust" arrangement by which requesting governments can obtain additional aid through the international agencies on a fee-for-service basis. Over fifty countries are now using this facility and there is probably no other way in which supplementary aid can be obtained with so low a drain on the exchequer of the country concerned.

Finally, it is appropriate to emphasize the very great desirability from both the practical and the psychological points of view of recipient countries increasing the size of their respective annual pledges of financial support to the United Nations Expanded Programme of Technical Assistance. The amounts involved are singularly small, even in relation to the general economic condition of the countries concerned, and even smaller in comparison with what many of these governments are spending on other and far less important (and sometimes shockingly less desirable) ends. The effect on prospective donors when their attention is directed to some of the forms of expenditure indulged in by beneficiary governments can only be detrimental to the future prospects of the countries directly involved and of the programmes as a whole.

It is at least equally important that recipient governments, having made pledges of contributions to the Expanded Programme, should also proceed to the practical step of paying the amount that has been promised. In a surprising number of cases in the past this detail has heretofore been overlooked.

Unless the recipient countries will make much stronger and more rationally concentrated efforts than they have made in most cases in the past, the value of the whole concept and programme of international aid will continue to produce only limited, occasional and scattered results. Regardless of what other countries, organizations and individuals may do there will have to be much more effort, much more sacrifice, much more determination and much more intelligence displayed by the governments and countries in need of aid, if the crusade that has now been started is to produce the kind of results that humanity so desperately needs.

CHAPTER NINE

The Prospects for the Future – II

If the main responsibility for their future progress lies in the needy countries themselves there is nonetheless much that can and should be done by the fortunate governments and peoples who are in a position to continue and expand their programmes of international aid.

It has repeatedly been emphasized that there is no clear and sharp line that can be drawn between donors and recipients of international aid. Almost every country in the world receives as well as provides assistance in one or another of its manifold forms. But by far the largest part of the total assistance for these programmes comes from a small number of comparatively wealthy nations—the United States, the Soviet Union, the older Commonwealth countries, Scandinavia, France, Germany, Japan—and the paragraphs that follow relate particularly to the policies that these countries could most beneficially pursue.

What the Donor Countries Can Do

1 / Increased Contributions

It is, of course, true that the adequacy of the resources being made available for assistance to the under-developed countries cannot be judged on the basis only of the gross amount of money involved. Many questions of timing, terms, purposes and other qualitative factors must be taken into consideration. But no matter how these aspects are evaluated, it is indisputably true that the present scale of contributions to the programmes of international aid is wholly inadequate to meet the urgent needs of the countries that must be helped if the present state of human society is to be substantially improved. Under existing circumstances many sensible governmental requests have to be refused. The implementation of others has to be postponed. Even among the projects that are approved, the money required to give them really effective implementation is often lacking. The United Nations Technical Assistance Board, after summarizing a long series of projects that had failed to produce the hoped-for results, reported that "perhaps as many as fifty per cent of the unsuccessful attempts at technical aid can be traced directly or indirectly to inadequate funds—inadequate to provide a mission with the supplies it needs—inadequate to carry out a national project on the scale initially conceived—inadequate to follow up reports and recommendations." (*United Nations Technical Assistance Newsletter*, Issue No. 53, May, 1959.)

As has been shown, not even the most generous and most enlightened of the participating governments is today making a contribution to international aid that imposes any significant financial burden on its own people. It certainly cannot be argued that the nationals of any of the wealthier countries are making anything that could properly be described as a sacrifice in order to help their indigent neighbours. The contribution of the cost of one packet of cigarettes a week by each adult person in the United States would enable the government of that country to multiply its economic aid programme by five times. The women of Canada spend six times as much on cosmetics as Canada does on help to other countries. One penny a week from each of the people of Britain would enable that country to increase its contribution to the United Nations Expanded Programme of Technical Assistance to about ten times the present size. Much more dramatic comparisons could be made for most of the other wealthy countries. So it cannot honestly be argued that any nation is tightening its belt by even a small fraction of a notch in its effort to assist those in need.

It is very clear that even a modest sacrifice by the taxpayers of the more affluent states would expand the dimensions of the programmes of international aid far beyond their present size. Until the people of the wealthier countries begin to contribute on a scale that can be felt at home, the results that can be anticipated in the slums of the world will be meagre, sporadic and dispersed. While it is perhaps impractical to suggest a general rule, it is probably realistic to believe that a diversion to aid programmes of about two per cent of the annual national income of the major nations will be required if the efforts to reduce human poverty, and the tragic ills that accompany it, are to be attended by any notable success.

To bring about an increase of this order of magnitude in national contributions to the general welfare of humanity, governments must themselves be convinced of the desirability of such a policy and must then present the matter to their people in such a way as to win their acquiescence. It cannot too often be repeated that the contributions of the wealthier nations to the programmes of international aid, while motivated in part by altruistic impulses, are very far from being simple instances of charity. To the extent that they are unselfish, they are worthy of praise. But it should be clearly recognized that their philanthropy will in the end be a source of solid profit. Barbara Ward has described the situation well:

> To me, one of the most vivid proofs that there is a moral governance in the universe is the fact that when men or governments work intelligently and far-sightedly for the good of others, they achieve their own prosperity too. Take our Western experience with the welfare state. We did not plan to do it as a good stroke of business. It was a moral decision with ancient antecedents. Yet one of the consequences has been to reduce business risks. Mass consumption, secured by social security, enables the economy to avoid the booms and collapses of the old economy.

> I believe we should see the same outcome if in the world economy we could determine to build up the purchasing power of the poorer nations. We should find that, once again, our own prosperity had been helped by the underpinning of world consumption and by the creation of a world economy free from the ups and downs, the uncertainties and incoherences, of the system as we know it today.

> "Honesty is the best policy" used to be said in Victorian times. I would go further. I would say that generosity is the best policy and that expansion of opportunity sought for the sake of others ends by bringing well-being and expansion to oneself. The dice are not hopelessly loaded against us. Our morals and our interests—seen in true perspective—do not pull apart. (Barbara Ward, op. cit., p. 150.)

Serious programmes of international aid can be established on a continuing and long-term basis only by appealing to the self-interest as well as to the idealism of the people who will have to pay the taxes. Today there are frequent and increasingly sharp complaints from the citizens of some of the larger contributors that the people of the beneficiary nations show an inadequate appreciation of what is already being done for them. When President Sukarno told the United States to take its aid programme and go to hell there were a good many Americans who were tempted to act with pleasure on at least the first part of his demand. Even more moderate indications of a lack of gratitude are likely to reduce the enthusiasm of donor governments and peoples. In such cases it is

well to remember that the role of recipient is a difficult part to play—
above all by people whose national pride is involved.

In spite of the fact that foreign aid is not always rewarded by affection
or even by acknowledgement or thanks, there is plenty of evidence to
support the conviction that dynamic and intelligent leadership, by a
government that is itself convinced that international assistance is both
imperative and right, will evoke an affirmative response from its people.
As Sir John Maud has said,

> the major problem in a wealthy country like Britain or America is
> to be imaginative enough—to increase our own awareness of the
> challenge offered to people in countries like our own (which have
> found the secret of growing daily richer through modern technolo-
> gical advance) by countries which are not yet growing less poor at
> anything like the rate at which we are growing richer, and to find
> ways of kindling the compassionate imagination of our fellow
> citizens. (Maud, op. cit., p. 23.)

That a great deal of compassionate imagination has been kindled in many
countries during the post-war years is obvious. The problem now is to
maintain and increase the momentum that has been achieved, and, as
human nature tends to weary of good works, the added impetus of self-
interest must, in the next few years at least, increasingly be stressed.

It is significant that in most of the more advanced countries today the
high leadership in the business community, in labour and in intellectual
circles is already generally receptive to affirmative proposals for increased
foreign aid.* The opposition to expanded efforts comes, typically, from
the small businessman, the local politician and the uneducated mass.
This does not mean, of course, that there is any large area of public
opinion in any donor country that would support a sudden and massive
increase in aid, under present conditions. There is too much evidence of
incompetent administration in the present programmes, too little confidence in the ability and integrity of the recipient governments, too strong
a conviction that not all the wealthy states are making, or are prepared
to make, an equal contribution. Until at least some progress can be made
on each of these fronts the hope that any major government will voluntarily and individually decide on a vast enlargement of its contributions
is almost certain to be disappointed.

---

* See for example the report from a team sent by the Federation of British
Industries (not be confused with the FBI in the United States!) to examine
the technical assistance programmes of the United Nations, published by the
Federation in London in 1955. The International Chamber of Commerce has
frequently adopted resolutions supporting the principles of international aid.

In 1953, Mr. Raymond Scheyven of Belgium was asked by the General Assembly of the United Nations to explore with possible donor governments the likelihood of their being able and willing to make substantial contributions to an international development fund. In his valuable report he said that before large grants from the industrialized countries could be seriously anticipated,

> the taxpayers [of such countries] must be convinced of the value of the sacrifices asked of them. Their efforts must not be compromised by bad political management [in the prospective recipient countries], and the tax they pay must not be a substitute for the taxes that an enormously wealthy ruling class, indifferent to the poverty of its fellow citizens, might be unwilling to pay. (Official Records, U.N. General Assembly Ninth Session, Supplement 19, New York 1954, p. 8.)

There is no reason to suppose that this situation has changed.

If a significant increase in the present scale of giving is to be achieved, it will probably have to be brought about by an international "fair-share" agreement between most if not all of the major contributors. This will probably mean action through or in some kind of active collaboration with the United Nations. Certainly the United States is presently providing too large a proportion of the whole. It is not surprising that opposition to an indefinite continuation of this situation is growing in that country. Fortunately it is true that the situation is changing. In recent years other western countries have increased their aid activities and have softened the terms of the external development loans. In the U.S.A., commitments have fallen and lending terms have hardened. It should also be noted that over a third of U.S. economic aid takes the form of donations of surplus farm products which involves no significant sacrifice. Nevertheless it is most desirable that other countries should increase their proportion of the total task.

A minor problem related to the size of the contributions is the limitations which some of the donors have placed on the use of their donations. In certain cases these relate to the non-convertibility of the currency; in others to specific restrictions on how the money is to be used; and sometimes to both. The Technical Assistance Board has repeatedly requested that all contributions be made in readily convertible currencies, but the response has not been notably generous. Participation by the Soviet bloc countries, for example, has been mainly in non-convertible rubles or related currencies. The Soviet Union itself has refused to permit more than twenty-five per cent of its contribution to be exchanged for other currencies, and then only for projects of which it has approved in advance. Since comparatively few Soviet experts are used by the Expanded Programme, and as no aid is given to the U.S.S.R., much of the Soviet bloc contribution can only be used for the purchase of supplies and equipment from the communist countries, or for fellowships. This greatly limits its value.

Another restriction that reduces the utility of some components of the financial assistance provided by donor countries, is the not infrequent habit of offering "tied" loans or grants. Even when the tie is not written into the agreement, it is sometimes present in fact. As the Development Assistance Committee of the OECD pointed out:

> It is important to understand that contractual tying is not the only condition which ties aid. Non-contractual factors favour procurement in the donor country in many different ways. Some countries provide much of their aid to countries with which they have monetary and trading links or long-established trade channels. When technical experts from a country assist in developing the specifications for a project, one can expect them to recommend equipment with which they are familiar. It is of course true that, in the case of many types of contributions, varying from transfer of food to export credits, the aid is tied by the form in which it is contributed. The same situation is particularly evident in the technical assistance field. (Report of the Chairman of the Development Assistance Committee, Paris, September 1963, Organization for Economic Co-operation and Development, pp. 35–36.)

An agreement among the major powers on a large expansion of the present scale of aid is most unlikely to be consummated until the prospective recipients give more evidence than in the past of their determination and their capacity to do more for themselves. This accentuates the great importance of the suggestions outlined in the previous chapter. The most effective way to bring about a significant increase in the dimensions of international aid is for the recipient governments to make better use of what they are already getting, and show greater determination to do more for themselves. The recent decline in United States congressional support for the foreign aid programmes has been clearly linked, in part at least, to rising doubts as to the value of the use being made of United States help. Increasing numbers of Americans are coming to doubt the sincerity as well as the capacity of some of the recipients.

As Professor Isaiah Frank has pointed out, a good many Americans now believe that the United States provides "aid indiscriminately to almost 100 countries regardless of whether promises of social reform and self-help measures are fulfilled. Much of the aid never reaches the ordinary people but ends up in the pockets (or the Swiss bank accounts) of the oligarchies." (Isaiah Frank: "Foreign Aid and the Liberal Dissent," *New Republic*, January 23, 1965, p. 18.) And there have been too many examples of the kind of things described by a Canadian doctor who, on his return from a mission to Ceylon, reported that "the Sultan of Pahang was building a $2,500,000 pleasure palace while trucks repairing roads on his estate were foreign aid gifts from Canada." (*Victoria Colonist*, July 23, 1964.)

The third change that is essential, if the people of democratic states are to be persuaded to accept the idea of heavier taxation to support increased contributions to mutual aid activities—and if the recipient countries are to make the efforts and immediate sacrifices that a development programme requires of them—is a marked improvement in the operation and administration of most of the present programmes. This improvement is very necessary among the multilateral agencies, as is indicated below, but it is of even greater importance in the bilateral or national programmes, because it is here that many of the present weaknesses are most flagrantly displayed, and also because it is here that they are most readily apparent to the taxpayer's eye.

If more of the recipient governments begin to display a greater resolution in meeting their own problems, and if more evidence of administrative competence is exhibited by the operating agencies, pressure on the governments of the wealthy nations to join in providing a massive increase in their scale of giving can be exerted with a clearer conscience and with more hope of ultimate success.

If such changes are long delayed the dispossessed peoples of the world will grow increasingly restless and impatient as they wait for the help which many of them have now come to consider their right. The dangers inherent in such a situation—dangers to the people themselves, to their governments and to the peace of the world—will increase with every flying year.

2/Improvement in Programme Design and Administration

The administrative shortcomings of the aid programmes vary from country to country, from agency to agency, and from time to time. In the United States, for example, while there have been certain failings that have been common throughout the whole period since the initiation of the Point Four activities in 1950, there have also been marked variations in the managerial competence displayed by the successive administrative units.

That there is waste, inefficiency and even corruption in the design and administration of the external aid programmes in some countries is known to everyone with even a cursory acquaintance with the facts. In too many cases the responsibility for developing and maintaining the programmes is assigned to ministers or departments that are unqualified by experience, capacity, or even interest, to handle the job. It sometimes seems to be looked upon as the poor relation in the family of national activities. Yet properly conceived, administered and explained to the people who provide the funds, it should be a show-piece and a subject of national pride. In some cases—as, for example, in the Netherlands, the United States and Scandinavia—the work that has been done has been marked by generosity, imagination and initiative; in many others these characteristics have been conspicuously absent.

In addition to the operation of conventional forms of international aid, the more serious governments can and should be expected to develop such original initiatives as the Peace Corps of the United States, or the Voluntary Service Overseas of Great Britain. Both of these and a number of similar organizations in other countries have taken advantage of the idealism, the enthusiasm and the intelligence of the youth of their nations to make significant contributions to the developing concepts of how help can be best provided. The "junior expert" scheme of the Netherlands and the training-centres organized in Copenhagen, show a similar willingness and ability to experiment with new ideas.

Perhaps the basic requirement if the maximum operational efficiency is to be achieved is a clear definition of policy objectives. If economic and technical assistance continue to be intermingled with military support, as in the case of the United States, or to be dealt with as integral parts of political policy as is most obviously the intent of the Russian programmes, or are to be influenced by persisting colonial considerations as in Great Britain and more particularly France, the difficulty of organizing a consistent, rational and efficient administrative structure and a correspondingly satisfactory technique is enormously enhanced.

If donor governments are to achieve the kind of administrative proficiency in their assistance programmes which they should, and presumably do desire, they should begin by establishing a much more clearly envisaged, and more sharply delineated, policy than has generally been the case in the larger countries in the past. They should then select enlightened and competent administrators and give them the kind of freedom from personal and political pressures which good administration requires. Finally, they should organize their financing in such a way as to give some assurance of consistency in support of the programmes, thus reducing the time that senior officers must devote to defending their activities and to seeking appropriations. There is too much truth in

Harlan Cleveland's summary: "Even though we know better we are still tackling twenty-year problems with five-year plans based on two-year personnel working with one-year appropriations." (Harlan Cleveland: *Address to AFL-CIO Convention*, November 14, 1964.)

If policies, machinery and financing can thus be established and assured, the officials in charge of the programmes can begin to concentrate a greater part of their abilities, their energies and their time on co-operation with prospective recipients in the devising and implementation of effective projects of aid. Fortunate conditions of this kind exist in only a comparatively few national capitals today and yet they are an essential element in any attempt to achieve maximum efficiency in the use of the money that is provided for assistance to the under-developed nations.

It is, of course, true that most governments do not organize their domestic affairs with the degree of efficiency that is here advocated for their programmes of external aid. But extravagance and maladministration at home usually bring some benefit to some people even when they are detrimental to the economy as a whole. Most of the wealthy countries, moreover, are able to afford incompetence. But when money is voted to assist countries and people who are in great distress, it is intolerable that it should be diverted to marginal uses, or that it should be wasted by personal incompetence or by the refusal of governments to act with an adequate recognition of their responsibilities.

Improved administrative techniques and the imagination to find and develop methods to apply new ideas, are among the results that can be expected from governments that conceive of international aid as something more than just a begrudged necessity, a salve to conscience or a half-hearted concession to an enlightened public opinion.

3/The Encouragement of Private Initiative

Closely related to what has been said about the Peace Corps and similar activities, is the value to be derived from governmental action which is designed to stimulate private participation in the general field of international aid. Whether this takes the form of direct subventions to such agencies as the Canadian Universities Service Overseas, or is limited to the provision of information and verbal encouragement to religious organizations, universities and related educational agencies, private foundations and other committed groups, such assistance has a significant value both at home and abroad.

A comparatively new element in this general picture of privately organized aid is the provision that is now beginning to be made in some countries for tax concessions to private business organizations that make a clearly identifiable contribution to the social betterment of the people of a foreign state. This kind of development may well become a valuable component of the aid programmes and it should receive all the support that can be extended to it by the International Chamber of Commerce and other agencies with comparable interests and objectives.

4/ Increased Use of the International Agencies

Reference has already been made (in Chapter Five) to the controversy as to the relative merits of bilateral and multilateral programmes of mutual aid—a controversy which has been going on for many years and which will undoubtedly continue for many more. The fact is, of course, that in choosing between them there is no single answer that is everywhere and at all times applicable.

There are many arguments in favour of the bilateral approach, the most persuasive being, perhaps, the fact that popular support can be more readily mobilized when the people concerned can be assured that their particular benevolence will be widely identified. Thus Canadian interest could more easily be stimulated when Canadian dollars were given directly for the construction of a hydro-electric dam in Pakistan or for the provision of Canadian fishing vessels to Ceylon, than it could when the Canadian government decided to give two million dollars to something as vague, as distant and as abstract as the United Nations Expanded Programme of Technical Assistance.

This kind of direct relationship between the taxpayers of the donor country and the users in the recipient area has a real value and it should be neither hindered nor discouraged.

It is also important that private agencies—universities, foundations, churches, business organizations—should be actively encouraged to initiate and maintain direct person-to-person and organization-to-organization relationships for mutual aid and encouragement. Donor governments should do far more than they have even contemplated doing in the past to support rational activities of this kind.

It is sometimes boldly asserted that the only reason that governments make any large allocation of funds to international aid is because they look upon this practice as an instrument in their struggle for political and eventually for military support. From this point of view, aid that is not given directly by the government concerned loses its value for its avowed purpose. Those who support the assistance programmes for such reasons can naturally see no value in providing aid through the United Nations or through any other multilateral agency.

While it is true that aid programmes have sometimes been used for political purposes, it is certainly not true that this is the only, or in most cases even the major, reason for their initiation and maintenance. Otherwise why do the Scandinavian nations, the Netherlands, and Canada rank so high in their proportionate contributions to international projects? Certainly the cold-war argument is seldom if ever heard in these countries. Yet the Canadians, Dutch and Scandinavians cannot be considered to be basically more generous or more enlightened than, say, the Russians, the Americans or the British.

Moreover, it is becoming increasingly clear that if economic and technical assistance is given in the hope of being an effective instrument in winning political or military support, it is being given in delusion. Very few governments are for sale in this way, and if purchased will not stay bought. The attitude of any national government when reminded of past favours is almost always—in substance if not in form—the same as that of the ward politician in similar circumstances who replied to his benefactor by saying, "But that was yesterday, what will you do for me today?" This may be regrettable but it is not untrue.

Although the great value of direct contacts between governments and countries is widely recognized, this does not alter the fact that most objective critics of the programmes of international aid are agreed that a very large proportionate increase in the amount of aid that is channelled through the multilateral agencies—the Colombo Plan, the Organization of American States, and above all, the United Nations and the Specialized Agencies—would bring beneficial results. The chief arguments in support of this view have already been considered (see Chapter Five), but it may be useful to summarize them here :

a/The fact that United Nations or other multilateral aid is, and is now recognized by the recipient governments as being, free from all political or other ulterior motives makes it uniquely palatable in the under-developed areas. Governments more readily accept assistance from an international organization of which they are themselves a part, than they do from a single country which by the very act of giving becomes inevitably open to the suspicion of moving in pursuit of its own special interests.

b/Not only is multilateral aid easier to accept in principle, it is also likely to be more beneficial in fact. When aid is received from a single country the experts are almost always nationals of the donor state, the fellowships are tenable in that state, the equipment is of its manufacture. When the aid is provided by the United Nations there is no such concentration of national influences: the experts will probably be of varied backgrounds; the fellowships will be tenable in whatever country or countries may be mutually decided; the equipment will come from any one or many states.

c/The diversity of the areas from which aid may be drawn under the multilateral programmes is likely to improve the quality of the assistance. In the United Nations Technical Assistance Mission to Bolivia in 1950, which was the first comprehensive mission sent out under the Expanded Programme, there were fourteen experts drawn from eleven different countries. They constituted a body with a variety of competence and a diversity of experience that could not have been found in a purely national group. They were, moreover, much more acceptable to the Bolivians than would have been a mission consisting entirely of Americans or Germans or even of Danes, Japanese or Canadians. It cannot be denied that the United Nations can provide a variety of choice that no national programme can equal.

d/Increased use of multilateral rather than bilateral channels has the additional advantage of putting pressure on all governments to bear a reasonable proportion of the load. It is true that in the case of the United Nations and the Specialized Agencies, the United States has from the beginning carried a disproportionate share of the financial burden, but this situation has gradually been rectified and it is quite obvious that the multinational character of the organization has compelled a wide participation.

e/There is also very real value in the fact that through the multilateral aid programmes, governments are brought together in a joint venture of both a practical and an altruistic character. That this experience may pay dividends in other fields is not, necessarily, an idle hope. The mutual practice of virtue may lead to new virtuous practices.

f/One way in which the donor countries themselves would greatly benefit from a more frequent use of the multilateral channels is sometimes overlooked. The British historian A. J. P. Taylor described this aspect of the problem very clearly when he said that when an under-developed country becomes directly and more or less completely dependent on another, "it is the former which can call the tune; it can threaten to collapse unless supported and its protector has no answering threat in return." (A J. P. Taylor: *The Struggle for Mastery in Europe, 1848–1914*, London, 1954.) A frequently used variation of this tactic is, of course, the threat to turn communist if additional aid is not forthcoming from non-communist sources.

Though less is heard of it, the converse is also probably true. Such threats are less useful to a government that is trying to play one donor against another, when the assistance that is sought is to be supplied by a multinational agency.

g/Finally, it is at least arguable that the international agencies give more value for the aid dollar, or pound, or ruble, or peso, than can be obtained in other ways. While it is not always or at all times true, it is generally the case that the technical assistance activities of the United Nations are more efficiently and economically administered than are the aid programmes of the national governments. Whether this is due to the degree of supervision to which these programmes must submit, to the enthusiasm and dedication of those engaged in their execution, to the absence of any very significant political, personal or corporate pressures, or to some other cause or causes, is difficult to estimate and impossible to prove. Whatever the explanation, it is generally accepted by those in a position to judge that, with all the shortcomings that still mark their work, the programmes of the United Nations and the Specialized Agencies are less open to criticism than are most of those under national direction.

5 / The Divorce of Economic Aid from Military Assistance

As has been suggested, both the communist and the capitalist-socialist countries have at times used technical and financial aid as an instrument in their rivalry for the adherence of the uncommitted nations. Although there is little evidence to support the belief that either side has won any solid and lasting advantage in this way, the competition still continues and is unlikely to cease. Of those who argue that international aid is essential to save selected recipients "from communism" or from falling under the influence of "the capitalist exploiters," it is undoubtedly true that many are firmly convinced of the validity of their arguments. But it is probably safe to say that this proposition is often employed because of its public relations value rather than because it represents a firm conviction. And any popular support that is won in this way is by its very nature as tenuous as it is transitory. Mr. Adlai Stevenson has written very clearly on this subject:

> A policy based just on anti-communism and military potency is not in the spirit of this great movement of the twentieth century and will win few hearts. The challenge to us is to identify ourselves with this social and human revolution, to encourage aid and inspire the aspirations of half of mankind for a better life, to guide these

aspirations into paths that lead to freedom. To default would be disaster. . . . We shall have to learn that we cannot buy agreement or effective alliance among the new states of the Middle East and Asia with economic or military aid. (Adlai E. Stevenson: *Call to Greatness,* New York, 1954, pp. 82–98.)

However, the anti-communist argument has undoubtedly helped the United States and other administrations to win support for their aid programmes and to this extent it can probably be argued that bad reasons have aided a good cause.

From very similar motives, some of the most powerful nations have interlaced their programmes of military and economic aid. In such cases it is argued that the latter is essential to support the former. In certain instances the intermingling is so complete that it is almost if not quite impossible to untangle the different strands. Moreover it is difficult to avoid the belief that economic aid is sometimes made contingent on the acceptance of military assistance; and military assistance is sometimes hard to distinguish from political control.

For anyone who has seen the process in operation, it is difficult to avoid the conclusion that the building up of the military establishments in the under-developed nations is almost always and without qualification, evil. It destroys values, makes democratic government almost impossible, introduces foreign political influences, and wastes the substance of the recipient nation.

Where in the annals of human perversity can there be found any more imbecile policy than that of pressing on Latin American governments the acceptance of large numbers of modern military aircraft and the equivalent hardware of the other services? These countries are in no danger except from each other; the introduction of modern equipment merely helps to ensure that any local conflict will be more vicious and sanguinary than would otherwise be the case. The very possession of the weapons increases the likelihood of war because of the natural tendency of the professional to desire to use the highly specialized instruments of his calling.

The acceptance of gifts of modern weapons ensures also the reception of large numbers of specialists to instruct in their use. The result in many cases has been that the influence of the donor government has become more than a threat to the independence of the recipient. This is more than ever true because of the swift rate of obsolescence and the rapid wastage that inevitably characterize the use of complex and highly sophisticated weapons. The reliance on the donor for replacements further subordinates the receiver to the continuing external influence.

It is sometimes argued that weapons should be given to the weaker countries to strengthen those that are on "our" (western, or communist) side, whereas, in fact, the result if not the object of supplying arms is almost invariably to assist the recipient government to put down "subversive" elements among its own people. Yet very often the only hope for national progress is that these subversive elements should succeed.

As has been pointed out in an earlier chapter it is becoming more and more obvious that in many of the under-developed countries the military forces are the only modern component in the national economy. In such states a contemporary army-navy-air-force complex is operating in an early medieval society. As an inevitable result the military, being beyond all comparison the most powerful element in the nation, soon feel the urge, as they possess the power, to take control of the country. Democracy, in such circumstances, becomes an impossibility.

The effect on the popular mind of seeing the military in power and of observing the prevalence of military concepts and standards, is an inevitable weakening of those human and intellectual values of which military authority is the antithesis.

In this connection Barbara Ward's repeated assertion that "again and again" it has been necessary for the "military leaders, coming in with a tradition of service and a reputation of integrity" to take over and try to pull the country together "to face the truly daunting problems of development" which the corrupt and rapacious politicians have been unable or unwilling to solve, is as historically unsound as, in such a remarkably acute observer, it is personally incomprehensible. For every Ayub Khan* there have been a dozen Batistas.

Finally there is, of course, the economic and financial argument against the diversion of the limited resources of the under-developed countries into the maintenance of a military establishment that is as wasteful and unproductive as it is almost certain to be brutalizing and despotic.

If there is one thing that the under-developed nations do not need it is increased military establishments. Except under most special circumstances no assistance in the building up of a national army, navy, or air force should be given to any such country.

It is probably for such reasons as these that Senator Fulbright, one of the most enlightened and responsible of American statesmen, refused in 1965 to accept the task of piloting the programme of combined military and economic aid through the United States Congress.

---

* This was written before the outbreak of the insane conflict between Pakistan and India in 1965.

6/ Increased Facilities for the Trade of the Under-developed Countries

Writing in the OECD *Observer* in December, 1964, Mr. Thorkil Kristen-sen, Secretary-General of the Organization for Economic Co-operation and Development, said:

> *Three requirements will have to be met if the developing countries are to approach the standard of living of the industrialized countries. They must have more knowledge; they must have more capital; and they must have wider markets for their product.*

The third of these essentials has until recently been the most neglected element in the study of the problems of international aid; there has been very little recognition of the improvement that an enlightened policy of international trade, and of monetary reform, could provide. A serious attack on the trading difficulties presently being experienced by poor countries would radically alter their prospects for progress in development. The Secretary-General of the United Nations, U Thant, recently pointed out that the total dollar value of the aid given to the under-developed countries during the past decade amounted to less than the fall in prices of the products exported by those countries during the same period. This would seem to give some substance to the wisecrack of Robert M. Hutchins that "the big myth about aid to the developing countries is that there has been some." (quoted by Anderson, *op. cit.*, p. 11.)

If the prosperous countries really intend to hasten the economic and social development of their indigent neighbours, they will have to adjust the terms of international trade to bring greater opportunities for profitable exchange to the people of the under-developed countries. As long as the rules of the international market-place are predominantly made by and designed to meet the requirements of the major participants, no permanent and salutary solution will be found for the problems of the poverty-ridden areas of the world.

Technical and economic assistance on a continuous and increasing scale will be necessary for a long time to come, but the impact of that assistance could be enormously increased if the trading policies of the richer countries were to be adjusted in such a way as to provide wider markets for the nations whose present opportunities are limited by the weakness of their own economies and by the barriers that prevent them from gaining profitable and effective access to world markets. Both trade and aid are essential elements of any programme designed to bring rapid and sustained progress in the under-developed countries.

As things are today, far too much of international aid is directed towards the creation of conditions the primary objective of which is to promote the export trade of the wealthy nations. Indeed, aid itself often takes the form of exports of wheat or other commodities that constitute a burdensome surplus in the United States or Canada or one of the other prosperous countries. Properly handled, such transactions can be of some immediate benefit to the recipient nation, but they are likely to provide little in the way of permanent strength to the developing economy unless they are very carefully used by the recipient government. It is in this connection that the plans being implemented by the United Nations' World Food Programme can be expected to make an important contribution. But the real need is for a reorganization of the patterns of international trade in such a way as to assist the poorer countries by increasing the effective demand, and prices now paid, for their products. In the words of a Pakistani professor at the University of London, "Year after year I have seen the cotton crops from my village in Jhang fetch less and less on the world market. Year after year I have seen the imported fertilizer cost more and more." (Quoted in Anderson, *op. cit.*, p. 11.) And Sir Michael Blundell has described this situation in Kenya :

> *While the West pours out aid with one hand it sets in motion with the other policies which progressively reduce the wealth of the un-developed areas. The creeping post war inflation in Western industrial countries, combined with a position of over production in most primary products, has meant a catastrophic fall in the real income of farmers in Africa, Asia and South America. In 1948 a medium-sized tractor cost in the Highlands of Kenya £500, while a ton of coffee could be sold for £600. Today the position is drastically reversed—the tractor costs nearly £900 and the coffee realizes slightly more than £300.* (Sir Michael Blundell: *So Rough a Wind*, London, 1964, p. 209.)

Unless this sort of thing can be changed, there is little prospect of creating those conditions of sustained growth which will eventually reduce the need for programmes of direct aid.

It was in recognition of these elementary facts that a United Nations Conference on Trade and Development was convened in Geneva on March 23, 1964. The calling of this conference—attended by over 2,000 delegates from 123 countries—was directly influenced by the almost catastrophic decline in commodity prices which has recently brought increased suffering to a large part of the already poverty-stricken areas of the world. A well-informed and admirably organized summary of the UNCTAD proceedings is H. S. Bloch: *The Challenge of the World Trade Conference*, Columbia University, 1965, 56 pages.

At Geneva it was pointed out that although world trade had increased one hundred per cent in the last ten years, the share of the under-developed countries had fallen from thirty-one per cent to just over twenty per cent of the total. Many of these countries were in fact in a worse position absolutely as well as comparatively, at the end of that decade.

Many of the weaker countries are largely dependent for their international credits on the market on a single commodity such as tin, cocoa, coffee or bananas. In forty-two different countries, in a typical year, a single product accounts for over fifty per cent of the national exports. But the producing countries have almost no influence on the prices these commodites command. Today many such countries find themselves in a position that is not only deplorable for the present, but that threatens still greater calamities for the future. This is true even in the case of some of those countries in which the price of their basic commodities has been slowly strengthening in the last few years. There is no assurance at all that this improvement will not be reversed tomorrow. If the trading position of such countries is to be permanently strengthened, this can be done only by raising and stabilizing the prices paid for their primary products and at the same time providing an increasing market for the output of their usually small, often even rudimentary but locally important, industries.

The great obstacle in the way of the latter proposal is the difficulty of persuading the highly industrialized countries to agree to the importation on any considerable scale of manufactured goods that will compete with their own production. The argument against the admission of goods produced by "underpaid labour" is invariably emphasized and the whole proposal is denounced as a plan for the "importation of unemployment." While in some cases there is an element of truth in this argument, it should nonetheless be possible for the affluent countries to admit a far larger aggregate of manufactures from the under-developed areas than is being done today without seriously affecting the industrial life of such countries as Canada, France, Germany, Great Britain and the United States.* It should be easier still for the U.S.S.R. The basic argument for proposals of this kind is very simple: a/if development takes place, everyone, including the great industrial nations, will eventually prosper; b/real development cannot take place without some significant degree

---

* In 1963 some 13% of Great Britain's imports of manufactured goods came from the under-developed countries—much of this as a result of Commonwealth preferences. The corresponding figures were, for the United States 8%, and for the countries of Western Europe from 1% to 4%.

of industrialization; c/it is therefore to the long-range advantage of the major trading powers to assist in the rapid growth of industries in the under-developed nations. The difficulty, of course, is that the short-run effects may be individually injurious to influential manufacturers in the larger nations.

M. Maurice Brasseur, speaking for the European Community at the Geneva Conference, agreed in principle that any "substantial increase of the foreign exchange resources of the developing countries will depend increasingly on the diversification of their exports." He also said that the Community agreed, again in principle, to the stabilization of the prices of primary products at a level sufficiently remunerative for the producing countries. (*European Community*, No. 71, May 1964.) The problem is to translate these principles into practices. Somehow it must be done.

Dr. Raul Prebisch, the distinguished Argentine economist who was the Secretary-General of the conference, after many years of experience in his own country and as head of the United Nations Economic Commission for Latin America probably knows as much as any man in the world of the problems of the poorer nations. At Geneva he proposed that the wealthier states, in addition to providing enlarged markets for the products of new industries in the undeveloped countries, should take the lead in arranging for the introduction of a wide range of commodity production controls, to be supplemented by a scheme for the payment of compensatory grants to under-developed countries that are seriously injured when sharp declines occur in their export prices.

Many of the representatives of the richer countries went to Geneva expecting to take part in a debate in which the standard East versus West competition for the adherence of the under-developed and un-committed nations would be continued. Instead, both the western powers and the countries of the communist bloc found themselves under vigorous assault from the representatives of the poor countries. In effect the whole emphasis quickly shifted from an east-west to a north-south conflict.

In the early days of the conference, the more prosperous nations began by arguing that some small concessions on products exported by the developed countries might perhaps be arranged under the auspices of the General Agreement on Tariffs and Trade. In spite of the fact that, as the Honourable Mitchell Sharpe has pointed out (Address to United Nations Association, Toronto, April 19, 1964), some forty of the developing countries are members of GATT, this approach was criticized as being ineffective by the representatives of the under-developed nations who, in many cases, tend to look on the 61-member GATT as being a "rich nations club." Such critics do not fail to point out that in the fifteen years of its

existence GATT has made no real contribution to the welfare of the under-
developed countries. Their critical attitude was intensified by the fact that
the United States, the United Kingdom and other great powers indicated
that they were thinking of supporting the plea for commodity controls
in relation only to three or four articles, none of them of any great
significance to the poorer countries. In any case the list was too short.
India, supported by the U.S.S.R., argued for agreements on at least twenty
items. Anything much less would be of very limited value. The poorer
countries also argued that a new, inclusive, world trade organization was
required if any effective steps were to be taken. Only under such auspices
could the drastic reforms desired by the under-developed countries be
expected to ensue.

The importance of the trade situation as a component in the general
problem of the development of the backward areas of the world can be
illustrated by summarizing the situation in Latin America during the
decade of the fifties. Dr. Prebisch quoted these figures:

Latin America: 1950–1961

Inflow of private and public capital:	$23,000 million
Outflow of interest, profits and dividends:	$13,400 million
Favourable balance:	$9,600 million
Cost of deterioration in terms of trade:	$10,100 million
Net *loss*:	$500 million

In other words, unless additional markets can be found, or sales can be
raised in some other way, compensatory payments will have to be made
if outside aid and investment are to make any significant progress possible.

The Geneva Conference did not provide any radical solutions for the
problems with which it was confronted, although an Anglo-Swedish
proposal for long-term compensatory financing may be the germ of a
valuable growth. What the conference emphatically did do was to convince every serious student of the world scene—including many of the
representatives of the major governments—that these problems cannot
be disregarded or swept under the tatami any longer. The delegates of
seventy-seven less-developed countries, whose united impact was far more
effective than most observers had expected, made it clear that they would
remain united and would press their demands until effective action is at

least attempted. The conference refused the demands of the poorer countries for a new organization which would in effect replace GATT, but in the end accepted a "compromise" proposal for the establishment of a Trade and Development Board. The board consists of fifty-five countries which will prepare a new "Geneva Conference" for 1966, at which the problems which the 1964 conference could not solve will be again debated. One of the better brief summaries of the work of the conference was that of the Honourable Paul Martin, the exceptionally able Canadian Minister of External Affairs who himself presented the views of the Canadian Government to the conference. In his summary Mr. Martin said, in part,

this Conference was called to consider how trade can play a greater part in the economic development of the less-developed countries. If the pace of development in these countries is to gather sufficient momentum, they will need to increase their imports of capital goods and raw materials. These growing import requirements must be financed in large measure from their own export earnings. In fact, the less-developed countries have experienced a continuing decline in their share of world trade and their export earnings have not provided them with resources commensurate with their import needs....

Most of these countries are still dependent on a narrow range of commodities for a very large proportion of their export earnings. The Conference has recommended a programme of action designed to improve the terms of access to world markets for these products. It also agreed that new efforts must be made to arrive at international arrangements which would assure producers of primary commodities a more dependable source of export income....

The Conference recognized that, however much the prospects for their traditional exports are improved, the less-developed countries would come to depend increasingly on exports of the products of their new industries. This underlines the need for reductions in the barriers to world trade being made on a basis which will afford these countries the fullest possible opportunity of expanding their industrial exports....

The Conference acknowledged that, whatever part was played by trade, the international community would have to continue to support by means of aid the efforts of the less-developed countries to accelerate their rates of growth....

It also recommended measures that the international community should undertake to aid the development of the less-developed countries and in this regard it recommended that each developed country *endeavour, within the measure of its capability, to achieve a level of assistance that would come as close as possible to 1 per cent of its national income. . . .*

The Conference also reached agreement that there should be new institutional machinery within the United Nations to carry forward the work begun at Geneva and to bring into focus the problems of trade as they affect economic development. The General Assembly of the United Nations, at its next session, will be asked to endorse the holding of similar conferences on a regular basis and the establishment of a new Trade and Development Board. (External Affairs, Vol. XVI, No. 7, Ottawa, July 1964, pp. 312–314.)

The real results of the 1964 exercise are to be found not so much in any specific and concrete decisions as in the establishment of what promises to be a permanent united front of the poor nations under, for the present at least, very practical and effective leadership. Dr. Prebisch may prove to be not only the Moses but perhaps also the Joshua of the under-developed peoples. The promised land however is still far beyond the horizon.

Important as it is in certain cases, the establishment of a simple and more or less equal reduction in tariff barriers will not by itself go very far toward solving the problems of the developing countries. In the nineteenth century Great Britain, the manufacturing centre of the world, had an import coefficient of as high as 36 per cent; that of the United States by 1939 was down to 3.2 per cent. *The Economist* has summarized the Prebisch argument on this matter in the following paragraphs:

The old order disintegrated. Agricultural self-sufficiency was encouraged in the industrial countries; as populations grew richer, less of their income was spent on the simpler foods; technological progress steadily tended to develop substitutes for many raw materials and to reduce the consumption of others relative to the output manufactured from them. Demand for and trade in manufactured goods is tending to grow rapidly, at a pace increasing with the rate of development (since developing countries, above all, need imports of manufactures). Exports of primary commodities, with a few exceptions such as petroleum, are expanding relatively slowly so that the countries producing them do not generate enough income to pay for manufactures or service their debts.

The free play of market forces, on this view, "is admissible in relations between countries that are structurally similar, but not between . . . the industrially advanced and the developing countries."

What Dr. Prebisch calls the "conventional reciprocity" enshrined in the Havana Charter (i.e. the principle that tariff cuts must be equivalent everywhere) has been partly abandoned in the Kennedy round. But to him "real (or implicit) reciprocity" would mean the advanced countries granting concessions in their tariffs or restrictions to the developing countries, while countenancing the continuance of greater protection in those countries, as the necessary precondition to a shift from agriculture into manufacture. In this sense, he sees the rules of the General Agreement on Tariffs and Trade as inadequate to the trading relationship between rich and poor countries. But he would add that even these GATT rules are not honoured, in the spirit, between developed and developing countries. The heavy protection of domestic agriculture, sometimes, too, of high-cost home production of industrial materials and energy, plus differential duties to discourage the processing of materials, load the dice further against the developing countries. (The Economist, London, March 21, 1964.)

7/ International Monetary Adjustments

While it is certainly true that the kind of programme outlined by Dr. Prebisch would do much to improve the chances of rapid progress in the under-developed areas, it must also be recognized that his suggestions will be less effective than they should be unless they are accompanied by radical measures of reform in the money system under which the world is labouring. The International Monetary Fund, especially under its current direction, can contribute to the stability of the more advanced economies, but it is unlikely to initiate and pursue policies designed to have a direct and significant effect on the under-developed areas. The management of the Fund has not yet fully accepted the argument that one of its primary responsibilities is to establish conditions that will accelerate the development of the poorer countries.

Reorganization of international monetary policies along modern lines may be even more difficult than the transformation that has taken place in domestic practice over the past generation, but its importance can hardly be over-stated. To quote again from *The Economist*, the Fund should be committed to:

. . . the invention of a proper international monetary system, one that would allow Keynesian policies to work across frontiers instead of merely within them. The under-developed countries should be given, on a discriminatory basis, large annual injections of purchasing power through the International Monetary Fund in terms of some new international unit of account. Those who object to the expense

of this should be told that there are in fact only two senses in which this credit could "cost" anybody anything.

First, it would cost the under-developed countries themselves something if the automatic covering of their import gaps so removed internal discipline from their own governments' economic policies that economic stimulation was pushed past the stage of genuine development into disruptive inflation. This can certainly happen but it could also very easily be stopped if the central international organization creating the credit showed any financial courage at all. Secondly, the initial cost to richer countries of such an aid scheme would show itself in an increase in their balance of payment surpluses, paid for by the transfer to them of these new and convertible international units of account. . . .

After a while, of course, these export surpluses forced upon the richer countries would involve some real costs, if they impose new inflationary pressures upon them. But it is important to remember the orders of magnitude involved. If some such credit system enabled poorer countries to spend an extra $5,000 million of new foreign exchange a year, this would double the present total of international aid to them; but it would add less than 4 per cent to the total value of demand entering into international trade, and much less than 1 per cent to the total of demand falling upon richer countries' resources from the internal expenditure of their own national incomes. As it would be given out in a way that would actually improve western countries' recorded balances of payments, instead of worsening them, this extra demand might in at least some western countries prove more useful in promoting expansion than deleterious in threatening inflation . . . a large extension of aid would bring economic benefit to the rich as well as to the poor.

But even if the economics of the matter for the richer countries were rather worse than neutral, the morals and politics of the case for expanding aid are transcendentally urgent. Historians will look back upon the failure to improve the international currency system, to fit it for international Keynesian policies, as the most extraordinary economic failure of this generation. They will regard it with the same blank astonishment and impatience as most educated people today regard the failure to follow internal Keynesian policies at the beginning of the 1930's. And this time, as anybody who follows events in Asia and Africa must know, the penalties of ignorant inertia could be so fearfully much greater. How can pressure be mobilized on

slow-moving western politicians to make them recognize this?
(*The Economist*, February 15, 1964, p. 580.)

David Horowitz struck the same note in his Geneva address, to which
reference has already been made, when he said :

> it should be borne in mind that the main obstacle to progress on the
> road to self-sustaining economic growth in the less-developed coun-
> tries is not objective conditions, but rigid, antiquated and obsolete
> economic thinking, utterly unrealistic in the age of the atom and
> space, in the age of one world. The stubborn adherence to economic
> ultraorthodoxy was, to a very great extent, responsible for the world
> economic crisis in the thirties and may frustrate the attempts to raise
> the standards of living of two-thirds of humanity today.
>
> An imaginative approach to the great tasks of our century could
> have the same result as the counter-cyclical policy in the developed
> world had in the elimination of economic crises in the post-war
> world. Such a policy would not only narrow the gap between the two
> halves of humanity, but make richer and more prosperous all those
> embarking on this great venture. (Horowitz, op. cit., p. 9.)

That the attitude of the IMF may be changing in the direction suggested
by *The Economist* is a not unreasonable deduction from the report published by the Fund in August, 1964. In that report it is recognized, for the
first time, that the existing policies with their basic reliance on gold,
foreign exchange balances, and occasional *ad hoc* and unrelated credits,
does not and cannot ensure adequate international liquidity in the future.
In its review of the various ways in which the Fund's contribution to
increased liquidity could be effected, the report includes an enlargement
of IMF credits and by the Fund itself taking the initiative in spreading new
investments. If such investments should be directed in significant amounts
to the less-developed countries—through the International Development
Association or other appropriate channels—the result would be of great
importance to the progress of those countries and of general benefit to
the world economy. That there is some disposition in Fund circles to move
in this direction has recently been made apparent. Independent economists, led by such experts as Professor Robert Triffin and Dr. Thomas
Balogh, are also engaged on a vigorous campaign to bring about a re-
consideration of the past policies and practices of the Fund. (See Triffin :
"From Waterloo to Tokyo," *The Economist*, August 15, 1964, pp. 657–
659.)

There seems to be a rapidly increasing measure of agreement that
eventually—and this may not be very far ahead—the IMF must take on

most of the functions of an international central bank, authorized to issue and to control a new international currency. Whether this new currency will be based on gold or not will depend, as one American journal has put it, "on how much magic the bankers think necessary." (*New Republic*, February 20, 1965.) But the finance ministers of the most economically influential countries have not yet been fully converted.

In a collateral field, it should be noted that at the Tokyo meeting Mr. Pierre Paul Schweitzer, the Managing Director of the IMF, disclosed that the Fund was now prepared to provide technical assistance for the establishment of new central banks. It would also assist in the recruitment of experienced personnel to serve in both an advisory and executive capacity in the new institutions. (*Survey of International Development*, Washington, October 10, 1964. p. 1.)

This is not the place to argue at length the validity of specific proposals for expansion of the trading possibilities of the developing nations. That was done in Geneva, and to some extent in the 1964 Fund sessions at Tokyo, and it must continue until some solution, or at any rate some partial solution, is evolved. Certainly it is clear that international aid in its now conventional forms will not by itself bring about the changes that must occur if real progress is to be achieved. Fortunately there is multiplying evidence that enlightened opinion in many of the major countries is coming to a recognition of this fact, and that proposals for special treatment of the under-developed countries in the terms of trade and the reform of the present system of international monetary controls, are being seriously canvassed. The danger is that action will be too slow and too half-hearted, in spite of the fact that the need is becoming every day more apparent. But the less-developed nations have at last organized themselves in such a way as to ensure that their demands are kept in the forefront of international debate. The search for solutions to the problems they have raised cannot be concluded by temporizing resolutions or by amicable assurances of good intent and goodwill. Delay or inadequate action after the problems have been so widely canvassed, and hopes have been raised so high, could easily result in the creation of new and critical dangers not only for the future of the programmes of mutual aid, but for the peace of all the world.

CHAPTER TEN

The Prospects for the Future — III

It has been said in an earlier chapter that on the average the international agencies engaged in economic and technical assistance—the United Nations and its Specialized Agencies—are probably better managed than are most of the corresponding organizations in the various national services. This does not, however, mean that they operate with such great efficiency that there is no range for improvement. Any such belief could arise only from ignorance of the facts.

A · What the International Agencies Can Do

1 /Improved Administrative Arrangements

No one in a position of responsibility in the United Nations or in any of the Agencies would argue that answers had been found for all their administrative problems. Even on the straightforward issues of mechanical organization and operation, there are improvements that can be made. Over-staffing, lack of clarity in job descriptions, excessive paperwork, waste and inefficient lines of communication and responsibility, avoidable delay—one or all of these weaknesses can be identified in the various administrative and operational units. In most cases their existence is recognized and efforts are being made to overcome them. Management being human, they will never be entirely eliminated, but much more can be done than has at present been achieved. Progress in this field is of great importance because of the effect of bad administrative practices on public opinion and on the governments in the donor countries. It is even more important because inefficiency and incompetence can only result in reducing the quantity and the quality of the assistance that can be afforded to the governments and the peoples who are praying for aid.

Among many aspects of the United Nations programmes that would repay examination is the administrative burden imposed by the present top-heavy system of supervisory committees, agencies, councils, and assemblies which makes efficient operation much more difficult than it should be. It is wasteful of time, personnel, paper, ink and money. And it is wholly unnecessary; the responsible governing bodies could be kept adequately informed, could give the necessary guidance and maintain the essential controls, with only a minor part of the present cumbersome machinery.

As matters stood in 1965, the Technical Assistance Board must report in detail twice a year to the Technical Assistance Committee of the Economic and Social Council. It must report to the General Assembly through the Second, Third and Fifth Committees. It must report to the Administrative Committee on Co-ordination. In addition, each of the participants in the Board must report to its own governing body. Special reports must be made from time to time to the substantive committees set up by ECOSOC. Thus a large part of the time, energy and imagination of the Executive Chairman of TAB, of his assistants, and of his associates from the various agencies is devoted to the preparation of a massive sequence of reports. The pressure almost never lets up. And few representatives of the various governing bodies read more than a small fraction of the reports that are compiled with such a wasteful expenditure of labour. Most of the recipients wouldn't note the difference if the reports were written in Erse.

The Administrative Committee on Co-ordination no longer performs any essential function in the management of technical assistance and it could without loss be eliminated from this picture.

A single inclusive, annual TAB report once a year could be examined in detail by the Technical Assistance Committee and then passed on to ECOSOC and the General Assembly and to the governing bodies of the Specialized Agencies in November of each year. For the remainder of the year the Board and the operational units of the Specialized Agencies should be left alone to get on with their work. This would reduce the number of delegates and officials who enjoy a holiday in Geneva each July, but no one else would be so disastrously affected. The amalgamation of EPTA and the Special Fund, and the elimination of TAC should prove a contribution to efficiency.

While changes and improvements of the character suggested are important for the correction of administrative weaknesses in the multilateral programmes, there is an even greater need of reform in the operational procedures of many of the national or bilateral agencies. While the United States should not be singled out for particular reference in this connection (particularly under the present administrative leadership) it is probably true that that country has, even proportionately, the most elaborate and costly mechanism for the handling of aid funds. But other countries also should re-examine their organizational arrangements. There are few, if any, that could not be greatly improved. The criticisms that have been addressed to the United Nations agencies could be underlined and sent, registered and by special delivery, to most of those responsible for the bilateral programmes.

2/Increased Inter-agency Co-operation

> For years it has been notorious that the Specialized Agencies, particularly in their technical assistance work, have operated in competition rather than co-operation . . .

This quotation from the *New Statesman* (London, February 21, 1964) represents an opinion that is widely held and that has had in the past more than a little justification in substance. However, it is equally true that there is today a good deal more co-operation and co-ordination among the agencies (including the United Nations itself) than was the case in the early days of the Expanded Programme, when mutual suspicion in some cases almost amounted to hostility, and when competition was both crude and, in certain instances, directly encouraged at the highest levels. Even today, there is more that might be done and further improvements that could be made if those in charge of the agencies, including their governing bodies, were to give something more in the way of leadership than they have done in the past. An occasional exercise of discipline and compulsion might still, in some cases, have most salutary results.

The work of the Administrative Committee on Co-ordination under the leadership of Dag Hammarskjold brought some improvement in relationships between the agencies. So did the related increase in the positive leadership of David Owen, when he became the permanent executive head of the Technical Assistance Board. The persistent determination of the Technical Assistance Committee that all agencies must be brought to use the services of the resident representatives resulted in a considerably expanded practice of co-ordination in the field.* As has been noted, men

---

* In this connection one of the most able and experienced of the resident representatives has made the following comment: "One important factor in strengthening the hand of the Resreps, and thereby bringing about more co-ordination as among the Agencies, has been the fact that the Resrep now represents the Special Fund—i.e., money, albeit in small amounts; and money is power. I have never felt more humiliated in my life than as a Resrep—I had nothing to offer the . . . government that would mean anything to it. Consequently it had absolutely no use for me."

like Sir Herbert Broadley of the Food and Agriculture Organization, Dr. Brock Chisholm of the World Health Organization, Gustavo Martinez Cabañas of the United Nations, were of exceptional value in helping to develop a practical working relationship that was mutually beneficial and was so eventually recognized. But local loyalties were, and to some degree still are, hard to overcome, and much more still needs to be accomplished.

Some help in this direction may well develop from the work of the "committee of wise men," set up under Professor Thacker (President of the 1963 United Nations Conference on the Application of Science and Technology for the Benefit of the Less Developed Areas) to examine the scientific and technological programmes of the United Nations and Specialized Agencies with a view to identifying gaps, to maintaining programme balance both within and between agencies, and to discovering how better co-ordination in these areas can be achieved. The reception of this committee by the agencies was generally affirmative and it may prove that practices effective in the fields of science and technology may be recognized as applicable also in other quarters.

But the only certain way of ensuring continued and increased co-operation among the agencies, and tighter co-ordination of their labours, is by the eternal vigilance of their supervisory bodies. Human nature being what it is, the threat of a minatory eye and the sound of a menacing voice will help to ensure administrative virtue. There has been too infrequent an application of each in the past.

Every practical effort should be made to increase the authority of the Inter-agency Consultative Board. Among immediate objectives, the World Bank and the International Monetary Fund, and their associated organizations, should be brought into the Board where they and the present membership should be subjected to a rule of really effective co-ordination. If the governments that provide the finances would take their responsibilities more seriously, they could enforce a degree of inter-agency co-operation that would mark a real advance in the administration of the aid programmes. Money would be saved, services would be improved, and conscientious personnel would be greatly heartened.

The really important factor in the search for increased efficiency, however, is the quality of those engaged in its pursuit and the measure of the professional pride they take in their work. Here, inevitably, the standard will vary from time to time and from organization to organization. About all that can be done is to preach, work and pray.

Another form of co-operation that should be maintained and encouraged is that within the United Nations units themselves. The way in which the services of the resident representative have been engaged to assist the Executive Director of the World Food Programme and the officers of the Special Fund is warmly to be commended. Improved relationships in the field between the technical assistance staff of the United Nations and the Regional Economic Commissions have also been developed. This has come about in part through the institution of annual meetings in Addis Ababa, Bangkok, Geneva and Santiago, in which the Chairman of the Technical Assistance Board and the Managing Director of the Special Fund participate; and in part through headquarters encouragement of frequent meetings between the resident representatives and the officers of the Regional Commissions. These things are all good; they should be continued and supplemented in every useful way.

3/ Improved Methods of Evaluation

During the early years of the Expanded Programme, those in charge of its development were so busy in trying to get the machinery established, and in meeting the initial problems of the applicant governments, that there was little time left for the evaluation of the results of the first wave of projects. Gradually the scope and the quality of the evaluation procedures were refined and expanded. However, it is still true, in spite of the improvements that have been made, that there is much to be done in the way of developing and standardizing the techniques for the critical review of projects, and in assessing the causes of failure or success. It is to be hoped that the resolution (1042) of ECOSOC requiring the development of new pilot studies on evaluation will produce beneficial results. The practice developed by the Executive Chairman of TAB of bringing before the Technical Assistance Committee examples of failures as well as of successes in the work of the agencies operating under the Expanded Programme, was a valuable innovation. An indefinite continuation of the old retailing (indulged in by almost all agencies) of honey-dunked success stories had long since passed the point of diminishing returns. Today they are given about the same credence as the more oleaginous of the TV soap-operas. What are needed now, to produce effective results, are sober and objective accounts of successes and failures, with at least attempted explanations for each.

4/ Concentration on the Most Important Fields and Forms of Assistance

Although it is formally established and fully recognized that the responsibility for deciding on the forms of assistance to be provided by the United Nations and its agencies "has been given," to quote David Owen (*Statement to the Second Committee of the General Assembly of the United Nations*, October 1, 1963), "without qualification to the Governments of the recipient countries," subject only to the "judgement of the Participating Organizations on the technical feasibility of the individual projects," it would be naive to imagine that the governments are not in fact greatly influenced by the views of the administrators of the programmes. This places a very heavy burden of responsibility on the United Nations and the agencies, and they would be gravely at fault if they did not use their best judgement in recommending priorities and in seeking to influence the governments in their selection of projects.

There can be little doubt that among the most important fields in which governments should be advised to seek aid are a/central planning of development programmes, b/industrialization, c/technical training as a component of general elementary education, and d/improvement in administration, including a greatly increased use of the OPEX principle. With appropriate modifications in each particular case, these are obviously the areas in which the developing nations most require assistance, and the participating organizations should use all their persuasive influence to encourage governments to give priority to them. Without planning, aid will be wasted; without industrial growth there will be no significant and stable progress; without technical training, economic and social development will be a hopeless mirage; without competent administration the success of every programme will be clouded in doubt.

B · Conclusion

It would be unjust to conclude this listing of ways in which the United Nations and the Specialized Agencies should seek to improve the quality of their service in the cause of human progress without paying tribute to the imagination, industry and dedication with which many of the officers of these organizations and many of the members of the various supervising bodies have devoted themselves to the conscientious discharge of their responsibilities. Without minimizing the weaknesses and failures that have accompanied their successes, it is not an exaggeration to say that there can have been few cases in human history in which so many men and women have been united in devoting themselves with such skill and conviction to the work of helping others to live better and more hopeful lives.

Despite the bitterness and the hostilities by which its governments are divided, despite the diversities of condition and belief, despite the contrasts of background and circumstance, the world is today as never in the past, a single community. Men have circled the earth in less than two hours; their words pass instantly from hemisphere to hemisphere. What affects one region affects all; when turmoil arises in one area all areas are concerned; the impact of local controversy carries the threat of general conflict. To quote again from Adlai Stevenson's last address to ECOSOC:

> *Joint action is, after all, the final significance of all we do in our international policies today. But we are still held back by our old parochial nationalisms. We are still beset with dark prejudices. We are still divided by angry, conflicting ideologies. Yet all around us our science, our technologies, our interests and indeed our deepest aspirations draw us more and more closely into a single neighbourhood.*

In such a world no man can view with disconcern the suffering of another. His own peace, his own well-being, are conditioned by those of his brothers in his own or other lands.

At long last these facts are being recognized, and in form accepted, by many people in every nation, and by the governments that represent them. A start has been made to translate this formal acceptance into the practical deeds of aid and co-operation.

But what has been done is only a start. The first and the greatest barriers—barriers of indifference and denial—have been surmounted and left behind. What still remains is the task of carrying into effective practice the concepts of mutual concern and mutual responsibility that have been accepted in philosophy, in theory, and in words.

Here too, a start has been made, but infinitely more remains to be done before the values that science and resources have made available to the few can be shared by the many—as eventually they must be shared if humanity is to survive the dangers by which all men are threatened.

That the task is not simple or easy is apparent, apparent above all to those who have been privileged to work in the early years of this new crusade. That it cannot be allowed to fail, or even to flag or languish, is manifest to everyone who has any knowledge of the facts of life in the world of today. To fail would be to invite the disaster that would inevitably follow. To avoid such a tragedy will require all the humanity, the intelligence, the goodwill, the generosity, the devotion, and the industry that the peoples and the governments of the world can bring to the task. But the prize is worthy of the effort. The penalty of failure will be the sacrifice of hope for the future of mankind.

The problem is one of morality. That it can be solved if those in positions of authority, and those whose lives they influence, are determined to solve it, is beyond question. But it will not solve itself. The real question facing the troubled world, and to which only the future can provide an answer, is whether the moral essence in human character is strong enough to overcome the adverse elements with which it is intermingled. In the testing days and years ahead, the answer to this conundrum will decide whether, in the words of the Book of the Dead, humanity will or will not "be found to be light in the Balance."

Index